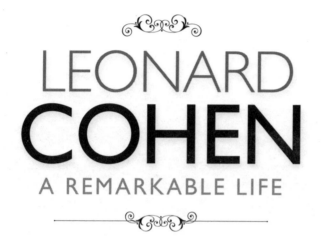

LEONARD
COHEN
A REMARKABLE LIFE

To Leonard D

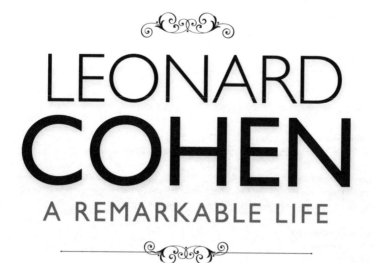

LEONARD COHEN

A REMARKABLE LIFE

ANTHONY REYNOLDS

OMNIBUS PRESS

London / New York / Paris / Sydney / Copenhagen / Berlin / Madrid / Tokyo

Copyright © 2010 Omnibus Press
(A Division of Music Sales Limited)

Cover designed by Fresh Lemon
Picture research Jacqui Black & Anthony Reynolds

ISBN: 978.1.84938.138.3
Order No: OP53163

Exclusive Distributors
Music Sales Limited,
14/15 Berners Street,
London, W1T 3LJ.

Music Sales Corporation,
257 Park Avenue South,
New York, NY 10010, USA.

Macmillan Distribution Services,
56 Parkwest Drive
Derrimut, Vic 3030,
Australia.

Every effort has been made to trace the copyright holders of the photographs in this book but one or two were unreachable. We would be grateful if the photographers concerned would contact us.

Typeset by: Phoenix Photosetting, Chatham, Kent
Printed in the EU

A catalogue record for this book is available from the British Library.

Visit Omnibus Press on the web at www.omnibuspress.com

Contents

FOREWORD

Last Night In Valencia

There has been very little promotion for tonight's performance. The show has not even been advertised by Cohen's own official website. Nevertheless the people have come to this mutant Spanish suburb named Benimamet. They have come to experience the poetry in person, to bear witness to a long life fully lived and to hear the man sing. A man who, amongst many other public and private victories has singlehandedly authored some of the classic pop songs of the 20th century; a man now deeply entrenched within the third act of his life. Tonight the dusky narrow streets of this ancient village ferry various nationalities. They are of numerous ages, miscellaneous faiths, non faiths and I count myself among them. Sitting outside the appointed and cavernous venue – the brutally named Luis Puig Velodrome – the sun goes down over crowds gently milling in the Mediterranean sunset.

I am sat shooting the breeze in the September evening with Leonard Cohen's current guitarist Javier Mas. We're outside the rear of the domed sports Hall, between the security guard studded 'artist's entrance' and a couple of enormously glistening freight trucks. Conversely, this air of subliminal security and efficient industry that surrounds the singer does not deter those who wish to gravitate toward Mr Cohen tonight, it actually attracts them. As Javier and I talk of everything and nothing a well dressed middle aged lady approaches us. She is German but speaks both Spanish and English with barely a trace of accent. "Are you with the Leonard Cohen band?" she asks politely, unsure exactly of whom to address. Her face is open and innocent. I point to the guitarist and smile, and disappear as she applies her focus exclusively to the Spanish guitar maestro on my left. Before Javier can even engage her she's talking frantically. "I know Leonard, from a long time ago, we were friends, many years ago and I know it's his birthday and do you think that I could perhaps…?'"

It's as if by reminiscing fast enough she will override any obstacle in her path to Mr Cohen. Javier shakes his head firmly and cuts her short sweetly. He is used to such requests. As if explaining to a child for the third time, he tells her it is impossible for *anyone* to meet Leonard tonight or tomorrow night or at any time during this tour and that in addition, it's not actually his birthday today. The lady stutters into response. "No, I know, it's on the 21st but you see… I…" As far as Javier is concerned this conversation has ended and he has a show for which to prepare. I intervene, asking the lady how she came to know Leonard. She begins her story too eagerly, perhaps against the disappointment blooming within her. "I met him at a show in Germany about 30 years ago… we wrote each other letters and I have many signed poems of his, I kept them all… I still have them… in frames… even now…" As she speaks she metamorphoses' into a young girl once more, it is 30 years ago and she is home again. Her patter soon trails off. There is a beat of silence. The spell is broken. We're outside a sports hall in Spain and it is 2009 and she is not getting backstage. The lady turns back to Javier with one last request. She offers him a Cohen *Best Of* CD and it dawns on me how badly designed such objects are for the purpose she has in mind. She wants Cohen to sign it. "Do you think at least you could…?" Javier again shakes his head, no, and says something quietly in Spanish. The lady nods, smiles sadly and walks off into the Valencian dusk.

Security is *very* tight on this tour. In Granada a few nights previously, local singer Enrique Morantes, invited to the show by old friend Leonard himself, was actually refused entry to the backstage area after the show. Leonard had specifically asked for Morante's company but the zealous tour manager would still not allow it. Many, including Javier was pissed off at this but it was not something worth causing a fuss over. The members of the current Cohen touring group are chosen not only for their musicianship but for the feng shui of their attitudes. Everyone needs to be relatively easy going in order to maintain the incredibly strong but deceptively mellow sense of equilibrium that lubricates a tour like this. Someone in Javier's position is obviously put under heavy extra curricular pressure by those seeking actual physical contact with his boss. If the guitarist so much as steps outside of the sanctuary of the hotel/bus/venue/circuit, he is hassled. Thus the itinerary follows a taut, high pressure schedule. Such an agenda is designed to make the whole experience as streamlined, economical and as friction free as possible for Cohen, a man who will be an elegant 75 years old in a few days time.

The singer's manager Robert Kory is the main power behind such a policy, and his insistence on tight security is based on a very personal experience. Kory himself was just one among many when introduced to Cohen backstage on the 1988 'I'm Your Man' tour. Presented by a friend to the tired and wine saturated singer – Cohen was drinking heavily at the time – Kory was acutely aware that to Cohen he was just another anonymous face among many that night. While the brief backstage meeting was amiable, ultimately it seemed pyrrhic and futile for all concerned. Yet the experience left an inedible impression on the then young lawyer. "It's probably because of that meeting that I've been so adamant on the current world tour about a 'closed tour' policy," says Kory. "Because those backstage meetings after a show with a crush of people are unsatisfying for those who go backstage and particularly for the artist. I mean, when we first met, what did Leonard Cohen know of me, right? I'm introduced to him by a friend and we've got seconds...A few minutes at most... in a crush of people... what's the point? There's no meaningful interaction. So a closed tour policy is a *good* policy I think." Kory is well aware of the demands made upon a performer, whom however fit is now nevertheless, technically elderly. "He needs this space," stresses Kory "to be able to perform at the level at which he is performing... in order to deliver a tour at the level at which we are delivering."

Sat in the dwindling Spanish dusk, I asked Javier exactly why Leonard does such very long shows of up to three and a half hours a night. A beaming Javier replies: "Because he's so generous."

Cohen himself had been hoping to still be singing at such an advanced age since watching jazz blues singer Alberta Hunter perform in New York in the early Eighties. "She was 82 at the time," Cohen would recall, "and it was really wonderful to hear experience in this woman's voice. You knew that she knew what she was talking about and when she said 'God Bless You' at the end of her set, you really did feel blessed."

While his manager is well aware of Cohen's age he isn't unduly concerned by it, or by the almost nightly marathon his friend and client insists upon. "He's perfectly capable. And his privacy, if you will, is not only for Leonard but for the benefit of all involved, including the audience, first and foremost, who pay every night. And it's worked out well, our policy. But we have to have no exceptions because once you have exceptions then where do you stop? We have so many wonderful stories, touching stories from friends, one after another and of course Leonard would love to see everybody but its just not physically, humanely possible."

Ultimately, Kory does not see Cohen's advanced age as a particular factor in this. "I don't feel any pressure regarding that," he says. "Early on I told Leonard that we were going to proceed with as few compromises as possible, hopefully no compromises. I don't need to do this and he doesn't need to do this. So if we're gonna do something we really should be aspirational and do it without compromising. This means he can take whatever time he needs and whatever vision he has and for that to be articulated. That's the process and it unfolds in its own time. The irony is that by proceeding with such a timeless agenda we get more done more quickly than he has done in many, many years. I don't even purport to understand it… but that's the way it is!"

Eventually the time of the show comes around. It is dark now. I have waved Javier 'adios'. Aside from this being the first time I'll ever experience Cohen in concert (I can't say 'in person' because I always felt that musically, listening to his records was the definition of a personal experience) tonight has an additional emotional resonance for me. Oddly, the Cohen band has recently hijacked my best friend in Spain. It's a story that deserves its own chapter in some other future book, but for now it is enough to say that the sudden absence of my sole vital companion in this country – a country I moved to almost exactly a year ago – has caused, even perhaps forced, me to decide to move back to Britain earlier than planned.

Cohen himself seems to have a particular, almost Zelig-like talent for simultaneously enjoying a unique affinity with many different countries and cultures. In Paris, he's an honorary French man. In Greece a Greek. In Israel, New York, Berlin… Cohen seems at home just about anywhere. One could write a book on Cohen with specific regard to his exclusive relationship to any one of these places. Beginning with his adolescent love of the poet Federico Garcia Lorca, Cohen had long since developed a mutual affinity with Spanish culture. My own estranged friend has arrived in her hometown of Valencia with Cohen and crew in their chartered jet. I see her all too briefly prior to the concert before she disappears into the mysterious underworld of the backstage area. Her head has been turned. It seems to me she has experienced less a seduction and more a conversion.

The briefly crepuscular Benimamet air folds into a warm, dark night. Finally, it is show time. I enter the hall with the rest of the faithful, accompanied by two friends. The sports hall is brightly lit, garish and teeming, about three quarters full and holding 600. My two companions and I have excellent seats, kindly and conscientiously arranged by Javier. We are front row, barely to the left. I have a private supply of gin to hand and disregarding all personal issues and even professional ones, I commit myself to enjoy the show in the capacity that originally brought me to this assignment – as a fan of Leonard Cohen and his music.

With no introduction and no announcement, the house lights fall to be replaced by beautifully discreet and evocative stage lighting. Within subtle but deep and powerful blues and reds, the place transforms from harsh and functional sports hall into some celestial and luxurious waiting room. As the band begins it seems that unfortunately it is not the music as such but the *sound* of the music that matched the waiting room analogy so well. As ' Dance Me To The End Of Love' ushers us into the show, the playing is so smooth, so groove worn (but curiously grooveless) and the sound mix so impeccable that the result is close to that of live muzak. Each player seems to occupy his space so politely and friction free that all egos, all court and spark, fire and magic have been airbrushed away. But then, when Cohen enters, all archangel elegant and dapperly eloquent in dress, movement and delivery and begins crooning you get the point. Live, the music is merely a tasteful scaffolding for the seductively subterranean graze of Cohen's singing voice. And the voice – comprised of warm honey and hemp – is a vessel for the powerful and quintessentially *lyrical* lyrics. I am reminded that Cohen was a poet and novelist a good decade before seriously embarking on a musical career. And today, arguably, the whole live Cohen experience is still ultimately geared toward the written word.

Despite seeming initially underwhelming, the whole experience nonetheless soon becomes sublimely exhilarating. There he is, a few feet away. The man who's been everywhere during this last half century is suddenly *here*. And the songs that bled from all our home stereos and headphones through so many romances, despairs and phases of our lives… those songs are alive and in front of us right now, at this very moment. The group, too, seem aware of this and curiously, appear to be an extension of the audience in some way. Everyone here is *here* but only one of us here is Leonard Cohen. The rest are witnesses. He's the (our) man.

Leonard Cohen himself is of course smaller than one imagined, and seems almost chemically reserved as a performer. But then at three hours, tonight is after all a marathon and not a sprint. Impeccably tailored it almost appears to me that it's his very suit that is holding Cohen up. Though seeming reasonably strong and confident he appears in some eerie way to be cradled by the actual lights that fall around him. Both he and the spotlights somehow seem acutely aware of both his age and the hours ahead. One also perceives a sense of duty in the presentation, both to the work and to the audience. Yet he also seems a little too withdrawn, a little frail, and even a tad fragile. Although this is the first Cohen concert I have seen in person, over the years I've watched hours of video performances, both bootleg and official. Through the decades he always seemed robust and rooted by a strong and healthy gravity. During the tours of the Eighties and Nineties the ballast was evidently provided by an excess of fine red wine.

Tonight he looks as if he could blow away on a sudden gust of wind. And now the third song begins. The elegance on stage invokes its own vitality. Things seem to be picking up. And then Cohen falls. There on stage, in the instrumental passage of 'Bird On The Wire', right in front of me, the audience and his band, he collapses to the floor in his gorgeous suit and stays there, crumpled, motionless and unconscious. From where I'm sitting it truly looks like Leonard Cohen has died.

Kory: "Leonard had food poisoning all day. He had the symptoms of food poisoning. He was eliminating from all orifices. You and I or any normal person would just not try to perform. He tried to perform. That was one thing upon which we would disagree. Afterward I said, 'Leonard… that's what a NBA Athlete tries to do. Koby Bryant from the Lakers. If he were sick like that and he were in the world finals he would go to the doctor's all day long and get IVs all day long, you know every few hours and get hydrated 'cos that's the medical issue. And then he'd take anti-diarrhoea medication just before game time and he feels fine and he plays the game, you know…' so I said 'Leonard next time you really want to do the show that's what you have to do. You have to call the doctor early. Not that I recommend it."

In the Luis Puig Velodrome Cohen is carried off by the band in the full glare of the house lights. I focus on his form. His body is limp, lifeless. He is completely out of it, utterly gone. His face looks ancient, like a death mask of itself. Cradled by his band the scene resembles the eerie significance of a religious painting. Carried limply off into the wings, Cohen looks like a dead saint.

Only the first few rows witness this up close. Confusion becomes alarm and then grief. The audience are on their feet. Mobile phones are being babbled into, faces are wet. Within an hour Javier has come onto the stage and addressed the audience in Spanish. Leonard is fine. He is on the way to the hospital. There is nothing to worry about. Tickets will be refunded. He is conscious. He wants to carry on with the show but we need a doctor to check him out.

We get a call from my friend. She is already in the ambulance with Cohen. There is talk of a heart attack. But he is fine, he is alright and his daughter, Lorca is with him too. Apparently, when he'd come to, he uttered the almost comically heroic line: "Give me a glass of water and put me back on stage." Always playing the tough guy. But friends, family and crew would not allow it. We're told to go to the Nueve de Octubre Hospital. In a fug of gin and cigarette smoke I slump in the back of someone's van and we drive through Valencia toward what…? To sit praying beside Leonard Cohen's hospital bed?

The next hour is orchestrated by a symphony of Spanish babbling into mobile phones. Cohen is in intensive care. My friend tells us to come as quickly as possible. We are stopped at the hospital reception. The ward is of course, private. Off limits. We are turned away as the newspaper people arrive. I am grateful for this.

Drunk, I decide to check out myself and get a cab home. Tomorrow I return to Britain.

I don't see my friend again and I never do get to see Leonard Cohen Live.

CHAPTER ONE

Genesis

"I didn't have a sense of who I was, or where I was going, or what the world was like, what women were like. The only thing I had a sense of is that I'm going to document this little life..."

LC 1992

Leonard Norman Cohen was born at a quarter to seven in the morning to Nathan and Masha in Montreal on the Friday of September 21, 1934. His first given name, followed the family tradition of occasionally using 'L's for their male offspring – his grandfather was called Lyon and his great-grandfather Lazarus. A sister, Esther, born in 1929, already awaited him. Leonard's father Nathan was a proud and proper man with a vague inclination toward introspection and intermittent romantic melancholy. Even for the era he was somewhat old fashioned; courtly, portly, moustachioed and always impeccably tailored, he sometimes sported a monocle and had precise ideas about manners and etiquette. Nathan was rarely seen out of a suit and tie and in the Cohen household everyone dressed formally for dinner each night.

By the time of his son's arrival he was a recent veteran of World War One, and had in fact been among the first commissioned Jewish officers in the Canadian army. Nathan had not come out of the Great

War unscathed. The newly industrialised primitive horror of trench war left an indelible stain upon the hearts and minds of anyone who experienced it but in Nathan's case it also weakened him physically, and he would never quite recover from the trauma. Nathan, or 'Nat' as he was known by those close to him, was deeply patriotic and originally an engineer by trade but worked mostly for the family clothing business – The Freedman Company. This was an appropriate environment for a reticent and mannered man who was at heart a dandy, with his wardrobe of spats, waistcoats and rakish hats. Such sartorial traits would be passed on, albeit in a somewhat refined form, from father to son.

As well as having rather a withdrawn personality and sense of style, Leonard's father was an actively proud and patriotic citizen who had been honoured to volunteer for duty in the Great War. (Perhaps as a consequence, even when later labelled with the terms 'hippy' and 'Buddhist' and all their subsequent 'peacenik' associations, Leonard would retain an almost contrary admiration for the military model throughout his life and would never define himself as a pacifist but quite the opposite. Indeed, if fate had turned another corner, if Nathan had lived, then Leonard reckoned that at his father's instigation he himself would have enlisted in military school). Being somewhat 'tone deaf', Nat was a confirmed listener as regards to music and song, his tastes centring on the comic operas of Gilbert & Sullivan and the traditional Scottish songs performed by Harry Lauder. He also had a strong interest in photography and film, and to this day many of his home movies of the young family still surface as footage in documentaries on his son.

Wife and mother Masha was dourly pretty, elegant, soulful and vital looking. Originally from Lithuania, then a part of Russia, having fled the Stalinist regime, she still carried the inherent melancholy of that region and its weather within her, even now in her role as a frequently contented Canadian housewife and dedicated Jewish mother. A trained nurse who had spent time in the Red Cross, she was well suited to being the wife of an often poorly war veteran. As a mother, and as her offspring grew older, she became more of a friend than a mere matriarch to Leonard and Esther, treating her children with uncommon respect and as they eventually came of age, as equals. Leonard would remember her coming downstairs to meet him and his teenage comrades as they rolled into her kitchen after a night in the city. Rather than fuss or admonish, she would sit at the table with them, making tea and cooking breakfast for all as the Quebec dawn broke over the green expanses of the adjoining Murray Hill Park.

As sister Esther matured, she would aspire to a (quasi) literary tradition of sorts and become both a librarian and a clerk for Colliers Encyclopaedia. She and her brother were never particularly close as children. "I never really got to know her until we were much older," Leonard would recall. "I discovered she's a great spirit; a great laugher, a great talker and solid in herself."

The family home was a two storey bare-bricked semi-detached house in Westmount, an upper-middle-class suburb of Montreal, located on the slope of Mount Royal. The house and adjoining park gave a fine view of the city, on the edges of which remained a native Indian Mohawk reservation called Kanawake. Some of Leonard's earliest memories of he and his father were of Nat taking him out to the reservation for walks. Leonard's bedroom for the first 15 years of his life was an undersized box room at the rear of the house, with a small window that opened up onto the lush verdant park where he would routinely walk his dog, a Scottish terrier called Tinkie.

Leonard would never forget Tinkie, a presence he remembered as "... the closest being to me during my childhood... the dog would sleep under my bed and follow me to school and wait for me... a great sense of companionship." Tinkie would die at 13. "He just asked to go out one night," recalled Cohen, "so we opened the door... it was a winter night and he walked out and we never saw him again. It was very distressing... we only found him in the springtime when the snow melted and the smell came from under the neighbours porch... he had gone out to the neighbour's porch to die. It was some kind of charity to his owners." Cohen would not replace Tinkie, never again owning a dog. A framed photo of his boyhood companion remains on a dresser in his LA home to this day.

As the Second World War raged in Europe, and as the horrors of what would become known as the Holocaust slowly surfaced, Leonard and children like him were shielded from the facts. When photographs of the concentration camps emerged toward the end of the war the local papers printed them only as part of a supplement that could be removed so as to protect the children. The young Leonard was aware of the war as a fact but it seems to have made little emotional impression upon him at the time. "Our favourite activities were the following," he would recall, "going to the movies, learning songs, going to Sunday school. It was during the war, there was no chewing gum so if you had any, or any chocolate, it was great." So Leonard grew from the rich cross fertilized soil of a strong and ordinarily unique family. The principal motifs of his rearing either implanted or surfacing now would manifest throughout his later life and career. He clearly inherited his father's sense of duty, decency and morality, endearingly juxtaposed with a love of shined shoes, cufflinks, a tailored suit and an impeccably tilted hat. From his mother's side there was the almost hereditary leaning towards melancholy that her people had harboured over countless East European generations and winters. From Masha, too, came a pronounced influence on her son as regards a love of story telling, the currency of song and the sense of history such music embodied. These potent and deeply impregnated spiritual and emotional nutrients fed into the boy and were bound together by an ancient, profoundly defined and recognisable faith – Judaism.

Such a religion, with all its exacting, specific customs and conspicuous characteristics was an inheritance that Leonard never seems to have seriously questioned, much less rebelled against, even as an adolescent. From the earliest age, he seems to have accepted the rituals, prayers and symbols – the very faith itself and all its outward gestures and mechanics – as his own given lot and wore this faith as if it were tailored specifically for him. He was, like many boys his age, bored by the ritual, in his case of attending synagogue and Hebrew school. But he ultimately wore who he was proudly. "I never had a moment of revolution against my family," he would remember. "They always struck me as extremely decent people." This religion, one in which "… the candles were lit, prayers were said", and in which "there was a very clear consciousness of a tradition", would help give structure, comfort and support to Leonard throughout his life.

Leonard's upbringing, like many others of the same faith and era was one where education was intrinsically linked with religion and where religion even superseded culture but this was nothing out of the ordinary for the time and place. "My upbringing was traditional rather than Orthodox," Cohen remembered. "It was a thoroughly Jewish home and a fairly good education." The family were well respected in their community but were also slightly apart in that they spoke predominately English − Masha retaining a slight East European accent − in a city where the common language was French. Masha, who had arrived in Canada as a teenager, had no sentiment about the 'old country', no urge to return to the place that she and her family had crossed oceans to get away from. This lack of sentimentality and an almost complete absence of nostalgia is something Cohen would strongly inherit.

Financially the Cohen's were comfortable enough to employ a modest and cosmopolitan ensemble of domestic aides, which included a black chauffeur-cum-gardener for the family and an Irish Catholic nanny (Ann) for their son. (Montreal far more Catholic than Jewish and still is, and Leonard was far from being beyond any Christian influence. Indeed Ann would sometimes take him to mass with her and this fostered in him an interest and affection for Catholicism if not a commitment to it). Although the Cohens certainly never flaunted their modest wealth they enjoyed the ultimate luxury − they were 'unconcerned' with money; rich enough to afford a certain indifference to it.

Outside of the family home and the synagogue Leonard attended Westmount High School where as part of the musical curriculum he took up the clarinet. He was no prodigy in any class and if remembered at all by his surviving classmates it was for his ultimate ordinariness. Rona Feldman Shefler, a fellow pupil and friend of Cohen's at WHS remembers an "introspective, quiet boy with a half-smile. He was gentle, not flamboyant, he never showed himself off." Beyond school, and again as was customary, on some evenings and Saturday mornings Leonard attended the occasional piano lesson with a Miss McDougal. Like many boys of his age he probably resented having to give up his spare time for such platonic pursuits. Leonard was not short of friends. As well as Rona, an early and subsequent life long friend made around now was Mort Rosengarten. Both he and Leonard grew up and played on the same street and would go on to live parallel lives as artists − Mort as a sculptor − and spend their tender years always in close companionship.

Potent seeds continued to be sown within Leonard throughout these early years, seeds that would eventually grow into an infrastructure that both supported and defined his adult life; in particular, the "… great Chekhovian spirit" of Masha, often expressed in her almost genetic melancholy by singing the traditional songs of her Lithuanian childhood around the home. She was in her son's own words, "A very good singer, much better than I am… she would sing around the house quite a bit." His religion also heightened his sense of music and its deep inherent power over heart and soul. "When I was standing beside my tall uncles in the synagogue and the cantor would catalogue all the various ways in which we sinned and die, that moved me very much." The family did not make a 'big issue' out of their religion. Indeed, Leonard remembers the actual word never being used. "They didn't make a big deal out of it," he would explain of his family's attitude toward one of the biggest presences in the household. "They weren't fanatics. It was all very ordinary and friendly. It was mentioned no more than a fish mentions the presence of water."

The most defining episode in the boy Leonard's life, perhaps the crux of his early development, was the death of his father at the age of 52 in the first month of 1944. Nathan had never fully recovered from his wartime experiences and since returning from the front had never again been in full, robust health. With a melancholy that matched that of his wife, he often mused – in public and at the family dinner table – on his suspicion that he would die before his time. "My son, Leonard, I'll never see his Bar Mitzvah," he once exclaimed sorrowfully to a relative in the synagogue. Nat was correct in this premonition and was dead before the age of 55. Leonard was nine. As affecting as this death must have been, Leonard even then was almost eerily pragmatic. "I didn't feel a profound sense of loss," he would say years later, at the same age on which his father had passed, "maybe because he was very ill throughout my entire childhood. He was at the hospital often. It seemed natural that he died. He was weak and he died… maybe my heart is cold. I wept when my dog died. But when my father died I had the feeling that that was the way it should be. In a way, it wasn't my business, it didn't concern me. Larger forces control all that. We can't argue with those forces. I'm not saying it was great but it seemed normal to me." The funeral took place, coincidentally, on the day of Esther's birthday. Both children were of course in mourning, but keeping with his father's tradition, the ceremony itself was no raging wake but rather a quiet, dignified ceremony distilled by a hushed sadness and a solemn acceptance.

Immediately after Nat was buried, Leonard made for his dead father's bedroom and went to the dresser there. He took a bow tie from a drawer, slit it with a knife and placed inside it a note he had written. He then sewed up the bow tie's scar, sealing the slip of paper and its words within. Walking out into the January snow, Leonard buried the bow tie in the garden. "I know that was the first experience I had with that kind of heightened language that I later came to recognise as poetry," Leonard would recall. Many many years later, he would suggest that he was in some way still digging in that same garden, still looking for the bow tie and its note, and had been all his adult life.

At nine years old and fatherless, Cohen was now at least symbolically expected to be the 'man' of the family. He seemed to handle the loss and the expectations put upon him stoically. The Cohens were still comfortable financially. Nat had, of course, been prudent in his investments and in addition there were regiments of uncles, cousins and aunts to help support Masha, Leonard and Esther. It wasn't as if Cohen would have to go out into snowy Montreal and clear driveways in order to support the remaining family himself. Naturally, from this point on his relationship with his widowed mother deepened. Their relationship would always be solid, and based upon friendship as much as genes. The boundaries of any discontent between them were moderate and down to Cohen's immaturity. "My mother used to annoy me when I was young," Cohen would reminisce decades later. "She used to tell me stories about her youth in Lithuania and I was too impatient to hear the whole story... it seemed she would jump from one event to another and I could never follow what she was saying." Only as he matured would Cohen be able to apply patience to his mother's very particular way of storytelling. For now he was preoccupied with not only the need to make his own stories but to immortalise them in his own words too.

Despite the absence of Nathan the family house was full, flourishing and nourishing with cousins, uncles and friends stopping by, passing through, staying for supper. Masha's father, Rabbi Solomon Klinitsky-Klein, who bore a resemblance to Sigmund Freud, lived for the last year of his life in the room next to Leonard. In his prime the old man had been considered 'a great scholar', a Hebrew Grammarian who wrote a dictionary of Talmudic interpretation, acquiring the shining title 'prince of Grammarians'. By the time he became his grandson's neighbour, Solomon was working on an updated edition of his dictionary. The two worked in adjoining rooms, bounded by a common pursuit. "I had started to write when I met him," recalled Leonard, "and he indicated some interest... some sense of solidarity and pleasure in the fact that I was writing... he was living in the next room to mine and I was tapping away on a typewriter and he was writing (too)..." In his advanced age, Solomon was also becoming steadily senile and 'slowly mad'. "He'd come into the kitchen," remembers Leonard, "and he had a cane. He'd set the cane on the edge of the table and sweep everything off of it and say 'Someone's stolen my watch!'" This was obviously deeply disturbing and upsetting for Leonard's mother who could still recall a time when people would "... travel a hundred miles to hear her father speak..." Despite the declining mental health of the old man, Solomon remained primarily a 'warm and impressive' figure to his daughter's son. The presence of the great Rabbi would stay with his grandson throughout Leonard's life, a figure whom almost three quarters of a century later Cohen still longed to properly remember in writing.* On the other side of the family and a generation older, Nathan's grandfather, Lyon Cohen was no less a character, regarded as a 'very competent community organiser' who founded many Jewish organisations that would still exist in the 21st century. He also set up one of the first Anglo-Jewish newspapers in North America. Leonard remembers Lyon as saying he believed strongly in 'the aristocracy of the intellect', a statement that would become imbedded in the boy as he turned to adolescence.

Music increasingly resonated with Cohen while, not untypically, he was put off poetry by school. As a child he had for a while become fixated with a plastic flute on which he attempted, whilst driving everyone around him crazy, to learn the song 'Old Black Joe', composed by Stephen Foster. His application to music would become a more serious practice in his life as he continued to mature. Three simultaneous

---

* He would use the situation in a fictionalised form years later. The piece, 'A Ballet Of Lepers', would never be published.

epiphanies occurred in 1949 when Cohen acquired his first 12 dollar guitar (acoustic and pawn shop variety of course) and seriously discovered folk music and poetry. "I moved into what they call poetry through folk music," he explained. "I liked the lyrics very much…"

Throughout the rest of his life, poetry would occupy at least as much psychic space within him as music. His personal patron saint of poetry would become Federico Garcia Lorca, whom Cohen discovered at 14 by 'accident' in a bookshop. Lorca's poem 'Gacela of the Dark Death' was an early and enduring favourite, and in a way a call out to Cohen, hooking him, reeling him in. The line 'Cover me at dawn with a veil, because dawn will throw fistfuls of ants at me' and the savage and intoxicating surrealism of the Spaniard's work in general held a particular and mesmerising attraction that would intoxicate Cohen for a lifetime. From the first moment of that first opening of Lorca Cohen was seduced. "I never left that world," he would say. Outside of the Spaniard, the verse of Yeats and Eliot also moved him, such men all united in that they became early role models for a pending life that Cohen was hungry to begin. The boy Cohen recognised a future and method of living for himself in the work of these dead men. "I had a calling," he would remember decades and decades on. "I wanted to be a writer. From a very early, early time I just knew I was going to be a writer… a writer whose allegiance was to those who were already dead." It was the hybrid of this allegiance, along with Cohen's unforeseen future role as part of the then unborn phenomena of rock'n'roll that would mint his utter uniqueness as a force in both the worlds of poetry and popular music.

Throughout this febrile time, Cohen was engaged as a full time student, enrolling at McGill University in the centre of Montreal on September 21, 1951. Not untypically for the time, McGill's had a discriminatory admissions policy, which required of Jews higher academic standards and severely limited their access to some faculties. This had begun to change only the previous year, 1950. Cohen came from a kosher household and one can only imagine how such an intelligent, aware and passionate young man, pragmatic and unhysterical as Cohen was, would feel about such outdated and outmoded bigoted traits. Yet paradoxically, it was this very obligation to academia that allowed him to dedicate the bulk of his energies to a pseudo bohemian lifestyle. At 17 (Cohen often remembered it as being 15) he had followed both his family's expectations and the requirements of the Montreal educational system by attending McGill. His self admitted goal at the beginning of such an academic 'career' was '... wine women and song', in the event as accurate a description of the future that awaited him as there ever was. He took to his new role with characteristic relish, soon becoming active in the drama group and rising to become head of the debating society. Other than this, he spent little actual time in class during the early years. "The disadvantage was that you had no way of knowing what you were going to be at 15 or 16... I hardly went to any of the classes. Nobody cared really whether you turned up or not. You wrote your exams and if you passed them it was OK... some professors took roll call but by no means all of them."

To a soundtrack of Ray Charles, country music and occasional doo wop, the nattily dressed and occasionally plump Cohen instead spent what time he could downtown, soaking up the booze and atmosphere in many of Montreal's lively, smoke fogged bars, the dives on Stanley Street being amongst his favourites. He and his childhood buddy Mort explored their youth and hometown in tandem. "We would drive through Montreal in the evening or along the lake. Just drive and listen to music, the jukebox. I knew what every jukebox in town played," remembers Cohen. When out alone he often took with him a notebook, pen and guitar, a trinity of tools that would eventually become among the most recognisable tools of Cohen's calling.

In the summer of 1953 Cohen expanded his adolescent horizons vividly when he took his first trip to America, visiting Harvard in Massachusetts to attend an experimental poetry course by French poet Pierre Emmanuel (aka Noël Mathieu). He spent a month there, mostly listening to field recordings of American folk music at the Widener library. This early important adventure in Cohen's young adulthood remains recorded only as a fragment in the poem 'Friends'. On his return to Montreal he solidified his feeling of new independence and moved out of the family home and into a suite of rooms at a rooming house on Stanley Street. His childhood buddy Mort came with him. At last they had a place to entertain women. Cohen had a natural if minor gift in this department and was equally naturally desperate to use it. One trait that distinguished Cohen from his mentors and peers, according to a associate Moses Znaivner, was Cohen's "gift of compassion… and a talent for intimacy that charmed both men and women."

All the while he continued to have his fledgling yet strikingly mature poems published in 'the little magazines'. And although possessed with a rich interior life and a passion for the written word and a muscular sense of his own destiny within the pantheon of that very tradition, Cohen was obviously no Emily Dickinson. Unlike other adolescent would-be poets, he did not spend his time exclusively among the dust of libraries, box rooms and the words of the dead. He was a sociable, even lusty fellow and continued to move as readily through his social world as he did his inner one. A favoured hangout of writers in downtown Montreal was Ben's, an all-night downtown deli whose owners would one day mark a 'Poets' Corner' there, eventually hanging framed photographs of Cohen and other locally renowned poets as if they were retired boxers or famous crooners. Although he had passionate aspirations in all these fields – bar boxing; Cohen seemed curiously neutral as far as any sports went – the idea of being a 'poet' already held some embarrassment for him. "At McGill I was interested in playing the very opposite role of the Monk," he would remember. "I was trying to get a date most of the time… (I was not) terribly successful."

Music was a more yielding phenomenon. In his second year at college, along with school friend Mike Doddman, Cohen formed The Buckskin Boys. The name of the group held no great mystery. "Curiously enough, we found we all had buckskin jackets," he said. "Then it was on the basis of that mutual discovery that we named the group. Mine I inherited from my father. Pretty beautiful jacket, it must be over a hundred years old. There was a convention in Montreal in those days where a lot of barn-dancing – square dancing – was done as a social activity," Cohen explains. "So, we played in church basements and high school auditoria, and we played conventional songs like 'Turkey In The Straw' that [bassist] Terry Davis would call to. You know, 'do-se-do.' I was playing rhythm guitar and Mike Doddman was playing harmonica, and we had these instruments amplified. So, we were doing just the appropriate square dance material."

The Buckskin boys were bound together by a spirit of pure fun. Outside of their locale and a mutual love of entertaining they didn't even share one common religion. Occasionally the three would gather at Terry's family home to eat. His mother wittily commented that she "… was never sure what single meal she could to serve a Catholic, a Protestant and a Jew." Beyond the hoe down, Cohen still read and wrote veraciously but playing music and playing it in public was equally as important in some ways. "I was a musician a long time before I was writer," he'd affirm, defining his particular love of such homely music precisely because it was homely. 'Folk' music was just that, music for the local community. "The thing I always loved about that kind of music is that the 'people' knew it and understood it as their own music." In time he would wish the same for his poetry.

As an audience member he had lost his live 'cherry' when he saw the black civil right activist, musician and singer songwriter Josh White at Ruby Foo's, a Chinese restaurant in Montreal, back in 1949.* "He knew how to bend a string," Cohen remembered admiringly. White was also the co-inventor of the first round bodied guitar. For Cohen, the guitar was as serious a sword as the pen and he actually took flamenco guitar lessons from a local Spanish immigrant whom he chanced upon in the park near his home. "I must have been 15, he was 19," remembered Cohen. "He played wonderfully. I asked him if he could show me the tremolo, certain key changes... But most of all he held his guitar in a certain way, played in a certain way." Cohen called on the guitarist for a fourth lesson, only to be told the young Spaniard had recently committed suicide. This event and the flamenco style with its inherent beauty sense of celebratory melancholy would haunt Cohen and his work for the remainder of his life. Cohen's unique guitar style, the rolling, fluent, seamless flow of notes which seem to tumble like water out over the strings and back into themselves, would become another important and instantly recognisable detail of his work. The origins of this particular

---

* Discovered by legendary A&R man John Hammond, White would eventually be cited as an influence by many more recognized figures, from Elvis Presley through Odetta and plenty in between.

'chop' have been attributed to being a hybrid of Cohen's (albeit brief) classical piano training and the similarly brief trio of guitar lessons.

In time Cohen would also go on to experiment with alternative guitar tunings. His particular style of guitar playing was just one manifestation of his affinity with Mediterranean culture, an empathy in direct contrast to the snowy topography of Montreal and to his family's history, and this was perhaps the very power of its attraction. His passion for music was yet another inroad to the local 'scene'. Meeting in bars and coffee houses with other poets, drinking, smoking, debating, arguing, reading each other their work. Cohen stood apart in one vital aspect – he was already setting his poetry to the chord progressions that rolled idiosyncratically from his Spanish guitar.

It was a lively, physical scene and Cohen's presence as a poet or otherwise was anything but metaphysical. In the autumn of '54, Cohen was actually knocked out and arrested by an overzealous cop when he protested against being manhandled by the officer. Having stopped to watch a pseudo riot by some overexcited sports fans, Cohen was shoved and told to move on. Angrily pleading the role of innocent voyeur he was struck unconscious and woke up in the police wagon. Tried in court a few days later for 'resisting arrest' he was given a suspended sentence and a criminal record. For a follower of the politically subversive Lorca, Cohen may have taken some pleasure in his brief notoriety, although his family were appalled.

A new friend, Irving Layton would have been impressed. Layton was another local, older poet and known more as a brawler, a man's man at a time when poetry was often seen as the exclusive domain of 'sissies'. Layton however understood the holy power of poetry and respected, studied and practiced it. He was also an expert as regards the power of positive drinking and overly fond of chatting up women. He and Cohen forged a strong and special friendship that would remain for the rest of their lives. Such a companion intensified Cohen's opportunities socially and along with Mort and other like minded Young Turks, they enjoyed a rich social life together which was balanced delicately with Cohen's time at McGill. He was still far from being a total absentee on campus.

By the fall of '54 he had become a committed pupil of Louis Dudek's 'modern poetry' course, and this tutor would soon come to recognise the poet in this particular pupil. In return Cohen treated him more as a peer than a superior which 'Louis' seemed to prefer, particularly when Cohen and Layton invited the staff to the parties they'd organised. "Professors were always there; there were no barriers, no master/student relationships. They liked our girlfriends," says Cohen. "They were in their thirties or forties; they liked the people we brought to their parties."

Dudek's class met in the Arts building on Mondays, Wednesdays, and Fridays from five to six pm. This was the hour when the regular university day was ending to make way for the apprentice accountants and other extension-school students. Around 50 pupils attended each twilight session, stacking their coats, bags and books along the aisles and walls. In the wintertime, darkness would fall as Louis passionately guided the students through the eternal works of authors such as Voltaire, Rousseau, Goethe, Schiller, Novalis, Nietzsche, Rilke, Thomas Mann; Turgenev, Dostoevsky, Tolstoy and Chekhov; Chateaubriand, Flaubert, Baudelaire, Gide, Céline; Marcel Proust and James Joyce, Samuel Butler, D.H. Lawrence, T.S. Eliot and Ezra Pound. Dudek was clearly a man with a mission, as he had explained in his entry of Canada's Contemporary Authors Autobiography Series. "It may be that the worst teachers, as well as the best, are teachers with a mission, but I came with the confidence that I had something very important to teach. There were in fact two things. The first was modern poetry and literature, which had evolved fully abroad but which had barely started in Canada with small groups of poets having a limited audience.... The second program was the massive movement of European literature and thought since the 18th century, with its profound practical implications, which students' minds had still to experience, like buckets of cold water thrown at them from a high lectern."

Although Cohen remained a persistently average student in terms of exam results and attendance, Dudek's progressive, soulful philosophy in teaching could have been tailor made for a pupil with Cohen's particular make up. Cohen and his friends were as passionate about poetry as the next generation would be about rock'n'roll. It was certainly not a purely ideological or even academic pursuit. "I remember I once recited a poem while walking down the street with Irving," remembers Cohen touchingly. "He just put his hand on my shoulder and said, 'How did you

do that?' It was very informal... That was our life, our life was poetry."
Yet Dudek had been neutral about the first clutch of self-penned work
that Cohen had shown him. This was a temporary aberration. Soon one
poem, 'Sparrows' resonated with the older man and Dudek responded in
high theatrical style, taking Cohen's rolled up manuscript and 'knighting'
him with it there and then in a college corridor. Symbolically, this
marked Cohen's beginning as a recognised poet. 'Sparrows' fulfilled its
own minor destiny, being printed on the front page of the *McGill Daily*
as a result of winning its 1954 literary contest that December.

Beyond the written word Cohen continued to flourish and was active
in many unofficial and official strata, even rising to post of president
of the student union in his fourth year on campus. He was also band
leader of Hillel, the Jewish section of the student's union which one year
presented a play in which Cohen played 'second guard' and he supplied
guitar accompaniment for another local theatrical production. Full of
hormone fuelled energy, the young Cohen also became involved in a
respected local magazine, *CIV/n*, which published further examples of
his increasingly accomplished poetry.

In October 1955, Cohen finally graduated from McGill. He had a
helpful if modest inheritance from his father of 750 Canadian dollars a
year which allowed a modicum of independence. Hoping to keep his
mother and uncles happy Cohen attended a term in law school with the
tenuous notion of becoming a lawyer. His heart was not in it. He had
by now been published in various magazines, and had a solid reputation
locally as a writer, poet and general 'face' around town. He was already one
of the biggest fish in the local pond and he remained a vital presence on
campus, with Dudek by now being easily as much a friend as a mentor.

Dudek practiced what he preached too. By 1956 he'd formed a small
'publishers', and decided to launch the McGill Poetry Series with a
volume of Leonard Cohen's poetry. Surprisingly, apparently because of
philosophical disagreement between him and Luis, Cohen was initially
reluctant to present the manuscript. Funds were limited for the project,
so Dudek adopted the stratagem of selling advance subscriptions, at $1
a book. An advance sale of 500 copies would guarantee at least a small
distribution, as well as covering initial printing costs. At this point Dudek
introduced Cohen to a fellow student, Ruth R. Wisse.

Wisse would go on to become a leading academic herself, ending up as the professor of Yiddish literature at Harvard. A self confessed 'intense' lover of literature, she was one of Dudek's most passionate pupils and just as practical too. "I was accustomed to the system of prenumeration, through which my parents supported the publication of several local Yiddish authors," she remembers. "Appointing myself head of Dudek's sales team, I went down to the nearest Woolworth's, bought a couple of receipt books, and lickety-split sold over 200 advance copies. My work as feature editor at the *McGill Daily* had brought me into contact with so many students and teachers that I was able to sell my quota strictly on campus among people I knew. Anyway, the name Leonard Cohen was already a draw... he was already celebrated by the time I knew him at college... Leonard Cohen was the undisputed star of the artistic Westmount crowd."

The promise of such a book alone further solidified Cohen's reputation. Wisse looked on, curious and enchanted. "If at first I accepted Leonard Cohen's status as a poet on faith, it was because Louis admired him," she says. "Only after I had undertaken to sell the poems did I begin to read them." She became a brief and minor character in the Cohen story. "One evening the three of us went out to dinner to talk about the (forthcoming) Book. I would have expected us to go to one of the small French restaurants for which the city is famous, or to the Rose Marie, first of the tiny Hungarian restaurants that had opened right near McGill. That shows how little I understood the aesthetic rules of the game. We went to Joe's Steak House on Metcalf Street, where your choices were with or without garlic and karnatsel (spiced sausage). The lack of such refinements as a tablecloth made it easier to use the tabletop as a desk while eating. In the absence of true aristocratic possibilities, Louis and Leonard preferred to eat where there were no pretensions that food was anything but food."

Once inside, the three talked shop, "discussing the physical properties of the projected volume, the thickness of the paper, the font of the type, the arrangement of the poems and their order and the accompanying drawings. We could not settle on a title then and there,' says Wisse, 'but Leonard's eventual choice, *Let Us Compare Mythologies*, had the Jew playing gracious host to other civilizations, with a touch of formality that was only slightly ironic at his own expense." Cohen's debut collection would indeed be entitled *Let Us Compare Mythologies* and came into the world that May 1956. The initial print run of 500 copies would sell out within the year. The book was dedicated to the memory of his father, Nathan B. Cohen.

The book was a critical success even if the print run on Contact press was modest. Cohen would recall that, "In the three magazines of the country that reviewed it, the reviews were very good. In general, it was well received. We were beginning to touch others besides our small circle; small groups in Toronto, Vancouver, Edmonton." Sales were not disappointing. Everyone knew that few poetry books ever seriously sold and the 22-year-old Cohen was far from disillusioned. He was in fact exalted, and at the start of what he felt to be a brilliant career. The content itself – dealing with death, hope, sex and women via the occasional language of myth – was a poetry that was reassuringly mature and real for someone so relatively young. The public perception of him cemented around this time – as sharp, handsome, literate, brainy, romantic and horny – would endure for years hence. "Leonard in those days had many admirable qualities that did not yet figure prominently in his ballads," says Wisse. "He was clever, shrewd, even a little sly, with a satirist's critical intelligence. I sensed that even then he had already gotten clear of Louis, not only because he considered himself the truer poet but because he was cannier all around, in his handling of people and in his understanding of markets and fame. In Leonard's presence I always felt alert as though I had joined a hunter on the trail. No one else I knew took so much license in speaking the truth. One day I saw him standing with his closest buddy, Morty Rosengarten, on the corner of Sherbrooke Street. 'Where are you going?' asked I, who was always on my way somewhere. 'We're watching the girls come out for spring,' he said, just standing there." As he'd matured Cohen gravitated towards men of poetic authority like Dudek who initially nurtured, affirmed and galvanised his character. Eventually they would become his peers before his own reputation superseded even this status as he transcended the mantle of local poet and conquered the world. *Let Us Compare Mythologies* sealed the apex of their friendship. Dudek would remain at McGill until his retirement while Cohen now began to seek a global audience. Of the many important figures he'd met in the last few years – Dudek, FR Scott, Hugh MacLennan and Irving Layton – he would outgrow almost all except for Layton. The two continued to socialise heartily; two poetic bucks intellectually competitive but bound by love.

Wisse, so instrumental in the birth of his first book, would also go her own way. She appreciated that Cohen was something special but had no regrets at not getting to know him more intimately. "I should confess that Leonard Cohen did not appeal to me as a lover," she says, "not even in his poems. By the time Louis introduced us I had been swept up in the romance that has claimed me for a lifetime... More than stirring romance in me, Leonard enlarged my sense of the here and now. His poems were heavy with loss in a way that made the present more valuable, the small experience more fragile and precious. I think I remember each and every time I spent with him, as if the moment itself were a poem I had to learn by heart."

By now, Cohen had already made a conscious, public decision to become a writer. The printing of his first book, as provincial as its distribution was, was more than enough proof for him. It was a pre-paid ticket for the journey ahead. Cohen's family, while essentially middle-class and conservative, still appreciated the honour of such a vacation even if the financial prospects of such a living (quite rightly as it turned out), concerned them. Cohen would later acknowledge that he was able to brush off his uncles' apprehensions much more easily than he would have his own father's. In some way the death of Nathan now allowed him a rare freedom to follow his poetic calling. "Occasionally my uncle, my grand uncle would take me aside and say 'This is a very nice hobby but are you going to be able to make a living do this?'" It would take Cohen almost a lifetime to answer such a concern.

The outlook of that winter of 1956, however, was good. In addition to publishing a book, Cohen had recently recorded eight of his poems for an album imaginatively titled *Six Montreal Poets* for the Folkways record label. "Sam Gesser was the producer of that album," notes Cohen, "a man who became a very benign and generous figure in the musical circles of Montreal, who became an impresario and brought in people like Pete Seeger and The Weavers and acts that might not have found their way into the city. He made sure that they came. Very nice guy, and he gathered a group of us called 'Six Montreal Poets' and we made that. I guess I was invited to participate in that project on the basis of that recent publication, which would have made me the youngest poet, I think, on the album at the time."

His voice is at this stage, if obviously not unbroken, then was at least an octave and a half higher than the singing voice we'd become familiar with. In recital, his early speaking voice has the stilted, airless and mannered quality of Sylvia Plath's tones, of someone who was brought up speaking 'American' trying very hard to speak in English. This was a common trait amongst English speaking poets and announcers at the time. Anyone being recorded or broadcast attempted to do so, using the worldwide accent of the BBC's world service as a template. But it also reflected the fact that Cohen wasn't American and that Montreal was in fact a kind of multi national interzone. Speaking specifically of his home town Cohen would in fact point out that, "If you stop anyone here and ask them what they are they'll give you a race or country. They won't say they're Canadian, they'll say they're Hungarian or Greek or Jewish... this city was designed to keep its European past."

While the album was mixed, compiled, mastered and packaged Cohen abandoned his earlier half-hearted, largely diplomatic strategy to study law in Montreal and moved to New York City where he enrolled at Columbia University to study literature. Living in a dorm near the Hudson river, he once again became part of the local 'scene', this time in Greenwich Village, where he shimmered on the outskirts of the then burgeoning beats movement. He attended at least one reading by Kerouac at this time. Witnessing the handsome and charismatic, often beatifically drunk Buddhist poet/writer recite his stuff over a pseudo jazz piano backing would be of immediate if temporary influence on Cohen.

Like many of the beats, Cohen was also interested in expanding and/or altering his consciousness by any means necessary. He'd begun experimenting with drugs in Montréal and continued the practice in NYC where they were more readily available. His preferences in particular were for hallucinogenics – LSD and Peyote, Mushrooms – and hash or grass. Amphetamine, usually in easily available pill form, was also common. Although he was much less reckless than most in his indulgences he still occasionally combined drugs (resulting in no matter how subtly, cross polypharmacy), and often washed the pills/tabs down with alcohol. Unlike some of his elders who disapproved, Cohen did not see getting high as being obstructive. "You can co operate with the vision that alcohol gives you," he would explain. 'You can cooperate with the vision that LSD gives you. All of these things are just made out of plants and they are there for us and I think that we ought to use them." He was once again a well-liked student at Columbia but he was once again uncommitted academically. Not only was his heart not inclined towards becoming a professor or tutor, he was otherwise engaged fully elsewhere by the realities of sex, drugs and poetry. He did manage; however, during his brief tenure as a student to write a term paper on *Let Us Compare Mythologies*. Even this one token academic achievement was somewhat coloured by an ambiguous surrealism.

Cohen returned home for Christmas.* Wisse had sent him an invitation for her engagement party at her parents' home which was held on New Year's Eve, 1956-57. "Cohen's arrival created a stir," she recalls. "He had brought along a couple of people I did not know, one of them his cousin Robert Hershorn... Hershorn reminded me of Robert Cohn in Hemingway's *The Sun Also Rises*, who becomes more thoroughly dislikeable the longer he tries to hang in with the crowd. Hershorn seemed to have no social scruples, at least not in the company of people he considered his social inferiors. He quickly got himself drunk, and it fell to my father, who was in charge of the bar, to deal with the ugly scene he seemed intent on creating... I remember standing beside the makeshift bar in the dining room, my father takes a coin from his pocket and holds it out for Hershorn to see. The bad boy grins. 'Mr. Hershorn,' says my father, 'I'm glad you're a betting man.' Instead of threatening him with the rules of the house, Father challenges his guest to abide by the rules of chance, which were likelier to command his respect: heads or tails – you go on drinking or you stop. Father's sobriety may have determined his win of the toss, allowing the party to continue without incident." Hershorn, a known drug dealer, would appeal to

---

* Such constant trekking between New York and Montreal was often done simply if uncomfortably by bus.

Cohen's more adventurous, Byronesque nature and also presumably supplied cousin Cohen with his occasional pharmaceutical diet. Robert Hershorn would die of a heroin overdose in Hong Kong in 1972.

Shortly after the release of *Six Montreal Poets* that January, Cohen returned to Columbia. His studies were slacking and even compared to his time at McGill, it seemed he put more effort into extra-curricular non-academic work. This did not just entail drinking and partying. He remained focussed on his own essential work, particularly his poetry but in addition he did start his own short lived magazine called *The Phoenix*, which existed for one issue, published during April 1957. Beyond the desk, typewriter and lecture hall, a major romance blossomed with a beautiful, statuesque brunette called Anne Sherman. Cohen was besotted and she was as much a muse as lover. Despite their ultimate incompatibility Cohen was not shy about letting his friends know that he would, if possible, marry Anne. Such a statement was probably flushed with the first true sense of sexual liberation outside of his hometown and such a union would never happen. Anna and Cohen would remain on good terms for some time after his spell at Columbia and most importantly, she would in part fuel a future book, *The Spice Box Of Earth*. With the latest New York winter retreating, Cohen abandoned Columbia and academia forever and headed once again for home.

Cohen was back in Montreal for the summer of '57. Inspired by his recent adventures in NYC, Cohen was hungry to travel again, and to do so applied for a writing grant from the local council that would allow him to go abroad in the name of research. Meanwhile he once more appeased his concerned uncles and cousins, and worked for the family. Diligently, he put in shifts at his uncle's brass works and at the clothing factory, where he and the other workers laboured to a soundtrack of classic 50s pop courtesy of the factory radio. Summer moved on and by early 1958 Cohen was becoming concerned about being sucked into the family business at the expense of his own art and destiny. Nevertheless, though uncertain about his future and despite the growing length of the new depressive moods he found himself facing, Cohen retained a basic love of life. As well as very physically earning a very basic living, he was also, along with Mort, helping to run a gallery, The Four Penny Art gallery. At nights he continued to work on his poetry as well as exploring fiction. "I was working in a factory in Montreal at the time and writing," he recalls, "having these wonderful evenings that would go late, and then I had to be at work at seven. It was a good hour drive, so [I was] sleeping very, very little and playing all night and working all day." In the spring of that year he was best man at Layton's 'mock' marriage (Layton was already married and couldn't face a divorce). Meanwhile Cohen continued to be an active, formidable presence on the local coffeehouse and bar scene, living the 'beat' life almost to the letter, reciting his poems in public when the opportunities arose, smoking at least a pack of cigarettes a day and gulping diet pills washed down with booze.

Another (temporary) poet of the time, albeit a less recognised one, Don Owen, remembers that, "I first met Leonard Cohen in the late Fifties, when he used to come down to Toronto with Irving Layton for the poetry readings that were held in the old Greenwich Gallery on Bay Street. There was a considerable literary scene in Toronto at that time, and once a month the gallery would be filled with Harris tweed jackets, viyella shirts, Karen Bulow ties, baggy grey flannel trousers and desert boots, mixing it up with peasant blouses and skirts with lots of crinolines under them. I didn't spend much time with Leonard on those evenings, though – held back, I suppose, by a certain resentment that he was coming on so strong on my turf. I could get used to the idea that he was a better poet than I was, but he always seemed to leave the gallery with the most interesting woman there, the one I'd spent all evening trying to get up enough nerve to say hello to."

Women were a constant, ongoing, minute by minute preoccupation with Cohen. They were the fuel for his desires, fantasies and ultimately his work. He still missed Ann Sherman but was nevertheless healthy in his appetite for bona fide experiences with any attractive and intriguing woman that came his way. And Cohen, like many men his age, went out of his way to make women come his way. He was soon to lose one of his most favoured companions in this activity, old drinking and wenching buddy Mort, who left to study art in London that year. Cohen saw him off after an extensive bar crawl, perhaps even knowing then that he would be following his art student friend to England soon.

As spring came around, Cohen took his public performances up a level.

A first important performance in this new mode, of Cohen performing his poem 'Gift' in a Kerouac inspired style over jazz piano, was recorded by local radio at Dunn's Birdland club on Saint Catherine Street. Although this style of vocal performance – neither singing nor reading – has since become familiar to the point of cliché, it was arrestingly fresh in post-war Montreal. "I don't think there were too many people doing it at the time," Cohen would point out. "I was working with a pianist and an arranger, Maury Kay. I did a few weeks with him... He used to write big band arrangements. He had about a 12- or 15-piece band and this little stage, and it was his gig. I'd come on at midnight, and I kind of improvised while he played. Sometimes he was playing the piano by himself and sometimes doing parts of arrangements or tunes played in a somewhat subdued way while I took my own riffs. Or sometimes I'd do set pieces, like a poem from *Let Us Compare Mythologies*. We did that off and on for a month, and then I worked with a great jazz guitarist from Winnipeg by the name of Lenny Breau."

Eagerly attending these examples of Cohen's new shtick, Layton was amused at Cohen's intense, almost self-conscious hipness but the audiences, in the vernacular of the day, dug it. So did Cohen. He had always found music in poetry and now he was finding poetry in music.

That summer Cohen worked as a youth counsellor at Pripstein's Camp Mishimar. A traditional 'overnight' camp for children of varying abilities and attitudes, it was located in the Laurentian Mountains at St. Adolphe d'Howard, Quebec, 60 miles north of Montreal. The 24-year-old Cohen was again a popular presence on site which was known for dealing with particularly troublesome youngsters that other camps would not admit. Cohen also showed a hitherto unknown talent for black and white photography at the camp, his preferred subject being the female nude. Not surprisingly, Cohen was particularly popular with some his fellow female colleagues at Mishimar. At season's end, Cohen returned to Montreal and let it be known that he would not be persuing a career within the family firm. The summer vacation had allowed him to come to terms with his vocation. And yet there were specific strains within that vocation that Cohen had not yet decided upon. During this period, he seems to have moved away from the public jazz/poetry/reading experiments and dug back into his writing and its necessary solitude. In the ultimate sense, he saw his vocation not in merely fulfilling his talents as either a poet or a vocalist but in following his heart.

Cohen was pretty much fearless in his approach to life and had a muscular practicality to back up his poetic prowess. In the spring of '59, after phoning ahead, Cohen walked into the offices of Jack McClelland. The dapper McClelland was son of John, co-founder and owner of one of Canada's leading book publishers, McClelland & Stewart. Cohen had apparently chosen them to be his lifelong publishers. Impressed by Cohen's jib and giving the manuscript Cohen proffered only a cursory glance, Jack did an almost unprecedented thing – he accepted Cohen's book there and then. Thus a lifelong relationship, between Cohen and McClelland & Stewart was born. It was, notably, completed unmarked by signed contractual agreements between the two. Continuing in the vein of the assembling of *Let Us Compare Mythologies*, Cohen was at once eager to be involved in the rudiments of how his book would be published, how it would look and how it would feel. He suggested that rather than go for a dour hardback for this first edition – which was the norm – the company should instead present *The Spice Box Of Earth* as a colourful, pocket sized paperback. As was baldly apparent by now, Cohen the poet was not interested in pursuing an academic career; he wanted his poetry to be easily accessible and as popular as possible, as omnipresent as folk music. His argument with his publishers to facilitate such a process would be ongoing.

Meanwhile, the acceptance of his book by a major and successful publishing house was the final affirmation Cohen needed (if he needed any), allowing him to give up his job at the family factory forever. Like sandbags from a balloon Cohen was intent on jettisoning many of the normal tenets of regular living, leaving behind Academia and now the nine to five. He did not, however, confine himself to his garret and a diet of air and ink. Rather, Cohen took some work with the Canadian Broadcasting Corporation, and also took on the odd paid translation job before once again heading for New York, this time accompanied by Layton. On November 12 they gave a reading at the Young Man's Hebrew Association on 92nd Street. The performance was a success and, simultaneously, other good news came through. He was now "…

awarded a grant by the Canada Council. A very generous grant at the time, it was about three grand, which was worth a lot in '59, and also a ticket to visit the ancient capitals, because on the basis of *Let Us Compare Mythologies*, I said I wanted to visit Rome, Athens, and Jerusalem. So, I had a round-trip ticket from Montreal to Tel Aviv." Typically, he chose to visit none of these places as his first port of call. Following in the footsteps of best pal Mort and countless others, Cohen chose first to go to London.

In December 1959 Cohen found himself in the city's pleasant, leafy, northern neighbourhood of Hampstead. Perhaps as a mission statement on that very first jet-lagged day Cohen actually bought himself a Green Olivetti 22 portable typewriter with standard issue black keys and white letters. It cost him what was then the considerable sum of £40. This was the beginning of a life long affair between the two and a necessary tool of his trade, particularly in the short term. Cohen had arranged to stay in London with Stella and Jake Pullman at 19b Hampstead High Street. Morty had recently vacated the home but Cohen had two other friends staying there awaiting him, a friend from childhood, Nancy Bacal, and Harold Pascal along with the Pullmans' cat, David. The house embodied a friendly, respectful congeniality. Then in his late 40s, Jake Pullman was a seasoned sailor and man of the world who had travelled extensively and flown long distance freight aircraft between America and Britain during the war. He and his wife ran a warm, open house but were nevertheless possessed of a strong work ethic which would serve Cohen well. He would retain a friendship with the former for the rest their lives.* "She (Stella) gave me a couch in her sitting room when I first got to London in '59," Cohen would remember, "and she said, you know, 'What are you supposed to be here for?' I said 'A writer.' She said, 'If you write your three pages a day you can stay.' So she supervised, tyrannically, the production of those three pages... Stella Pullman had this wonderful and nourishing influence and trained me to be a disciplined worker... she said she was going to throw me out on the street if I didn't do those three pages every day!"

---

* Jake would die of a heart condition in 1973.

Some of the other activities required of him were less metaphysical but just as practical. Almost on arrival Cohen felt the climate disagreeable. In England, everything is very humid. "The beds are humid at night [which] is why the women are so strong!" he reminisced. "The first night Mrs. Pullman gave me a hot water bottle. 'Why?' 'Undo your bed and you'll know why.'"

After spending the night sleeping on his cot in the living room, bathed in the sodium light of streetlamps, Cohen would have very specific chores to fulfil in those chilly pre-central heating mornings. In a reverse echo of his future duties as a monk in a monastery in LA, he "… had certain duties, like getting the coal in and lighting the fire." In effect he was living a kind of monastery life or at least a prelude to one, were it not for the rampant social life Cohen enjoyed at this time. Nancy Bacal was the perfect companion. "My higher education began in London," she would remember at the time. "The timing was perfect. I'd fled Montreal because the code of behaviour was too parochial and confining, because I knew instinctively there was no one set of values that was intrinsically right. At least that's what I hoped."

This challenging, fearless attitude must have matched Cohen's attitude in many ways and the two explored north and west London's cafes, pubs and libraries accordingly. Cohen was initially enthused by being in the capital that had a history of so many great writers and even more excited at his imagined part in that very lineage. Yet he would be initially disappointed by many aspects of a London that was still very much 'pre swinging' unless you knew the right doors to knock on. "In London I never found the night life except at a West Indian club called The All-nighter with great music and great pot and dancing."

Neither did Cohen have much luck romance wise in London, a situation that was as much to do with the etiquette of the day as it was with any lack of charm on his part. But his latest drinking and cafe partner had no such problems. "My friend, Nancy Bacal…, knew the town and took me there. She was dating Michael X, a disciple of Malcolm X, who later founded the Black Muslim movement in London. He told me he was going to return to Trinidad and take over the government and he wanted me to be a part of the government (laughs)… I said 'Listen, Michael, you are going to make a nationist black government, how could I be part of it?' He responded, 'Permanent Advisor to the Minister of Tourism.'"

A white, middle-class Jew befriending a radical black extremist was not, at least in Cohen's case, as incongruous as it seemed. "In most times and places it would have been extremely odd for a man like Leonard Cohen to have been friends with a man like Michael X," explains Michael's biographer, John Williams. "But the sixties in London – and other major cities, of course – were not most times, and Michael X's circle of friends included the dope priest Alexander Trocchi, Bill Burroughs and Ronnie Laing, as well as Cohen and Judy Collins and John Lennon. What brought them together was, on the one hand, the simple matter of Michael's girlfriend of the time being Leonard's childhood friend Nancy Bacal, and, on the other hand, the fact that Michael was a decade older than most of the hippies running round London at the time, and his closest friends tended to be other older hepcats, like Trocchi and Cohen, who had seen a bit of the world and liked the new hippie scene but were not completely seduced by it."

Apart from extremist, militant political figures, Cohen established a small lively new social circle that included the soon to be eminent Jacob Rothschild. Under Stella's watchful eye Cohen blackened his quota of pages daily, continuing to toil at the book of poems that he now owed to his new publisher thousands of miles away in Montreal. Generally Cohen was enthused to be walking in the footsteps of such great English writers as Tennyson and Milton and similarly excited to make a pilgrimage to Dublin in honour of Yeats and Keats, whom he toasted with more than one glass of Guinness while he was there. Bereft of bars, London's teeming pub life nevertheless suited him. His lodgings were comfortable, his social circle amicable if lacking romantically.

Yet ultimately, London did not suit Cohen. Although he'd been raised in part by Montreal's ruthless, vividly beautiful winters there was something about blustery London's constant rain, and occasional pea-souper fogs that oppressed him. Such greyly tyrannical damp weather, however, did force him to buy one particular key item of clothing – a pale blue, Burberry raincoat.

CHAPTER TWO

Hydra And Phaedra

"There is a hand at work in everybody's life".

LC

It was the month that Elvis Presley returned home to Memphis after a two-year stint with the US Army in Germany. The UK pop charts were a monochrome patchwork of inoffensive ballads crooned by the likes of Max Bygraves, Jimmy Jones and Anthony Newley. Such somnolent saccharine sounds chafed scrumptiously up against the still primitive sounding rock'n'roll of Gene Vincent, Fats Domino and England's own Cliff Richard & The Shadows. In America, the first patent for a laser was approved while back in London, Jacqueline Boyer would win the fifth Eurovision Song Contest for France singing the instantly forgettable 'Tom Pillibi'.

Meanwhile, in that same cold and teal coloured March of 1960, following the 'brutal' extraction of a wisdom tooth at an East End dentist, Cohen took a wander. "I was walking on Bank Street with a huge cavity in my mouth," he remembers. "It was raining, I wasn't dressed properly..." For whatever reason, his walk through the financial district and its oppressive dual combination of slate grey buildings and climate, led him to the national bank of Greece. The soaked Canadian seemingly entered on a whim. The random teller he did business with there was both heavily tanned and wearing aviator shades. Such a quixotic appearance – particularly the latter adornment – was arguably more political than fashionable. Perhaps the teller considered the bank, like embassies, to be an actual part of Greece itself and was dressing accordingly. Possibly it was a subliminal protest against the shabby English weather outside. Either way, Cohen was intrigued by the man's get up, and the two began talking, Cohen asking the clerk what the general climate was like in Greece. "Springtime," the teller replied. Seldom had Cohen been more effectively or speedily seduced. He made immediate plans to leave the UK, finishing his work on *The Spice Box Of Earth* manuscript and posting it off to McClelland & Stewart with some relief. By the April 15, after some rudimentary sightseeing in Athens, Cohen had taken a five-hour steamboat journey and arrived on the island of Hydra, which translates as water.

Yet Cohen wasn't arriving at this particular island purely on impulse. To anyone with even an arbitrary interest in poetry, philosophy and mythology, the idea of Greece itself would have already occupied a unique if marginal physic space within the imagination. While in London Cohen had already spoken of Greece, and its satellite island Hydra in particular, with his friend Jacob Rothschild. Jacob's mother co-owned a house on the island, and Jacob had urged his friend to visit, promising that he'd write his mother in advance letting her know of Cohen's arrival. It was this very recommendation, in fact, that prompted the curious Cohen to wander out of London's drizzle and into the bank of Greece in the first place. "I had heard a lot about Hydra, of that very beautiful island," he'd recall. "I said to myself that I should go somewhere completely different in order to see how they live."

Unlike Athens, the island that Cohen arrived on that spring resembled the ancient Greece of its mainland much more than its increasingly metropolis like capital city. The harbour and housing of Hydra were arranged in a classical Greek style, following the design of an amphitheatre. The atmosphere was busy but not frantic, the town quietly thriving and alive but still basically rustic. Although not agricultural, Hydra had no inherent industry other than small scale fishing activity. For those areas set up to receive it there was an hour of electricity available once in the morning and once again at night. Most homes were lit by candles and/or paraffin lamps. After having recently lived in Montreal, New York and London the effect of such spare lighting on the island would have a welcome and seductively romantic effect on Cohen. There were even biblical echoes evident in Hydra's public transport system: the main mode of transportation along the rough tracks up into the main mountain area was by donkey, palm leaves optional. The absence of traffic noise was almost deafening. Like the electricity and gas supply, plumbing on the island was still a relative novelty and telephones were a scarcity.*

But what Hydra *did* have was much that money and 'progress' couldn't buy: atmosphere, congeniality, a beautiful climate and a population that had for centuries practiced and refined a very particular Mediterranean genius for living. For most of its sparse population, life on the island involved basic physical work which was fuelled by a rich diet of fresh organic food and wine and was relieved by the greatest and simplest pleasures in life. Live music, intoxication, making love against the backdrop and beauty of the climate and island itself satisfied most needs. Hydra was no mere obscure idyllic backwater either. At the time of Cohen's arrival, the island had a history of hosting a healthy contingent of European and American ex-pat artists. As well as the locals, there was a small population of international writers, painters, poets, architects and choreographers. In many ways Hydra was at this time the Greek equivalent of Spain's Ibiza.

At 25 years old, Cohen in his current role of wandering poet was, either consciously or not, following a minor tradition in his pilgrimage to Hydra. His spiritual forebear, Henry Miller, had been enraptured by the place just over two decades before. Writing in *The Colossus Of Marroussi* in 1939 he described a place that had changed little by the time Cohen had discovered it. "Hydra is almost a bare rock of an island... there are only two colours, blue and white and the white is whitewashed every day, down to the cobblestones in the street...

---

* Cohen couldn't know it then but the introduction of a full scale telephonic system some years later would be the inspiration for one of his most legendary and most covered songs, 'Bird On The Wire'.

aesthetically it is perfect, the very epitome of that flawless anarchy that supersedes because it includes and goes beyond all the formal arrangements of the imagination. This purity, this wild and naked perfection of Hydra is in great part due to the spirit of the men who once dominated the island."

On arrival Cohen roomed with two friends of friends, a couple already well established on the island, the Australian novelists Charmian Clift and George Johnston. George was tall, slim and dashing with a forelock of dark thick hair falling romantically to the left side of his brow. Charmain had an almost modelesque beauty about her. They made a handsome, attractive couple. "The Johnston's were central figures," their guest remembered. "They were older. They were doing what we all wanted to do which was to write and to make a living out of writing. They were very wonderful, colourful, hospitable people. They helped me settle in. They gave me a table and chair and bed and really helped me out."

The guest soon took their gift of furniture to a rented house of his own at the cost of $14 a month.* Once Cohen had settled somewhat, he took up Jacob Rothschild's offer, climbed up to the great 40-room mansion overlooking the sea and introduced himself in person to Jacob's mother Barbara, had divorced their father some years previously when he'd renounced worldly goods and joined the Labour Party. Had Cohen known this he may have taken it as an omen. By the time he called at her luxurious abode, Barbara was married to the Greek painter Nikos Ghikas who owned the house.

Cohen's meeting with Barbara was not a success, so it was just as well that he had taken the time to make himself independently comfortable before approaching the big house on the hill. Jacob's mother had received no letter from her son, and no one in the grand residence had any idea who Cohen was, and furthermore were uninterested in knowing who he – or 'his sort of Jew' – was. Disgusted and rejected, Cohen returned to his rented house. This snub however, made little lasting impression on him. The crystal waters, warm air and translucent

---

* In 1960 over half the houses on Hydra were estimated to be abandoned and this obviously affected prices in the tenant's favour.

sunshine of Hydra had already utterly enchanted and beguiled him. It was as if he belonged there, as if he'd already spent time in this paradise in a previous incarnation. There was a spiritual calm to the place. "When I arrived in Greece I really did feel I'd come home," he recalled. "I felt the village life was familiar although I'd no experience with village life."

Through his initial hosts and his own courteous, low key charm Cohen was made consummately welcome by the ex pat/artistic community on the island and had no need for the approval of the old money contingent represented by Barbara and Emma Rothschild. While Cohen's hereditarily cold Canadian bones slowly thawed under the same sun that had once scuppered Icarus, he made friends easily with a wide range of colourful characters, almost all of whom were continuously intoxicated by a combination of their relative youth, talent, and the inspiring climate of an alien environment and its native cheap and potent local booze: Retsina wine.

Along with his original Australian hosts, among those that Cohen would hang out with at Katsika's bar were the painter Anthony Kingsmill, the Norwegian writer Axel Jensen, the philosopher-musicologist George Lialios and a floating cast of musicians, poets and writers including Paul Desmond, William Lederer and even on one fleeting occasion Alan Ginsberg. (The two poets had already met briefly at a party in New York a few years previously and would meet again in the future under very different circumstances). Another writer, David Fagan, would move to Hydra and befriend Cohen more than two decades hence, but he states that the island of then was the same as the island of now in many fundamental ways. "It's such a very small place," he stresses, "just a rock in the sea, really. It has no roads and thus no cars or motorbikes or even scooters. People are forbidden to use bicycles after the age of 14. It's such a small place that you are almost forced to become part of the community." Ironically, by 'fleeing' to Hydra, Cohen had placed himself within the heart of an almost inexhaustibly rich and catholic social scene, one that compared with almost any capital city on the planet, albeit in microcosm. By putting himself into a kind of exile upon a relatively tiny and obscure Greek Island, Cohen had somehow found himself at the centre of the world itself.

Of all his new friends, the blonde and tautly handsome novelist Axel Jensen would prove to be amongst the most important in one profound respect: he would introduce Cohen to the girl who would become not only his great love for the next few years but who would, in a far off life, also gain minor fame as one of Cohen's most important and beloved muses. Jensen's wife and mother to their child Axel Junior, was a 25-year-old blonde Nordic beauty and one time occasional model called Marianne. Cohen, who remembers being introduced to her by Jensen himself, would eventually fall in love with her. Before that, within the fashionably friendly and open atmosphere of 60's Hydra, Cohen would gallantly go on to look after Marianne and her child while Jensen parlayed with another female companion in Athens.

Marianne Ihlen herself, however, would remember the moment of their first meeting emphatically vividly. Compared to Cohen's casual reminiscence and considering his reputation, it's ironic that she remembers it so much more romantically. She recalls their introduction vividly, albeit as if via a misted and cracked segment of cine-film. Whilst queuing in a shop waiting to buy water and milk, she became aware of a presence behind her. She turned and remembers seeing Cohen standing in the shop doorway with the sun behind him. Marianne couldn't make out his face; he was shadow cast from flesh and bone. The silhouette spoke from a mouth she couldn't focus on, his features were indistinct. "Would you like to join us, we're sitting outside," he said. The language was English but the accent neither British nor American. Moments later, when Marianne met properly with him outside in the sunshine, there was an instant chemistry between the two, accompanied by the silent far off sound of destiny falling into place. Marianne's grandmother, who raised her, had told her as a child that she would meet "a man who speaks with a tongue of gold", and Marianne recalls that first meeting with Cohen as "utterly incredible".

Cohen was equally as impressed. "There wasn't a man who wasn't interested in Marianne," he would remember. "She was a traditional Nordic beauty... but she was also very kind... and modest about her beauty." As he came to know her, Cohen was also beguiled by her talent for living. "She knew things," he said, "about the moment, about graciousness, hospitality, generosity..."

Typically, the subject of Cohen's ardour did not share his appreciation of her physical allure. Speaking decades on, Marianne would state modestly: "I never felt that I looked like much at all. I didn't believe it when Leonard said, 'You're the most beautiful woman I've ever seen', but what I mean is that... I think I had too round a face. So I have gone round looking down all my life. But after all I did have... you know the sun bleached my hair, and after all you were ... in Greece you were so blonde, so blonde, so blonde, because there they were mostly dark. Skinny. Almost no boobs... To my great regret."

She was, however, as enamoured of her beau as he was of her. "Oh, he was beautiful!" she says. They had another endearing quality in common too, a natural modesty: "Neither did he think that he looked like much," she remembers. "We both had problems. You have no idea."

With Axel senior now more or less out of the picture Cohen, Marianne and her little boy moved in together. The romance was not instant. Cohen's behaviour toward the abandoned mother was initially dictated by compassion for both her and her situation and he remained as ever, courtly and also physically distant. But after nights of eating together and of the poet reading her his new work, much of which was inspired by her, they eventually became a family, first within her house and then in Cohen's, which he bought using an inheritance from the recent death of a grandmother. With this windfall he was able to buy a three-story house halfway up a hill, for $1,500. By late September, he Marianne and her child had moved in. This was the first of many homes Cohen would own around the world and one that he would both retain for the rest of his life and with a particular affection. "I like my desk there," said Cohen, "I don't know what it is but there's something about the light and my desk and my kitchen. It always gives me something."

Acquiring a property on an obscure Greek island at his age was not a casual thing for a young Canadian to do. On some level Cohen must have decided that he would be spending serious time on Hydra. The new home was sparse and elegant with matted floors, surrounded by solid and mostly bare stone walls. He evidently had an obsession with sparseness even then and disliked too many paintings obscuring the purity of a bare wall. The furniture was basic and sturdy. His heavy desk was anointed with a gardenia, replaced lovingly by Marianne each morning. Lit by lamps and candles, the bedroom was dominated by Cohen's robust, Russian-made iron bed.

Now in a more or less solid relationship, Cohen and Marianne continued to mix and mingle with their shared friends at the numerous bars and cafes on the island. Like any other couple they divided their time between an established, harmonious home life, and a rich, flowing social one. On some warm nights, the air heavy with night stock, Marianne took particular delight in getting merry on Retsina and dancing traditional Greek dances in the café's courtyard, often accompanied by a happy local. Usually Cohen would wait at a nearby table, patiently drinking and quietly smoking beneath the stars, enjoying the spectacle of his woman cutting loose until she had exhausted herself. "And then we went home together," she recalls sweetly. "And then it would be so incredibly peaceful and so harmonious to be with him, because there was such tranquillity."

It was around this time that the *Life* photographer James Burke (who would die tragically in a work related accident only four years later) accompanied a journalist on an assignment to interview Cohen's novelist friend George Johnston. The resultant beautiful black and white photographs he took capture perfectly the seemingly free and easy going bonhomie that Cohen and Marianne enjoyed. One picture in particular randomly captures a beaming, guitar hugging Cohen surrounded by a group of multiracial, seemingly classless, friends all bound together by an obvious love of their libertine life. Years later, when Cohen reminisced once again in particular about the impression his original hosts the Johnstons had had on him, he could have been speaking about many of his Hydra friends when he said: "They drank more than other people, they wrote more, they got sick more, they got well more, they cursed more and they blessed more, and they helped a great deal more. They were an inspiration."

Most significantly, such a poised balance of a social and domestic life and the resulting harmony that ensued provided Cohen with the perfect routine within which to work. His labours were the ultimate background to everything he did. Beyond the romance, the socialising, the intoxication, artificial and otherwise, at the very core of Cohen's existence there was the unremitting dedication to his work. This was the focal point of his life, the cornerstone upon which all other relationships and activities rested. During this idyllic time with Marianne and her son, he continued as ever to hone his poetry and even songs, although musically he was at this time more of an interpreter, often learning and playing other people's compositions, mostly folk tunes, than practising as a committed songwriter himself. Pictures from his life of this period habitually show him either with or in close proximity to an acoustic guitar although his main instrument during the early 60s was the typewriter and his preferred form was poetry and prose. He continued to work on the manuscript of his first novel, which would come to be known as *The Favourite Game* and kept up a vigorous correspondence by letter with friends, family and editor Jack McClelland.

Cohen's drug intake was as intense as his work rate during this period. Given the lack of narcotics as a natural resource on Hydra, (with the exception of the light opiate buzz of the commonly brewed poppy tea), the drug use showed a real commitment on Cohen's part. David Fagan, an expert on the history of Hydra, confirms that, "No, he wouldn't have scored much on the island itself, despite its port. He would have had his own supply, or had it posted to him or whatever. But drugs would certainly not have been easily available on the island then."

Some of Cohen's favourite drugs, however, were easily available over the counter of the local pharmacist, particularly two of his favourites, Maxiton and Mandrax. The latter would gain as much fame in the 60s as Cohen himself, particularly for its use (illegally) as a recreational drug.* Mandrax was a potent sedative-hypnotic drug that worked as a muscle relaxant and general sedative; it was a major downer. Mandrax was easily available and among the youth culture enormously popular (by 1965, it was the most commonly prescribed sedative in Britain). Particularly when used with wine it gained a reputation as a 'party' drug, and as such soon became known by various affectionate nick names: 'mandies', 'mandrake' or 'mandrix'. Cohen would indulge heavily in 'mandies' over the next few years, obviously seeking the ultimate, smooth, levelled out mood. Sometimes he'd mix the downer with the upper, taking both

---

* In the seventies it would gain even greater infamy in its incarnation commonly known as Quaaludes.

Mandrax and Maxiton. In this way he was chasing the ultimate artificial neutrality, as both drugs fought to cancel one another out, resulting in a state of eerie pseudo neutrality. Another favoured combination, with the same goal in mind, was smoking hashish on top of the speed. The twenty-seven-year old Cohen was no pharmacist and he mixed such substances via instinct. He did smoke to becalm himself, admitting how "a few crumbs of hashish", provided "relaxation and receptivity", allowing him to listen to the cricket song as the sun went down, but unlike many of his mainland peers his goal was not just to "trip out" but to ultimately help him blacken pages. Cohen's main aim in getting high was to get down to work.

Cohen also altered his consciousness by fasting, going so far during one abstinence that he actually made himself ill. "I was wiped out," Cohen recalled. "I didn't like my life. I vowed I would just fill the pages with black or kill myself. After the book (which would eventually be known as *Beautiful Losers*, his second novel) was over, I fasted for ten days and flipped out completely. It was my wildest trip. I hallucinated for a week. They took me to a hospital in Hydra. One afternoon, the whole sky was black with storks. They alighted on all the churches and left in the morning... and I was better."*

Unlike the drugs, which often inspired his condition to work but ultimately impaired that condition, the constant presence of Marianne and her son did not in the main disturb Cohen's routine or schedule. In fact, particularly during the earliest phases of their romance, Cohen was inspired and nurtured by life with his Norwegian love. Their life on Hydra would be summed up decades later by Marianne herself: "We lay in the sun, we walked in the sun, we listened to music, we bathed, we played, we drank, we talked... there was horse riding and there was lovemaking..." She would also claim that for five years she had the unique luxury of not wearing shoes.

Cohen remembered her gratefully. "She brought a tremendous sense of order into my life," he said. "It was really a great privilege to live in a house with her. She had been brought up by her grandmother in the

* The storks were no hallucination. Thousands of these birds actually did stop over on Hydra for a break every year en route to Africa.

war so she had the education of an older generation. Just the way that she laid a table or lit candles or cleaned the house… (But) it wasn't just that she was the muse, shining in front of the poet. She understood that it was a good idea to get me to my desk."

It was not all paradise in the Garden of Eden however. Cohen was an attractive young man and other women often courted his company, particularly during tourist season. "There was this fabulous young model from New York, who came to Hydra," remembers Marianne, "and they disappeared for an entire day. And so I imagined all kinds of things. I curled up like a small foetus, and built a large wooden coffin around me, an imaginary one, of course. People who passed by actually thought I was dead."

Even when not playing dead, the cost of living on the idyllic island was cheap, Cohen calculating he could get by on $1,000 Canadian a year. But however inexpensive life on Hydra was, it wasn't actually cost free. Although mostly removed from the commercial sector physically – hardly any existed on the island anyway – Cohen continued to play his part within that world. Even sat shirtless and speeding at his typewriter in Aegean sunshine, he was still technically a commercial poet and a published writer. McClelland & Stewart were major players, and despite his earlier wishes for them to present *The Spice Box Of Earth* to the public as a cheap and accessible paperback edition, when Jack actually offered Cohen the choice between this or a more expensive and substantial hard cover publication, Cohen went for the latter. This meant the book would not be released until the spring of 1961. While the poetry book was being painstakingly prepared for printing in Montreal, Cohen finally completed a first draft of the novel he'd been working on since London. Burnt out by the writing process and the substances ingested while completing it, Cohen sent the original copy of what would become *The Favourite Game* to Jack McClelland at the end of that year's summer.

By winter Cohen was restless and broke yet again and that November he took the boat across the sea to Athens and flew to Montréal. From there he and a friend took a stoned and intoxicated rented limousine ride to Ottawa where Cohen made the most surreal application for a grant ever. "When they arrived in Ottawa they somehow managed to get their hands on a wheelchair," recalls Owens. "and took turns pushing each other in and around and about the Canada Council offices, serenading the secretaries and causing a big uproar." The Dadaesque performance paid off and Cohen would receive his grant early the following year.

Money was a constant issue for Cohen during this time, the yearly trust fund of $750 inherited from his father not even covering the cost of one year of living on Hydra. As Christmas approached he partially turned his energies to other means of making money through writing, principally scripts for television dramas and plays. Ideas leapt from the keys of his typewriter as Cohen awaited the arrival of the next grant cheque but none ultimately brought home the bacon (although Cohen was a vegetarian at this point). Meanwhile, across town, the galleys of his second poetry book were mounted and set for printing by McClelland & Stewart, while at the same time his editor there received "reader reports" on Cohen's first novel. They were not favourable. As a consequence, that December came the surprising news that McClelland were actually returning his book; they would not be printing it in its current form. Jack had, after all, taken Cohen on as a poet and not a novelist and even as a novel the work was unconventional, baffling the readers paid to assess it. Until now the young author had had a uncommonly positive response to his work from both Dudek and McClelland.

Cohen was surely disappointed by this new rejection but appeared to be firmly philosophical. "Since hearing the news I have been strangely exultant. I feel free again, the way I felt before a line of mine was ever published." This noble proclamation was somewhat betrayed by the fact that Cohen immediately began rewriting the book. Buoyed by the interest in the novel from yet another publisher, an American firm by the name of Abelard-Schuman, Cohen continued to revise, refine and remodel the manuscript into the New Year. As with the songs Cohen would soon be completing, the book went through various stages, titles and forms, haunting him on a daily and renewed basis.

By March 1961 Cohen felt unbearably physically stagnated by the intense cerebral that a life of writing (and the need to make money) had imposed on him. With the new grant from Ottawa in his bank account he decided to shock himself into feeling again and headed for Cuba. Bussing it to Miami from Montreal, he took a March 30 flight from there to Havana. On this very day, back in Montreal, Jack McClelland, sat in his comfortable book cluttered office, received the proofs for *The*

Spice Box Of Earth, ready for printing. Cohen, meanwhile, had flown into another world.

The Cuba of the late 50s and most of the 60s was a place in violent flux. The year before Cohen's somewhat reckless visit, Fidel Castro had led an armed revolt to overthrow the country's infamous dictator Fulgencio Batista. By 1961 the newly established Cuban Revolution had drifted towards a Marxist-Leninist political system and as an obvious consequence, relations with Cuba's neighbour – the communist fearing US – grew conversely frigid and agitated. Diplomatic relations between the two ended abruptly in early 1961, just prior to Cohen's arrival. In addition, the effects of the trade embargo that the US had placed upon Cuba in 1960 had seriously escalated and by now, desperate Cuban citizens were forced to scuttle and scramble for food and consumer goods. Relations with the Soviet bloc had also intensified, and Cuba got centre-stage attention from the whole world as it tried to survive hostilities from both the US and its own counterrevolutionaries.

All this was happening as Cohen arrived. As the middle-class Canadian poet disembarked his plane, hundreds of Cubans were clamouring past him to go the other way. Upper class and professional citizens were leaving the island in droves, as the new government began to practice a disturbing new ideology which sought to "re-educate" some minority groups – including homosexuals and free thinkers – by executing them.

Cohen booked into the local version of one of his favoured run down hotels and unpacked. Architecturally, the place around him was in glorious decline, with once colourfully ostentatious buildings and homes now crumbling magnificently, their pastel painted walls peeling and warping beneath sloppily pasted propaganda posters and thickly painted graffiti. Socially, too, the city was in an intoxicated uproar. Amidst the Caribbean heat, multitudes of beautiful, expansively hipped whores moved through the early morning hours amid banks of thick cigar fog, lubricated by potent sugary rum and whatever drugs were available. All such fraternization was played out in the midst of continuously threatening civil unrest and violence.

Dressing for the occasion in pseudo military khaki garb and growing a beard to match, Cohen hopped the bars after midnight in a rich, fecund atmosphere that utterly inebriated both him and his poetic sensibility. But behind the seemingly impulsive, almost Byronesque, thirst for adventure there were personal questions Cohen sought to answer, and he hoped the Cuban experience would force such answers upon him. "I went down there. I don't know how much of a supporter (of the revolution) I was. I had this mythology of this famous civil war in my mind. I thought maybe this was my Spanish Civil War, but it was a shabby kind of support. It was really mostly curiosity and a sense of adventure."

His presence in Havana did not go unnoticed by the new regime. Nevertheless, Cohen's first visit from a mysterious government official at his hotel late one night would turn out to be more comic than Kafka. Calling on him at his room, a man informed Cohen that his presence was needed at the Canadian embassy immediately. Cohen was thrilled and anxious, feeling no doubt that in opening his hotel door to the dark suited man he had let himself into the plot of a Graham Greene novel. The man and Cohen were driven to the Embassy through the dark and perfumed Havana streets. On arrival Citizen Cohen was ushered into the office of the Vice Consul. Cohen stood before the man's desk anticipating some tricky questioning or accusation. Instead the official merely admonished Cohen with the statement: "Your mother is very worried about you"! Masha, back in Montreal, had become disturbed by exaggerated news stories of Cuba's civil unrest and had been in touch with the Embassy as a result, pleading with them to locate her son. Cohen would experience more dramatic action days later when he was out wandering at night on a white sandy beach ninety miles east of Havana. "I was walking on the beach in the middle of one night," he recalls, "and was suddenly surrounded by about 11 guys with Czechoslovakian submachine guns. I was an American who didn't speak Spanish, and they thought I was the first guy off the landing boat. I was the first guy arrested. It was a bit tricky to sort this thing out. But they happened to be very gracious. Wherever they took me, by the end of the night we were drinking toasts to each other and 'the friendship of the people', and they let me go."

Cohen had managed to charm and convince the authorities of the truth even if he wasn't sure of the truth himself. Years later he would gently mock his Cuban adventure, joking that "I felt that I was defending the island against an American invasion and planning that invasion at the same time. I was the instigation of the whole scandal…"

The next day he and two of his new soldier friends returned to Havana. As they escorted Cohen to his hotel they were caught for posterity by a street photographer who sold the photo to Cohen; he picked it up off the man a few days later, placing it in his knapsack.

His thirst for danger and adventure satiated, Cohen decided to make his mother happy and return to Montreal. It was April 26 and Cohen was standing in line for the next available seat on any flight to Miami. People were desperate to leave the country and the atmosphere was one of subdued and restrained hysteria. Under these circumstances, Cohen's nerves must have been seriously jangled when he was called to the airport's security desk. The reason for him being pulled out of the queue was the discovery among his effects of the photograph showing Cohen – complete with beret, bullet necklace, beard and khaki trousers – smiling blissfully with his two diminutive soldier buddies. The authorities saw this picture as proof enough that Cohen was actually a Cuban with a forged Canadian passport. As such he would not be allowed to leave the country under any circumstances.

While his fate was decided by the authorities, Cohen was guarded by a heavily armed 14 year old. Such a situation was surely more macho frisson than Cohen had bargained for, but by a stint of pure luck, the adolescent soldier was momentarily distracted by some other commotion on the runway. Cohen was told to stay where he was as the 14 year old ran off to investigate. Nerve wracked, Cohen simply recovered his knapsack and made slowly for the nearest plane. Acting as coolly as he could he got aboard and found himself a seat. The plane's pilot was in too much of a hurry to have the stewards check tickets and had soon cleared the runway. Within hours of being arrested, Cohen had escaped Cuba. In addition he'd finally found his point of view. "It was not a fiction. They were under a threat of invasion, so you have to take that into consideration. But just a society that well organised turned me against it. I didn't like the loudspeakers on every corner, and the general sense of gung ho. There were articles in the journals about the bourgeois individualists – artists and that sort of thing. And I found myself characterised very accurately in a lot of these polemics. Because – that's really where I am: I am a bourgeois individualist."

His body and honour intact, Cohen left his Havana adventure with a reinforced sense of his masculinity and ideology. A handful of poems were also forged from the experience.

By early May, Cohen was back in Montreal where his mother no doubt slept soundly once more. That month he gave a brief reading to commemorate the forthcoming publication of what would be his second collection of poetry and his first by a major publisher. When released, *The Spice Box Of Earth* was, certainly by poetry book standards, more or less an instant success. The reviews were unanimously if sometimes esoterically positive. "There are poets, passionate men by definition, who can never in their poetry communicate sexual passion. I do not believe Leonard Cohen is among them," read the review in *Canadian Literature*, No. 10. "He will probably have to write less about love, and think about it longer... Above all, he brings the impression of good health to his poetry. The afflictions mentioned here are curable, and once Cohen has freed his sensibility from what West called 'the thick glove of words' he will be able to sing as few of his contemporaries can..." This last line would prove spookily prophetic in the most literal sense. The first edition would sell out within three months.

Following a misadventure with some opium brought by the visiting Alex Trocchi, a well known London 'beat' and drug imbiber, Cohen once again left Montreal and set sail for Hydra. He had recently received $1,000 from the Canadian Council arts scholarship a couple of hundred of dollars of this bought a ticket aboard a freighter. Headed for Genoa, Italy, the freighter made numerous stop offs among them Greece. The sailing took three weeks and by the end of the summer Cohen was back on Hydra with Marianne. Cuba had realigned him in some ways and he was ready again to relish life on the peaceful Greek island, refreshed as he was after his recent purifying adventures. Rejuvenated, he threw himself back into the regular routine of drug consumption, lovemaking and typing. Time away had also refreshed his relationship with the ever beautiful Marianne and that same year they visited her family in Oslo where he was as usual inspired and piqued by a different climate. Marianne would have surely introduced her beau to family and friends as a writer or even a poet. To all appearances this is exactly what Cohen was at this period and all he was. Music seems to have been but a hobby at best. During the early Sixties, for Cohen the published and acclaimed poet there was little suggestion of the future that awaited him.

In March of 1962, Cohen returned to the great 'cabbage' – as he would later describe it – of London. He once again stayed at 19b in Hampstead with his friends the Pullmans. Yet he was almost instantly homesick, as his letters to friends abroad so poetically attest. Yet where *was* home? Cohen felt drawn to both Montreal and Hydra if not exactly equally then at least as deeply. *The Favourite Game*, the obtuse and perverse novel, the one that McClelland had turned down, had eventually been accepted by the London firm of Secker & Warburg. They urged him to stay on in London and work on revising the book further.

He took the time to reacquaint himself with London's leading black freedom fighter. "Michael X I knew very well," Cohen would reminisce. "I had many talks with him. For some races there are men of imagination who are really oppressed and there is absolutely no other way. They have got to take up this position whether they really believe it in their hearts or not... There's no argument you can have with them. You can't say 'cool it'. But he himself knew the limitations of this position. Michael said to me – he was completely against arming the blacks with guns in America... He was even against knives. He said we should use our teeth. Something everybody has. That was his view of the thing. It was a different kind of subversion... He would invite me over to his place and he would serve me a drink, a delicious drink, I would say, 'God, how do you make this?' He would say, 'You don't expect me to tell you. If you know the secrets of our food, you know the secrets of our race and the secrets of our strength.' You know it was that kind of vision that he wanted to develop. Pretty good one."

Despite such stimulating company Cohen could stand the dreary winter of London no more and once again he flew to Athens and sailed to Hydra. Once ensconced in the daily sunshine bathed routine he continued to toil on what would eventually become his first published novel. He still had numerous distractions, one being when his mother and sister came to visit him in the summer of '62. True to Jewish custom and out of respect to his mother, Marianne – a divorcee and not married to Cohen – had to temporarily move out. While Cohen recognised the necessity of such a palaver he complained to friends about how such visits and manoeuvres killed his concentration. Secker & Walburg were eager for the new manuscript and Hydra in the summertime offered too many distractions, attractive female tourists who were intrigued and attracted to the tanned, trim Canadian poet being top of the list.

Cohen didn't help his situation by moving around the planet almost constantly. "Change is the only aphrodisiac," he observed. In October his old friends at CBC invited him on all expenses paid trip to Paris. The idea was that Cohen represent Canada as part of a radio panel discussion on the state of crisis in Western culture. Despite his commitment to Secker & Walburg and ultimately to himself, Cohen was eager to go. "I was doing it for money ($600)," he would explain in an account of the trip written up and printed in the magazine *Partisan Review*. "And to get out of a very sunny place where there were no books and no prospects and a couple of women who knew me too well."

Strapped for cash as ever but packing a small lump of green Lebanese hashish (which he would subsequently lose), on arriving in Paris Cohen had to check into a "coffin-sized, coffin-colored room in the Hotel Cluny Square" on the north-west corner of Blvd. St. Germain and Blvd. St. Michel. Expenses could not be claimed for another two days – Cohen arrived 48 hours early – at which point he would be allowed into a more opulent room at the Hotel Napoleon. Cohen's brief, meanwhile, was to familiarise himself with a sample of books written by the other members of the panel, as he would be moderating the event. No doubt exaggerating his account for comic effect, to this end he claimed to have read for 30 hours straight, consuming five books by Mary McCarthy, four by Romain Gary, "and about a thousand articles by Malcolm Muggeridge." Cohen eventually left his coffin-room for something to eat, taking with him the last of the books and made for a late night café where he was no doubt transported into ecstasy by the many Ray Charles songs on the jukebox. Cohen picked up a girl in the café and the whole episode was recorded in bittersweet style in the short story he would write two years from that day. The radio broadcast itself went without a hitch although Cohen was not particularly impressed, either by the 'dryness' of the discussion or his fellow panellists.

The New Year found him in New York once more where amongst the usual activities he stayed with sister Esther who now lived there with her husband. He continued to write wherever he was, almost completing the final manuscript of *The Favourite Game* by the winter of '63 when it was accepted by both his London publisher and their North American distributor, Viking. True to his rampant productivity Cohen was already mining a new seam of poems by the time the proofs of his first novel were delivered to him.

The Favourite Game was finally published in September 1963 by Secker & Warburg in the UK and by Viking in North America.* Reviews were as expected with critics intrigued, complimentary, appreciative, their style often inspired by the tone of the work itself. Yet sales remained poor. The *Tamarack* review read: "It's a beautiful story, joyously physical, witty, and introspective, written with a wonderful surging intensity. A few poems from *The Spice Box Of Earth* are included, but the real poetry of *The Favourite Game* is [leading character] Lawrence Breavman's passionate, lyrical zest for life, for the beauties of molten brass and fresh fish in ice, for the individuality of people and places, noses and dawns." *Alphabet* magazine wrote that "At the best, Mr. Cohen reveals a gift for creating outrageously comic situations and startling and illuminating metaphors. His ability to crystallise the inter-relationships of these metaphors allows many of the chapters to be read as individual poems. When the author suggests, on the last page, that all his characters' lives are like different kinds of blossoms springing from a common source, he displays an imaginative power which makes one puzzle all the more at the novel's weaknesses. They seem so unworthy of his talent, so unnecessary."

Books often record and express a certain specific era in an author's life, one that would be left behind on publication. The first phase of his life with Marianne on Hydra seemed to be winding down. Cohen was as ever restless and money was an ongoing, inexorably exhausting concern. The same month that his novel was released, Cohen was on assignment for *Holiday* magazine in Montreal. The brief was to meet and interview the hugely celebrated classical pianist Glenn Gould. Cohen achieved

---

* Intriguingly, the book exists in various versions, written both in the first and in later editions the third person.

at least 50% of the brief, meeting Gould in a hotel bar and becoming utterly entranced by him. The account of their meeting, however, would remain unwritten.

This stay in Montreal did however allow fate to step into Cohen's life yet again when he made his initial contact with Suzanne Verdal. Cohen's impressions of Suzanne and their brief times together would one day world famous. They first met while Suzanne was "... maybe several months into my relationship with Armand (Vaillancourt), which was mostly based on being dancing partners together." She remembers: "And he (Cohen) would watch us dancing, of course. And then I was introduced to Leonard at Le Vieux Moulin, I think in the presence of Armand, in fact. But we didn't really strike a note together until maybe three or four years later."

Until then Cohen continued to work, travel and hustle. He gave readings often, including, occasionally one on Hydra although these were rare. His profile was building in Canada and he was invited to make publics addresses and attend literary functions. Leonard Cohen was by now generally considered in Canada as standing for *something*. He travelled the country on a reading tour that November, an unremarkable trip that nevertheless refined and solidified his national reputation. He was already speaking about his next 'lunatic' novel and continued to work away at another book of poems, provisionally entitled *Opium For Hitler*. Yet although his reputation as a poet was growing incrementally amongst ever slightly increasing circles, on a real popular level he was unknown.

There was an establishment firmly in place in Canada and on one trip to Montreal in '64 he countered its conservative, disdainful face. That year Cohen attended the filming of one of Oscar Brand's *Let's Sing Out* TV shows, aired from a different location each week on the CTV channel. Brand was already a legend in American and Canadian folk music circles and a hugely popular radio and TV presenter. "I was sitting with Carly Simon," remembers Brand, "who had been on the show doing with her sister their hit song, 'Wink 'Em, Blink 'Em And Nod'. So we were sat talking about what her prospects were and they were pretty good I think, her having a rich father... and then a young man came over... well... I wouldn't know how old he was because he looked so *sloppy*. He looked beaten up. He didn't look neat. He didn't look as if he was worried about his looks and in that regard he didn't look as if he had anything to worry about. Anyway he says 'Excuse me are you Oscar Brand'? And I say 'Yessir'. So he says, 'Mind if I sit here'? I say, 'Sure'. So he sits down and I keep talking to Carly Simon. Anyway, eventually I say, 'What can I do for you'? 'cos he was obviously sat down for a reason. And he said, 'I'm a poet'. And I said 'Congratulations. That's very useful. This is a country that likes poetry. I'm glad to hear it. Have you written anything?' So he gets out his papers and I read it. And I thought it was 'stumbling'. So I told him that. And he said 'Oh'. But I said, 'They are good and if you work on them you'll probably get them better.' And he was very hurt. So he took the papers and folded them up and put them back in this big wallet. And he left. And I felt bad about it."

However sensitive he might have been, Cohen was too busy surviving, working and living to let such trite rejections get him down, although he did occasionally get angsty in a surreally humorous manner. "I once had drawn a bath and I put pine oil in it and I noticed the pine oil stained the water the same color as my Olivetti (typewriter)," Cohen recalled. "I was in a mood of some extravagance and I put the typewriter in the bathtub and tried to type under water. Then I threw my manuscript for *Flowers For Hitler* in the bath and tried to scrub it with a nail brush. This was during a particularly tense period one winter in Montreal. Then I took the typewriter out of the bathtub and in a rage over some imagined injustices a woman had done to me, flung it across the room."

Typewriter abuse aside, Cohen's nervous energy was mostly channelled into his work. By February that year he'd he began a fourth novel, *Beautiful Losers*. With his relationship to Marianne waning slightly, and fuelled by cigarettes, Maxiton and Cognac, he wrote intensely through the Hydra months to finish the book. Further distractions and opportunities assailed him. McClelland & Stewart had organised another reading tour of Canada. At the same time he gratefully picked up a $4,000 literature prize awarded for *The Favourite Game*. The poetry tour, taking in Toronto, Kitchener, London, Kingston and Montreal began on October 25. Cohen and fellow poets Layton, Earle Birney and Phyllis Gotlieb set across Canada in two cars. Aside from old buddies Layton and Cohen, the poets did not particularly mix. "Let's just say I was pretty much suppressed by my companions," Gotlieb would remember, adding that after the tour ended: "Last I saw of Earle, he was in the back of a taxi, with his thumbs at his ears, waggling his fingers at Leonard and Irving." Gotlieb herself was not the aim of any such gesture. "Oh no," she says, "If I'd thought that, I'd have given him the finger."

The adventure, what there was of it, was initially filmed by poet turned filmmaker Don Owens. On reviewing the rushes it was felt that everyone but Cohen and Layton's presence was negligible. Gotlieb's personality obviously did not come across in her readings. As Cohen explained, "They were stuck with a problem. They had invested a lot of bread in it and they had to make a film, so they decided to make one on me and it was a kind of salvage job so it took all the pressure off the production in a way because it was a salvage job." Subsequently, new footage directed by Don Brittan would be added to the film and the whole thing re-edited and become better known as the famous documentary *Ladies and Gentlemen... Mr. Leonard Cohen*. The economic aspect of the tour left the poets deeply unimpressed. Months later, once the accounts had been processed, each participant received $37.50 for their trouble.

A third book of poetry, the controversially titled *Flowers For Hitler* had been released earlier during the year, and such was Cohen's status that the critics were now beginning to review the author rather than the book. The University of Toronto quarterly wrote: "By an untalented poet such a book would be a bore. But Cohen is potentially the most important writer that Canadian poetry has produced since 1950 – not merely the most talented, but also, I would guess, the most professionally committed to making the most of his talent. What we get in a great deal of *Flowers For Hitler* is the retuning of a virtuoso instrument, elaborate mnemonic devices, a series of techniques for the extraction of selves, a disciplined fulfilling of irrational tasks, a combination of derangement and restoration within the poetic process. I am sure that for Cohen this is (among other things) the necessary means to poetic survival. But for the reader who is convinced of the fineness of the instrument, *Flowers For Hitler* can be an exciting book in its own right."

Cohen the writer was by now undoubtedly a serious proposition. Witnessing the presence of his own books on the shelves of friends and family made an obvious impression on him. For a perfectionist like

Cohen – someone for whom Stephen Spender's maxim of "A poem is never finished but abandoned" seemed tailor made – being able to come across his books as the property of others provided a sense of release and closure. "In terms of history the work always belongs to history," he said. "There's a dual ownership. Yet as soon as the artist shows it, publishes it, sings it, then it takes its place amongst all the other things in the world and is subject to all the modifications that things are subject to in the world…" Yet it was hard to gauge if he was successful as a writer. That year Cohen brought in $17,000. This was a more than respectable figure for any poet, particularly one who sold as modestly as Cohen. But much of that income had been via grants and awards, money that could not be counted on on a yearly basis. Such fiscal uncertainty continued to agitate him.

Back on Hydra, in April of 1965, a burnt out Cohen finally finished *Beautiful Losers*. He'd made himself physically ill during the process and on completion had to take to his Russian bed to recover. He now weighed 116 pounds and the effects of the speed he used as writing fuel had almost broken him. The manuscript was greeted by both Viking and McClelland & Stewart with some bafflement but they were ultimately convinced by the quality of the actual writing and both firms accepted the book.

That same year *Ladies And Gentlemen… Mr Leonard Cohen* was allowed a limited cinematic release. It was a charming, tautly edited piece showing its subject at rest and play. It also includes valuable footage of Cohen recording his poems – again a la Jack Kerouac and Steve Allen, with occasional piano accompaniment – for the Canadian Broadcasting Company. Cohen sits demurely during the sessions, alone on a stool, dressed casually in trousers and shirt – no jacket or tie – the only others in attendance being the sound engineer, who is sat besuited and grave at a bank of militaristic recording equipment. Of course we only know this because there is CBC film footage of the event, which also meant that Cohen was always aware of the film crew in attendance. Filming such activities as a poet recording recitals of his work was a fairly recent development. Poetry had only recently been afforded the privilege of actually being sound recorded. But by Cohen's third book, not only was he being asked to read his poems into a microphone, the whole process of recording was *itself* was being recorded on film. Cohen seems to take this whole process – the externalisation of the inner whilst being filmed and recorded on dual levels – completely naturally. It also brought home the fact that despite his Canadian Council endorsement and funding and unlike much previous Canadian poetry, Cohen had the chutzpah to write mostly about himself. There was little evidence of patriotic duty in his poetry or its reading (although there was some). This again was part of Cohen's uniqueness and his critical success. This trait would remain throughout his life's work. "I was never able to move out of my private life," he acknowledged.

Even at the time of its release, the film had the sense of being an instant archive, as if it had been around for decades. But among the dated and fading billboard posters and quaint traffic scenes in the background, the 'young' – Cohen never appeared truly young, except as a toddler – Cohen strikes a curiously ageless, even timeless figure. The film was well received in Cohen's home country. The screening at the main McGill Auditorium was almost full, which was apparently rare for the genre of film being shown. In addition the audience responded as if Cohen were actually giving a live reading, clapping and quietening in the appropriate places. As for the subject himself, Cohen's interest in himself on film was mostly endearingly fantastical. "I've always had a fantasy that some director will find me sitting at a drug store counter, like Hedy Lamar or who ever it was." he mused. "I always wanted this to happen. Some very perceptive director would see that I stood for something very, very particular. I would take all the work away from it. I thought I would not have to create myself as an image. I would be cast as some kind of detective with wide lapels." Ever keen to be modest, Cohen would ultimately come to consider *Ladies And Gentlemen's...* greatest interest as being limited purely to his own family.

There were grants, there were critical notices, there was recording sessions, and now there was a film. Such attentions repaid his and his family's confidence in a life that in some ways he felt was already mapped out for him. And surely, as long as he was true to that map, things would work out ok. "I felt there would be money in my life," he would recall years on, having by then experienced every extreme of money there is, "not in any abundance but there'd be enough for me." Despite his productivity this was still not the case. He continued to criss-cross the country and its borders, promoting his forthcoming novel in NYC, that February. This was not the usual performance. Cohen was still witty, reading his poems sincerely and clearly, introducing them with a comic's timing but he also made public his new role as singer/songwriter.

It was Valentine's Day at The 92nd Street YM-YWHA (The Young Men's-Young Women's Hebrew Association) Hotel, New York City. The event had started in the usual manner but Cohen concluded the set by picking up his guitar and performing an entrancing version of a song then called 'The Traveller'.* The introduction of an actual *song* amidst a poetry reading was a subtly startling occurrence. None of his contemporaries was capable of moving from reading to singing so easily, much less while accompanying themselves on guitar. Most would not even have considered such an activity. Yet by picking up his vinyl stringed Spanish acoustic guitar, and singing a strange song in a plaintive, oddly pitched voice Cohen had launched himself into a brave new world.

Back in Canada, his second novel, *Beautiful Losers,* was released that March. To Cohen it was a spiritual if not religious work. "I would say that *Beautiful Losers* is a redemptive novel, an exercise to redeem the soul," he explained. The critics did not agree and the book was heavily criticized for its "obscene" sexual content. "I've just read *Beautiful Losers* and had to wash my mind," exclaimed the *Toronto Telegram's* reviewer. while the *Toronto Globe and Mail* simply branded it "verbal masturbation". Cohen was, as ever, philosophical. "I'd feel pretty lousy if I was praised by a lot of the people that have come down heavy on me," he retorted. When it was put to him that he was "a mild man who writes brutal, startling poetry", Cohen not unreasonably turned the accusation its head. "I thought I was a brutal startling man who wrote mild, lyrical poetry," he grinned

Despite, or perhaps because of, the visceral and largely negative reception to his latest book, his profile as a writer continued to grow in his home town. He even appeared on national television to 'defend' his work. The critics were hardly bashful in their damnation of the book

* It would come to be better known as the immortal 'Stranger Song', a classic which he'd written only recently at the Penn Terminal Hotel :"A gruesome establishment'," Cohen reckoned.

but Cohen did not respond in kind. His reaction was hard to gauge. He seemed neither affronted or particularly moved either way. But neither was he amused or scornful. The book's language and descriptions had even allegedly upset Canada's official 'censors' but Cohen recognised this for what it was. Such reactions marked an advancement in terms of what was acceptable in art and a general progression in thinking. The fact that his book would outlive and even help redefine any censorship was, as he construed, it "a triumph for 1966". He also considered the idea of "selling ones anguish" through books as one of the best things one could do with such negative feelings, whatever the authenticity of such distress.

As with all commercial ventures, however, the bottom line, even in the rarefied world of poetry publishing, was money. The books would sell much less than enough to justify further ventures in this field. This was a profound stumbling block for any published writer, *particularly* a published writer. No one would have predicted it then but *Beautiful Losers* would be Leonard Cohen's final novel. As his personal literary ambitions waned, a quiet reputation as a songwriter bloomed, like moss on some hitherto unnoticed windowsill.

Around this time, local group The Stormy Clovers were amongst the first beyond Cohen himself to perform his songs. (Cohen had increasingly been practicing his song writing if not actively promoting it.) Cohen himself performed with the group, for the first and only time, at the Venus de Milo cafe on Sherbrooke Street, Montreal, shortly before his first CBC performance on Adrienne Clarkson's *Take 30* TV show in May 1966.

In the wake of the critical furore surrounding his latest book, Cohen returned to Hydra, Marianne and her son. Cohen had to face the facts: he was a nationally respected but essentially marginal Canadian poet and novelist. He had originally arrived on the island at 25, full of promise, words and music. He had, to all intents delivered on all fronts. Yet the reality was harsh. He was returning to Hydra as a 32 year old who was, in his own words 'broke'. "I just came to the realisation that I couldn't make a living," he stated flatly. Although he had never persued it for his own sake or been particularly motivated by mammon, Cohen had expected money to occur as almost a natural phenomenon in conjunction with both the effort and realisation of his own work. If he followed his heart, maintained an integrity and wasn't lazy, then surely one of the side effects would be to attain what everyone else seemed to take for granted – the simple phenomena of making a living. "I thought if I wrote well and the books were published – and they were – then there would be enough to finance the next book." The last part of the equation did not happen. Cohen's books were much more successful than the vast majority of works published – they were after all reviewed, they were hip and they gained him a reputation and most importantly they were published. But they had not sold in any serious amount, and neither had Hollywood intervened. Many an author of Cohen's modest profile had seen their standard of living be somewhat artificially bolstered by ancillary rights to the work being bought out but as yet no one had purchased film rights to the novels. In his own way, Cohen worked as hard as any of his forebears had back in Canada in their Montreal factory and yet he earned barely enough to put sufficient quantities of fruit and nuts on the table of his house in Hydra. And Hydra was a place where the cost of living was as cheap as it got. He was obviously a writer of talent and more importantly one with a unique voice. Good or bad, the reviews had acknowledged as such. Perhaps it was only a matter of time before sales picked up. Cohen no longer felt like hanging round to find out.

Back in Montreal CBC were courting Cohen, offering him a job as a TV presenter. However broke he was, whatever wall he seemed to face, one thing was certain in Cohen's mind and that was that it was still too early to give up and go back to the 'air conditioned' nightmare of Montreal. So Cohen looked around inside himself for viable alternatives. Music had always been a parallel passion to poetry and now, faced with the reality of not being even able to pay the bills, Cohen began to explore the possibilities of what was perhaps his second calling. He even considered changing his name before embarking on what many would have considered a risible venture. If this was true then his new moniker reflected this opinion. Alas, the pop folk singer 'September Cohen' would never come to be and he quickly reverted to Leonard. He never did get the tattoo he talked about either.

He had of, course, been 'collecting' songs – learning country and western and folk tunes via the shortwave static of armed service radio, and playing guitar and singing (in a fashion) since he was 14 but Cohen didn't consider himself much of a musician, either as a singer or guitarist and few others who heard him did either. Like most people he was more an aficionado of music than a maker of it. He wasn't even, particularly, a fan of the makers of the music he loved. As a patron of cafes, diners and bars, he'd "lived beside jukeboxes all through the fifties. There was 'The Great Pretender', 'Cross Over The road'. I never knew who was singing. I never followed things that way… I wasn't a student of music. I was a student of the restaurant I was in… and of the waitresses."

Yet despite having such a pure relationship with the art, there was the occasional face and name that Cohen could put to songs, names he would remember forever. Both Hank Williams and Ray Charles inked tattoos upon on his heart. And although, even as his own singer songwriter star eventually rose, he would always lack the confidence to stand comfortably beside such greats, Cohen did have a steely belief in the basic craftsmanship of his own songs, in both the lyrics and the melodies in particular. Even so, sat in his modest house on Hydra wondering how to pay the outstanding grocery and bar tabs, he saw himself launching into music as a purely experimental and financially motivated venture. He knew he was no great singer in the accepted sense and he was generally unsure about what he was getting himself into or even how he was supposed to get himself into it. What he certainly knew however was that "I feel free when I'm singing". This evidently was enough.

In October of 1966, at the age of 32, with money borrowed from cousin Hershorn, Leonard Cohen set off for Nashville to become a country music star.

CHAPTER THREE

Here It Is

"Luck has so much to do with success... and failure."

LC

On his arrival to New York City in the fall of '66, musically at least Cohen was an innocent abroad. Future peers and friends such as Judy Collins and Bob Dylan were certainly familiar names, even to a French Canadian who had lived in Greece for the last few years, and Cohen did retain some vague grasp of their work. But as actual people and as to what they represented, the individuals who made up the new breed of singer songwriters were essentially vague entities to Cohen. "I was totally unaware of the folk music renaissance," he claimed. "But I was ambushed in New York by this whole phenomenon."

Cohen had, of course, heard not only of Dylan but had listened to Dylan's records back in Montreal, becoming actively interested in Dylan's magic and alchemy the previous January. But until Cohen was press ganged in NYC by this whole new movement in the early winter of '66, he had been unaware that Dylan was no longer seen by many as a mere novel curiosity. Dylan had now transcended, in establishment terms, his notoriety as a goofily powerful and eccentric young song writer, singer and poet and was now becoming recognised as the figurehead of a powerful new demographic, a demographic that was rapidly metamorphosing its underground into an over ground. Cohen would later recognise this as a temporary 'crack' in society that gave an opportunity for mavericks like him to 'make it'.

"I have a terrible voice, can't even carry a tune," he reckoned at the time. "Also, I'm very small, emaciated, with the residue of acne. And I'm demonstrably Jewish (Dylan is not). The only thing going against me is that I play the guitar too well."

Although musically, Dylan and Cohen were already splitting apart (Dylan had gone electric less than two years previously while Cohen's musical vocabulary remained skeletally acoustic), Cohen had felt an empathy if not outright competition with Cousin Zimmerman from day one. "I was living, in a certain sense in the same kind of universe that he was living in so that when I heard him, I recognised his genius… but also a kind of brotherhood," said Cohen, who until recently had appeared to have much more in common with the poet Dylan (Thomas) than he had the folksinger. In effect the kind of 'new' music that Dylan was pioneering – musically basic, heavily lyrical, simple in its complexity (and tangentially opposed to the current rock'n'roll of Elvis and Jerry Lee Lewis and/or the lounge music of Sinatra and Bobby Darin et al) – had in fact superseded a specific type of youth's interest in a particular kind of *poetry*. Cohen himself didn't know it but fate was cuing him up, preparing to place him centre stage among the hearts and minds of this new and youthful demographic. As the New York critic writer Robert Cristgau put it, Dylan, Phil Ochs and Collins (and soon Cohen) and more now provided "… the kind of poetry enjoyed by people sitting on their backpacks, reading Yeats and William Carlos Williams."

The entire western pop scene was plum ripe for a figure of Cohen's experience and credentials. This would come as much as a surprise to the man himself as to anybody. Handsome and quietly charismatic, his Montreal upbringing and the Authentic Beat life he'd recently lived in Hydra and London – and even partially in Fifties New York – only compounded his air of genuine poetic allure. This was a time when the previously explicit counterculture philosophies of Ginsberg, Kerouac and Burroughs were just beginning to be absorbed into the academic mainstream. While he admired some of their work (Burroughs' *Naked*

Lunch) and was friendly with certain key figures (Ginsberg), Cohen would recognise that he was never made welcome into the Beat circle, citing that he felt these new poets didn't consider his own poetry 'good enough'. It was, in fact, neither a question of good nor better. Cohen was simply too traditional, too lyrical, too plainly romantic in his poetical form compared to the new experimental techniques and poetic politics of Ginsberg and Hubert Selby et al. At the same time, the romantic and overtly confessional poetry of Sylvia Plath, John Berryman and Anne Sexton was all the campus rage across the country. With his dark, dapper looks, and weighing in at less than 140 pounds Cohen was an utterly contemporary mix of all these components, framed beautifully within the tough silhouette of a black leather jacket and the rough hardwood body of a battered acoustic guitar.

Cohen would eventually make it to his original destination of Nashville, but not for another two pivotal, life changing years. In New York he was lean, losing his tan, tense and restless. It was if he were shedding a skin. The metamorphosis from mystic mandraxed poet of Hydra to hustling singer songwriter of the big apple, would be an uncomfortable one. It was also a perfectly natural and necessary transmutation. "I've always felt very different from other poets I've met," explained Cohen. "I've always felt that somehow they've made a decision against life. I don't want to put any poets down, but most of them have closed a lot of doors. I never felt too much at home with those kind of people. I always felt more at home with musicians."

While in NYC he soaked up all he could, actively seeking out the Warhol crowd on arrival and wandering (on this occasion with Danny Fields), as so many of that group often did, into the hippest venue of the moment, The Dom. There, amidst the clouds of cigarette smoke and in the weird glow of black light, Cohen was struck by a Teutonic vision. "... an incredibly beautiful blonde woman singing, the apotheosis of the Nazi earth mother...' he would remember. The chanteuse Nico appeared to him as an erotically and narcotically corrupted angel "who looked like she inhabited a Nazi poster." Thus Cohen became infatuated with the post modern Goddess of Tragedy and sometime singer of the Velvet Underground, herself, Nico, who on this occasion was playing a set with her latest young beau, the then teenage Jackson Browne.

Watching dumbstruck with lust amongst the predominantly indifferent audience, Cohen was smitten. "I said, 'Forget the new society, this is the woman I've been looking for'." By his own admission, Cohen, who was 33 in an age where it was Uber-hip among those who mattered "not to trust anyone over 30", followed Nico around like a love sick bobby soxer. When introduced, Nico, in her stiff, dead voice, immediately rejected him on these very grounds. "I managed to meet her," recalled Cohen, "and within five minutes of our conversation she told me to forget it." Romantically, Cohen was simply too old for her. She preferred young, pretty boys, like Alain Delon, Iggy Pop (who recalled how she taught him how to give head) and current musical foil Jackson Browne. Cohen was as old as Satchmo by comparison.

The Canadian poet and the German one time *Vogue* model did, however, decide to be friends after a fashion. Cohen thought that the acquaintanceship was at least a basis from which to reach her and turn her around, a platform from which to ultimately seduce her. It would never happen. "I was madly in love with her," he says. "I was lighting candles… performing incantations… anything to have her fall in love with me, but she never did."*

When Cohen was first introduced to Nico, she was of course better known, (in the right circles) as being a kind of occasional member of the Velvet Underground. Thus, Cohen's painfully platonic relationship with her did at least help widen his social circle and as a result some sort of solace soon came in a sincere recognition from another poet and author. One night Cohen found himself sat at a table in the hip NY hangout Max's Kansas City being gently hassled by some (no doubt amphetamine fuelled) guy. Despite a growing irritation, Cohen kept his manners and responded gently to the annoyance. From across the other side of the table, a dark haired, slightly built dude in Ray Bans leaned over to Cohen and told him, "Hey, man you don't have to be nice to this

---

* Years later, with Nico having seemingly mellowed, Cohen would at long last make his move, going so far as to daringly place his hand on her wrist as they both sat talking on a bed in her room at the Chelsea. Nico was not impressed by Cohen's courtly, gentle advance. Screaming, she punched Cohen out and the police were called.

guy.You're the man who wrote *Beautiful Losers*'!"The ally was Lou Reed. (Reed would remember the first meeting slightly differently, citing the bar at the Chelsea hotel as the location. But he would always attest to his admiration of Cohen as a poet and a writer, comparing the impact of *Beautiful Losers* on him as being on a par with William Burroughs's *Naked Lunch*. Neither men at the time ever dreamed – even in their wildest occasional hallucigenic states – that decades on, a sagely Lou Reed would be inducting an elderly Leonard Cohen into the Rock and Roll Hall of Fame.

Although socially Cohen admitted that he felt 'frozen out' at this time, he was enjoying a minor, growing reputation as a poet and songwriter in certain circles. Introduced via Mary Martin, Judy Collins had already heard 'Suzanne' over the phone. (Cohen had called Collins from his mother's house in Montreal, somehow selling his live rendition of the song to her over the long distance telephone wire). Now Cohen was invited to Collins' apartment to 'audition' in person. Within weeks she had recorded 'Suzanne' for her *In My Life* LP, released almost immediately afterwards in November of 1966. (She would record and release another three more of his compositions, 'Sisters Of Mercy', 'Priests' and 'Hey That's No Way To Say Goodbye', all for her follow up album *Wildflowers*, the subsequent year.)

Such activity was monitored by one of NYC's leading musical lights, legendary Columbia A&R man John Hammond. "'Suzanne', of course, was his great tune..." he opined, "and there was one artist who was very enthusiastic about him, Judy Collins. And, also... Joan Baez loved him, too... yeah, those two. Women all feel very protective about him, because he's a very dark, gloomy-looking man, you know; and they all want to protect him."

Lacking the constant presence of a girlfriend since Marianne, 'protection', perhaps wasn't exclusively what Cohen was looking for in women at this point, but their versions of his songs would present to the wider listening public a strong idea of Cohen's force as a songwriter and perhaps even an inkling of his work as a poet. Compared to Cohen the singer and performer himself, the sweet and pretty interpretations by Collins would make his own recordings sound sinister and almost beautifully abnormal by comparison. His mild reputation as a published poet and novelist had allowed him the brief and futile audience with Nico but in a wider sense, the eternal 'Suzanne' and his subsequent blossoming reputation as a songwriter would become his calling card.

'Suzanne' had been written back in Montreal as the result of "a sheer act of desperation – of a desperado". It was "… a documentary song. It took a few years to write but it's just documentary… like all decent poems or songs… it's just the evidence… the ash of a flame that burned well."

God was in the details. The subject of the song was Suzanne Verdal, the wife of a Quebec sculptor, who Cohen had initially encountered a handful of years previously. Suzanne did indeed live by the river, near the St Lawrence, and the particular brand of tea was 'Constant Comment'. Suzanne herself would remember: "One of our mutual friends mentioned to me, 'Did you hear the wonderful poem that Leonard wrote for you or about you,' and I said no, because I had been away travelling and I wasn't aware of it…" The subject of the song acknowledged that she was "… flattered somewhat. But I was depicted as I think, in sad terms too in a sense, and that's a little unfortunate. You know I don't think I was quite as sad as that, albeit maybe I was and he perceived that and I didn't."

Considering the perfection of the song, it is remarkable that the subject matter of the piece came almost as an afterthought. "The song could have been called by any name because I had the guitar pattern before I had the name of the woman," Cohen said. As a whole, this perfect marriage of words, chords, harmonics and melody would go on to re-create the landscape of snowy Montreal itself within countless listener's rooms for decades to come.

Cohen spent that Christmas back in his home town, staying at a modest rented apartment on Aylmer Street. New York, exciting, visceral and ultimately essential as it was to Cohen's destiny, also had the effect of somehow amplifying his sense of isolation. Cohen had no one regular romantic partner during this time. Marianne and her son had visited Cohen a few times at the Chelsea Hotel and they continued to spend time in Montreal together (where she sometimes took a job in a boutique) when the circumstances allowed. But outside Hydra and with Cohen now entering a new phase in his life, for their romantic relationship seemed to flounder. Cohen would also approach Verdal around this time, she claiming that, "Once when he was visiting Montreal, I saw him briefly in a hotel and it was a very, very wonderful, happy moment because he was on his way to becoming the great success he is. And the moment arose that we could have a moment together intimately, and I declined."

In an absence of a steady lover, one of the most important female influences in Cohen's life (aside from the agonisingly unrequited yearning for Nico) came via the continuing relationship with his 'manager' Mary Martin, a former associate of Bob Dylan's manager Albert Grossman. Although she would open many important doors for him, her business advice in key respects would prove to be questionable.

Meanwhile, on returning to the Chelsea, as Cohen continued his further explorations of the local scene and its cast of regal bohemians, he still felt something of an outsider. Cohen was now in his thirties and yet was as adrift as a teenager. There was absolutely no guarantee that he would ever get a recording deal. As a writer of novels and poetry he had seemed to have succeeded in every sense – except for sales and financial reward. Although his song writing had taken great leaps in the previous months and was being noticed and utilised by other more successful artists, the future, particularly financially, was uncertain. "I wasn't deeply aware of an impending explosion," he stresses, alluding again to the blooming folk renaissance in retrospect, one in which he would play a notable if late role. "But there was a sense of freedom and opportunity in the air."

Cohen used such freedom to express the muse in any way he saw fit and was by now even experimenting in painting, dabbling with watercolours and oils. Poetry, novels, painting... not one activity justified financially his avowed removal from the successful Cohen family business(es). The prospect of solving this problem by going into pop music was, as he would freely admit, a 'mad' one. Yet he was gaining a real reputation as a singer/songwriter based almost completely on Collins' popular version of 'Suzanne' alone. In addition, Cohen had already recorded demos of some of his early songs for the Polygram label at NYC's Vanguard studios, with The Band's organ player, Garth Hudson. These sessions included what Cohen would identify as his 'first ever song', one that he had begun writing back in the late 50s, the unremarkable 'Tonight Will Be Fine'.

Nevertheless, despite the uncertainties, this was, as ever a prolific time for Cohen. There were other songs from this period that, while registered with ASCAP at the time, never would see the light of day. These included 'Middle Of The Night', 'Blessed Is The Memory', 'Love Is The Item', 'Splinter' and one that would eventually resurface as 'Story of Isaac', the heartbreakingly titled 'Nine Years Old' which was, of course, Cohen's age at the time of his father's death. Despite his productivity, life alone in New York City was a sometimes relentless and uncomfortably intense time for Cohen, particularly compared to the kind of poetic idyll and harmony he'd so recently enjoyed on Hydra. Far away from the perfectly lit desk that Marianne would anoint with a Gardenia every morning, Cohen was now deep within the belly of the beast itself, and a willing participant in the selling of his own fate to Babylon. It was if his destiny had changed gears, moving into a speeded up version of itself and Cohen was finding it hard to keep up, despite the occasional self administered dose of Maxiton. Important figures were appearing in Cohen's life on a daily basis and exiting it at a similarly heady rate. In the flurry of such rapid new experiences, Cohen made many misjudgements. Jeff Chase, a self proclaimed music publisher and arranger worked with Cohen on his early demo recordings. The two men did not gel on any level but 'got along' by a warped combination of Cohen's business ignorance and Chases' low rent cynical savvy. Subsequently Cohen signed over the rights to three songs ('Suzanne', 'Stranger Song' and 'Master Song') exclusively to the arranger who in return promised to tout the demo to labels on the singer's behalf. When Cohen wished to withdraw from the relationship completely, Chase claimed the rights to the songs as his own. Cohen made a half hearted attempt at getting further advice from Mary Martin who bizarrely – given her experiences with Dylan et al – advised him to concede to Chase's demands. Thus, Cohen handed over the publishing rights to three key songs, one of which at least, 'Suzanne', would soon become a modern day pop hymn. Yet the fate of such compositions was far from apparent at the time.

In the fullness of time he would be fortunate to make the acquaintance of music industry lawyer Marty Machat, who would go on to become a profound figure in Cohen's life and in doing so rescue the songwriter from future business catastrophes. Marty's son, Steven Machat, points out today that, "No one then had the slightest idea of what 'Suzanne' would be or was… no one *then*, in their right mind would believe that anyone would be discussing 'Suzanne' 40 years later… we didn't think it would last that long."

Leonard would later joke that back in Montreal his mother had actually warned him about people who might take advantage of his ignorance in business matters. "They're different from us," she had told him sweetly. At the time, the son was embarrassed at his mother's 'squareness' but would eventually admit that "… she was right. Some of the renaissance folk singers I met pretended to represent my interest and love my work and eventually pilfered a lot of my work – stole my songs. They tricked me…" If Cohen had had the actual songs themselves stolen from him, he did however retain ownership of the demos, i.e. the actual recordings themselves. Evidently an acetate of these sessions found their way to the offices of the already Cohen-conscious A&R man John Hammond, the Columbia executive who signed Dylan to Columbia, and Mary Martin arranged a meeting between the two.

"I was heard by a very great A&R man called John Hammond, who signed everybody from Billie Holliday to Bruce Springsteen," remembers Cohen, who was well aware of Hammond's reputation before meeting with him. "He was a very kind man. He had heard Judy's version of 'Suzanne' and he invited me out to lunch near the Chelsea Hotel. Afterwards he asked me if I would mind playing some tunes. So I did, very nervously, and he said just three words to me: 'You got it.' About the best words I ever heard."

Hammond, who had recorded the audition, had to fight a little with the powers that be at Columbia, the main obstacle being Cohen's age and general air of 'otherness'. He simply did not come on as a rock singer or even a traditional folk singer. Hammond had expected Columbia's reaction from the first mention of Cohen, from Mary Martin who had told him: "John, there's this poet from Canada, who I think you'd be interested in." recalls Hammond. "She said, 'He plays pretty good guitar, and he's a wonderful songwriter, but he doesn't read music, and he's sort of very strange. I don't think Columbia would be at all interested in him, but you might be…'."

A man with an impressive and proven track record, Hammond had every right to trust his gut instinct. The one on one audition at the Chelsea had sold him. Now all he had to do was convince the label. This was, after all, his job. "I thought he (Cohen) was enchanting... because that's the only word you can use!" he remembered. "He was not like anything I've ever heard before. I just feel that I always want a true original, if I can find one, because there are not many in the world; and the young man set his own rules, and he was a really first-class poet, which is most important. They all looked at me at Columbia and said, 'What, are you...? A 40-year-old, Canadian poet? How are we going to sell him?' I said, 'Listen to him...' and, lo-and-behold, Columbia signed him." Cohen was now officially a Columbia records recording artist. Nashville would wait.

With Cohen still in residence at the notorious, blessed, infamous and conveniently located Chelsea Hotel, the sessions for his debut album sessions began in stop/start fashion at Columbia's Studio E, on 49 East and 52nd Street in early '67. The veteran Hammond himself was initially involved as producer. "John had arranged for some musicians to be there," recalls Cohen, "and we started playing a few songs. After one of them, I remember John saying over the speaker, 'Watch out, Dylan!' He had a very curious... a very curious way of affirming the singer, in the studio. First of all, he would sit behind the console, at the side of the console, with a newspaper. And that took the edge off it. You didn't feel that he was surveying every move you made. It was a very compassionate kind of 'lapse of attention' that he would display, which I'm sure was a very highly-engineered and very well-tested way of putting the performer at ease. He would appear to be reading his newspaper, and I'm sure he was reading his newspaper; but it just took that edge of pressure off, so that you could feel you could make a mistake, without him looking at you – because when you're in the studio in the first days, you really think that everything you do is wrong; and a lot of things that I did were wrong."

In these earliest sessions, Cohen ran through the songs, laying down tracks with jazz bassist Willie Ruff, both he and Cohen recording their guitar parts together. "Well, Willie Ruff is a great, bass player and a French horn player," said Hammond. "He's a full Professor of Music at Yale. He's a black guy from Sheffield, Alabama, and somebody I trusted immediately. Leonard always needed reassurance, of some kind, and he recognised that Willie was a supreme musician; and it was a wonderful combination, the two of them... Willie was not upset by the fact that Leonard couldn't read music, and he just realised this guy was a genius of his own kind."

The exotic two man combo duly put down bass and vocals for 'Suzanne', 'Master Song' and 'Sisters Of Mercy'. At this stage Hammond was still a benevolent, fatherly figure at the studio. "You know, he [Hammond] never said anything negative," stresses Cohen. "There were just degrees of his affirmation that you could pick up, very quickly, as you got to know him. Everything you did was 'good', but some things were 'very good'. When it was only 'good' – and that 'good' came out of a real goodwill, but if it was just 'good' – just the enthusiasm that was attached to 'good', you knew you had to do another take."

As the next step, Hammond had arranged a studio band of "dynamite New York studio musicians" (in the singer's own words) to accompany his new signing, without Cohen being consulted on the exact personnel beforehand. This was a minor misstep on Hammond's part. The dynamic between Cohen and Ruff had been intimate and natural but the arrival of more anonymous personnel unnerved Cohen, the studio novice put off by their proficiency. "I really don't know how to sing with really good professional musicians that were really cooking," Cohen explained, although he would stress that he had nothing against such men personally. Ruff exited at this point. "I don't remember anything, in particular, that went down between me and Willie, during those sessions," he states, "except that I was able to do them with a sense of confidence. The support that Willie Ruff brought to those sessions was crucial. I couldn't have laid down those tracks without him. He supported the guitar playing so well. He could always anticipate my next move; he understood the song so thoroughly. He was one of those rare musicians that play selflessly, and for pure and complete support."

Cohen didn't feel comfortable continuing in the same manner with the new crew. He now tried to find himself a mental, physical and musical place in the studio space by manipulating the environment in very specific ways. At Cohen's request, and without Hammond batting an eyelid, candles and incense were brought into Studio E as well as a full length mirror. This was not to snort drugs off. "In Montreal I'd always thought of myself as one day becoming a singer," said Cohen charmingly, "and I used to stand in front of the mirror and sing to see how I looked." This Cohen did as he ran through his vocals, often accompanying himself on guitar too. Singing and playing simultaneously while recording in a studio was an activity that would become rarer and rarer in time, and even in 1966 – the year before *Sgt Pepper's Lonely Hearts Club Band* was released, after all – such practice was already bordering on the archaic. Surrounded by his smoke and mirrors, Cohen eventually settled into a means of recording wherein he felt confident and comfortable.

At which point Hammond took leave. It had soon became apparent that the much in-demand producer was clearly too busy – some reports said ill – to commit full time to the album, or perhaps Hammond felt that stage one was complete and his work was done. Polite and patient as ever, but frustrated at the stop/start approach, Cohen asked Columbia for another full time and committed replacement and John Simon was appointed as producer. Simon was both almost a decade younger than Cohen and infinitely more experienced in the studio process but was nevertheless immediately struck by the new signing. "He [Cohen] wasn't the kind of guitar player I was used to listening to," he recalls. "Most of the guitarists I knew came up listening to pop music… Leonard had apparently learned to play classical guitar." Simon took to his client immediately, perhaps precisely because of his unusual background. "He was smart. A lot of these acts I recorded weren't too smart but Leonard was smart and fun to be with and full of insight…"

Simon was at the time experimenting in various production techniques and came up with the idea of using female voices (one of whom was actually his wife) employed not in their traditional duet or sole harmony roles but purely as instruments in themselves. The result was the plaintive, ghostly textures that seem to occupy the space between rhythm and melody, vocal and lyric that is usually sweetened by strings (strings would also occasionally feature, adding to the intoxicatingly sweet effect). Cohen liked this vocal effect very much, relishing its ethereal nod to the classic all girl pop music of the Fifties, wherein female voices were often layered as a dominant texture. In addition, Cohen was never particularly enamoured by his own singing voice. "My own voice sounded so disagreeable to me when I listened to it, I really needed the sweetening of women's voices behind me," he explained.

Despite the new fluency that Simon brought to the sessions, there were of course further tensions within the studio, this being a natural, even necessary part of any recording process. In particular Cohen quarrelled with Simon over an arrangement of 'So Long Marianne'. "He had a certain approach where the song began and then he stopped it for a few seconds and it would then begin again...," remembered the songwriter. This was a common musical device which many arrangers and bands used, often unconsciously, to 'alert' or help 'hook' the listener. Cohen understood the value of such a device but didn't want it on his album. "It's unnecessary," he told Simon. "It interrupts the song." Simon stepped away from the argument and diplomatically told Cohen that he was off on Christmas vacation and that Leonard could mix it in his absence. This, Cohen subsequently did, stripping the album of many of its unnecessary adornments, including the producer's piano part on 'Suzanne'. Cohen was progressing at quite a rate. From being persuaded to become a singer by Judy Collins only a few months earlier, Cohen was now asserting himself as the record producer of his debut album.

Yet Cohen still wasn't satisfied with the sessions. One night, while attending yet another Nico gig, this time at the Scene club, he was impressed by the support group, who were a kind of blueprint pan-world music fusion folk combo named Kaleidoscope. So impressed was Cohen by their performance that he approached bass player Chris Darrow as soon as the group came off stage. "After the first set this guy comes up to me and introduces himself," remembers the bassist. "I had no idea who he was. He was wearing a black leather jacket and carrying a black briefcase, he had short cropped hair and he was so pale. He was one the palest guys I've ever seen. So he comes up to me and says 'I'm Leonard Cohen and I'm making a record'. Now, at that time in the sixties he did not look like anyone who would be making a record. He was older, and conservative looking. We were in from the west coast and had long hair and that look hadn't even gotten as far as New York then. But where we came from, it was all organic and loose and... seeing this guy with the cropped hair, it looked like he was maybe a jazz musician or something.

And it was so weird to see a guy walking around in a club with a black leather briefcase. I didn't ask what was in it. So anyway, he says 'I really like your band… would you guys be interested in playing on my record?' So I said, 'See those guys over there? They're our managers, go and talk to them and they'll set you up'."

Cohen did indeed set things up and before leaving the Scene that night addressed the group personally. Darrow's friend and band mate, the ace harmonica player Chester Crill remembers Cohen explaining to the group the problems he was having in the studio and thinking that to him at least, Cohen looked like the epitome of a folk singer. "Anyway, he was very specific about why he liked us guys," says Chester. "He said that he thought we had all kinds of combinations of sounds that he himself hadn't been able to achieve with the guys he was working with. He was after a certain detail, as well as an intimacy."

After Cohen shook hands and left, someone passed Chester a copy of Cohen's recent poetry collection, *Parasites Of Heaven*. "I looked at it," remembers the harmonica player, "and thought… 'Geez! This poor guy'!" The very next day Chris and Chester and one other fellow band member, David Lindley, rendezvoused at what they assumed was Cohen's apartment. "I don't remember where it was exactly," says Darrow. "This was my first time in NYC. I didn't know the place. We were just led up to this place by Leonard. It could have been a hotel room for all I know. It had a generic feel to it."

Cohen, as ever, routined the songs simply, by playing to the musicians from the couch, accompanying himself on a nylon stringed guitar. "He was very straightforward, as a man," recalls Chester, "and very affable. But his songs were irregular. They weren't constructed in a regular form. You know, standard ballads can take the form of A, A, B – verse, bridge, chorus etc, but his weren't that straightforward. And so learning 'em off cold was kinda hard'.

Darrow: "He was a nice guy, pretty matter of fact. But I was 22 at the time (Cohen was approaching his mid-thirties). I had no idea who this guy was, we were just there to get paid. So we just sat around trying to figure out his songs. It was all acoustic. He had this guitar style that was kinda… 'amorphous'. It was like there was no kind of fixed time in it. It flowed and I think a lot of people were having trouble trying to figure out where the downbeat came and where the changes were supposed to come. Now, we all came out of folk music and there was indeed a good folk scene in NYC then but we got the impression Leonard was having trouble getting folk musicians to work out how to play his kind of folk music. [Cohen would recollect that 'Master Song' in particular proved difficult]. I got the feeling he wasn't having a lot of luck with his album sessions. But you also gotta remember we were doing folk with a kind of Middle Eastern feel, which was rare at the time… we had a guy who played the oud and we had a flamenco guitarist… and I think that even then, Leonard wanted something a little out of the ordinary."

The musicians turned up at the studio the next day. "It was a real corporate building," recalls Chester. "Columbia owned it. And the studio Leonard was in was right next door to the radio studio – CBS radio. All on the same floor. So when we got off the elevator, there was a huge sign saying 'Its Arthur Godfrey Time!' He was a famous DJ then, did the morning show. So we'd get out of the elevator at one in the morning and it would be 'Arthur Godfrey Time'! And we'd get out of the elevator at six and it'd be 'Arthur Godfrey Time!'… It was the most corporate studio I was ever in."

Interestingly, Chester remembers the recording sessions being mainly at night; Darrow during the day.

Chester: "When we got to the studio, I remember that they had already filled up pretty much every track available on each song. They put everything they had onto each song… real diverse stuff, girl singers, strings, percussion. Although it wasn't all used in the final mix, it was on the original tape and that didn't leave a lot of room for us. They filled his songs with everything you'd figure the industry associated with 'male vocalist' at the time."

Darrow: "I think there was a definite problem with his sessions up to that point. I mean… he already had several producers on that album… so we ended up, the next day in the studio and it was pretty much, just 'knock it out'."

Chester had the impression that they were retained on extra time and that the initial budget had already been spent. On Cohen's insistence, he and Darrow had been brought in as part of some sort of salvage operation. "I don't even remember there being a producer there by the time we turned up," he affirms, "but I do remember that there was kind of like a feeling of 'There is no time to do this'! I have very little memory of it, it was pretty unremarkable. I remember an engineer behind the glass and running the tape and us just getting going. I recall there was a window in the studio and you could see the city skyline."

Chester explains that although 15 of the available 16 tracks on the tape were already full, when he added his harmonica part during the playback he heard Cohen's voice and guitar only. "He [Cohen] would say, 'Do this, and this and this'," says Chester, "but there were hardly any tracks left, so the three of us would have to get together around the microphone together at the same time. We were cool with this. We were used to it. We were tight together. And remember, we were just supplying top lines, sweeteners, ear candy. We weren't involved in the basic foundations of the song. And our response was purely emotional. There were no lead sheets, no charts, we were given no scores. Leonard might say 'There's a hole there, fill it, follow the guys coming right before'. And within that we just responded as we saw fit. You know, I hated the New York scene at the time," he adds, "but there were a few people who did us great favours then and Leonard — who to me looked absolutely like a folk singer the first time I saw him — he was one of them."

Toward the end of the album sessions, takes were being recorded hastily. No musician credits would appear on the subsequent album sleeve, and there was some confusion as to who had played on what. "I think I played on everything," says Chester, "but they only used it in the mix of one or two."

Darrow: "I later found out that I was on 'So Long Marianne' and 'Teachers'. Some of the other guys played on other tracks."

For the three members of Kaleidoscope hired by Cohen, the sessions were fleeting, a mere few hours in a young musician's intense day to day life and their memories as such remain vague. No one then knew they were recording the classic debut album of a future modern day star, and eventual inductee into the Rock and Roll Hall of Fame. At the time, for Darrow and his colleagues it was just another hectic day in the life, merely one more session to help with the rent.

Despite its relatively difficult birth, both the material and Cohen's vision ultimately prevailed and the actual finished album was a testament to the integrity of both. Captured to tape in an appropriately 'Church like' studio, the very opening note of 'Suzanne' in particular is a portal into another, complete and perfect world. The song, and specifically this original studio recording of the song, passes through the speakers and brings into the listener's room something utterly whole and consummate. What is striking is that all of this is apparent in the very sound of the opening note. The tone of the guitar and its subsequent placement amidst incensed air in relation to the microphone and the voice is both perfect and magical. The song is as precise and intimate as it is universal. Fittingly, and not accidentally, it was chosen to be the opening song of Cohen's first album.

It is a curious incongruity that although Cohen would come as close to marriage as he ever would with a woman named Suzanne (Elrod, who would also bear their children), the 'Suzanne' of the title was of course, another Suzanne altogether. The first incarnation of the lyrics had been as pure poetry in *Parasites Of Heaven* published the previous year, while another, earlier, poem, 'Suzanne Wears A Leather Coat', dating from 1963, appeared in the same collection. The use of Christian imagery in the song was particularly striking yet had its origin in raw reportage: "Notre Dame de Bon Secours [the church that overlooks Montreal harbour] is a church for sailors," explained Cohen. "Inside the church there are models of ships hanging and the sailors are blessed from that church. So the very next verse moves very easily to the idea that Jesus was a sailor..." Whatever the workmanlike facts of its origin, 'Suzanne' was the perfect entrée to Cohen's debut album, containing within its mystic blueprint the code and symbol of every song that would follow.

Outside of the studio, Cohen didn't actively pursue the friendships of the musicians he worked with, although he was warm and congenial and enjoyed the company of their kind. "I saw him about three times after the sessions," says Chester. "I saw him socially but it was always music related in some way. My impression was that he had very little sense of the business. And I thought 'they' were screwing him royally. But outside of his taking control in the studio, he kinda went along with it, it seemed to me. Record companies used to charge everything to the artist then, the guy who arranged the strings, the strings players themselves, and remember they even owned the actual studio itself. It was Columbia's studio and they would charge you to use it. They owned the guys who ran the tape and they even owned the tape! They manufactured the recording tape. And Leonard was paying for all of this. So if he ever got even a dime back in royalties that would be a rarity. And Columbia thought they were recording a pop rock vocalist. Which he wasn't."

Chester saw Leonard in person one last time when the singer invited some of the contributing musicians up to his apartment to listen to a finished acetate of the album. "It was real late at night," recalls Chester. "And we listened and sat around and talked about it. And I remember he had this chick there with him. She wasn't famous or anything… just good looking! I remember it being four in the morning and thinking 'Man… she's good looking!'" Chester was less enamoured of the actual finished work that he heard that night. "I thought that if he had been presented in the correct milieu – that is naked – then it would have been an awful lot of a better 'launch' for him. As it was I thought that first album – as a introduction – was horrendous. Because it didn't really represent what he was. It was schmaltzy. Way over the top. I've heard a couple of his later albums which were well produced and they are very effective. But that first album sounds like someone trying to shout over a traffic jam. And I think that's why he was so concerned during the making of it. There's not much of a coherent structure to it."

The album was good enough for John Hammond to approve the final mix, and after track sequencing was confirmed it was mastered and its artwork collated and printed. In anticipation of the album's release Columbia's press office arranged interviews, circulated acetates and reel to reel copies of the album to DJs and helped co ordinate the offers of TV spots that were coming in.

Appearing on these early TV spots in his new guise as a singer songwriter, Cohen still sounded as if he were merely reciting poetry over his own guitar backing rather than accompanying himself and singing. The various versions of 'Suzanne' already released had done much to prepare audiences for his shift from poet to folk singer. Judy Collins had of course already released 'Suzanne' and 'Dress Rehearsal Rag' on her 1966 album *In My Life*. She would follow these a year later with her own plaintive interpretations of 'Sisters Of Mercy', 'Priests' and 'Hey, That's No Way To Say Goodbye' on her *Wildflowers* album.

Intriguingly, English singer Noel Harrison, son of actor Rex, would also record a version of 'Suzanne' and perform it on the *Ed Sullivan Show* on TV. His subsequent recording reached a respectable number 56 in the US *Billboard* chart in October 1967. Outside of the (predominantly Canadian) TV spots, Cohen's own personal musical appearances were still rare. Having eventually come into his own as a reciter of his own poetry, he was still a nervous performer in the role of songwriter/singer.

In between the recording sessions for his debut album that year, Cohen pulled off various one man live attacks on both intrigued audiences and his own nerves. That April at the State University in Buffalo he performed in front of a capacity crowd. Here he fused three disciplines – reading from his novel, reciting his poetry and singing a clutch of songs with guitar. While he hadn't yet seemed to have accepted his new fate of performing troubadour completely – perhaps doubting that the public would be as convinced by his own conviction as he occasionally was in private – he continued to encourage and bestow confidence on his friends. He was a personal inspiration to Judy Collins, discreetly pushing her toward developing her own song writing during this period even as he lacked the confidence to perform his own songs in public. A platonic friendship had deepened between Cohen and Collins and in late April 1967, during a break in his recording sessions, she 'forcefully' invited him to play at a Town Hall rally to benefit The National Committee For A Sane Nuclear Policy.

The audience that night was apparently aware of who Cohen was even before the build up that Collins gave him in her preceding set. Cohen was particularly edgy and nervous and this seemed to be transmuted into his acoustic and vinyl stringed guitar, making it seemingly untuneable as soon as he walked on stage. The handsome, besuited singer struggled to make the strings obey the basic laws of concert pitch beneath the callously hot stage lights. Eventually he started singing, 'shaking like a leaf'. Although the guitar was temporarily obedient something else wasn't quite in tune. Audaciously, Cohen stopped the song half way through, letting his arms drop dramatically to his sides. "I can't go on," he exclaimed, beaten, and turned and walked off the stage. The audience loved the avant garde drama of it and screamed encouragingly for Cohen's return. The fellow artists backstage were sympathetic towards the terrified singer and comforted him as a group. They urged him to go back and somehow, having reset the occasion to his own particular emotional wavelength, Cohen did just that, going onto 'slay' them. Collins looked on proudly from the wings, later pointing out that for Cohen, "This was the beginning of a gruelling life as a travelling troubadour."

His loose guitar strings had been testing that night but ultimately, Cohen was unconcerned with technical excellence or in being able to sing like Mario Lanza or Maria Callas. "I thought it was about truth... and telling your story," he said, describing in a nutshell the shtick of the phenomenally popular Bob Dylan. Other more musically adept contemporaries of Cohen were able to analyse his 'failings' in terms of musical theory. Buffy Sainte-Marie commented on Cohen's style at the time: "He is obviously not a product of the G-E-D7th school of song writing. Almost all of his melodies start in one key and go through progressively more outrageous modulations, which often end up in a key entirely unrelated to the original one... He has the delicious gall to ask us, who do not even know him, to follow him into a completely original and sometimes scary mind of words without the aid of any of the old folksy musical clichés we are used to holding on to as a guide-rail."

Cohen also stated that he considered himself as working particularly in *pop*, not folk or rock. As a pop singer he was untypical in the extreme. Short haired and clean shaven, allergic to denim and armed with an almost debilitating musical uniqueness, Cohen would just have to work out the particular means of 'telling his story' in a brutally competitive business. "I wouldn't call myself a folk-singing personality," he'd said just a few months earlier. "I really don't care what they call me. I'm not a particularly good painter but I'm doing a little painting now, putting together a collection. I have this feeling that if you liberate yourself, anything you lay your hand on can sparkle. Professionalism is the enemy of creativity and invention."

Cohen continued to practice his creed and lever himself into any appealing opportunity that beckoned. That year Leonard wrote some music for old friend Don Owens' 1967 film *The Ernie Game* and appeared in it as himself, in a party scene, singing 'Stranger Song'. Another Cohen-related film was also televised that year: *Poen*, a five-minute cornucopia of various strikingly graphic images, both blessed and secular, edited and directed by Josef Reeve, to the sound of Cohen reading from a passage of *Beautiful Losers*. He made an unaccredited appearance in *Angel*, a seven-minute film by Derek May.

Apart from his modest celluloid presence, Cohen notched up a more major musical appearance in that summer of '67 when Cohen appeared the Newport Folk Festival on Rhode Island on July 16. The night before the concert, he and Judy Collins had 'played all night' together in a hotel room, with Cohen introducing her to his recently written 'Hey, That's No Way To Say Goodbye', a song he would record as soon as his album sessions resumed later that summer. It was another newly minted classic drawn from a variety of sources and a composite of muses. It's commonly thought the 'golden hair' in the song belonged to Marianne although she would dispute this. Suzanne Verdal, a brunette when Cohen knew her, would also later reminisce of their time together: "We'd walk down the street for instance, and the click of our shoes, his boots and my shoes, would be like in synchronicity. It's hard to describe. We'd almost hear each other thinking. It was very unique, very, very unique." This echoes the song's lines, "Walk me to the corner/Our steps will always rhyme".

Despite the personal respect of his soon to be peers and contemporaries, without an album release, Cohen was still very much an unproven quantity compared to the rest of the well established and popular names on the Newport bill. These included Judy Collins, Pete Seeger, Arlo Guthrie, fellow Canadian Gordon Lightfoot, and Buffy Sainte-Marie. That same afternoon, Cohen was asked to participate in Judy Collin's songwriter's workshop along with yet another Canadian, Joni Mitchell, Janis Ian, David Blue, Mike Settle, Tom Paxton, Eric Anderson and Collins herself. Collins introduced Joni and Cohen and the two hit it off almost instantly. At this time Joni, who was Cohen's junior by nine years, was also living in NYC, at the Earl Hotel in Greenwich Village. The two began a brief and intense affair which although traversing NYC and Montreal had burnt itself out within weeks. They would remain friends Joni in particular acknowledging the small but real influence Cohen had upon her own work. "Leonard was an early influence," Joni would say decades later. "I remember thinking when I heard his songs for the first time that I was not worldly. My work seemed very young and naive in comparison. At the time I met him I was around 24... But thematically I wanted to be broader than he was. In many ways Leonard was a boudoir poet."

Immediately prior to the release of his debut album, the poet laureate of the bedroom continued to test himself live, with varying degrees of success, in a Montreal supper club (where he was apparently received with some suspicion) and again on CBC's *Camera 3* current affairs program. This show, long since lost, featured Cohen's only known performance of the song 'God Is Alive, Magic Is Afoot' and was broadcast that autumn, just prior to the release of Judy Collin's partially Cohen authored album *Wildflowers*. It featured Cohen lip synching to 'Suzanne' with the CBS orchestra as accompaniment, while he 'played' a fake guitar painted blue so that images could later be projected onto its body during the broadcast. When aired, the show once again proved Cohen's unique ability to provoke audience/listener/reader/viewer response. The *New York Times* reported: "[Cohen] ... sang a few songs, read some poems, and was pictured peering sensitively into several tawdry Broadway store windows. The impression he made was strong enough to elicit the greatest audience response in the show's fourteen-year history." One viewer berated the network for "letting this cancer loose" on the Sabbath, but most of those who wrote in wanted to know more about Cohen. Who was this ambiguous and tortured poet who prowled the urban slag dump proclaiming "God is alive. Magic is afoot"?

With several recordings of 'Suzanne' shimmering from AM and FM radio across various states, buoyed by the steady support of Judy Collins and backed by the mighty music machine that was Columbia, even such occasional negative reactions as this proved the adage that any publicity was good publicity. There was a healthy buzz around the forthcoming release of *The Songs Of Leonard Cohen* album, now pressed, packaged and ready to go with a release date scheduled for the end of the year.

As review copies of the album were mailed out by Columbia offices worldwide, reviews of *Beautiful Losers* continued to appear throughout the summer in various obscure periodicals and 'little magazines', and an anthology of his poetry was being prepared by Viking Press for release in 1968. Yet on some level it must have been galling to Cohen that his decade long career as a poet and novelist hardly seemed to figure at all now, dwarfed and eclipsed as it was by the new and totally unexpected life in music that awaited him.

CHAPTER FOUR

The Smoky Life

"You want to hear a guy's story, and if the guy's really seen a few things, the story is quite interesting. Or even if he comes to the point where he wants to sing about the moon in June, there's something in his voice... when you hear Fats Domino singing, 'I found my thrill on Blueberry Hill', whatever that's about, I mean, it's deep."

LC

*T*he *Songs Of Leonard Cohen*, featuring a cover portrait courtesy of a Montreal photo booth, was released on Boxing Day 1967. True to its incongruous birthday – because of Christmas and the holidays this was one of the worst times in which to release any album – the record was no immediate hit as such but a 'sleeper'. Critical consensus, as it trickled in from around the world was mixed. A collection of songs with no rough edges, this immortally titled debut nevertheless found its way into listeners' blood streams via osmosis, not puncture. One possible criticism, especially by those familiar with Cohen's recent literary life, was the claim that the LP was merely Cohen's next book, transcribed into pure sound and thus almost a novelty record. Yet compared to the novels in particular, there was something consummately coherent about Cohen's debut album. It sounded whole and complete and of itself. And just as 'Suzanne' embodied in part every other song on the album, so the record presented a microcosm of the singer's sensibility and universe with all its poetic and musical vocabulary and all of its established symbols and language. The record came completely formed and was authorative, with its own climate and gravity. It sounded both like someone's first and last album. (Ultimately, decades on, playing it would be like playing a compilation, an early 'Best Of'.)

The Songs Of Leonard Cohen owed much of its potency to Cohen's previous decade of devotion to poetry and prose. There were also various voices unique to Cohen on the album – the mystically modal chord changes, the idiosyncratic style of guitar playing, the turn of phrase and the singing voice itself. That voice – as unique as a fingerprint or bruise, something between an incantation and a groan – was the epitome of the term 'acquired taste'. And yet it conveyed sincerity, truth and intimacy as believably as any Frank Sinatra or Marvin Gaye. The difference between Cohen and such artists is that, ultimately, they were professional singers. Cohen was a vocalist, a stylist in the manner of Jacques Brel and Bob Dylan. As a singer and musician he was undoubtedly committed to himself but still unsure as to what that self was. With the long term commercial fate of his debut album still undecided, Cohen was uncertain as to what he was doing or if he even wanted to do it.

"Around 30 or 35 is the traditional age for the suicide of the poet, did you know?" he pointed out shortly after his album's release with typical humour. "That's the age when you finally understand that the universe does not succumb to your command." If at this point in his life Cohen had disappeared into a Mandrax induced eternal sleep, walked into the sloppy tides of the Hudson River or drank himself into a fatal coma at the Chelsea Hotel bar, then this one perfect record would have established his pop immortality. As it was, the most notable casualty from this period would be Cohen the novelist. Scores of songs, concerts and poems awaited him through a long long life but Cohen would never again publish another novel.

Immediately prior to the album's release, Cohen had been nervous and downbeat and by the time it was released he would be anxious and gloomy.

"I think my album is going to be spotty and undistinguished," he'd

Backstage on the 1976 European Tour. (JOHN MILLER)

Cohen bought bassist John Miller a Nikon Camera who took these previously unpublished photos on the European and UK tour of 1976. (JOHN MILLER)

Cohen and German promoter Marcus celebrate a mutual birthday, September 1976. (JOHN MILLER)

Cohen with the late Laura Branigan, a backup singer on his '76 tour. (JOHN MILLER)

...ft to right: Road manager, German promoter, Sid McGinnis ...itarist) and Cohen after the tour bus has broken down on a German autobahn in 1976. (JOHN MILLER)

Cohen (left) poses with John Miller outside a London phone box in 1976. (JOHN MILLER)

At the Sound Ideas Studio in New York during the aborted *Songs For Rebecca* sessions of 1975. Backing singer Lori Zimmermann can be seen behind Cohen. (JOHN MILLER)

Sightseeing (above) and onstage (below) during the 1976 European Tour. (JOHN MILLER)

'My mirror twin/my next of kin': backstage at Musikhalle, Hamburg in Germany during the mid-Seventies.
(HANS-JURGEN DIBBERT - K & K/REDFERNS)

Backstage at the Starwood, Los Angeles, with members of Devo and photographer Martine Getty.
(BRAD ELTERMAN/BUZZFOTO/FILMMAGIC)

A great white hope: Cohen onstage in the mid-Seventies. (LFI)

'Come over to the window/My Little darling'. (GEMS/REDFERNS)

told a journalist that Christmas. "I blame this on my total unfamiliarity with the recording studio. They tried to make my songs into music. I got put down all the time… It was a continual struggle… continual… they wanted to put me in bags. I thought I was going to crack up." Such nerves were understandable for a man who spent too much (or maybe not enough) time alone in his shabby hotel room.

Columbia's marketing was low key but clearly visible if you were hip enough to read the right magazines. A typical advert for the album showed an incongruous photo of a reclining and awkwardly smiling Cohen accompanied with the slightly self conscious quote, "I've been on the outlaw scene since I was 15. I had some things in common with the beatniks and even more things with the hippies. The next thing may be even closer to where I am." Beyond such dubious statements (it sounds like the last thing Cohen would have said) Cohen was not completely unfounded in his anxiousness. *Rolling Stone* critic Arthur Schmidt for one was underwhelmed by the debut album. "There are three brilliant songs, one good one, three qualified bummers, and three are the flaming shits," he said unpoetically.

The album made little impression upon the *Billboard* chart, reaching number 83 on its release although in the UK it eventually reached number 13 by August '68, staying on the charts for a very creditable 71 weeks. (According to its author it would not 'go gold' in the UK until 2001 by which point it had sold one and a half million copies.) But unlike the vast majority of debut albums released, particularly those by ex poets in their mid-thirties, Cohen's album was a true success. It sold slowly but steadily and was both heard and beloved.

Future music writer and raconteur Harvey Kubernick was a young college student at the time in Los Angeles. "I discovered Leonard Cohen from reading magazines like *Eye* and *Cheetah*," he remembers. "These were big music magazines of the late Sixties. And even then I thought 'Wow! Here's a guy who's over 30 and just making his first record!' We'd never seen someone over 30 come out of the poetry world and record a musical album… I mean, we were all huge Doors fans and we loved Dylan so the idea of poetry in music wasn't foreign to us. So, you know, someone like me was ready to be really into Leonard Cohen. And I remember that his first album was particularly popular on FM radio in California. Particularly on 'underground' stations like KTTC FM."

Such exposure could be replicated across the globe. Columbia was an efficient and well established international operation. Although Cohen spent much of his time in NYC while his album was actually physically released – sat in a diner supping coffee or swimming at the local YMCA pool, writing in his room at the Chelsea – he had the advantage of a huge company working on his behalf, distributing his words, voice and music worldwide.

In London, future Cohen collaborator and film maker Tony Palmer was amongst the first to sit up and take notice, both personally and critically. At that time Palmer had a musical review column in the *Observer*. He also had a prescient ear, as he recalls. "I was the first person to review Cream, Bowie etc in a broadsheet newspaper. And I was the first journalist whose review of The Beatles was reprinted on one of their record sleeves. [Palmer's 'White Album' review appeared on the back of *Yellow Submarine*.] So when Leonard Cohen's first album landed on my desk, I listened and thought 'There is something really special going on here.' I liked the direct connection between what the man was singing about and the emotion with which he sang it." Palmer instantly recognised a correlation between Cohen and Dylan but at the same time the unique quality of Cohen's voice, in a dual sense. "He was singing about something very personal but in a universal way... I mean 'Suzanne' was clearly about someone called Suzanne but it's also about a love which has passed and gone, or so it seemed to me. Joan Baez had had a similar effect on me a few years earlier and that's a sign of genius I think, touching on the universal through the personal, in art. Another thing that struck me was 'This man is a poet'. He had an ability to communicate to you before you even understood what the song was about. Of course, in time I came to realise he actually *was* a poet and had been for years before this record." Not all of Palmer's peers and friends shared his clarity or enthusiasm. "The reaction from most people I played it to was puzzlement," he says.

Broadsheet reviews, radio and TV exposure were familiar channels for pop music at the time, even for a record as seductively esoteric as Cohen's. Yet one didn't have to be part of Columbia's mailing list or tuned into underground FM stations for Cohen's siren song to reach you. Anne Riise was an ordinary 12-year-old Norwegian girl and on midsummer eve 1969 was walking home with her grandparents when she remembers passing by "… bonfires and happy people along the lake…We passed a bonfire with many young people, singing and playing guitars. Beatles songs. I recognised them. But there was another song I hadn't heard before. It captured my attention. What was it? I couldn't forget the song and wanted to hear it again. Later that night, after my grandparents had gone to sleep, I sneaked out. I just *had* to hear this song again. I had luck. The singing company were still there, and I learned that the song was 'Suzanne'. Who had made this beautiful song? I didn't know. I went home, and I was able to play the song on my little flute (very quiet so as not to wake up my grandparents) and could then write down the melody line. I repeated the song many times, but I still didn't know who wrote it. Until one day when I heard it on the radio. I recognised it from the first guitar chord. This was the song that had made such a strong impression on me. And then I heard the voice. The *voice*! Wow! Couldn't believe it! I did not understand all the words he was singing, but I knew he was speaking to me! Felt it in my heart, spine and mind. And his name was Leonard Cohen."

'Suzanne' was actually released as a single, and although it was a 'radio hit' in some states it did not sell enough to make the chart.

The slow sales, spotty exposure and the occasional scathing review were deceptive of Cohen's growing popularity. In truth, Cohen had people intrigued. There now began a slow flurry of letters to Cohen from the sad, embittered and beguiled the world over. One of the earliest called Cohen her 'beautiful creep', which brought a tear to his eye. "That's what I am," he admitted, "a beautiful creep." This peculiarly personal method of communication between Cohen and his audience would endure throughout Cohen's life, and it signified that although in the best tradition his work was beginning to divide people – you either loved it or hated it – he was at least being taken seriously. That January Cohen flew to London at the invitation of the BBC and, more specifically, at the bequest of Julie Felix. An American living in London, Felix had her own 'variety' show which she used to introduce an incessantly tasteful parade of musical guests to the British public. As an introduction to quintessential Cohen, his performance on her show was astonishing. Sat stock still like some monument from Easter Island, he concluded a flawless performance of 'Stranger Song' by shedding one solitary tear, caught exquisitely in camera close up. The image brought to mind photographs of holy statues weeping in dusty churches. Static apart from the ceaseless fingers and the almost motionless mouth, Cohen had given a TV performance every bit as powerful and affecting as Jimi Hendrix's 1969 *Lulu* appearance.

Rainy, dour Britain was particularly sympathetic to a man of Cohen's demeanour and tempo. He returned to London again that summer at the invitation of the BBC, by which time the album had climbed to its highest chart position. In a studio expertly set up to record him, Cohen took to the stage of the Paris Theatre in Lower Regent Street with a handful of invited musicians to record over an album's worth of songs live before a slightly bemused and very English invited audience. Thorough and careful versions of 'You Know Who I Am', 'Bird On The Wire', 'Hey, That's No Way To Say Goodbye', 'So Long, Marianne' and 'Dress Rehearsal Rag', were all performed, the last song apparently included at the request of Fairport Convention singer Sandy Denny who was present in the studio at the time. On July 9 Cohen also recorded a live session for John Peel's *Top Gear* Radio 1 programme. John Peel: "It really was one of the nicest sessions we've ever had, it was just incredible…. if Leonard Cohen ever comes back to this country I vote that they give him an entire *Top Gear* to himself." The first four songs were broadcast five days later; 'Rag' was aired on August 11. With Dave Cousins of the English group The Strawbs on banjo, three unidentified backup singers, drums, piano and bass, the sets were efficient and professional but if anything Cohen sounded almost too relaxed, too mellow… too stoned.

Back in the US, Cohen kept up his extracurricular activities. He attended meetings with film directors in LA, where he discussed doing a soundtrack for a film called 'Suzanne' and caught up with Joni Mitchell. The meetings with 'movie people' did not go well – most producers he met with wanted Cohen to supply soundtracks for their self consciously 'hip' and arty movies and confused Cohen as being of the same ilk. He was, of course, made of more classical stuff, a man whose work and vision had merely synched with a passing fashion of the day. Cohen shared certain traits with his folk singer/hippie brethren but was ultimately beyond such categorisation. He was still searching for 'the answer' at any available opportunity.

After clocking a sign above a doorway on Sunset Boulevard while driving along with Joni Mitchell one afternoon, Cohen became, briefly, a Scientologist. Over two decades on Cohen would still retain a marginal interest in the subject. "I looked into a lot of things. Scientology was one of them," he'd say. "It did not last very long. But it is very interesting, as I continue my studies in these matters, to see how really good Scientology was from the point of view of their data, their information, their actual knowledge, their wisdom writings, so to speak. It wasn't bad at all. It is scorned, yes. I did look into that and other things, from the Communist Party to the Republican Party, from Scientology to delusions of myself as the high priest rebuilding the temple."

1968 offered the first summer in which Leonard Cohen was properly considered a singer. It was also the season in which he and Marianne finally, amicably and sorrowfully parted. It had been a long and fruitful partnership for both and was beautifully immortalised in song and verse: this was a much more precious fate than many couples experienced in their breakup. 'So Long Marianne' was as beautiful a 'Dear John' letter as there ever was. There had been no bitter or acrimonious falling out; their season had merely ended. The two had drifted apart as Cohen became entrenched in his new life and the two would continue to drift apart, eventually losing touch completely. While Cohen had had plenty of casual affairs over the years he had never met anyone to match the intensity of the relationship he'd had with Marianne until he met Suzanne Elrod. Cohen first encountered his latest muse, and the mother of his children, in an elevator at the elegant Plaza Hotel in New York. There was a powerful and mutual attraction and she almost immediately moved into Cohen's room at the Chelsea Hotel. Suzanne was less passive than Marianne, more predatory, more self assured and urban. Compared to Marianne and Hydra, Suzanne and New York made for a more visceral, kinetic and inspiring proposition. "God, whenever I see her ass," said Cohen. "I forget every pain that's gone between us."

As Cohen threw himself into his new life and love, demand for him and his work was at an optimum. While Columbia enquired about the next record, Viking Press published *Selected Poems 1956–1968*, which was published in the UK the following year by Jonathan Cape, The anthology – actually compiled by Marianne Ihlen – sold well in the first three months after publication, much more then the previous books, and would go onto to win its author the Canadian Governor General's Literary Award for Poetry in 1969. Cohen however refused it, sending a telegram to the board: "The poems themselves forbid it absolutely," although he would later admit that he himself wasn't exactly sure why he had turned it down.

When Cohen had left Hydra in late 1966 his intention had been to become a country singer in Nashville. His diversion from this path had been immensely fruitful albeit temporary. As the New York winter approached, Cohen donned his cowboy boots and headed once more for Nashville to hook up with a new producer to record his second album. Cohen had met Bob Johnston, a Nashville based producer best known for his work with Johnny Cash and Simon & Garfunkel, in LA. Since at this point in time Cohen was something of a hybrid of both these acts, Cohen moved from the Chelsea in New York to Franklin, Tennessee, where he lived on a farm 30 miles from Nashville itself, with the 19-year-old Elrod in occasional residence. Using a basic domestic reel-to-reel tape machine, Cohen recorded some demos on the actual farm and otherwise immersed himself in a version of the country life. The farm was surrounded by 1,200 acres of virgin forest and at its heart were Cohen and his teenage girlfriend, a Spanish guitar, a typewriter, a newly acquired jeep, some hash and a lame horse which Cohen would soon immortalise in song.

With Johnston appointed as producer the recording sessions began in the fall of '68 at Columbia's Studio A on 16th Avenue, Nashville. It was unusual that no major live dates had punctuated the space between albums but at this point Cohen was still reticent to tour. "If I could do it, I'd do it," he confessed at the time, recalling his first New York appearance a year before. "My fingers wouldn't move, my voice wouldn't open up."

His confidence in the studio wavered but Johnston was hip enough to concentrate on Cohen's strengths rather than his weaknesses. When the validity of Cohen's tortured croon was brought up his new producer was insightful in its defence. "What legend has a voice? Does Chevalier

or Johnny Cash or Dylan?" said Johnston. With such an experienced
and tactful engineer guiding him, the sessions for what would become
Songs From A Room soon took on a rhythmn and shape. "He created a
hospitable atmosphere in the studio," Cohen noted of his producer. "He
is a very forceful and very hospitable man. He wasn't all that naive and
all that primitive in terms of what he was doing. Southerners [are] often
very deceptive in their personal style. They invite you to think of them
as country bumpkins. They're very far from that. Bob Johnston was very
sophisticated. His hospitality was extremely refined."

The range of personnel was less plentiful than on the previous work.
By comparison, Johnston used almost a skeleton crew, among them
session musicians Ron Cornelius playing acoustic and electric guitar,
Charlie Daniels playing bass, fiddle and acoustic guitar, Elkin 'Bubba'
Fowler contributing banjo, bass and acoustic guitar, while the producer
himself played rudimentary keyboards – mostly single notes on a B3
organ. "He found very good musicians," Cohen says. "I mean, you were
being accompanied by Charlie Daniels and other great players. He knew
the scene very, very well. He found the accordion player for 'Partisan
Song' and those three girls to put on the overdub. So, his contribution
when requested was really quite thorough."

The sessions were intense but punctuated by the occasional break. In
October Cohen returned to Montreal to seek out (in vain) an apartment.
Even at this late stage he confessed that he had... "no idea for the sound
I'm looking for. Almost all my songs can be sung any way. They can be
sung as tough songs or as gentle songs or as contemplative songs or as
courting songs." It was this very fact that illustrated the need for a strong
engineer/arranger/producer on Cohen's records.

The trip to Montreal allowed Cohen a useful and immediate
perspective on the process as he was in the midst of it. He had at this
point already made a start on the classic 'Bird On The Wire'. "I tried
many versions," he said in Montreal. "I tried it in many different ways.
At about four in the morning I sent all the musicians home except
for my friends Zev who plays Jewish harp, Charlie McCoy who was
playing the bass... and Bob Johnston... I asked him to just sit at the organ
from time to time. And I just knew that at that moment something was
going to take place. I'd never sung the song true, never, and I'd always

had a kind of phony Nashville introduction that I was playing the song to and by the time I came around to start my own song I was already following a thousand models. And I just did the voice before I started the guitar and I heard myself sing that first phrase, like a bird..., and I knew the song was going to be true... I... I sang it through and I listened to myself singing, and it was a surprise. Then I heard the replay and I knew it was right."

Cohen returned to Nashville and soon completed the recording. Compared to the relative 'party' of the previous album, *Songs From A Room* is the hangover of the morning after. Starker and lacking drums, less anchored and tilted so the focus is on Cohen's words, the sounds and arrangements around his language are eerily spare, melodies hanging like bejewelled cobwebs from bones and parched tissue. Yet there was a voluptuousness in the album's austerity, a richness of the 'less is more' variety. As to his original manifesto, Cohen had moved to Nashville to make less a country album and more something that sounded like tranquilized folk music. It was however, quintessential Cohen, and Columbia accepted it as such.

Beyond the birth of his first Nashville album, Cohen's meeting with Johnston was important in ancillary ways. As he slowly became acquainted with the business side of his new art, Cohen had come to realise the grave mistake he had made as regards his publishing. Not only had he lost three of his key songs for nothing (he hadn't even received an advance for the publishing rights to the songs), he had been given this disastrous advice by the very person who should have been looking out for him, Mary Martin. Even she was losing out on the mistake, owning as she did a share of the publishing company (Stranger Music Ltd) herself. Cohen now wanted to be free of Martin and set about firing her as quickly as he could. Painfully, he would be haunted by Jeff Chase for years to come through the loss of those songs. While recording, Johnston suggested that Cohen speak to Marty Machat who at the time was Johnston's lawyer and a rising star in rock'n'roll management, having become adept at renegotiating contracts between record companies and their poorly treated in-house producers – such as Johnston who were, despite the fame, sales and success of the artists they produced, paid no more than a basic wage.* This was clearly unreasonable. Johnston could put his heart, blood and soul into a Johnny Cash record that sold millions and yet he would receive only his standard weekly wage. It made no difference to Johnston's bank balance if he was producing hits or flops, Cash, Cohen, Simon & Garfunkel or a relatively minor selling act. "After [Dylan's] *Highway 61* and [Simon & Garfunkel's] *Sound Of Silence* I got $3,000," remembers the producer bitterly. "After *Parsley, Sage...* and *Blonde On Blonde* I got $6,000. For those records? Screw that."

Marty Machat would represent and orchestrate Johnston's eventual move from mere working stiff at Columbia to that of independent, freelance producer for whoever paid the most. "My father told Columbia 'Fuck that' remembers Steven Machat," Marty's outspoken son. "Anyway, Bob eventually introduced Leonard to my father because I believe Leonard wanted to extract himself from contractual obligations... he wanted to part company with his then management who was Mary Martin."

Marty Machat was instantly smitten with Leonard; love-struck, even. "My father projected onto Leonard," says Steven Machat. "He projected an idea of whom he wanted Leonard to be. Leonard told him he was a Buddhist. My father was besotted." He was now officially Cohen's manager.

As more money came in, Cohen was increasingly practical about his business affairs. He'd been impressed with his own family's attitude to running a business when he was growing up and he both trusted and was impressed by Marty Machat's chutzpah. Despite the mistakes he had made, he was as financially comfortable now as he ever had been. By June of 1969 it was estimated that he'd sold 92,000 copies of *Selected Poems 1956-1968* and approximately 300,000 albums, and in the US he was still selling approximately 3,000 copies a week. These were decent if not awesome figures and, along with publishing royalties earned from both his own versions and cover versions of his songs, barring those – including 'Suzanne' – still owned by Jeff Chase, were enough to keep him afloat. "My intentions," he said that year, "run all the way from

---

* Beatles producer George Martin was in exactly the same position on the other side of the ocean.

making a living to the highest and most arrogant aspirations of spirit seeking."

Aside from financially, 1969 would be another landmark year for Leonard Cohen. That year, at a friend's wedding in LA, he met Kyozan Joshu Sasaki Roshi, a powerful, diminutive and bald Japanese Rinzai Zen teacher, who would become a profound, active and vital presence in Cohen's life from that day on. More than any romantic partner or musical colleague, Roshi would become Cohen's lifelong companion, sage and seer, guru and drinking partner. Born on April 1, 1907, Roshi had entered the United States in 1962, and founded the Mount Baldy Zen Centre, near Mount Baldy in California, where he was Abbot. Mount Baldy would also play an important role in Cohen's life and personal mythology. Roshi became a monk at the age of 13 under his teacher, Joten Soko Miura. (It would take Cohen an additional 30 years to reach the same level under Roshi.) Even at the time that Cohen met his master, Roshi was well on his way to being considered one of the most influential teachers of Zen Buddism in the USA. For someone as vividly Jewish as Cohen, his interest in Roshi was taken by some as a conversion to Buddhism, but the attraction was simpler and in some ways more profound than that. In effect, Cohen had fallen in love. "I wasn't looking for a new religion. I had a perfectly good religion," said Cohen almost defensively. "I had read Freud and that solution didn't seem inviting to me. And I bumped into a man who I didn't know what his position was or his version of the cosmos or reality... what his model was but I noticed in him at ease with himself and at ease with others."

Songs From A Room was released in April 1969. Although dark, Spartan and for the most part non-seductive, it did as ever contain at least one instant classic – the enduring, hymn like 'Bird On The Wire', inspired by the introduction of a telephone system into Cohen's beloved Hydra. As a commercial musical commodity, by now Cohen had a ready made audience waiting, with a saleable identity and a public profile already in place. The brisk sales reflected this – the album charted at number 63 on the *Billboard* chart and number two in the UK. Although even less commercial sounding than his previous album, Cohen's career was at this point fuelled by its own momentum and momentarily transcended good and bad reviews. There was now an increasing public demand for Leonard Cohen that more or less demanded that he tour. He was still reticent, however, and while the album did good business, Cohen promoted it with interviews only while continuing to lead his country life with Elrod, punctuated by occasional trips to Montreal, NYC and Hydra.

Around this time Marty Machat called Tony Palmer. Both he and his favourite client had been impressed by Palmer's *Observer* review of *The Songs of...* and wanted to let the journalist know personally. "He phoned me and said, 'I really want to thank you for what you did,'" recalls Palmer. "I said 'What did I do'? Marty told me: 'Two things: you treated Leonard with respect both as a musician and as a human being.'" Palmer was known for treating pop music – something that many in the establishment then considered a lower art form – with a respect normally afforded to fine art and classical works. "After all," says Palmer, "not all musicians were drugged out hippies. And they wanted themselves and their work to be taken seriously. And I did. You have to remember that when I started my column in the *Observer*, I hadn't been doing it very long when I was summoned by the editor to be told, 'I have something very serious and complicated to discuss with you'. I thought I was going to be fired! He told me, 'Since you began writing your column two months ago' – and he produced a folder at this point – and said 'this is 360 people who have cancelled their subscription to our newspaper – because of you! And... I am very pleased that that should be the case. Can we have a lot more'! And I think that's forgotten. When Leonard released that album, 'pop' music was struggling to be taken seriously." Machat had earmarked Palmer as a useful ally and he would be in touch with a serious proposition within the next few years.

Meanwhile, Cohen was beginning to acclimatise to his new life, moving in the ever rarefied circles that his celebrity afforded him. He finally met Dylan in the autumn of 1969. Cohen has gone to see Tim Buckley perform at The Bitter End folk club in Greenwich Village, and Dylan, made aware of his presence, asked the owner of the club, Paul Colby, to bring Cohen into his presence. The details of this historic summit remain unrecorded.

Such a meeting was proof alone that Cohen had 'arrived'. When he'd first booked into the Chelsea he was an aspirant, a wannabe. Returning there after his trip to Nashville, he was now something of a 'face'. Barry Miles, the writer and all round hipster, had himself moved into the Chelsea in late '69. "I was in New York making a record with Allen Ginsberg," he recalls, "and I was staying at the Chelsea. One night we went down – as you do – to the El Quijote bar which adjoined the hotel. It was full of Chelsea regulars, Harry Smith the film maker, Amy Biderman, an assortment of characters… And Allen introduced me to Leonard. I'd been aware of him since his first record of course. I had been on the editorial board of the *International Times*, the underground paper, and wrote about half their record reviews. So I was getting every album released by Columbia Records throughout the Sixties. I sold most of them but I didn't sell Leonard's. I enjoyed playing them. There was a quality to them that I liked. In Britain he was seen as a 'bedsit' singer, gloomy. My wife liked to play his records quite a bit but he didn't register with me in any major way. Anyway, so now I was introduced to him at one of the big tables at the back where a bunch of people were drinking… he was very much 'around' the Chelsea then. He was seeing a girl – one of many as I recall – called Anne Biderman, a daughter of one of the residents there, Amy Biderman. She was young, 16, 17, and he was her first boyfriend. But my main impression of Leonard was that he was extremely *generous*. You'd often have a big table of people who were running up quite a big bar bill and Leonard would just slip away and pay it, very quietly. And he did that on a number of occasions. He wasn't being flash either, just generous. I was very impressed. I remember Harry Smith saying to Leonard one time, 'As you're the richest Jew here you should pay'. And Leonard thought that was just fine."

Back in New York Cohen met with John Hammond and other staff at Columbia. The label with happy with his work and reasonably satisfied with sales but they felt that even more could be achieved if Cohen would only go out and promote his work like everyone else. It was pointed out to him that he was putting himself at a distinct disadvantage by not competing with his peers in this way, so later that year Cohen finally bowed to the inevitable and agreed to tour.

In the meantime, however, Cohen and his new group went back into Studio A in Nashville to record the follow up to *Songs From A Room* which would be titled *Songs Of Love And Hate*, work on which began in late 1969. Produced once again by Bob Johnston, the other personnel included guitarist Ron Cornelius who acted as band leader of 'The Army'.

Cornelius remembers the initial sessions vividly and although he'd played with Cohen at length already, it seems that only then did he realise exactly what he was getting himself into. "Day one... all I knew was I was getting involved with somebody that was an intellectual, classical guy that doesn't sing very well... it took me a while to understand what it is we're dealing with here... we were on a mission." The sessions introduced another slew of Cohen classics, almost all of which would go on to be reinterpreted by scores of other, wide ranging artists, down the years. Among them 'Joan Of Arc', 'Avalanche' and 'Famous Blue Raincoat'. The latter, in particular, would both fuel and become enmeshed within Cohen's personal mythology. Cohen explained that song was apparently about "A man writing a letter to a man who has had an affair with his wife", but on a more prosaic level, the song actually related to Cohen's own attire. "I had a blue raincoat. It was a Burberry," he said. "It had lots of buckles and various fixtures on it... it was very impressive. It always resided in my memory as some glamorous possibility that I never realised... it stood for that unassailable, romantic life... the opposite of a cloak of invisibility... it was something that could lead you into marvellous erotic and intellectual adventures." Adventure was what Cohen now craved most of all, and thus recording sessions were interrupted for the occasion of Cohen's first world tour.

Assembling the touring group was Cohen's next chore and Bob Johnston was his first choice as musical director. The producer remembers his transformation from studio engineer and producer to touring band leader with typical southern nonchalance. "I ended up on the tour almost by accident," he recalls. "'He asked me to manage him; then he asked me to get his band together. Getting ready, I had said to Cohen, 'Man, I'll get you the best piano player in the world.' 'No, I want you,' Leonard insisted. I protested: 'I can't play piano. I can bang around, but I can't play, and you've got great musicians here. They're wonderful people.' 'Either you come and play, or I won't go' was Cohen's response. I thought, 'Hell, I'm not gonna miss this.' So we started off. I just played piano and guitar and organ, whatever. I couldn't play very well, but he couldn't sing very well."

The touring group, mainly compromised of the players on the album, came to be called The Army. After three low-key US gigs, one in California and two in Washington, vocalists Corlynn Hanney and Susan Mussmano joined Ron Cornelius (electric and acoustic guitars), Charlie Daniels (acoustic guitar, bass, fiddle), Bubba Fowler (acoustic guitar, bass, banjo), Bob Johnston (piano and organ) and Cohen himself (acoustic guitar and lead vocals/poetry recital).

The tour proper began in Europe, opening on May 3 in Amsterdam and closing in the UK on the 19th. Each set included roughly 20 songs from Cohen's two albums plus the occasional poem and new song not yet recorded. Audiences were appreciative and substantial. It had been worth the wait. Not only did Cohen sell out the Paris Olympia and London's Royal Albert Hall, but interest in him was such that other presentations of his work ran concurrently with this tour. In the summer of 1970 the Royal Winnipeg Ballet brought a ballet, *The Shining People Of Leonard Cohen*, to Paris, where it was very well-received. Choreographed by Brian Macdonald, the piece also featured the reading of several of Cohen's poems.

The summer was a feast of festivals for Cohen and band, and spent exclusively in Europe. The intimacy of Cohen's voice and music was surprisingly well suited to outdoor venues, the loose yet potent gang like vibe of The Army fitting in well with the mindset of the largely stoned, drunk and tripping audiences. Cohen's appearance at the legendary Isle of Wight festival at the end of August is now regarded as both legendary and mystical. Awoken in the early hours and required to go on stage without delay, Cohen did so in his pyjamas, which were hidden beneath the legendary raincoat. Sounding stoned but in control, Cohen calmed the rowdy audience with seemingly minimum effort, particularly with a somnambulant reading of 'Suzanne'.

Steve Andrews, a rangy Welshman and an aspiring songwriter himself, was among the thousands witnessing Cohen's hypnotic performance. "Leonard was my hero even as a young guy of 17," he recalls, "and I had to see him at the Isle of Wight so was thrilled when I did. I can remember he lit a match and held it up and said, 'Let there be some light in all this darkness for a while.' Others in the crowd copied him and held up lit matches too and they fizzled out as he launched into 'Seems So

Long Ago, Nancy'. It was audience participation on a symbolic level and respect for what Leonard was saying. It's a memory I kept all these years.

"I saw The Doors too and many other big names but can't remember anything about them. Leonard made that much [more] emotional impact on me. I saw Led Zeppelin at rock festivals around that time, too, and they had loud applause, encores and people dancing, but I remember that strangely they bored me to tears. And I saw Emerson, Lake & Palmer's first performance at the Isle of Wight and some American hippie was sat next to me saying, 'Man, it sounds like a fucking spaceship.' For me it was just a lot of loud noise on stage and a bunch of guys showing off. I couldn't get into it at all.

"For me, I suppose, what Leonard has, and had, is a direct communication with the individual. His words and performance speak to us all somewhere and it's not about anything more than that. It wasn't about freaking out to some loud music and freaky sounds but more about recognising in Leonard's words what we could relate to. There was a lot of awe and reverence for him at the IOW, and it was a shared appreciation for a great poet and writer. His audience listened. There was great respect shown. It's almost a religious experience and very different to the reaction a rock band generates. It is why I remember seeing Leonard but have forgotten the performances of the big-name bands."

Onstage itself the band was the archetypal fist of laurel leaves that made up the greater whole. "If anyone wasn't there, it didn't work," says Cornelius. The focus remained the lyrics – so the audience had to hear Cohen's voice, conversely what was naturally the quietest sound on stage. The band had to play accurately but quietly. This was an agonisingly hard feat for a rock group.

That October the tour continued in America. This leg of the tour was as unique as the European leg had been successful, with one deliberately unpublicised aspect of it being occasional stops at various mental hospitals. Cohen had initiated these very private and intimate concerts not from any sense of charity, but because he claimed simply to enjoy them. There was, he said, none of that "sense of work, of show biz, of turning people on." He felt a particular affinity with the patients in these institutions. "Those people are in the same landscape as the songs come out of. I feel that they understand them."

Apart from the hospitals the shows were more traditionally rock and roll. At one North American show, Cohen knelt down on the lip of the stage, reached out to the crowd and pulled someone from the audience onto the stage. This started a chain reaction. "He started waving to people, come on up, and all of a sudden there are 30 or 40 people up on the stage, with the band, while he was singing," recalls audience member Steve Zirkel, who would go onto play with Cohen in a future incarnation. Panicked, the auditorium staff cut off the power to the microphones and chased everyone off stage. Zirkel continues: "So Leonard tells us, 'Go back to your seats. We'll finish the show. But I notice you have a great park across the street. After the show, let's just everybody go over there and have a party. Me and the band will meet you over there.' And that's pretty much what happened. Everybody went to their cars and their bottles of wine and their stashes of whatever. We all converged at the lake. I ended up talking for a long time to Charlie Daniels, who was the bass player then. There was a guy in the band who rolled 'the fastest joints in the world.' Cohen was there, mingling with the crowd, a big party on Auditorium Shores. I remember this huge haze."

Despite the attendant pressures on Johnston's denim shod shoulders – if anyone in the band had a problem, they came to him, not Cohen – the tour remains a jewel in his memory. "It was some of the nicest music I've been involved with," he would say decades on. This first proper touring band would be the blueprint for Cohen's touring and performing for the rest of his life. The singer and his musicians would travel together and play together, as an on the road community, an army, a family – a true faction. Doubtless Leonard felt that such a set up both played down his weaknesses as a singer and musician – the constant trouble he had pitching and projecting his voice – while accentuating his strengths – the uniquely sparse power of the voice and lyrics. He even went so far as to incorporate straight recitals of poems within the performance.

Harvey Kubernick, a fan since the debut album, was an eager attender at these early US shows. He remembers how striking the presentation was, with Cohen reading texts as well as performing songs. "I'd not seen anything like it at a rock concert before," he states. "I mean, I'd seen The Doors at the Forum and he [Jim Morrison] read something as an introduction which went into their 'Celebration Of The Lizard' but we'd never really seen this kind of presentation. It was remarkable... he wasn't even a singer as such... it was something between rock and roll singing and crooning but was neither."

Kubernick and his buddies were part of a mixed-sex, adoring audience and were soon backstage. "At the end of the show he invited us all backstage," remembers the journalist. "That's the way he is! I'm telling you – of the 3,000 people 1,500 came backstage. And I had never seen that. There was no security, laminated passes none of that 'to the manor born' stuff... when I got backstage there were lots of people, mostly girls bringing copies of his books to be signed... as well as the debut album. He was very handsome in the flesh, dashing even, with his black hair, and he was very trim. For myself, I was more interested in meeting girls there – girls with miniskirts who smelt of patouchli oil – but they didn't want to speak to me because I wasn't a 'lit' major."

Kubernick was impressed by the Cohen operation as a whole, not just by the man himself but also by those surrounding him. "Their US agent during this phase of Cohen's career was Stan Goldstein," recalls Kubernick. "Live agents are overlooked generally, but Stan was... he treated the 'proletariat' like us – little writers for local magazines or whatever like me – he treated us as if we were writing for the *New York Times*. He wasn't like, 'Yes, you may see Mr Cohen my son', but he seemed to be someone who was instrumental in ushering in this new breed of singer songwriter. He also managed John Stewart [formerly of The Kingston Trio] and Janis Ian, and this kind of person was important to Leonard at this stage of his career."

With the tour over, the group returned to Nashville to complete the interrupted album. Many of the musicians involved were now, after their recent and extensive adventuring, closer to family than an army or group. Cohen had been right in his instincts to have Johnston graduate from producer to musician during the tour but in the studio he reverted to his original role. Among the more accomplished musicians, Cornelius recognised that Johnston had no traditional music ability – "Didn't know one note from another' – but was nevertheless impressed at the producer's ability to bring out the absolute best in musicians. "He was born with the ability to make you want to do the best you've ever done, right here tonight," he says.

Despite the tightness of The Army, such a group was by now perhaps more suited to on-the-road work than to creating an experience unique to the studio. The album was completed (mostly in Nashville but with a children's choir and strings, arranged by Paul Buckmaster overdubbed at Trident studios, London), mixed, mastered, packaged and released quickly. Featuring a hideous cover design it came out in late January 1971. Cohen seemed ambiguous about the record, "It is a return... or maybe not even a return, a claim, another kind of strength," he rambled.

Songs Of Love And Hate sold strongly on release, again charting higher outside of North America, reaching number 145 on the *Billboard* chart, number four in the UK and number eight in Australia. In Canada, however, it sold less than its predecessors. In some quarters it was the album that seemed to seal Cohen's reputation as being something of a downer, to say the least. From the *Songs Of Love And Hate* era sprang all the corny clichés that at first raised interest and even amusement but which by the Eighties would be fouling the very critical and commercial streams Cohen attempted to wade through. "It's true I started to break down around the time of that record," Cohen would confess. But when he was asked specifically to comment on the morbid, depressing criticism levelled at him, Cohen countered that he did not see these as "bad qualities for a singer to have".

In some ways, and to many of his fans, Cohen as a man was somehow greater than his music. Steven Machat, son of Marty, was now old enough to pick up on the subtleties of his father's life. "Did my dad like Leonard's music? Dad liked Leonard," he says. "And Leonard's music *was* Leonard."

CHAPTER FIVE

New Skin For A New Ceremony

"I've always tried to make a documentary of the interior landscape. I say to myself, 'What really happened? What is really happening now, that you are thinking of this woman?' That's what I've tried to do, is make it authentic and accurate. And precise."

LC

The first two years of the Seventies had seen Cohen approaching a peak in this early phase of his career, and he and his manager were determined to both capture and cash in on the phenomenon that he had become. In the winter of 1971 Cohen travelled to Toronto to oversee the sale of his early papers to the university there. This was an unequivocal sign that Cohen was now being taken seriously by the world of academia. Such interest was solely down to his earlier literary work but nevertheless the sale of his manuscripts and letters to such a major university was still a rare occurrence for a pop singer.

Cohen had also made a small impression on cinema when segments of music from his debut album were used by Robert Altman in his seminal 'western' *McCabe And Mrs Miller*, released in the summer of '71.

Cohen had given permission to Altman to use his music after being impressed by the maverick director's *Brewster McCloud* movie. Cohen did not compose or record any new music for the film; instead outtakes and off cuts were taken from his debut album's original recording sessions and then embellished and remixed. The players who had performed on the original sessions did not get paid any extra for hearing their work turn up on the soundtrack of a major Hollywood film. Chester Crill's harmonica – recorded solely for *The Songs Of Leonard Cohen* – was prominent on what there was of the soundtrack. "Nah, it didn't bug me that it turned out that way," he says. "I mean you'd hear something you came up with in a few hours in a studio for another session altogether, you hear that pop up on some big movie and it – and your melody line – has been embellished by strings or whatever and you think – hey! Doesn't that count as a composition? But in the end I was just flattered."

Marty Machat and Cohen were moved by the use of his music in Altman's work and it made them realise that cinema was a potent media with which to get Cohen's vision across. Tony Palmer, who had piqued interest among Cohen and co with his perceptive and complimentary *Observer* review, also happened to be an accomplished film maker, who had trained under another movie maverick, the noted English director Ken Russell. It was in this capacity that Palmer once again received word from Cohen's manager. "I had done quite a few rock and roll documentaries by then," explained Palmer, "and although I really wanted to focus on classical music, I did find rock musicians absolutely fascinating."

Since Machat had first got in touch with Palmer a few years previously, Palmer had gone on to make a handful of well received films on rock music on subjects such as Cream, their master drummer Ginger Baker, and Frank Zappa. Machat had seen some of these films when they were broadcast in the US on the PBS channel and had been impressed by the work of someone who as well as obviously being a gifted and even innovative documentary film maker, was in addition a Leonard Cohen fan. "Marty wrote to me in the autumn of 1971," recalls Palmer, "and said 'We're gonna do a European tour in '72. Would you be interested in filming it?' I wrote straight back and said 'Absolutely! Try and stop me!'" Palmer was intrigued by what he might achieve. "As far as filming went, I was always far more interested in people – the subject – than I was about all the nonsense that goes on around them. And Leonard was a special subject."

In October 1971, Palmer finally got to meet that subject. "I met with Marty in his New York office," he remembers, "and he introduced me to Leonard there. I had a sense from his music that I would like him, so the fact that I did instantly upon meeting him didn't surprise me at all. What did surprise me was that he was extremely self effacing, extremely humble, almost apologetic. And although he'd done some live work he'd never been on a tour that was as extensive as the one being planned. We sat and talked and he was very worried about how he would be received. Although he had most of his group then, he still felt unprepared."

Cohen had enjoyed the previous tour with The Army and was confident as he was ever likely to be in his role as a pop rock singer performer. When asked why he was a reticent live performer, Cohen answered plainly: "I think I'm always afraid of failing. I think that's one way of putting it. It's just that I have this sense that to take up people's time with anything but excellence is really too much to think about... Compel them to come and then bore them for hours. If you can really give and give the total gift it's worthwhile, but you don't feel you can demand their grace every night."

He also had other plainly practical worries. "One of his main concerns," says Palmer, "was how would we record the music? So I came up with a master plan. I suggested that there's no point in me recording every song at every concert. Leonard said, 'That's good 'cos we haven't rehearsed them all yet!' So I said, 'Why don't we record the fifth, tenth and fifteenth concerts? No point in recording everything...' Leonard said, 'What if we do a great show and you miss it', so I just said, 'Well, that's sod's law!' As it turned out, Cohen's people, who were recording the songs for a possible album, had a lot of problems with their sound equipment and on more than one occasion we – the film crew- helped *them* out."

All of this was in the near future. At this point, sat in Machat's cramped office, with New York roaring indifferently outside, Palmer was still under review, as it were. As he and Cohen talked, he got the sense that Cohen wasn't particularly familiar with his film work but that he was going on Machat's word. "He was less concerned about my work and more concerned if he and I were going to get on," explains Palmer, "because he and I were gonna be in each other's pockets a long time." Machat also made it clear to Palmer that he didn't want Cohen involved directly in the financing of the film. "Marty wanted to protect Leonard from that and so funded it himself."

Having passed Cohen's low key personality test, the filmmaker was asked to present Machat and Cohen with a (as it turned out, very reasonable) budget. It was accepted immediately. The film was on. Cohen had one last stipulation. "He made it clear to me that nothing was to be off limits," says Palmer, "that I should film whatever I deemed to be appropriate."

Cohen then left New York, stopped off in London to drop off some 'baby clothes for a friend' there and moved on to Hydra. He returned to America shortly after and prepared himself for the tour rehearsals by spending five weeks with Roshi at the Mount Baldy monastery. Suitably rejuvenated he then drove down to Nashville in his Toyota jeep to reconvene with his band and prepare for the coming adventure.

Cohen and his group rehearsed where they recorded – in the high-ceilinged rooms of Columbia's Studio A in Nashville. There were issues. The original female backing singers booked for the tour were not successfully meshing their voices with Cohen's. Thus "Lee from Toronto" and "Stephanie from England" were let go perilously close to the first date of the tour. Compounding such problems was the fact that after the high altitude invigoration and purity of Mount Baldy Cohen was not particularly pleased to be back in Nashville and on the rock'n'roll treadmill once again. Having given up his residence on the farm he was, as usual, staying in a hotel, and he seemed irritated to be there and clearly not looking forward to the tour.

Despite the presence of Elrod and his band mates Cohen was often tense, sometimes working out twice a day at the local YMCA gym to alleviate his very physical anxieties. He would later consider himself at a physical peak during this period, working out in the morning, rehearsing in the afternoon and often working out again in the evening. He was conscious of his diet and exercise and how this impacted on his state of mind. His band mates were grateful for his efforts, even as Cohen was frustrated. "He taught me more about how to take care of my guts than anyone," said guitarist Ron Cornelius bluntly.

Cohen himself was going through one of his habitual depressions, telling a visiting journalist at the time that: "I lived a lot better when I had less money. A lot more luxuriously, and so it's very confusing, as you might imagine. My standard of living went down as my income increased. Believe me, it's just the nature of money. Money in the hands of some people can only decrease their standard of living. I mean I lived a lot better when I had no money. I was living in a beautiful big house on a Greek Island. I was swimming every day; writing, working, meeting people from over the whole world and moving around with tremendous mobility. You know, I can't imagine anyone living any better and I was living on about $1,000 a year. Now that I spend many times that I find myself living in hotel rooms, breathing bad air."

Despite his depression or perhaps because of it, Cohen was still writing prolifically. At this point he had ready a manuscript for his next poetry collection, titled *The Energy Of Slaves*. Though caught up in the maelstrom of being a popular singer and an in demand product of Columbia records, the literary side of his work still mattered deeply to him. "I am interested in this book's reception. I'm interested in how it will be received almost more than any other book," he said that March, "because I have the feeling that by making it public I may be making a mistake. I hope that I will find that this gnawing feeling is wrong or that I have misread it."

Cohen soon got to gauge public reaction to his work first hand. In March of 1972, beginning in Dublin, Cohen and The Army, accompanied by Palmer and his film crew, began their second tour in two years. Jennifer Warnes had met Cohen the year before and was joining him on this tour for the first of many. She had, in fact, only joined the group two days before the first gig. She would recall that: "The experience of touring with Leonard Cohen in 1972 was mind-boggling. I've never seen anything like it before or since. It was like being in one of those big poetry books, inside the relationship between (Jack) Kerouac and (Neal) Cassady, being way deep inside something live, like Hermann Hesse's magic theatre. I was 24 years old, new to the world in every way. I'd never seen Europe. We went all over Scandinavia, ended up in Jerusalem. There was absolute worship for him in Europe. He was like François Villon, flower children, everywhere. I'd never seen people on trips before... in these beautiful opera houses..."

Cohen himself now felt something of a veteran. Touring, he opined, was "like an Italian wedding. You kind of know the bride and maybe you've met the groom once or twice, but you've never met anyone else that's there. And everyone gets too drunk and eats too much. [On] the morning after you don't remember much about the wedding."

On the first night in Dublin someone called out for a poem. Cohen responded with a few jokey lines. This expressed his awkwardness at inserting recitals of the written word into a music concert. "I never really enjoyed myself doing poetry from the stage," he'd later explain, "but I'm sorry I didn't have a book of poems with me because people were so hospitable and interested and I did feel so relaxed. I might just have said, 'Well here are some poems I've written, if you want to hear them.'"

Palmer observed all of this as both a film maker and audience member. 'It seemed to me that he looked upon the performance on the stage as a collaborative effort and if everyone on stage was together, if it was a real community, then the performance was good. If it wasn't together – if someone had a row, if there was tension – the usual on tour stuff, then the performance would still be acceptable but not as special. It mattered to Leonard very much that everybody pulled their weight."

The tour had a celebratory feel, a sense of Cohen spreading the word on behalf of some unnamed political party concerned only with the state of its people's heart and soul. In April, toward the end of the sold out tour, Cohen and The Army played at the sports stadium in Tel Aviv. The concert began as any other, with Cohen and the group now sounding solid and slick whilst retaining a grainy, ethereal patina. On this tour the female voices in particular sounded locked into each other, a bouquet woven from beams of light yet as strong as vine. Such were the harmonies that at a distance the voices take on the sheen of strings. There was tension at this particular show when the security guards attempted to confine the audience's movements toward the stage. Cohen was perturbed at this and improvised a new protest song there and then. Accompanying himself with his familiar rolling style on the Spanish guitar, a slightly stoned sounding singer intoned 'I feel like I'm singing to machines… Come on machines/Move a little closer to me/I know you got souls machines/But you've fallen into slavery… machines/Throw off your wires/Disintegrate your tubes/And come much closer/Don't just stand there…' As the crowd laughed uncomfortably, Cohen abruptly changed person and began singing from the point of view of the security guards: 'Why don't you come a bit closer/So we can beat you up/And teach you a lesson/There's gonna be the final solution for the machines'. This brave and surreal improvisation drew a gratified applause and Cohen, having acknowledged the disturbance caused by the harsh security guards, felt he could continue the show as normal.

His band, too, was impressed. "Here I am," recalls Warnes, "standing behind this man who thought it was brave to invent songs in front of people, right there. And he did that! We invented a song in the middle of every concert, just for that audience."

Cohen then attempted to segue gently into 'Sisters Of Mercy' with the cryptic comment "I feel like Ed Sullivan'." But this song too collapsed into a comedy, "I like spending the night with two girls," he crooned. "It's better than one/It's better than none…" Eventually the show got back on track, with the inclusion of "a new song we wrote just a few weeks ago: 'Chelsea Hotel'". Cohen was already alluding to Janis Joplin, even at this early stage in the song's life. (At this stage the song differed considerably from the recorded version, with a whole different repeating section and several different lyrics including the line 'My friends of that year/They were all getting queer').

Introducing 'Suzanne' as 'pure documentary' there was a hint of bitterness about his loss of the song's copyright. "I wrote it for this person and she accepted it. And after that, you accepted it. And after that, lawyers accepted it, and after that, agents accepted it, and after that, banks, financers… and I just wanna remind any songwriters here you really must remember the birthplace of your song."

Cohen was in a subtly volatile mood throughout the Tel Aviv concert and his introduction carried an underlying subtext that he considered this song had been stolen from him. As if in response to his sunken anger there was a small but vicious scuffle between the orange-clad guards and the mainly student audience immediately after he completed the song. Cohen and band had wanted to dedicate 'Tonight Will Be Fine' to the guards, imploring them to "just enjoy the concert" but matters were turning ugly, too ugly to ignore. "I know you're trying to do your job," he said, addressing them directly, "but you don't have to do it with your fists. We can bring 6,000 people down into this place!" Predictably, Cohen's statements did not bring harmony. The guards reacted even more violently. Cohen and band launched into a spirited rendition of the traditional American workers union song 'We Shall Not Be Moved'. Cohen and the band eventually collapsed off stage amidst a montage of cable hums, feedback and half discernable shouts and curses. He vowed never to return to Israel again.

Despite his willingness to stand up and be counted, Cohen did not see his own music as 'marching music' or music to rouse the rabble. "I don't think anyone is gonna march off to war with my music," he said. If his music could be classified in political terms then it was, according to its author, "Music of personal resistance".

Palmer looked on from behind his camera and film crew, noting concerns that were more practical than political, more perfunctory than poetic. "He was sometimes a troubled soul," he says, "and if there were problems with the sound etc., then that too caused a lot of anxiety. He was very concerned that the group give a great performance, not just a professional one, and so was very concerned that they bonded. The number of times he said in the dressing room, 'That concert didn't go well. Something happened today. You went to one museum and I went to another museum. We split up. We had no unity as a group.' And I could see exactly what he means. They would always give a professional performance but when it was in lift off they all… went to the same sauna together."

When the tour ended in Jerusalem in late April, Palmer had more than enough footage for an extensive documentary and even at this late stage there was some debate as to who actually owned the footage and resulting film. "Marty's production company owned the controlling interest in the film. We had some interest in it but it was not significant," Palmer explains. "Marty put out what we call the 'above the line costs', the musicians and sound engineer travel, accommodation, lights etc. We put in the below the line costs, which means all the basic filming facilities. That was the arrangement." Palmer seemed unaware that most of the tour would have been financed not by Cohen or Machat (in the short run, at least; expenses were usually recoupable) but by Columbia Records as part of the 'tour support' clause in Cohen's recording contract. Despite the usual legal and technical hassles that accompany any commercial venture, Palmer considered the venture up to now a resounding success. He also considered himself on good terms with his subject. "You couldn't help but like and admire him," he says of Cohen. "When you were sat next to him on a plane or whatever he was very hospitable. I'd say we became close friends by the end of it. The problems started afterwards."

Cohen had clearly defined hopes for the film. "We hope it (the film) will emerge out of the performances, I think it's going to surprise me. I would like it to be a kind of essay and I would like the character, who'll be me, to emerge as a surprise. I don't think it will really be anything I am." Like so many musicians in the first flush of musical success he already had cinematic pretensions, although he was more realistic than most in this regard. "I would love to be a great filmmaker, it's a wonderful notion. I would also like to be a great mason, but I would like to find areas in which I can summon energy. If it's films it would be wonderful but I myself don't think it will be, I don't think I have the talent for it."

Palmer, a lauded and experienced filmmaker, immediately began editing the film. He had a lot to draw from. "I've got to stress," says Palmer "that Leonard placed no restrictions on me whatsoever." Once the edit was completed, as was the industry norm, Palmer invited Machat and Cohen to the screening room to see the rough cut. Cohen's reaction was powerful. "He cried a lot," remembers the filmmaker. "He wept. He was very emotional, tears running down his cheeks." Apart from this Cohen seemed subdued. "He was very complimentary about the quality of the sound recording," says Palmer, who perhaps should have taken this as a warning sign. "But then we took a lot of trouble over it. Some was four-track, some eight-track and some even 16-track."

Columbia themselves had requested recordings from this and the 1970 tour to be mixed down to releasable quality. An album had been collated from both and was released in April of 1973, to hardly any commercial reaction. *Live Songs* was a collection of just that. Beautifully recorded and surprisingly atmospheric, Cohen was very much the focus – belligerent, rousing, stoned and quietly powerful. At times he sounded almost overwhelmed, as if not sure what to do with his new found popularity and power.

Also, for someone whose songs were being covered by other artists at a pleasing rate, Cohen himself was shy to return the favour. That Christmas he explained why this was: "The reason I've stayed away from it [performing other people's songs] mostly is because I started writing my own songs because I couldn't really learn the tunes of other songs. I would love to and if I could really sing well I'd sing everybody's songs, but I feel if I sing my own songs nobody can complain. I think if you sing your own songs you can really embody the vision in the song but I wouldn't like to try it with 'O Sole Mio'." (He did, however, perform at least one well known cover version on this tour, aside from 'Passing Through', a busked version of the romantic classic 'As Time Goes By'.

Palmer had officially delivered the film to Machat and Cohen approximately six weeks after the tour was finished. He had also delivered it well within budget, costing as little as £30,000. Following the private premiere of the first cut, the three people in the screening room seemed very happy. "Marty proclaimed it a masterpiece," says Palmer. This was surely a bad sign. "And then," continues the filmmaker, "a few days later he calls me and says 'We have a problem. Can we talk?'" Palmer half sighed, half groaned. "I said, 'Sure'. So Marty tells me 'Leonard feels that the film is too confrontational. You begin the film with the riot in Tel Aviv. Is there no way we can start the film in a more gentle way?'" Palmer was slightly nonplussed but agreeable and said he could do just that. "Of course we opened with that riot because it was so dramatic," explains Palmer, "and what you see is Leonard calming it down. Marty then told me that Leonard was very worried about the poetry. I was a bit surprised because at his request he asked we film him reciting some poems. One particular reading was given at a café in East Berlin with officials stood right by him!"

Palmer responded coolly to Machat and offered to give the film to Cohen so he could look at it again in his own time. "After all we're not in any hurry," said the filmmaker. "Actually we are," responded Machat.

"I want this thing out and earning money." Palmer went one further, offering to let Cohen and Machat "fiddle about" with the work if they wanted to. "I was experienced enough to know that when people are worried about how they come across in a film, its easier to simply say 'OK, why don't you have a go,'" says Palmer, "'and if you can come up with something better, I'd be delighted'. On the whole, they don't. But it wasn't a bluff as such. It was out of courtesy to Leonard. It was very personal to him, so let him have a go."

Cohen did just that, setting himself up with another editor, Humphrey Dixon (whom the usually gentlemanly Palmer actually describes as "Someone who should burn in hell, I'm sure he manipulated Leonard with typical editor bullshit"). The two used editing suites in London, Toronto, New York and Los Angeles, a tour in itself. Cohen and Dixon spent six months re editing the material. Palmer sat it out patiently while Cohen and Dixon ran up bills close to half a million dollars. At the end of this laborious and costly process, they came up with what Palmer would refer to as "version two". "They included a lot of version one," he says, "but it has none of the poetry or improvisations or the revealing interviews he gave and much less humour. But still, between the two versions there was only about 10% difference. But it was an important 10%."

Marty was civil enough to let Palmer see the film. After watching it, the filmmaker let it be known that he thought something important was missing. Marty agreed, saying "But Leonard is so exasperated with it having spent six months on it – longer than the actual tour – and a lot of money that he now just wants to wash his hands of it." Palmer was amazingly mellow in his response. "I said, 'If that's what Leonard wants, fine'. I thought, as soon as he gave birth to it he would forget about it. And that's what happened. That's why it disappeared."

The resulting film (version two) ultimately had a limited UK cinema release and would eventually be shown once on German TV. "The BBC asked to see it," remembers Palmer, "and we showed them version one, which was the only one ready at the time. They loved it and offered Marty a lot of money to show it but this was when version two was being made. So Marty asked them to wait. When he finally showed them Leonard's version the BBC refused it, saying they wanted my version. And that's why it was never shown on UK TV. It was a cock up."

Consigned to a few art theatres and with Cohen wanting nothing to do with it, the film's release went by largely unnoticed. This was a shame because as a "fly on the wall" view of Cohen's early peak (as Palmer describes it), it was a riveting and deeply enjoyable movie, easily comparable in quality to D.A. Pennebaker's Dylan movie *Don't Look Back*. Cohen was a fascinating subject, both inscrutable and embarrassingly open at the same time. Palmer caught him swimming naked in a pool, chatting up female fans backstage and shaving before an encore. Various stories abound from the time that Cohen was regularly indulging in downers, pot and the occasional tab of vintage acid but Palmer says that, "Very rarely was he high. In fact I remember he got cross at one point because Bob Johnston was an inveterate smoker and was always puffing away on a joint in front of the camera and offering it to Leonard."

Despite the inherent tensions of such a venture, subject and filmmaker became close. 'Very close," says Palmer. "He and I never had a cross word the entire tour which is unusual considering. The nearest we came to an argument was when he said to me, after the Manchester gig, 'It's not going very well.' And I said, 'You're joking! That audience was totally transfixed by you!' and he said, 'Yes but it's not going well for us.' And that was the closest we came to a serious disagreement. During the making of the film, at least."

By the time he'd finished work on the film, Cohen was drained. September '72, was a tumultuous month for Cohen. He bought a house in Montreal yet continued to move around the word at an unhealthy pace. That month he almost simultaneously received news that his cousin and friend, Robert Hershorn – the man who had lent Cohen the money to move to NYC in late '66 – had died (of a heroin overdose it would later transpire) in a hotel room in Hong Kong. In the same month Cohen's first child was born to Suzanne Elrod. Abandoning his family tradition of giving males names beginning with 'L', Cohen called his son Adam. That month saw Cohen mourning the death of his old friend whilst celebrating the birth of his son. His feelings were mixed, his moods up and down. In retrospect, it seemed that the birth of their first child would instigate a fault line in Elrod and Cohen's relationship rather than enhancing it. To cap it all, he was apparently broke. "Well, this film's been a blow financially, but I don't have a great deal of bread,' he confided. "My lawyer tells me I have money. But I never see it... I know damned well I haven't got any money."

1973 seemed a grim year for Cohen, so much so that he spoke sincerely in the press about his impending retirement. "Well, I wish everybody well on 'the rock scene', and may their music be great. May there be some good songwriters – and there will. But I don't wanna be in it," he said in New York that February. Of course, Dylan had also enjoyed a kind of temporary semi-retirement, from which he would soon emerge on his legendary final tour with The Band, and so had Frank Sinatra whose comebacks would become almost as legendary as they were numerous. Neither of these very public withdrawals from showbiz seemed applicable to Cohen: "It's not like I'm announcing my retirement. No, not at all. It's a totally psychic thing, on a very private level. It may turn out that the public won't realise any difference. It may turn out that the records still keep coming, and the books keep coming. But I won't be there, I won't be part of it."

As if confirming his disquiet, *Live Songs*, released that April would flop. By August that year he and his family had retired to Hydra. From there he flew to Athens where he planned to involve himself in the Yom Kippur war between Israel and Egypt that October. He offered his services to the Jewish state as an "entertainer for the troops" but really, as with his trip to Cuba years before, Cohen was actually attempting to reconfigure his sense of macho self. He had become disgusted with his role in the music business and the birth of his child had left him feeling chained to a woman like never before. Yet whereas in Cuba he was a relatively young man on an adventure, leaving a mother worrying in Montreal, now he was a father of a newly born child. The situation he threw himself into seemed reckless, to say the least. Embarking on numerous affairs as he did so, Cohen did indeed play for the troops in bunkers and hangers and also came under fire. He returned to Hydra and his family after a month of duty. He returned unharmed and with perhaps what was his original goal – fresh material, 'Field Commander Cohen' being the most obvious trophy of his wartime experiences.

By September, Elrod, Adam and Cohen were back in their Montreal home on Ste. Dominique Street. It was now – and purely by chance – that Cohen began a fruitful working relationship with John Lissauer, then in his early twenties and a rising producer who had only recently graduated from college. One of his earliest assignments had been recording the then unknown jazz guitarist Al Jarreau and when he met Cohen for the first time some months before in Montreal, Lissauer was playing a concert there with another of his artists, Lewis Furey. "We were playing at a little place in downtown Montreal called the Nelson Hotel," remembers the producer. "Lewis was almost punk rock, like a Lou Reed vibe but without guitars. Just the funkiest drummer and bass player and a jazz banjo player, a kind of Kurt Weill, raw and punk like. Oh and we also had three gorgeous female backing singers. And it seemed this show was a real event; the whole of Montreal had come along it seemed. Things were really bubbling up there. Anyway, Leonard was there and he introduced himself. I knew who he was but I didn't know much about his music. I wasn't into folk music which is what I would have considered him doing at that time. I considered myself a serious composer and I'd done some jazz stuff and some other edgy stuff. He was well dressed in a dark anonymous suit, as if he were dressed to disappear into the night or something, and he was softly spoken, extremely polite and complimentary about the show. He was devoid of attitude and posturing and would remain that way. He was very aware of how he was considered in Montreal and he was trying not to upstage Lewis or the moment. He struck me as exceedingly humble, almost cap in hand like. I'm not even sure I knew who he was in that first instance. He presented himself to me as a fan of Lewis' music. But the girl I was with – when she saw Leonard her jaw dropped and hit the table. But he was extremely discreet, very humble. He was just saying how much he loved the show." Lissauer was as impressed by Cohen's demeanour as Cohen was by the show. The producer gave Cohen his NYC telephone number and the singer promised to be in touch the next time he was in town.

By the time Cohen came over, Lissauer had a big loft on the fourth floor of an apartment building on 18th Street in New York. "It was the coolest place to hang out," he remembers. "It was above an old Mafia after hour's club." Cohen had phoned ahead and was now downstairs. "He rang the buzzer and I had to throw the key out of the window to let him in. And when he came up he was carrying a pizza. My neighbours had ordered a pizza and Leonard had met the delivery guy at the door and he offered to take it up for him. The pizza was for a jazz musician's wife across the hall. And she was at that time a huge Leonard Cohen fan! So she comes out to meet the pizza guy and meets one of her idols, Leonard Cohen! It was one of the great moments. She was in a hysteria! It was like *Candid Camera*. She talked about it for a year!"

Cohen sat down on Lissaeur's couch and the two got talking. This soon graduated, in time honoured fashion, to the usual manner in which Cohen presented new material to potential producers, simply playing the songs live, in person. "So, anyway he played me some songs and we decided there and then to do an album together. I was 22 or 23 at the time and was a relative unknown. Why he had faith in me, I don't know," says the producer modestly. "But even so, Marty Machat wanted me to 'audition' for it, so it was agreed that we'd do two or three songs to begin. So we went over to the CBS studio for a month and cut a handful of tracks. It wasn't a particular place I would have chosen, as a studio. You know there were guys in lab coats there, union guys not hip guys. It wasn't a happening place. And John Hammond was overseeing things – he and I hit it off instantly, by the way – and the three tracks were quite exciting. Leonard had never done anything like it before. We cut 'Lover Lover Lover', 'There Is A War' and 'Chelsea Hotel'."

These initial recordings were approved by Marty and Hammond and without ceremony (or singing any contract, the deal was done on a handshake between the producer and artist), Lissauer had the job. The three demo tracks were not discarded and reconstructed like with most demos, but built upon as the album sessions began proper. Lissauer was, of course, glad that the three tracks had been approved but he didn't actively seek out Marty's opinion anyway. "I didn't see him much," he says, "He was kind of a scary guy. In fact he was the scariest. You didn't mess with Marty. He was from another place. He would whisper but that would carry something."

They relocated to another NYC studio, Sound Ideas, and the producer began to call in musicians. Among them was the 29-year-old double bass player John Miller. "Was I happy to get the call? Hey listen, as a freelance musician living in New York, I'm always happy when the phone rings!" Miller had worked with Lissauer on the Furey project and was familiar with Cohen, although he was at this point an admirer rather than a fan. "Sure, I knew his stuff," he says. "I used to play with various folk groups and singers in New York and we'd often do versions of 'Suzanne' and 'Bird On The Wire'. So when John asked me to come over I packed up my double bass in its case and walked over there. I used to like walking with my bass."

As the musicians arrived, Lissauer was setting up the studio. "One good thing I learnt about recording at the Columbia studios was that Leonard's voice sounds incredibly present when recorded by a Neumann 67 microphone," says the producer, "which Columbia had in abundance, being an old studio. They had those old classic tube microphones, these great old microphones that came from World War Two Germany. They sounded so great and from then on we always used them. I didn't like Columbia's recording studio but I did get that from them." The irony of Cohen using what was in effect a Nazi microphone could not have been lost on him but he didn't remark upon it. Neither did Cohen mention why he was no longer working with Bob Johnston or even speak of any previous producer he had worked with, although Lissauer did get the impression that the whole Nashville experience and especially the tour with The Army had been a bit overwhelming for Leonard. "It was like a big wave picking him up and while he had fun it didn't quite have the artistic sensibility that Leonard needed. The focus then had been more on this Nashville energy thing."

Cohen had moved on from that sound and the choice of musicians in attendance reinforced his new aesthetic. Miller arrived and unpacked his double bass, remarking that 'it was more like a jazz combo set up, almost, except there was no drummer there. Miller had worked with Tim Buckley as part of his classic drummerless combo line-up and saw the familiar potential for this Cohen album immediately. He also warmed to Cohen instantly. "He was open and genuine," he remembers, "and short. I was surprised that he was short 'cos I was a short guy and I didn't expect it. But he was friendly and so real – I felt that this was a man I'd like to get to know."

The atmosphere at the studio – essentially a gathering of strangers – was at once congenial and civil. Lissauer had a strong vision for all those present and was untypical in that not only did he produce the albums but he also (part) engineered and (completely) arranged the songs. Most producers would usually hire an arranger – particularly a string and brass arranger – separately. "I came into it with the music written," says Lissauer of the string scores. "And I would conduct the players. Of course I trusted my engineer and it helped I had a great one, a guy called Rip Rowel and the assistant engineer was Leanne Ungar who as we know would go on to work with Leonard for evermore, a really great engineer."

"I read music, so it wasn't a problem," says Miller. "It was what you expected. I had no problem with my parts presented to me but I was very impressed by them – the whole set up was so spacious. The music was about what not to play as much as it was what you played. I'd describe my first impression of Leonard as being through his music – it was the music equivalent of a haiku poem."

The fifteen-year age difference between Lissauer and Cohen – more prominent with the two men at their then particular ages – was not an issue. "He was never avuncular or became a father figure or anything," says Lissauer. "I mean he was very experienced but he loved what I brought to the table and we were partners."

Miller: "I had been in a lot of sessions you know, and this one was very relaxed, very amiable and loose and cool by comparison to many I'd experienced."

Lissauer: "We talked about the sound we wanted for the album, not track by track but overall. We really wanted Leonard's voice to be big and God like, imposing without him singing loud or strong. We wanted him to sound effortless rather than effortful."

The sessions began on time and the players moved through the songs and scores and arrangements quickly, and Cohen was present throughout. The album's sound would go on to be compared by some to John Simon's production of Cohen's album but Lissauer didn't consider it to be as dense as that album although he didn't go out of his way to familiarise himself with Cohen's previous work. "I didn't really want to be influenced by what had gone before," he says. "I wanted it to be fresh and I didn't want to do a 'folk' album."

As such, 'The Army' was replaced by a completely different set of personnel. In common with Simon, Lissauer saw Cohen's songs as individual pieces that together would make up a whole. At the same time those pieces should also be treated as mini albums in themselves, and framed as such. Lissauer considered the 'Nashville' albums – what he'd heard of them – to be a bit static. Starting with *New Skin For the Old Ceremony* he was very conscious about adding 'colour' to Cohen's work. He was also aware that Cohen was writing "new songs, not just another 'So Long Marianne' or 'Suzanne'. Those kind of songs were out," says Lissauer. "He was writing more upbeat and attacking stuff now."

While Cohen had always used female vocals in his sonic palette, the new producer sought to put a twist to this element. "The female backing was my idea," says the producer. "That sultry mix of New York and Montreal female voicings... it was just something I was comfortable with. I was obsessed by the idea of painting pictures, of drawing images in sound and I thought Leonard had these incredibly vivid images in his lyrics. They took me places. And I wanted to frame them. I treated them like individual little pieces of art. It wasn't just about a bunch of songs."

Miller had worked with Lissauer on the Lewis Furey album and held the producer's aesthetic in high regard. "His take on music was very particular, European, simple but complex, highly imaginative. This applied to both his arrangements and production. It was crystal clear to me why Leonard wanted to work with him."

'Is This What You Wanted', the aggressive, confrontational song that would open the album, confirms the producer's opinion that Cohen had by now turned a corner. The vocal is one of Cohen's rawest and most damaged sounding to date. "We got a couple of takes on that vocal," confirms Lissauer, "and we found one that was *raging*. He was into it. It was after about three hours of doing it and he was trying to get his intensity up and I think he wanted to be bleeding. Not actually bleeding but essentially his throat and his heart was ripped." No click tracks were used to bind all the musical elements together; the tightness and syncopation of the parts were down to Lisseur's impeccable arrangements. "And what I had to do was conduct them correctly," he adds.

Lissauer was going for a more cinematic effect for this album, juxtaposed with and enhanced by his unique use of Moroccan and African percussion. On one of the few up-tempo songs, 'Lover Lover Lover', Lissauer wanted an 'Ethiopian' backing and the result is unsettling and exotic. Bassist Miller saw the music as "being like Japanese calligraphy, it was about what's not going on as much as what is".

Lissauer was lucky in that this album contained its fair share of new Cohen classics. His version of 'Chelsea Hotel' was tighter – or perhaps more skilfully edited – than the fledgling version that had been presented on the recent tour. Using himself and Janis Joplin as characters in the song, Cohen investigated and expressed his problems with the ideal of physical beauty. Asked to comment on the famous lines "We are ugly but we have the music" and "You told me again you preferred handsome men but for me you would make an exception" decades on, Cohen finally and awkwardly forced himself to admit that, "There were times when I thought I was good looking... but the damn thing is, it's comparative. There are always people around you who look better."

'Who By Fire' would become another standard, and in Tony Pamer's opinion, "was one of his most profound songs". "The first time you hear it, you're struck by the power of the imagery... the simplicity of the music – which again, is a characteristic of Cohen – there's nothing ever arty farty about the music." The stark and perfectly poised arrangements heard on this track apparently "came easily... because his songs inspired me to think that way," says the arranger. This haunting, eerie hymn like song did in fact owe its origins to the eleventh centaury Jewish prayer known as the Unetanneh Tokef or Unesanneh Tokef but Cohen rarely spoke of the background to his songs and the musicians and producer responded to them purely as music. "I'm not really a lyric man," says John Miller, "which might sound strange if you're playing with Leonard! But really, I just react and play along to the rhythm, the chord changes and the melodies." Miller didn't have a particular problem playing without the anchor of drums. "They were so well scored and arranged that I just followed the charts and John's direction... plus, when you got into Leonard's own particular kind of guitar playing... once you get into it, it kind of suggests to you where the song was going." The album was Cohen's richest, musically, so far. It was also oddly, his sparsest.

Lissauer: "We used so many combinations. Sometimes we used 10 strings (a quartet or octet would be the norm) and different singers on different songs. The strings were the New York Philharmonic, really fabulous musicians who followed me well. I could usually rely on my charts but occasionally I'd get verbal: 'Make it sound like ice shimmering in sunshine' or whatever, but mostly if you write a score well enough that does the job."

It's worth noting that for all the material's richness and depth, as far as the string players were concerned this was just another gig. Often they would have come from a TV advert soundtrack session and be en route to a Barbra Streisand appointment. "But we kept a core band throughout," explains Lissauer. "I was playing keyboards and we had John on bass throughout pretty much. If you start with a consistency then there's a running thread throughout the material. If you then start to colour the tracks with all kinds of flavours, then at least they don't sound like a 'Whitman' sampler. There is a familial feel to the album even though they are free to go where they go. A lot of what I do depends on the personalities of the musicians I use. So especially with the strings I got the guys who followed me best. I liked using musicians I had a bond with. I can write for them and we can attempt something special."

The album progressed song by song with work being done on groups of songs before starting afresh on new ones. "In all it probably took six or seven months," says Lissauer, "We'd start on something, go back and do vocals and then start on something new. We considered everything, we lived with rough mixes and the treatments. The main thing was the vocals 'cos after all that is in Leonard's case so important. It – and the words – are really the focus. What I was doing was colouring them, framing them. It wasn't the kind of album where we'd do rhythm tracks on seven, eight songs and then overdub vocals... nah! We were too artistic for that." As usual Cohen played along with the musicians while they learnt the songs and recorded their takes. "His guitar playing was interesting," says Miller. 'He was no James Taylor or John Martyn, or even Joni Mitchell. But there was something very very compelling about his playing. When he started you knew what to do."

The mix was very dry in that reverb and echo were hardly used, or if it was then it was employed so sparingly that it wasn't noticeable.

"Dryness is intimate," opines Lissauer. "If you really want to believe someone have it dry. And because I was doing a fairly colourful album in terms of the surrounding instruments we didn't wanna turn it into some schlocky reverb Hollywood sounding thing. We wanted it intimate and close. We wanted you to be forced to listen to, to live every nuance of Leonard's voice, we wanted you to be forced inside of it. No safety nets. No distractions. It forced you to take it seriously. I wanted his voice to be under a microscope," he stresses. "It made some people uncomfortable and I guess we were being brave. But I liked what we were doing."

Overall, the recording sessions had a civil, orderly, professional and almost academic air. For mid-Seventies New York this was something of an anomaly. But it was a method that suited all involved – and most importantly the material – well. "Session times were different. But I don't think we ever went past midnight," remembers Lissauer. "We'd finish at one at the latest. We'd start around 4pm. We didn't overdo it. No one was getting high. We were serious about our art. Cohen was tireless. He never complained. If there was a technical issue he just let me fix it, and would wait and then get on with it. We worked. We rolled up our sleeves and got on with it."

Cohen was serious about his singing too, more serious and confident now that he had a tour behind him. "As regards to his vocals," says the producer of how Cohen was recorded, "sometimes Cohen went in with cigarettes and wine, sometimes he didn't. Some days he was up and boyish, other times he'd have a darkness. Sometimes he'd even have a girlfriend with him."

Cohen of course always entered the actual vocal booth alone.

"When he sang he always had his hands up as if he were looking up and reciting something. It wasn't like he had his hands behind his back crooning. Sometimes he'd be moving to the music, contrary to what you might think... but there was nothing dramatic, no cigarette in one hand scotch in the other and a Sinatraesque hat... he really was there just to sing."

Unlike many other vocalists who demanded lots of reverb in their 'cans' (as for example John Lennon) or who went the other way completely (Marvin Gaye recorded his vocals from the control room couch with a hand mic), Cohen was by comparison, "very undemanding in terms of the sound mix in his headphones. Unless there was a problem he wouldn't say anything. Some singers with insecurities sometimes get obsessed with headphone mixes but Leonard doesn't go through any of that." More attention was focussed on how Cohen was recorded than on previous albums. "We wanted to capture every nuance," says Lissauer, "and so we had to record him in complete isolation. There could be no other sounds bleeding into that booth. No disruptive vents of air, headphone leakage nothing. If we did then we couldn't have exposed his voice as much as we did."

There were occasional breaks in the schedule. John Miller in particular had bonded with Cohen. "We would go out and talk," he remembers. "I don't drink, so I couldn't say he was a good drinking buddy but he was certainly a good buddy. We'd have tea or whatever. I remember one time we got into the actual Japanese tea ceremony." Lissauer did go boozing with his artist. "We discovered the joys of this very particular drink, a Korean liquor which he had been introduced to by Roshi [who also attended the sessions, telling Cohen that he should 'sing sadder'] and we scoured Chinatown to find this stuff and it was quite nasty but pretty wild. So yeah, we had a few instances at the end of the night where things would get a little nutty. I think one such night may have led to the vocal on 'Green Sleeves'. But we weren't smoking dope and snorting coke with empty bottles of scotch lying around."

"We knew what the mission was," adds Miller. "And that was to lay down some killer tunes."

Cohen had clashed with John Simon but on *New Skin* he seemed happy to trust his producer completely. As testament to this Lissauer states that, "Leonard stayed out of all production aspects. I would do my thing and for the most part he would say 'Yeah'. We never had a disagreement or anything, we just sort of evolved together. Things seemed to work magically. We talked a lot during the making of the record. There was a lot of philosophy involved, talking over coffee."

Apart from the carefully assembled group there was one high profile guest on the album. "Janis Ian came along because I was supposed to do some arrangements for her and we'd become friends," says the producer, "and I needed another singer. I was making calls and I ended up talking to her about something else and I said to her 'Hey! Why don't you come

and sing with Leonard'. It was that casual. There was no star humping
going on. Leonard himself, as a singer, might be attached to a vocal
for a while and then suddenly change his mind and he'd wanna do
it again, change it, make something different." Aside from this one off
cameo by Ian, the studio was a closed set as the producer confirms.
"Generally, we didn't have people around anyway. When you have extra
people around in the control room somebody is trying to act the part or
impress someone. No one came in, not from the label or anything, no
one messed around. When the musicians were done they left. The singing
was basically just me and Leonard. Occasionally his girlfriend might be
there but he preferred it just me and him. It was about concentration. We
were very good at concentrating."

Miller: "It was certainly a challenge but not in the sense of 'Oh God,
can I run this marathon.' I felt an immediate connection with his music
and with Leonard. I was drawn to what he saw when he looked out of
the window."

The album and sessions concluded with one of Cohen's most eccentric
and unhinged vocal performances to date, on the barely subdued,
alcohol-fuelled sneer of 'Leaving Green Sleeves'. "He was letting it out,"
confirms Lissauer, 'You heard more emotional more colourful stuff than
on what I would have called a 'yawny folk album'. I really was trying
to do little vignettes both of his songs and within his songs. I wanted to
take you places. I really love it when great art places you in the scenes."

The album sessions were completed without rock'n'roll casualties;
no dramas and no punch ups. Lissauer was happy, Cohen was happy
and if Cohen was happy, Marty Machat was happy. "The great thing
about Musician Union scale gigs like this," says Miller, "is that everyone
gets paid and on time. There's no banging on someone door's weeks
later screaming, 'Where's my money, man'. Not when you play with
Leonard. And as for his manager, I liked Marty. I thought he was cool."
A few new friendships were born too. "We became buddies," says John
Miller. "I loved talking to Leonard. He introduced me to many things,
just through conversation, the idea of Zen being one of them." Lissauer
concurs: "The whole experience was incredibly enjoyable and it was like
Leonard and I had been working together for years. He even introduced
me to sushi. Sushi was just hitting New York and we went out all the

time. There were only two [sushi] restaurants in the whole of New York when we started the album. He introduced me to all kinds of other writers. I was never really interested in poetry for instance, until Leonard introduced me. He was a wealth of information to me and I introduced him to a lot of music. He had a lot of energy for things." Miller, who has played with everyone from Tim Buckley, through Gil Evans to Frank Sinatra, sums up the experience thus: "It affected me profoundly. I think every musician should have a chance to play at least one song with Leonard. It would teach them so much about what not to play."

Producer and singer were both excited by what they had achieved in the studio and wanted to take it to the people. The album was released in August and an extensive tour – Cohen's biggest yet – was planned for that September. This was a strange time for Cohen commercially. "We could only afford two female backing singers," explains the producer. "There was no money. Leonard didn't have the popularity he'd had or would have again."

Lissauer was to be appointed the musical director for Cohen's next two tours, and he relished the job. "Putting the group together was just a matter of putting together the right people who also got along together. Basically the people who were on the record. Their personalities worked together well and they understood what was gonna be happening."

John Miller was bassist on this tour and his first impression of Cohen was merely confirmed as they travelled together. "He was very genuine, very relaxed, you can't help but recognise that Leonard is a deep cat. I happened to enjoy his company a lot. I looked forward to it. He was certainly not a distant type of guy. I got to know him properly on tour. I found out that he was both an interesting guy and a guy who was *interested*."

The schedule was testing, with Cohen taking on 29 concerts in Europe alone during the first leg. Yet Lissauer states that, "That first tour was effortless because of who we chose. A small group but we all did a lot of different things on stage. The girls played guitars too, recorders and things, and I played piano, organ and saxophone, percussion. We went out without a drummer. Two girls, a guitarist, bass player and me. And Leonard of course. We also had a melletron so we could do some of the string things, 'Who By Fire' in particular. We had about 35 songs in our repertoire. We were small and disciplined."

In November the tour moved on to North America where the dates were confined to New York and Los Angeles with Cohen and band playing multiple nights at the same venues. There had been some debate as to how popular Cohen now was in the US and smaller venues had been booked in advance just in case, with extra shows added to meet any further demand. "We did maybe smaller venues, 3,000 seaters," says Lissauer, "but every one was sold out. We couldn't be that true to the studio versions because we were such a small troupe. Marty Machat *lived* with Leonard on tour. He was always there in the wings, beaming, in London at the Albert Hall and in Paris at the Olympia... that was where Marty had his tuxedoed elegant moment... Leonard was the most special thing that Marty had come across in terms of class and intellect." If Lissauer was perturbed at the constant presence of Machat, bassist Miller was a happy camper: "It was the greatest touring experience I've ever had."

That December they played six sold out concerts at the Troubadour in LA. Harvey Kubernick was once again among the smitten crowd, which also included Dylan. Indeed, Cohen would be invited to Dylan's LA home after the show and the two shared dinner and a long night's conversation. A few days later Cohen would say: "I admire Dylan's work tremendously, especially the later work. I also like Van Morrison very much, including his superb *Veedon Fleece* effort. I'm always interested in what Joni Mitchell is doing."

Kubernick noted that among those in the auditorium there was an awareness that playing such a venue, size wise, was a 'step down' for Cohen, compared to the bigger halls and theatres of Europe. This in turn would have accentuated and sharpened his set, tightening it, compressing it. "It was such an adoring atmosphere," remembers Kubernick, "but it wasn't like your typical fanboy or fandom stuff. I mean, Cohen was connecting with chicks and some dudes too – but mostly girls – on a cerebral level that I had never seen before. I saw him back stage talking with fans asking him sometimes dumb questions and he willingly subjected himself to this. He wasn't elitist and he was accessible. I saw no bodyguards or even his manager. And he wasn't taking phone numbers of girls or anything either... it wasn't one of those trips. And I thought that was kind of cool. But then he wasn't 22 years old, you know? He was an adult."

Kubernick upped his intimacy level with Cohen after one of these very shows when he and his friend Justin Pierce finally got to meet with their hero in his suite at the Continental Hyatt House on Sunset Boulevard for a one-on-one conversation which would run in the UK's big selling music weekly *Melody Maker*. "It was the cleanest, most orderly hotel suite I'd ever seen," laughs Kubernick. "Even the vitamins he was taking, packs of vitamins, were stacked meticulously." Although this was just part of another press junket for Cohen, co-coordinated by Marty Machat's girlfriend, Avril, 22-year-old Kubernick and 20-year-old Pierce did feel that they had struck up a particular intimacy with the interviewee. "He was just charming," remembers Kubernick. "I was his what – eighth interview that day? And remember he was playing a show every night! This guy had a work ethic and he enjoyed the interview process. We spoke a lot about Tony Palmer and his films. He was fascinated about the process of film and rock'n'roll documentation. He didn't seem at all disgruntled by his lack of comparative success in America compared to Europe. He was aware that he was doing pretty uncompromising – even for a singer songwriter – work in music and that he was and sounded a lot older than some of his contemporise. But he didn't sit around kvetching about it."

"Harvey and I would conduct the interview as partners," remembers Pierce. "We'd take it in turns asking him questions and I recall that he was very sincere, very polite. I'd go on to meet a lot of stars – Bowie, Rod Stewart, Paul McCartney – but Cohen among them struck me as a very pure artist."

Kubernick: "He was very pragmatic and workmanlike. And hospitable. I remember when the interview wound up, Avril came in and said that he needed to go to the Canadian embassy to work out some passport stuff. And he said to us 'Would you like to come along with me?' So we went out and got into his limousine. This was the first time I'd ever been in a limo! So we rolled down to the embassy and the conversation Leonard and I had became one that was very important to me. We spoke off record – of poetry. Allen Ginsberg, Lewis Furey, Peter Orlovsky. And at one point I broke off and asked him: 'Why are your songs so bleak, Leonard'? And in reply he quoted Ezra Pound: 'My betrayals are as fresh as yesterday'. So basically, that limo ride through LA was a discourse on poetry by Leonard Cohen! He was riffing on Lorca and Greece... he was exactly who he appears to be. Yet I can't say that ride was a major revelation for me. It didn't awake my calling as a poet or anything like that... but it was obvious to me that this guy was very erudite, smart and... more than this... here was a man who had a grasp of the human condition. He seemed like someone who was a 100 years old instead of 35. He seemed like a wise man down from the top of a mountain. He'd had a life. And yet I got the sense that he had never planned this music career thing that was happening to him. He almost hadn't expected it. He certainly was no careerist, that's for sure."

Pierce was less enamoured of poetry and spent much of the time gazing out of the window as the limo made the 30 minute trip downtown. But he remembers that when Cohen returned from the embassy he had gifts for both him and Kubernick. "He'd brought us these Canadian lapel badges," he remembers. "Just the kind they give out to tourists or whatever. But it kinda showed how sincere Cohen was."

Even in the midst of such extensive touring, Cohen was already considering his next foray into the studio. "Leonard said to me one night, 'We should collaborate on the next record'," remembers Lissauer. "He said, 'You write the music and I'll write the lyric'. A full on collaborative effort between the two was an interesting proposition, given that Cohen was clearly coming from a well defined ballad tradition whereas Lissauer's roots were firmly within jazz and classical music. Cohen was enthusiastic about his new writing partner when someone bothered to ask. "John Lissauer is fantastic, people are going to know about him way beyond the contribution he makes to my scene," Cohen gushed.

With the tour breaking for Christmas, on returning to New York, Cohen presented the arranger/producer with a batch of lyrics and asked Lissauer to put them to music. Thus, rather than sitting across from each other in the style of Lennon & McCartney, Lissauer and Cohen were writing in the tradition as practiced by Bacharach & David, and Bernie Taupin & Elton John, where lyrics and music would be composed separately from one another. Lissauer would sit alone at the piano with Cohen's lyric sheet and compose very specifically with Cohen's voice in mind. "The main thing was, could he sing them comfortably?" Lissauer explains. "Would he sound like himself singing them? I mean if I wrote a song in a setting that did not seem appropriate for him, like a big Elton John style tune or a big pop tune... these were not things Leonard could do and sound *real* doing. So a couple of the early things I wrote were a touch off in that respect. But I eventually got the melodies within his area of comfort. That said I would write the song in the key that I felt comfortable singing it and then we'd move the key around for Leonard so that he was comfortable." Neither had much time to get particularly comfortable in their civilian lives at this point.

In the New Year they set off once again on another tour performing 14 shows across North America and Canada.

With the final leg of the *New Skin...* tour overe by the end of March, Lissauer and the now 40-year-old Cohen relocated to LA and set up residence at the famous Chateau Marmont Hotel, complete with a piano in their suite. Here they fine tuned the pieces that the producer/arranger had been working on since last Christmas. "I'd play 'em to Leonard and he'd approve them. This was the summer of 75," recalls Lissauer. "Well, I think it was summer. It's always summer in LA. We wrote five or six things that were pretty good and I was aware that this was the first time he had ever collaborated equally on something."

While Lissauer was careful to write in character for his collaborator, keeping most of the pieces at a slow pace and often in a minor key, it might be truer to say that Cohen did not have an issue with uplifting songs in themselves. Rather, more up-tempo numbers in general did just not suit his voice or vision. "That's true," concurs Lissauer. "He's essentially a dark poet. And songs about 'the human condition' don't tend to be up-tempo numbers, if you think about it. Heart break and loss, difficult decisions, mortal dilemmas... don't tend to be uplifting and high spirited disco numbers." Most of Cohen's more successful songs were indeed written at an almost funereal pace. Lissauer was aware of this and was trying to write things that Cohen would respond to, structures and arrangements that he would immediately feel comfortable within. Lissauer was not especially concerned with challenging Cohen's sensibilities. "I was very young and exuberant then and in hindsight I may have used a slightly different approach in terms of the actual writing. Leonard would sing very safe intervals. He wouldn't sing like a singer he'd sing like a tough poet. Which is why some of the songs hardly modulate in terms of melody He's not even a crooner, he wouldn't write a melody like 'Somewhere Over The Rainbow' because he wouldn't sing a song like that. He sang in the same range in which he talked."

Once they had the basis of this handful of songs, the two put together a band to road test them. "We put together a different group and went out on the road. I believed in the practice of the early days where bands went out and played their stuff and whatever got the best reaction was then recorded. So I put this to Leonard – rather than record them and then try to recreate that live, let's do it the other way round."

Thus, Lissauer and Cohen set out on a mini eight-day tour of North America where they showcased mostly new material. Once satisfied with the new songs, studio time was booked back in NYC under the project title of *Songs For Rebecca*. "Out of seven songs that we'd decided upon we recorded five," says Lissauer. "We also recut three other earlier songs (from *New Skin*), 'cos we were using a drummer now rather than just a percussionist. We started getting a little more groove orientated… things were going swimmingly actually, so well in fact that we were saying, 'Wow this could be really successful, this could break through'. This could be an American record as opposed to European or Canadian… and then… then the plug got pulled."

Things were happening behind the scenes of which Lissauer was unaware. Cohen was signed to a major label and furthermore was in debt to that label. He also had a powerful manager who protected him and adored him but also had his own interests at heart; interests that were not always artistic. All Lissauer knew was that he and Cohen's manager had never seen eye to eye.

"Marty Machat and I did not have a great relationship," he says. "I had no respect for him because he was quite the well dressed thug. Very powerful. And Leonard was his boy and he was protecting him but he also wanted to possess the diamond," Lissauer continues. "Marty was attached to a lot of sleazy things and the only class he was ever connected with was with Leonard and that's where he got his precarious elegance and class. The project just evaporated. We were taking a break and were on a high about the possibilities of this… when suddenly Marty announced that he wanted Leonard to work with Phil Spector! 'What this kid needs is a star producer!'"

This project was the first not fully authored by Cohen, and Machat wasn't happy at splitting the potential royalties. Lissauer: "Marty also wasn't keen on sharing the publishing. He didn't publish my half of the songs but he *did* publish Spector." Machat did at least offer to buy Lissaeur's share of the songs from him. "I told Marty, 'No, Leonard and I have co-written these songs and I don't want you to publish my half.' He had a fit. He told me that because of Leonard I should defer my publishing, and I said, 'No'! It was another flare up we had. I wasn't taking his thuggish, bullying behaviour. He thought I was lucky to be involved with someone like Leonard and I *was* but nonetheless this didn't mean Marty could abuse me."

The project was officially cancelled. Columbia would not pay for further sessions. Cohen was no doubt exhausted by the last few years (Elrod had also recently borne another child, a daughter they called Lorca) and did not rush to the defence of the project or his new song writing partner. "Leonard would distance himself from such confrontations," reasons Lissauer philosophically. "He'd say, 'That's Marty's area and I don't get involved'. Leonard didn't like that kind of confrontation – which is why he *had* Marty. Marty was tougher than anyone else, any other lawyer, period, which is why he was great for his clients."

Marty subsequently confiscated the tapes and they disappeared forever. "We had recorded eight songs in total, "Lissauer sighs. "Some would show up eventually... on other people's records. 'Came So Far For Beauty' would show up later in another form [on the *Recent Songs* album] [and] there was another lovely south American song called 'Guerro', one named 'Trader Song', and we did a great new version of 'Diamonds In The Mine', a killer ass-kicking reggae version... really wonderful."

Lissauer, a recent veteran and contributor to numerous tours, and also the producer and arranger of one of Cohen's most strikingly beautiful albums, was left high and dry. Yet he bore Cohen no malice. "It *was* painful but I was doing a lot of different artists at the time and I said, 'Oh it'll come back around' and anyway Leonard was suddenly gone.

I couldn't get in touch with him. I assumed he'd want to finish the project, but then weeks turned into months, into years… it was never explained to me. The record business is not filled with wonderful people. The business itself is pretty slimy, pretty cutthroat. The making of records is a wonderful art but the business is awful, run by lawyers… there was nothing I could do about the situation so I carried on and dealt with it by continuing to work with other people. I respected Leonard not to try and peddle the songs elsewhere."

In April 1976 Cohen headed off on yet another tour. For obvious reasons, Lissauer was not aboard and Cohen's bass player, John Miller, took over as musical director.

There were 55 shows covering Europe extensively and with Cohen (looking like 'a curious cross between Lenny Bruce and an Old Testament prophet' according to one critic) and band sometimes playing the same sold out venue on consecutive nights. "I got to know Leonard very well on that tour," says Miller, not unsurprisingly. "I have so many memories. I introduced Laura Brannigan (as a backing singer) to that tour… no one knew who she was of course. We had so many good times… I recall vividly one night when we were in Spain, it was late and Leonard called me. 'You want something to eat?' So we went out and eventually found a place. It was about two in the morning. And we ended up playing cards with the bar staff there, until dawn… Another time, he knew I had an interest in photography and we had a day off so he took me into a camera shop and bought me a state of the art camera, a Nikon. He handed it over to me and said, 'Get to it!' And in Germany soon after, on the autobahn we broke down and while they fixed the bus or whatever I took photos of him doing yoga on the autobahn…funny stuff… and when we got going again, in the distance we saw these two people sticking their thumbs out. It was a mother and a daughter. Leonard told the driver to stop and pick them up. It turned out they were going to see our concert! For the next 48 hours we looked after them, Leonard put them up in hotel, got them free tickets… he was like that… he was genuine. That was when I realised Leonard was one of the few mentors I ever had. I became very good pals with him."

They also took time off to rush record a single at Musicland studios in Munich, the up-tempo disco on downers groove of 'Do I Have To

Dance All Night'. Funky and hoe down horny, it remains one of Cohen's great lost songs, released only on seven-inch in Europe. "We had a lot of fun doing that," says Miller. "It would be amusing to have a hit with it," said Cohen dryly.

That June, as the Cohen tour wound down Harvey Kubernick found himself at a loose end in London and in tune with the innocence of the times, called Avril, Marty Machat's PA and girlfriend, and the lady on the picture sleeve of 'Do I Have To Dance All Night') to ask about a bed for a night. She suggested Cohen's temporary flat, then in Bayswater. This was not as daring as it sounds. Kubernick was well known to Marty Machat, having both already met Cohen as journalist for *Melody Maker* and having worked as 'a food runner' on many Phil Spector sessions back in Hollywood. "I was almost family," he explains, "not just another journalist." This was another time, another place and, most profoundly, pre John Lennon 1980. 'It's true that the Seventies were different," says Kubernick. "Often you'd interview musicians and it would be at their house or in a hotel room. It wasn't just phoners and press conferences, there wasn't a lot of mollycoddling'." Cohen was in Europe at the time but Kubernick remembers it as "a very nice apartment, spacious and lots and lots of books". Although not particularly voyeuristic or snoopy by nature, anyone curious about Cohen would rummage around his flat, given the chance. "And I would have," says Kubernick, "if Avril wasn't there with me! All I remember about it is that there were so many books. Just like tons of books."

CHAPTER SIX

The Birth Of Death Of A Ladies' Man

"I don't feel emotional about it anymore; I think that in the final moment, Phil couldn't resist annihilating me. I don't think he can tolerate any other shadows in his darkness."

LC

By the mid seventies, Phil Spector – once considered the uber-Fuehrer of pop musical geniuses and the monster maverick patron saint of record producers – was widely considered to be an oldies act. Admittedly, it had been over a decade since the famously Wagnerian maestro had given the world the immortal pop symphonies of 'Be My Baby, 'You've Lost That Lovin' Feelin'' and 'River Deep Mountain High' and by now the capricious pop public had consigned Phil exclusively to the dusty sun bleached bargain bin of yesteryear. Nevertheless, during the late Fifties and throughout much of the Sixties the diminutive and always tastefully bewigged Phil Spector had singlehandedly rebooted production standards in popular music. Such a reputation may have endured or lingered longer in other media – in painting perhaps or in the fields of photography or science – but in pop music it was hits that mattered, and recent hits at that.

The beginning of the Seventies had started with much promise. Spector had been brought in to work on the tapes of the final Beatles album *Let It Be*, a commission that famously upset Paul McCartney when the producer added lush orchestration and dubbed female voices on to 'The Long And Winding Road'. Spector had also contributed profoundly to John Lennon's fledgling solo work, notably the classic *John Lennon/Plastic Ono Band* and *Imagine* albums, as well as the aborted *Roots* project (which would in part eventually evolve into the *Rock'n'Roll* album). In retrospect one could see that the sessions with Lennon had been the first browning of the apple, the inauguration of Spector's slow shift into a personal and professional winter.

The Lennon-Spector *Roots* sessions were designed as a well paid, enjoyable and exquisitely recorded trip down memory lane for all concerned. In the event, though, Spector twisted the merry jaunt into a clash of egos between himself and Lennon. As a result, the skirmish collapsed into a messy debacle with the producer hijacking the unfinished tapes and holding them hostage, causing Lennon precisely the kind of headaches and hassles that the *Roots* sessions had sought to avoid.

This was not a one off freak out. Spector would repeat such shenanigans with Cohen just a few years later. Yet the invitation by someone as revered as Lennon had came with an encoded misnomer. *Roots* was Lennon looking back to both the golden age of his youth and to the glorious childhood of rock'n'roll. In choosing Spector as the facilitator of such nostalgia, Lennon wanted Spector precisely *because* the producer could re-create and authenticate the 'retro' vibe Lennon needed on an album of hoary old rock'n'roll numbers. Unlike the progressive nature of his earlier solo albums, for a then troubled Lennon these sessions were something of an in-studio holiday, a means of letting off steam, a bit of a lark, as its drunken wailing outtakes so amusingly illustrate. Lennon recognised that Spector, while still an immensely proficient producer technically and one who was ever game for a laugh, was nevertheless no longer what he had been at his zenith. When the diminutive genius had cut The Ronettes and Ike & Tina Turner he had been a ferociously talented visionary, an eccentric electric alchemist at the top of his game and a renowned pioneer at using the very studio itself as an instrument. It cannot be stressed enough that both in his prime and in his field,

Spector was an innovator who not only pushed the sonic envelope but exploded it.

Dan Kessel, a young guitarist and son of the highly regarded and much in demand jazz guitarist Barney Kessel, had come to know Spector during his golden age. "I'd known Phil since I was 11, back at Goldstar studios in the late Fifties, early Sixties," he says. "My dad was a jazz guitarist and he was a hero of Phil's when Phil was a teenager. And Phil would always use Dad for his own recordings when he was in LA and when Dad went he would take me along. I actually performed handclaps on 'He's A Rebel'. I'd been going to recording sessions with my dad since I was six, since the late Fifties – these included dates with Ricky Nelson, Eddie Cochran, Elvis, Frank Sinatra, Doris Day, Jerry Lewis, Judy Garland. So by the time I got to meet Phil it all seemed pretty normal. In fact I appreciated Phil more after witnessing these other people at work. And I mean, like, Elvis was *God* to me when I was a kid. But I could see immediately that Phil was brilliant and hip. He was funny, smart and he dressed great and he had a great personality. He had a lot of charisma and star power. When I first met him it was the same effect that The Beatles had on a lot of people. He was kinda out of this world to me, just amazing."

Occasional Cohen confidante and one time lover, Joni Mitchell had been an occasional and casual observer at the Lennon/Spector sessions (which Kessel had played on) and warned Cohen of the potential perils of working with the increasingly, as she saw it, deranged producer. Ultimately, by the time Cohen and Spector did come together, the former was a troubled man too. Trussed in a rut, directionless and adrift, Cohen was longing for a new direction in both his life and his work, both of which were on the wane. Despite Phil's reputation and Joni's warnings Cohen would, steered by his manager Marty Machat, eventually allow himself to drift into Spector's unconventional orbit, consequences be damned.

Spector and Cohen had been formally introduced by their mutual manager-cum-lawyer backstage after Cohen's three-night stint at the Troubadour Club in Los Angeles back in December 1974. After the final show Spector had hosted a dinner for a select few back at his nearby Spanish style mansion. The meeting between him and Cohen was more than agreeable and while Spector declared himself 'impressed' by Cohen's 'mystery and technique' during the concerts, the prospect of collaboration was never seriously proposed on this occasion. Within a few years, it would be grievous circumstance – not any artistic aesthetic – that would bring the two men together in the studio.

By the mid-Seventies Marty Machat and Phil Spector had a simple but serious problem. Characteristically, Machat had recently negotiated Spector a generous label deal with Warner Brothers Records that required Spector to deliver future product, getting paid up front as an advance on royalties being the industry norm. Just as typically, for Phil at least during this point in his career, the producer had failed to deliver the promised product and now Warners were making loud noises about wanting their money back.

By now, even the producer's most faithful friends and fans were worried for his future. Commercially Phil hadn't been able to find his footing in the market for some time. In the last few years America had succumbed to Bowie-style glam rock, James Taylor-style confessional singer songwriters, Eagles and Fleetwood Mac-style AOR and Bee Gees-style disco, and Spector just didn't fit in with any of them. "Spector could no longer control the music," says Marty Machat's son Steven, who at the time was just coming of age and intent on following his father into the industry. As such Steven was a first hand witness to both his father's and his father's client's triumphs and troubles. "Spector was now working with artists but treating them as he used to treat his session musicians," he says. "He wasn't writing the songs and creating the sound, he was producing those who had a sound and wrote their own songs. He was not the man for that job. His ego was way too big for him to be just the producer."

Exacerbating the situation was the threat from Warners. Machat Snr. knew that if his troubled client was forced to repay the Warners advance, then that client would fire him and hire another lawyer to get him out of the mess. As fond as Machat was of all his clients (and in the final analysis, Marty Machat was surely all heart), he could not afford to lose Spector financially. By merely administering Spector's publishing rights throughout the world Machat was earning a commission of up to $150,000 a year. Spector's old hits still did the business on vinyl and tape and were played on enough radio stations in enough parts of the world to earn all concerned more than a reasonable living. As far as Machat was concerned, having to pay back the Warners advance and thus lose Spector and all associated revenue was not even an option.

Chain smoking cigars in his rented bungalow on the grounds of the Beverly Hills Hotel – usually while standing: Machat didn't use a desk – he had a 'eureka' moment. He would put Spector together with his other flailing client, Cohen. In addition Machat would assign his hip young son Steven to coordinate the whole project and under Steven's tutelage, Phil Spector and Leonard Cohen would record an album together and then deliver that album to Warners. Machat wouldn't even have to be involved as his son would deal with any problems head on. It would be the best kind of work experience for the boy. Steven was excited by the trust his dad was putting in him and by the responsibility endowed but less than enthused by the actual artists who'd been assigned to him. "My dad told me that Leonard and I were so alike," says Steven, who was initially both confused and unimpressed by his dad's favourite client, "and that Leonard was a Buddhist. What was a Buddhist? To me it was these guys in orange robes singing and chanting while I was trying to get laid at Woodstock. And I'll never forget that the first time I met Leonard, he couldn't look me in the eye."

Not only did Steven dislike the singer, he didn't dig the songs either. "I never liked Leonard's music," he adds. "It had no energy, no love of life. It was all inward looking." He also had a practical challenge ahead of him. "Both Spector and Cohen were commercial suicide in the US," states Steven stoically. "Cohen was signed to CBS worldwide but they wanted nothing to do with this [Spector-Cohen] concoction. We got him released from the US portion of his CBS contract and the deal was that he would be a free agent in the US starting with this album."

Whatever the potential for disaster, it was a truly inspired move from Marty Machat's point of view. If Steven could get Spector and Cohen to make an album and then get Warners to accept it, Marty Machat would be fulfilling Spector's outstanding contractual debt, saving his relationship with the producer and giving Cohen's ailing career a new jump start, three birds killed with one stone. Sadly, there would be other, innocent casualties. As a consequence of pairing Cohen with Spector, the project in progress between Cohen and John Lissauer, *Songs For Rebecca* was ruthlessly blown out of the water, with no explanation given to the shocked producer/arranger either by Cohen or Machat. "It just stopped," said Lissauer, "and at the time I had no idea why… It was..weird."

Beyond the sad fact that both were by now considered "box office poison" in America, and that they mutually shared a deep love for the vintage years of rock'n'roll, Cohen and Spector seemed poles part in most other ways. Personality wise Cohen was, of course, low key to the point of being medically introverted while Spector, despite his paranoia about appearing in public, seemed inclined to play out his life in the style of a twisted and intoxicated performance artist. Widely known for turning up at sessions dressed as a cowboy, a surgeon or a sheriff, regularly packing heat and on occasion so altered chemically that he appeared to be higher than God's hairline, Spector's idiosyncratic working methods were increasingly overtaking the legend of his music making. This new reputation as a hell raiser only seemed to feedback into his very life, refuelling and intensifying any apparent neuroses. Yet now, like two dateless geeks on prom night forced into an uncomfortable slow dance below a dilapidated mirror ball, it was Cohen's very lack of rock'n'roll smarts that intrigued Spector. Both also shared an affinity, perhaps more so in Cohen's case, with the Jewish lifestyle, and perhaps even more profoundly, both had lost their fathers at an early age.

At the start of the venture, Cohen was optimistic. "I thought my instincts were right in working with Phil," he'd say a few years later. "He's a musician, a writer and musical mind I have enormous admiration for. I've listened to his music all my life."

It helped that Cohen was a self confessed jukebox junkie, the ultimate medium for Phil's "little symphonies for the kids", as he referred to his great wall-of-sound productions. Cohen fondly recalled listening Spector's earliest hits, not least the very first, the beautifully aching 'To Know Him Is To Love Him', the words of which were inspired by the epitaph etched on Spector's gravestone – "No one knew it was a song about death," explained Spector – when Cohen was doing time on the workshop floor of his uncle's Montreal factory in late 1958. "In those songs, the story line was as clear as clear could ever be," said Cohen. "The images were very expressive – they spoke to us all. Spector's real greatness is his ability to induce those incredible little moments of poignant longing in us."

It was now late 1976 and without any US label firmly committed to the project, the odd couple nevertheless began an intensive work schedule. At Phil's invitation, musical possibilities were explored during a month of hardcore and nocturnal co-writing sessions at Spector's low lit and freezing cold LA mansion.* Phil was a gregarious if imposing host. Fuelled by an occasionally intimidating energy and, mixing booze with the kind of exaggerated ego that comes with a high school nerd made good, the producer was as much a performer in his living room as most rock stars were on stage.

During one early visit, although amused and engaged by Spector's boisterous long day's journey into night, an exhausted Leonard eventually made to leave. High and happy, Phil was having too much fun and simply locked the doors, trapping Cohen. "It was tedious," the cornered poet would recall. "I asked to be let out of his house. He locks the door from the inside once you come in, and he didn't want to let me go." Exasperated, the imprisoned guest caved in to Phil's enforced hospitality and the two decamped to the piano with liberal supplies of alcohol and cigarettes.

The very first night, the duo worked out a new version of Patti Page's 'I Went to Your Wedding'. They were still at the keyboard come breakfast. There they would stay – presumably with Leonard being let out occasionally when Phil went to the bathroom or succumbed to sleeping medication – for a month. "It really was too dreary inside that dark, cold house in Hollywood," lamented Cohen. "The Medici pose with guns and bodyguards isn't rock'n'roll glamour; it's kid's stuff."

Phil's then part-time lover and full time assistant, Devra Robitaille, confirms Cohen's memories of the house. "It was Dickensian," she laughs. "Very drab and gloomy. Big velvet curtains, always kept shut. Never any sunlight. I kept expecting to find Miss Havisham in one of the rooms, wearing her wedding dress and covered in cobwebs."

Cohen and Spector were soon joined by brothers Dan and David Kessel, both old friends of Spector and now accomplished guitarists in

---

* He kept the temperature hovering around 68 degrees Farenheit.

their own right. "When I heard we were going to be working with Cohen, yeah, I knew who he was," says Dan, who was then in his mid-twenties. "The first time I'd become aware of him would have been back in the Sixties, like most people, through Judy Collins version of 'Suzanne'. A wonderful record. And I used to read the music newspapers, so I knew Cohen was a real writer and I'd listened to some of his records. I thought he was a great songwriter. A good singer too, although I'd never actually go out and buy his records myself. But sure, by the time I got to be in a room with him at Phil's, I knew who he was."

Spector didn't need to explain to the Kessels (or anyone else) the business motive behind the project although he would later.

Dan Kessel: "Phil just said 'I'm doing this album with Leonard and why don't you come over'. You know, I'd been doing pretty much everything with Phil since The Beatles onwards anyway, so it was no big deal. As well as guitar I was one of Phil's assistants so to speak as well as production co-ordinator, I was there when Phil needed me."

Kessel, along with his brother, would arrive most nights around 7p.m. and was present throughout most of these pre production warm ups. "I met Leonard at Phil's house for the first time when they we were writing and we were helping them rehearse the songs as they were written," he confirms. "My first of impression of Leonard was that he was a dignified, good looking gentlemen. And I soon came to appreciate him as being all of these things, as well as his artistry. We were in a huge room at Phil's house. In fact all of the rooms there were huge. We would work in the living room. As they were writing I'd be there with my 12 string acoustic guitar, as would my brother David. Phil and Leonard would be at the grand piano – it was white of course – and when they knocked something together my brother and I would play along on our acoustic guitars. Leonard would be standing generally, pacing as Phil played. He would sit occasionally, but usually he was hovering around Phil, pacing and chain smoking. Me and my brother were on the couch and we were very sensitive to the situation. There was never any question of us actually contributing to the writing. We could have, we had the talent but it was never requested and we aren't the pushy type.

"I was glad to be there as a musician. If it felt like they needed to be alone or if Phil asked, we'd leave and go into the next room, give 'em some privacy. So it was kind of a combination of writing and rehearsal. We'd start at seven and go until six in the morning."

Despite the rumours and despite the nocturnal work method, Kessel did not see any evidence of drug use. "Speaking for myself, no, I absolutely did not use anything," he says. "And I'm not being evasive, I'm just telling the truth. I've no idea what Leonard was or wasn't taking and as far as I know Phil wasn't using. He wasn't a druggie at all. I mean there was *alcohol* involved."

Kessel was unaware of Cohen's past drug use or of his enduring fondness for Quaaludes but isn't surprised by the idea. "Oh, well, he was pretty low key that's for sure! But it wasn't a drug party or anything and if either of them were doing anything they were doing it on their own."

The writing sessions lasted close to a month, comprising three or four days a week. Once sufficient basic material had been prepared, Phil's office began booking musicians. For this project Spector would use up to four studios, although only three would be credited. The main base was Spector's favourite Goldstar Studio complex situated at 6252 Santa Monica Boulevard near the corner of Vine Street in Hollywood, with extra time eventually booked at the Disney Studios at Burbank, the MCA-Whitney studio in Glendale and at Devonshire Sound Studios. Once the actual locations were fixed Spector called for a version of his own 'army', the regiment of ace session musicians that he would use to actually make the record.

The album was largely coordinated by the British born Devra Robitaille, then Spector's full time 'administrative director' at Warner-Spector Records. Despite his apparent reputation Devra had few problems with her boss. "On a one to one basis Phil was actually very sweet," she remembers. "Phil was very intelligent and very interesting to talk to. He loved to philosophise, he loved to joke. He had a quirky sense of humour and he had a highly developed sense of irony which was very English in its way... very dry, wry and ironic... he was funny and interesting on a one to one."

Sadly, it was in front of an audience that Spector's megalomaniac tendencies played out and Devra's next step was to recruit that very audience in the form of the session musicians needed for the album. Devra consulted a Rolodex stuffed full of familiar and trusted names to attend the sessions. In some cases she would apparently then inquire whether a particular booked individual would "arrange a horn section for Phil". Dan Kessel confirms that, "Phil would tell her who he wanted, absolutely. He wanted top jazz and session players, he knew who they were and they knew him. These guys were the cream of the crop in Hollywood and he would go and see them play. He was a fan of them himself."

The incoming cast therefore included many familiar (and some unfamiliar) faces. Amongst the most familiar were the omnipresent Kessel brothers. "We'd show up at Phil's house beforehand, and go into the studio with him," explains Dan. "We'd hang out at his place first, having drinks, watching TV, having something to eat or whatever. Meanwhile they'd be setting up at the studio."

As the horn players, woodwind players, bassists, keyboard players, violinists, cellists, viola players, percussionists, guitarists, drummers and backing singers trooped into the appointed studio, feelings among them were mixed. Art Munson, a guitarist, was one of the many underwhelmed at the idea of contributing to – as he saw it – the "peculiar" Spector/Cohen cocktail. Not that such a coupling ultimately mattered. For Art and many of the other session musicians, the job was just that – a job, another day in the office. "I was doing many sessions at the time so it was basically just another gig," he states evenly, "but you know, I was always happy to have the work. I had heard of Cohen of course but you have to remember that I had been working with a lot of big names so his name didn't particularly stick out. Nevertheless it's always flattering to be called to work with an artist with a recognisable name."

Unlike the guitarist, some of the other musicians were at least slightly intrigued, their interest piqued at such a quirky combination. Pianist Al Perkins confirmed what many in the business were thinking when he opined that... "I did think it was an unusual pairing of producer and artist... Then again I think pairing Spector with anyone at that point in time was odd. Why? Because I knew of Phil's reputation, that's why... but still, you know, it didn't put me off in the slightest. I was eager to work with them."

Dan Kessel concedes that, "Yeah, I can see why people may have thought them an odd couple but then that's just a matter of opinion, ultimately."

Although nearly all who got the call were familiar with the name, few of the musicians employed were actual fans of Cohen's work. Spector was a more familiar quantity, but even so his reputation as an eccentric now outweighed his artistic achievements. Whatever the expectations, the various drummers, bassists, keyboard players, guitarists and backing singers had no idea of the carnival that awaited them.

"I didn't know Cohen's records," recalls pianist Bill Mays, sounding like a rookie going into battle for the first time, "and it was the first time I'd worked with Phil Spector!"

Spector's presence would dwarf the sessions even though each of the "50 or so" musicians would come face to face with Cohen in the actual studio, most during their very first session. But like a star against the sun, next to Phil's maniacal supernova the quiet unshaven guy in grey slacks and dark blue blazer made little impression on the various seasoned musos setting up at Goldstar. As ever, Cohen dressed 'elegant-casual' throughout, whereas Spector wore essentially the same with a twist, wearing denim blazers emblazoned with marijuana leaves on occasion. "They both looked casual, elegant and hip," says Dan Kessel, "but Leonard was continental hip and Phil was Hollywood hip."

The neighbourhood itself was rough and funky, a dying part of town in a fading corner of Hollywood, an area that arguably had more presence than the artist being served. Asked what impression Cohen made on him, Art Munson replied: "None. I may have met him but... if I did... there was no communication. He was... very... laid back." Others treated it solely as just another Spector session. Devra, however, vividly remembers meeting Cohen. "He wore a beautifully tailored black jacket. He looked very classy... white shirt and his hair was impeccable, well combed back but a little long over the collar. His whole demeanour was very classy and elegant. He had such a gorgeous and sophisticated and charming air about him. I liked him very much although I didn't really get to know him... he wasn't particularly outgoing."

"The man seemed quite quiet," concurs Bill Mays, "especially in contrast to Phil who was... shall we say, uh... pretty out there."

Al Perkins: "It was the first time I'd met LC... he was friendly to us. As I recall, Phil called for everyone to arrive at 7p.m., but it wasn't until midnight or later before things got underway."

Phil would have his engineers come into the studio prior to his arrival, setting up music stands, organising the placement of the musicians, setting up microphones and powering up the big analogue reel-to-reel recording machines. "Phil would tell them to be ready at seven," says Kessel, "and that's when the money starts, that's when you start paying both for the studio and the musicians. The clock starts at seven and you'd better be ready to roll. Everything has to be set up with the musicians sitting in their seats, tuned up and their amps plugged in and a pencil sharpener in their hand! Ready to record. They'd have chord sheets but not symphonic scores, no. But it helped if you could read music."

Spector wouldn't waste time and energy having his vision and concentration clouded by such menial tasks as helping oboe and timpani players get comfortable, and he knew that the setting up would invariably run over. "At seven we'd still be at home with Phil," says Kessel, "watching *Sanford & Son* or whatever. And then the bodyguards – armed bodyguards – and me and my brother would go over to the studio with Phil. And he would bring his own tapes. So the bodyguard would have these boxes of 24-track two-inch reels of tape, maybe 10 or 12 of them. Put 'em all in a dolly and wheel 'em into the truck and take 'em over. So we'd show up later, about 7.45 or so."

Schedule wise, the sessions would follow the pattern of the earlier writing shifts at Phil's house. "I left in the wee hours of morning the next day," recalls Munson. "I seem to remember no more than two songs being recorded that first evening… Leonard was in there throughout. We musicians had music charts and Cohen would sing a guide vocal along with us. Between takes we all chatted and waited around a lot. When Phil did playbacks they were so darn loud in the control room that most of us would have to go outside."

Much like he had back in 1967, while recording his debut, Cohen felt a little swamped by this new regime. "I've found that some of his musical treatments are very… er… foreign to me," said Cohen. "I mean, I've rarely worked in a live room that contains 25 musicians – including two drummers, three bassists, and six guitars."

Although a line up as full as this was foreign and intimidating to Cohen, it was par the course for a Spector session, while the fact that the producer arrived and left the studio under armed guard seemed to pass without comment. "I guess for a producer to have a bodyguard *wasn't* normal," admits Kessel, "but... it *was* normal for Phil."

Aside from this armed presence the sessions seemed to be relatively routine. "Phil would greet Leonard in the control room and Phil would make some mike adjustments," says Kessel. 'I'd say hello to everyone, grab my guitar and go out onto the floor with all the other musicians and then things would start to roll." The live room at Goldstar was a "medium to small sized recording room" and Phil liked to conduct the sessions from a modestly sized control room that was low-lit and inexorably swathed in thick cigarette smoke from the attendant musicians. In order to get a working sound mix and a good balance of instruments in his monitors, Spector would start by directing the musicians as individual groups, calling out to each section in turn – "Horns! Section A! Go!" – and once he was satisfied with the mix, he would begin running the musicians through the pieces as a whole.

"We would be given brief directions and start with a chord chart." explains guitarist Art Munson. "We sometimes didn't know if the tape was rolling or not but when Phil said 'Go' we went. We would start playing what we felt would fit. From there it would sometimes change if Phil had anything specific in mind. Other times whatever I came up with would be fine. I don't remember hearing any demos... I would always start the take by playing what I felt. Sometimes that would be fine or as I said, it might be modified. I do remember Phil asking me to do an old trick where you would weave paper across the guitar strings. In that way whatever you played would have a muted sound – a dampened effect. Later on over at Burbank studios I was doing guitar overdubs on already recorded tracks and maybe a few basic tracks [drums and bass]. I actually thought the tracking sessions were small for a Spector date."

As the recording progressed Spector began relocating to the other studios. With the initial tracks recorded, Spector perhaps began to relax and kick back a little. According to some present at the sessions, "kicking back" for Phil Spector at this point mostly meant snorting several grams of cocaine while drinking steadily throughout and waving around pistols and wine bottles. (The relatively mild Manischewitz Concord Grape Wine was the booze of choice). Such behaviour was humoured by most but not all.

One of the many backing singers, Venetta Fields recalls "I truly remember that session... yes, Spector had his bodyguard in the room with us, at the mike with a gun in his holster, with his jacket off." For the short time Fields was actually in attendance at the sessions she recalls first hand Phil's routine. "Every time we would record a take, he and his bodyguard would go to the bathroom and do more lines [of coke] making us wait for him..." Eventually some of the musicians, even at a relatively high profile gig such as this, would vote with their feet. "I walked out!" remembers Fields. "Phil was so rude and coked up and drunk, making racist remarks. I could not take it any more." No repercussions, professional or otherwise, would follow such drastic reactions. Phil would simply have his assistant call in replacements.

Devra, although confirming that Phil could be 'insane', doesn't actually recall him taking drugs. "I was at every session for five years," she states matter-of-factly. "Maybe stuff was going on behind the scenes that I wasn't aware of but I can tell you for sure that I never saw him do coke. That said I can confirm that he was pretty much drunk at every session."

The music writer Harvey Kubernick, who had by now been adopted by Machat and Spector as a kind of studio gofer, also claims not to have seen any evidence of Spector abusing drugs. "That is so hard for me to comprehend," he says of Spector's alleged coke use and racist humour. "He liked his particular brand of wine, that's for sure... but I was there a lot. I mean, I even handclapped with Rodney 'Mayor of Sunset Strip' Bingenheimer on the song 'Iodine'. I was *there*. I mean I'm not saying it was a serene Buddhist scene at those sessions but it was nowhere near as chaotic as it's always been presented. It wasn't sin city but then neither was it Hayley Mills in *Pollyanna*. Phil has a very caustic sense of humour... sometimes his rants are misinterpreted but they are always highly informative and educational and entertaining. And I never knew him to be racist. That was so against his code of life."

Dan Kessel: "Well, if that's her [Devra's] recollection, who am I to argue but... did she follow Phil in and *see* him do any coke? No, she didn't. But I do remember her walking out. And Phil's humour was very British and very ironic, she probably just didn't get his sense of humour. Racist? He worked with black artists all his life, he certainly wasn't racist." (It's worth noting that as well as producing Ronnie Spector, Phil also married

Cohen with preferred mode of transport, Hydra 1982. (ALBERTO MANZANO)

Cohen with his daughter Lorca, on Hydra in 1982 (above), and at work (below). (ALBERTO MANZANO)

At a soundcheck in Toulouse, France, 1980. (ALBERTO MANZANO)

In a Montreal pharmacy during the early Sixties. (ROZ KELLY/MICHAEL OCHS ARCHIVES/GETTY IMAGES)

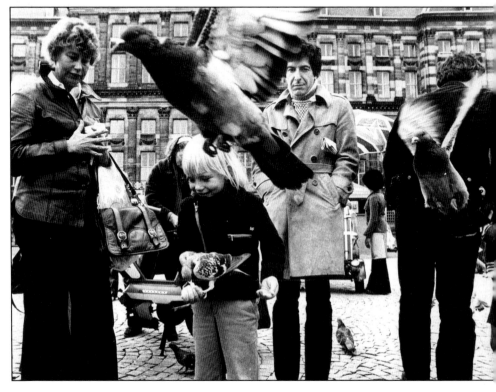

'Un Canadian errant' in Europe during the early Seventies. (SUNSHINE/RETNA PICTURES)

Cohen with The Army, 1972. (COURTESY CLAUDE GASSIAN FROM THE COLLECTION OF DOMINIQUE BOILE)

Meditating in the early Seventies. (PETER MAZEL/SUNSHINE PHOTO/RETNA PICTURES)

Cohen approves the master acetate of an album, sometime in the mid-Seventies. (IAN COOK//TIME LIFE PICTURES/GETTY IMAGES)

Channelling *Midnight Cowboy*-era Dustin Hoffman in 1985. (LENNART PERLENHEM/REX FEATURES)

The dapper Bohemian, late Sixties. (GEMS/REDFERNS)

and had a family with her). Kessel continues: "It wasn't unusual for the people Phil was producing to be drinking more than him. Lennon drank much more than Phil when they were working together. I remember at the Cohen sessions the backing singers themselves drinking, I remember him specifically sending out for a bottle of Southern Comfort for them.* It wasn't a big deal. But I never, ever saw Phil do coke. There were sober evenings and less sober evenings."

Whatever the truth behind Spector's behaviour his moods were temperamental and powerful, dictating the very emotional weather within the studio – weather that swung this way and that but always to extremes. Cohen was not so much at the centre of such shenanigans but more of an observer during the making of his own album. In some ways he felt that he'd been sidelined at his own gig. "In the studio he took over completely and there were a lot of armed guards around," Cohen affirmed. In fact Spector was treating him as just another hired hand, sometimes ordering Cohen to lay down a vocal at 2.30 a.m., as was the case with the title track. Cohen, considerably more in tune with his own body clock than Spector, loathed being forced to sing at such an ungodly hour.

Bruce Gold, the main engineer on the sessions, stated: "Phil is really a 'take charge' type of man. He wants to be in control of the situation. He's an artist with a palette holding the brush and… Leonard Cohen was the subject. Phil ran the show."

Ray Neapolitan, bassist on many of the sessions over several months, confirmed Cohen's demotion to that of walk-on actor in his own movie: "When you work for Phil, it's a Phil record, and Leonard was incidental and I think he felt that… he'd just come in… then he would do a live vocal, but he would pretty much stay out of the fray… there was 40 guys in there and Phil would just, Phil was 'on'… it was like theatre…"

Among the large supporting cast, Dan Kessel was one of the few who articulated his admiration of Cohen's lyrical talent to the man himself. "I loved his lyrics and kept complimenting him on them," he says. "I thought they were so great. I remember we were in the studio one time,

---

* In fact, one of the credits on the eventual album read, "All liquor purchased from John & Pete's liquor store. All pizza from Piece O' Pizza."

having a break after a run down prior to a take. Most of the musicians had gone outside for a break and Cohen and maybe Art Munson were the only two guys in the studio, sat amongst all these empty chairs. Cohen was lighting up a Gauloise cigarette. He'd just been singing and I don't remember if it was a take or a run through but he had the lyrics printed out in front of him. I think they were for the title track. And I was knocked out by them and I said, 'Leonard I just gotta tell you, man, your lyrics are just so great!' And he took a drag on his cigarette, looked at me and exhaled the smoke from his cigarette and said: 'It's a living'."

Both Cohen and Spector were singular talents in their own particular fields. Cohen wasn't the greatest singer technically but his lyrics were in a class of their own. The same could be said of Spector with regard to his adequate musicianship yet genius-like production skills. Devra: "Phil had an alchemist like approach to producing at times. He would just let things happen... he used a weird synergy. I remember at one point [drummer] Jim Keltner fell off his stool and clattered onto the floor mid track. Phil left that in as a drum fill! It was a really weird sound – *ka ka-ka ka boom ka!!*'... and it *worked*. Those are the kind of things I remember... that kept me going with Phil... it was magical."

At the end of each session, Spector would take the tapes home, again under armed guard. As eccentric as these manoeuvres were, Cohen himself would later admit that the sessions were even weirder than had been recounted. "Much weirder. I'm too ashamed to tell the whole truth of what happened there," he said. "There were a lot of guns around. Phil had bodyguards and he liked guns. So did I*, but I didn't happen to have any armed bodyguards. But you've got to understand, there was a lot of wine and other stuff around, so it wasn't just that there were a few guns around the place. People were skating around on bullets, guns were finding their way into hamburgers, guns were all over the place. It wasn't safe. It was mayhem, but it was part of the times. It was rather drug-driven."

While Spector, after a brief sojourn into sobriety, had very visibly fallen from the wagon, Cohen for the most part stuck to the more acceptable vices of booze and pills. "I've looked into most of them," he

---

* Cohen had nurtured an interest in firearms during his 'cowboy in Nashville' phase.

would say. "I never really got into cocaine. I tried it but I don't really like ingesting things through my nose. It always seemed so undignified for a chap of my stature." A long time devotee of Mandrax, Cohen did occasionally cross-pollinate this and the booze with an upper. "I always liked speed," he'd admit.

Cohen still considered the record they were making to be the most autobiographical of his career and having the largely anonymous session musicians lend an ear to his torment at ear drum busting levels would not have been easy on his nerves, frayed as they already were. "I was flipped out at the time," he said, "and he [Spector] certainly was flipped out. For me, the expression was withdrawal and melancholy, and for him, megalomania and insanity and a devotion to armaments that was really intolerable. In the state that he found himself, which was post-Wagnerian, I would say Hitlerian – the atmosphere was one of guns – the music was a subsidiary enterprise ... At a certain point Phil approached me with a bottle of kosher red wine in one hand and a .45 in the other, put his arm around my shoulder and shoved the revolver into my neck and said, 'Leonard, I love you.' I said, 'I hope you do, Phil.'"

Dan Kessel confirms that some individuals at the sessions were undoubtedly armed but does not recall... "any gunplay or anyone firing a gun. But if you're not a 'gun' person and are easily disturbed by guns then its gonna be a freak out for you. I happen to own guns and so to me it's no big deal. But I never had a heart to heart with Leonard about how he felt about guns."

Al Perkins again confirms that the sessions were... "unusual, at the least. I don't recall them being actually volatile, but Phil did have his pistol on him. Most of us were there for eight hours as I recall, and by the way I was paid for one 'demo' session only."

There were lighter moments too. "The atmosphere could be quite jovial," says Bill Mays. "I remember Phil waving a lit baton, leading us through the studio on a 'march' at one point. But that was Hollywood in the Seventies, you know? Quite a zoo!"

At one point during the height of the recording sessions Phil exclaimed rapturously, "This is great fucking music we've made!" before launching into a bout of serial huggings in the main room. Kubernick remembers watching Cohen sit gingerly before a microphone in the recording booth whilst Spector's distorted voice screamed out of the speakers to no one in particular, "This isn't punk rock... this is rock punk!" Such exclamations could be taken various ways. On this occasion it was actually the cue for Cohen to sing.

Despite such theatrical events, the material suffered most not from Spector's occasionally dysfunctional behaviour but from the indifference of the session players drafted in, as Art Munson would confirm. "I don't actually remember much about the songs to tell you the truth but we simply addressed the material in the best way we could in order to complement them..." The musicians brought little in the way of personal emotional commitment to the sessions. "Ultimately... I had no sense of it," he continues. "Being a session player requires a high degree of professionalism. You show up early, set up and be ready to play at the downbeat. You leave your ego at the door and devote yourself to doing the best job you possibly can for the time you are there. When you are done you are off to the next one"

Such an ethic was akin to contractors working on a building project but what Cohen's songs needed were emotionally involved craftsmen, as in his previous sessions with 'The Army' and producers Johnston and Lissauer. "But that was normal for a Spector sessions," says Dan Kessel, "and doing it any other way wouldn't have crossed our minds. In fact for a Spector session, an emotional investment in the songs isn't particularly crucial. If you were doing a small combo, where you can hear every instrument individually, then that could make a difference. These particular musicians were hardcore, super efficient, technically and professionally proficient musicians. So if their heart and soul wasn't into it, you wouldn't normally notice."

Arguably, for sessions that depended on so many different multiple parts making up a whole it was perhaps better that, as in an orchestra, no particular solo instrument *did* stand out. "Phil actually let them play the song for an hour before he started the tape rolling, precisely so the musicians would get all that personal expression stuff out of their system," explains Kessel. "He wanted just one big voice." Unfortunately, a singer and writer of Cohen's very particular pedigree and nuance was unsuited to such a system.

As the sessions appeared to near completion Cohen was becoming visibly disgruntled. He felt the producer wasn't affording him proper respect and was making himself 'inaccessible'. He also reckoned that his contributions – lyrics and voice – were being swamped, both by the producer's ego and the over orchestration. "I wish at times there was a little more space for the personality of the story-teller to emerge," he opined, not unreasonably. The staff at the studio were sympathetic. "I got along fine with everybody," says engineer Stan Ross, "but Phil couldn't get along with the artist… Phil was into his 'thing' at the time and so any distraction would distract him… anything would bother him… and even being on time bothered him. And that bothered Leonard."

"Leonard deserved better than he got," states Larry Levine, another of the engineers in attendance. "Both Phil and Leonard were very unhappy with what was coming off."

Devra thought that Spector's weaker, darker nature was simply exploiting and abusing a golden opportunity. "He had so much going for him," she remembers with true sadness, "fame, fortune, talent, the respect of his peers and along comes the opportunity of working with truly great artists, true artistic souls like Lennon and Cohen and it breaks my heart when I saw someone of that stature abusing that privilege. Leonard came in with so much creative poetry and it kinda' got stomped on."

Harvey Kubernick remembers it differently. "People were having a good time! They were getting paid to make a record. I don't remember anyone stomping out."

On the contrary, people were stomping in. "I brought The Ramones in one time," says Dan Kessel. "I'd been to see them and Phil knew them and Leonard was interested in them. I'd been talking to him about their song 'Beat On The Brat' and in particular the lyrics, 'Beat on the brat… with a baseball bat', and he was kinda intrigued by them."

Cohen also brought Roshi along to the sessions on occasion although if the 70 something Buddhist monk did meet The Ramones, his impressions of them and 'Beat On The Brat' remain unrecorded.

There was conceivably some grain of method in Spector's madness. Back at his height he had, after all been known for making stars out of complete unknowns. Perhaps by treating Cohen, whose career was now, at least in America, on the rocks, as a protégé of sorts, Spector could weave such alchemy again. "Even though Phil was always the boss," says

Levine, "he still made stars out of the people he worked with and if he could have he would have made a star out of Leonard also but he wasn't at his creative best at that time."

As the atmosphere began to sour there was some light relief when Bob Dylan and Allen Ginsberg turned up to add raucous vocals to 'Don't Go Home With Your Hard-On'. "Spector was taking a lot of cocaine," Ginsberg later remembered, "and was in a kind of hysterical frenzy, totally Hitlerian and dictatorial and sort of crazed – he started pushing us all around, saying, 'Get in there, get on the microphone!' – the whole thing was total chaos."

At one point Spector screamed, "Anybody laid-back in this room, get the fuck out of here!" thus turning the intensity up to eleven. Devra, an accomplished musician herself rubbed shoulders with Ginsberg at the mike, joining in on the chorus. On her other side was Kessel and Bob Dylan. "He was so drunk," remembers Devra. "He couldn't stand up. They lowered down the microphone to the floor and he sang from his back."

For some, such larks were proof that they were part of a myth in the making. "It was a wonderful experience," beamed backing vocalist Ronee Blakely. "Can you imagine yourself in that situation – being in a studio with Bob Dylan, Leonard Cohen, Allen Ginsberg and Phil Spector... isn't that heaven!" Blakely's memories are perhaps blurred as tellingly, most remember Cohen not even being in the studio at this moment, having put down what he considered a rough guide vocal to the song some time before. When Cohen got to hear the almost finished track he felt he was at last approaching the kind of rough and ready, gritty raw rock and roll style of singing he had long aspired to. Kubernick looked on as Spector and Cohen sat listening to a deafening playback of the album's most (s)punky song.   Swigging from a bottle of tequila Cohen proclaimed with some satisfaction: "I can really belt 'em out you know!"

Cohen and Spector would sometimes still be listening to playbacks at well past 6a.m., the producer no doubt wired to the gills with Cohen occasionally speeding and both, at times, drunk. Calling the session to an end in broad daylight, the two legends would battle with their relative comedowns alone and in their own ways.

"We'd travel home with Phil," says Dan Kessel. "And he'd be in a different mood on each journey, like anyone. I remember him being utterly whacked and tired one night and on other nights really up and ready to go for hours longer." Spector would usually succumb to sleep later than Cohen, often continuing to play the mixes back at his mansion well toward noon. "Ain't none of us ready for the glue factory yet," he exclaimed to a journalist on one such occasion. "I'll go one-on-one with any producer in the world, anytime...We can still kick ass!"

Finally, as the sessions played themselves out, a sense of mild bewilderment and the faint atmosphere of a wasted opportunity hung over everything. It was as if a communal coke comedown was enveloping everyone involved. "There was always a turning point with Phil...a point it never should have got to but Phil went beyond it," explains Devra. "I mean... when you consider all the talent in the room, all that potential power. But it always turned wrong with Phil... always turned bad. It was his demons, the negative, paranoid, schizophrenic parts of his personality that were to blame."

As the scores of players departed the studio, no one involved was swapping numbers or promising to keep in touch. "That's the way it goes day after day so you don't have much time to socialise," says Art Munson. "I really had no impression of Leonard. As a session player one is going from one session to another and sometimes it's just another job. It just depends on the mood and who you are working with. If I had known Cohen better or had worked with him before it might have been more intimate."

The sessions did not even 'officially' end. One day Phil just failed to return to the studio, keeping all the tapes (as he had also done with Lennon's masters) and going on to mix them alone. Cohen was aghast. He did not consider his recorded vocals to be anywhere near definitive. As far as he was concerned they were merely 'guide' vocals for the benefit of the musicians. He had expected to be able to take time on his singing but with Spector holding the tapes hostage at an unknown location this now seemed impossible, unless he brought in his own bunch of heavies to take on Spector's. "I had the option of hiring my own private army and fighting it out with him on Sunset Boulevard or letting it go... I let it go."

Dan Kessel: "I don't remember any discussion about that… I got no sense at the time that Leonard was unhappy. But I'm sure it was a completely different recording experience for him at the time. Completely alien to any kind of other album he'd made before. I mean he and Phil collaborated equally on the song writing but once that was complete – and maybe Leonard didn't understand this about Phil before he entered into the bargain – Phil always has control over whatever recordings he's produced. I was there and Phil just did what he always does. Phil is not the kind of guy who will ask you 'What do you think?' Because he doesn't *care* what you think because he already knows what *he* thinks. And he does that without apology. Cohen loved some of Phil's earlier work, right? And the guy he got to work with was that very same guy that made the records Leonard loved. You think any of The Crystals or even John Lennon would have said to Phil, 'Hey, how about some more trumpets'?"

In retrospect, the situation was perhaps equivalent to Cohen signing on to act in the movie of a famously renowned film director (Sam Peckinpah being the appropriate equivalent) and then with the shooting over, further expecting to be part of the editing process. One wonders if Cohen would have embraced the Spector collaboration at all if his manager hadn't wished it so. "When I heard the final mix, I thought he had taken the guts out of the record, and I sent him a telegram to that effect," Cohen recalls. "I asked him to go back in the studio."

As far as Spector was concerned this would not happen. "Phil had an obvious controlling and manipulative side to him," confirms Devra. "He'd say 'I'm not gonna let him mix it! I'll mix it myself! I'm the great Phil Spector'! It'll be the way I say it's gonna' be'! There was a lot of cat and mouse involved and it must have been frustrating for Leonard to seeing his creative children not flourishing."

Cohen himself was far too reticent a personality to actually engage or confront Spector on any comparable level. He recognised the extremes at war within the producer. "(He's) done some very soft and beautiful tunes, like 'To Know Him Is To Love Him'. That was when he was in his Debussy phase. But I met him in his Wagnerian phase."

Devra, closer to Phil the man as opposed to Phil the myth, had her own take on Spector's dysfunction: "Spiritually he came in already wounded, and hurt emotionally too as a child… and yet with all that talent and ability I would have expected him to have the strength to prevail… he should have taken the role of mentor to someone like Leonard and he didn't do that and that's his crime. He should have been the enabler not the disabler. It was carnage."

Given the actual physical, sonic results of such a debacle, Steven Machat had had little luck in finding a home for the album. Even his father stepped in to help. Marty had "… approached Warner's, but his plan began falling apart because label boss Mo Ostin wanted nothing to do with it either. Word was spreading. I actually shopped it to every LA label… in June and July of 1977."

By this time Cohen and Spector had officially fallen out. Marty's master plan was beginning to look as much like a screw-up as the album seemed to be. That September, attempting to bring some artificial positivity to the squalid mess, Marty tactfully informed a despairing Cohen that his son was right behind the project, on the case and a huge fan of the music. Not only was Cohen unreassured by such bullshit but he was actually furious at such a spin. "Are you out of your brains?" he asked Steven with the regret of someone coming to terms with the morning after a particularly nasty and intoxicated one night stand. "This album is junk. It's your father's masturbation. I love Marty. He's my brother. But I never want to see that man Spector again. He is the worst human being I have ever met… We were drunk and stupid. I do not wish for this album to see daylight."

Over at the Spanish mansion, Spector was by now no Cohen fan either. "That man might as well be a member of the Partridge Family," he'd screamed at Steven. The Partridge Family, the vehicle for pop idol David Cassidy, represented the squarest of the square, the uber-unhip, a coven of uncool. By comparison the Partridge Family made the Brady Bunch seem like the Manson family. As far as Spector was concerned, this was the ultimate insult that he could bestow upon anyone. Although the album was now, to all intents, finished – some would say abandoned – neither Spector nor Cohen wanted anything to do with it – or each other.

For the rest of the enormous cast involved in the record, each took away something different. "I really got to appreciate Leonard's artistry and writing through that experience," says Kessel. "I appreciated his persona and his style. I mean I wouldn't say he's the world's greatest vocalist in the style of Sinatra but he has a definite style and a sound and I appreciated all of that. I thoroughly enjoyed him as a human being and I respected him, I was glad to be working with him."

For Cohen the album painfully added to what was becoming a hellish time for him. The disastrous album that now bore his name seemed to mirror and even amplify all the negativity happening in his private life. On the domestic front his troubled relationship with Suzanne Elrod, the mother of his two children, was coming to an end, while in Montreal his beloved mother was succumbing to leukaemia. The irony was that up until now, Cohen's work had been a city of refuge for him through much less disturbing times. Yet now, during one of the most testing times of his life, even the once sacred sanctuary of his work seemed to be mocking him, punishing him and acerbating his predicament. In addition he was also under pressure to complete the manuscript for a forthcoming book, perversely entitled *Death Of A Lady's Man*.

Yet, although by now Cohen must have been envying the Old Testament's Job for the comparatively easy ride God had given him, he refused to complain nor confide any of these pressures to anyone in the studio. "He never mentioned any of this as far as I'm aware," remembers Devra. "I simply remember him as being quite together and a consummate gentlemen. A calm in the hurricane... although that said I do remember him on one occasion sort of seething, quietly."

As soon as it became apparent that there was little left for Cohen to do on the record – he couldn't even reach Spector let alone the tapes – Cohen took his disintegrating family and moved back to Montreal where he would concentrate on the final draft of his book and, more importantly, on nursing his ailing mother, who would succumb to her cancer in 1978.

In the coming years Cohen would recall her as: "A big person. A Chekhovian heroine. She laughed deeply, wept deeply... a great figure. My friends loved her very much. She was always there. We'd come home at three o'clock in the morning... and my mother would come in and sit around with us. She was a very large, warm generous person."

For the Machats, business continued as usual. "In 1977 my father had called me up from London and asked me to listen to a record by a British singer called Leo Sayer," remembers Steven. "[It was called] 'When I Need You'. Dad smelled an infringement suit. It was a straight rip off of Cohen's 'Famous Blue Raincoat'. 'When I Need You' was beyond bad as a piece of music in my opinion, but it was a number one on both sides of the Atlantic. It was credited to a songwriter called Albert Hammond. Anyway, the melodic similarities were obvious and we immediately launched a lawsuit. Hammond's people, Sayer's people... they didn't have a leg to stand on and they knew it. So, we were looking at substantial damages and royalties. But then we hit a problem: Cohen! He refused to testify. He told us that he would never submit himself to cross-examination in a court. He said: 'That's not what my spirit is there for.' So, we had to settle out of court and the deal we got was 15 per cent of the royalties when we would have got 100 percent in court. Cohen said he wanted nothing to do with the case or the money. We could have whatever was going. The money was paid into our joint company Stranger Music because my father was worried that if we didn't, this would alert the other side to the fact that Cohen had chickened out, because then they would not have settled..."

Cohen obviously had enough on his plate at this time. His own mother was still terminally ill, his relationship with the mother of his children was breaking up and as he saw it, he'd just been jointly responsible for a grotesque musical abortion. With Cohen and Spector having split the scene of the crime as such, Steven was left holding an ugly unwanted mess of a baby. The placing of such a deplored musical bastard was giving both Machat Snr and Jnr serious headaches. With every label in LA having passed on it, Steven determined to return focus on the original victim: Warners. Showing admirable chutzpah, he decided to avoid the boss, Mo Smith, altogether. Instead Steven concentrated his considerable charm and attention on someone much lower down the label's ladder, someone closer to his peer group, his demographic. Steven was 25 years old, and had managed to convince a junior product manager of the same age at Warners that having the names Spector and Cohen a record could only be a good thing. With this insider on his side, both managed to convince the boss, Mo Ostin, that if two hip young cats like themselves believed in such an album then surely the rest of the world's twenty-something's would too. Eventually, after a troubled labour and an unwanted birth, Warner's finally adopted the orphan that was *Death Of Ladies Man*.

Notwithstanding the problems surrounding its creation, the record has aged well and at least has value as being the least typical record in both Cohen and Spector's canon. The songs are essentially solid, melodically strong pieces that swim woozily within a hugely lush panoramic and paranoiac sea of sound. Despite his criticism of Spector's mix, Cohen's vocals are at the forefront of the tracks in most cases and every word is audible, even if the actual singing itself is not pitch perfect and often sounds blearily stoned and self conscious. But it's clear from the finished product that Spector was committed to the project; it does not sound half finished or undernourished – exactly the opposite in fact. The track 'True Love Leaves No Traces', in particular, is as incandescently beautiful as anything either man would ever commit to tape. Cohen's voice is married lushly to that of Ronnee Blakely's, like two halos mating, and he rarely sounded sadder or more sorrowfully seductive. The Cohen-Spector collaboration is a towering, mad monolith of an album and one that while at the time must have seemed perverse and bizarre in its late Seventies context, has since matured into a beautifully ugly monster.

Death Of A Ladies' Man was eventually issued in a gatefold sleeve on Warners in November 1977 and greeted with the expected bewilderment and derision. "It's either greatly flawed or great and flawed – and I'm betting on the latter," said *Rolling Stone*. "Too much of the record sounds like the world's most flamboyant extrovert producing and arranging the world's most fatalistic introvert." The reviewer did go on to praise certain aspects of the record, the lyrics in particular, but pointed out that as a whole, the venture did not convince.

The poor sales matched the confusion that the record met. Some long term Cohen fans were appalled by Spector's 'intrusion', although not all. "Unlike many Cohenites, I loved this album from the very first time I heard it," says long time Cohen devotee Andrew Darbyshire, then living in London. "The 'wall of sound' made it a richer musical experience to some degree. I felt so much of the melancholy of romance and love through it: a real sense of pain and frustrated longing. Every track was meaningful to me."

The cover of the album was one of Cohen's best, showing a documentary style photo of Cohen and Suzanne Elrod with their friend Eva La Pierre, a Quebecoise model Cohen had met on Hydra. All three are sat at the table of a 'Forgotten Polynesian Restaurant'.

Spector wasn't around to promote his latest tragedy, although either through a sense of duty or distraction, Cohen went through the usual rounds of promo interviews for the album. Even at his most philosophical he had little good to say about it. "The album's about the death of a ladies' man. You just can't hold that point of view anymore," Cohen mused. "Phil saw it immediately. Anybody over thirty, I imagine, who's had a couple of marriages and a couple of children, as Phil has had, would see that it's authentic. I don't know what it could possibly mean to a twenty-year-old."

In time, Cohen would grow tenderer toward the album, stating specifically that it was the mixes he had a problem with, not the songs or even the recordings themselves. As for the issue of the first take vocals, Cohen would eventually acquiesce to Phil's method, finding the good in the bad, saying, "It's true that record. It's raw."

Devra, a musician herself... "Liked it. It had some good stuff on it but... Phil's production habits by then had become too self aggrandising, too ponderous, too busy, to much reverb, too many overdubs. The beautiful heart of Leonard's music got lost in too much ego tripping."

The general public were indifferent. At the time, the album was a commercial and critical flop. But it had in effect served its original purpose. "My father was so lucky that Spector and Cohen didn't fire him," says Steven. "He was even luckier that Warners forgot to ask for their advance back. Or chose not to..."

For years to come Cohen would occasionally dine out on his tales of having worked with Phil Spector and lived. Whenever he was asked if the producer was as crazy as people said he was Cohen unhesitatingly responded with classic comic timing: "Crazier". Dan Kessel doesn't agree with this but remains philosophical. "The way I see the whole Leonard/ Phil thing is ... you know that joke about five blind men trying to explain to each other what an elephant looks like? One of 'em feels the elephant's leg and says, 'Oh! It's like a tree trunk'. Another guy feels the trunk and says 'It's like a snake'! And the other guy feels the tusk and says

'You guys are wrong, it's like a sword'!' So, everyone who was at those sessions, the way they describe what they saw it's…they are all right but they are all wrong'."

Despite the friction, Cohen always stressed that he liked Spector on a one-to-one level; it was just that when Phil had a larger audience he "becomes a performer of a Medici magnitude. He becomes a medieval tyrant and then it gets a little tricky."

A weary Cohen, obliged to attend the launch party for the doomed album did try to be courteous about Spector the person. "Incidentally, beyond all this, I liked him. Just man to man he's delightful, and with children he's very kind."

CHAPTER SEVEN

Recent Songs And Towers Thereof

"Men think constantly of women. And they think constantly of us. I think it's the divine scheme."

LC

With Suzanne Elrod gone and having taking the children with her, and with his mother Masha now dead, by late 1978 Cohen must have sought solace and sanctuary in his work like never before. The latest 'perfect offering' would be produced by Cohen himself, assisted by Henry Lewy and the in-house engineers at A&M's Hollywood studio: Derek Duncan, Greg Falken and Skip Cottrell.

Unlike Lissaeur or Spector, Lewy was not native American. Henry Lewy, a German Jew was a man with past, a mature and dedicated artisan who had fled to the US from Germany as a teen in the early Forties to escape the Nazi regime. Thin and rangy, by the time Cohen met him in 1978, Lewy had become a modestly known but well respected and established producer/engineer who had been working regularly with Joni Mitchell since 1970. On the most recent Mitchell tour, he had used a band called Passenger, a Texas-based fusion-rock-R&B group formed by Texan bassist Roscoe Beck. Utilising his healthy relationship with the group and in tandem with Cohen's obvious respect for Mitchell and her work, Levy hired Passenger for the album that would eventually and prosaically be entitled *Recent Songs.*

Thus, Mitch Watkins (electric guitar), Paul Ostermayer (sax), Steve Meador (drums), Roscoe Beck (bass), and Bill Ginn (keyboards) joined violinist Raffi Hakopian, oud and mandolin player John Bilezikjian, along with vocalists Jennifer Warnes and Sharon Robinson, at A&M Studios for recording sessions. For at least two of these players – Roscoe and Sharon – this marked the beginning of an active working relationship with Cohen that would endure until the present day. Roscoe recalls: "I had only fleeting knowledge of him [Cohen]. At the time, I was coming from the techno-chops side of things, where it's all about the note… but here was this whole other world, where everything was in the lyrics. Leonard's songs had an immediate and profound emotional impact on me, and they changed my musical perspective."

Among the other musicians, the committed and refined Bilezikjian would also enjoy more than a decade-long working relationship with Cohen, stopping only in the mid Nineties when ill health would limit the oudist's activities. Two of these more exotic musicians came through a friend of Warnes', bassist Stuart Brotman. "I was acquainted with Jennifer Warnes in the Sixties, and played a number of demo recordings on upright bass for her," he remembers. "Jennifer, her friend Leonard Cohen, and I were all at a concert at McCabe's, the guitar shop and folk music cabaret in Santa Monica around 1978-9, and they asked my recommendation for an exciting musician to add to the band. I got them in contact with John… and I introduced them to Raffi. At that time I was playing Fender bass at Athenian Gardens in Hollywood, where Raffi was a frequent featured artist."

Bilezikjian confirms the connection. "I was introduced to Leonard through Stuart Brotman, a very good friend and bass player," he remembers. "He in turn had gotten a call from one of his friends, saying that Leonard was looking for something 'unusual'. So Stuart mentioned me and Leonard invited me to a recording session. Right after that he came to hear me play at the Trojan Horse restaurant in Long Beach… it's long gone now… but at the time I had my own show there. It was a Greek restaurant, and I had belly dancers. I got Leonard to get up and sing with me. You have to remember that prior to this I had never even heard of Leonard."

The fact that John – an Armenian and classically trained violinist of the Russian school and maestro of the oud – had never heard of Cohen is much less unusual than the ignorance of the session players at the recent Spector sessions. In North America, Cohen's presence as a current, contemporary artist was now way beyond the wane, his career now receding into a beautifully rendered footnote to the Sixties. The recent Spector debacle had only compounded his obscurity. In addition to this, Bilezikjian moved in a relatively specialised market. "I didn't even know who The Beatles were until I met my wife," he admits.

The idea that Cohen wanted someone like Bilezikjian in his band specifically because of their vaguely shared Eastern European heritage is not one to which the oudist particularly subscribes. "We hit it off on a personal level," he counters. "He was very kind and hospitable. In terms of him being drawn to me because of his mother's influence… I think he was aware that I was ethnic, yes. But I'm Armenian not Lithuanian. But we didn't really speak of this. It never got that deep. It was simply very natural and spontaneous. He was a gentleman to me. I had heard stories about him subsequently… that at some point he was into drugs and so forth but I never saw any evidence of that. But we hit it off. And you know, I don't and never have drunk, smoked or taken drugs. Which is really saying something out here in Los Angeles. I mean, in the Seventies you almost had to have a drug habit to get invited to the right parties."

In addition to the soloists like Bilezikjian, English string arranger Jeremy Lubbock came to the sessions via his work with Joni Mitchell and Lewy. Lubbock had worked in the initial stages on Mitchell's *Mingus* album and had deeply impressed both her and jazz bassist and composer Charlie Mingus himself. Consequently, Lewy thought this particular English arranger could bring something unique to the Cohen album.

"He was a strange mixture, was Henry Lewy," recalls Lubbock tactfully. "He could be wonderfully nice and he could be wonderfully not nice, if he chose. As for Leonard, ultimately I preferred his songs to his singing. The singing was an acquired taste but the songs were just amazing."

As a man, Cohen impressed Lubbock further with his natural grace and old world class. On meeting him for the first time, Lubbock, only recently a player in the cut throat LA music scene of the time, remembers Cohen as being… "absolutely the anthisisis of the music business; he was like Joni in this respect. They are just above it all. Neither of them would have any truck with all of the crap that goes on in the music business. They were beyond it all, a law unto themselves. And that's partly what makes them iconic, you know. Leonard was very much a gentleman and that's a very rare quality in this business. The only other chap with such manners, that I worked with, was Michael Jackson. Of all the chaps I worked with, Leonard Cohen and Michael Jackson were most similar in terms of being gentlemen."

Once Lubbock was a confirmed contributor, another meeting was set up, one on one, between him and Cohen at the latter's spartan LA apartment. Cohen was of course, amenable, courteous and open during the visit – the perfect host. In direct contrast to the relatively recent Spector pre-production sessions, Cohen and Lubbock discussed the relevant songs – in this case 'The Traitor' and 'The Smokey Life' and their potential arrangements, with clear sober minds and in the clean sunlight of a late LA afternoon. Following these discussions, the arranger was given a basic demo tape of the songs and left to his own devices. He had only two weeks at most to arrange and score the two songs for a 16-piece string section. "No, deadlines or pressure wasn't a problem," states Lubbock. "That was what I did. That was my job."

Compared to the psychodrama surrounding Spector, work on *Recent Songs* was extremely civilized, sober and orderly. "Sessions started in the afternoon and we'd go into the evenings," recalls Bilezikjian. "No drinking, that I saw, no visitors. Finished at a reasonable time, no early hours stuff. I was a family man remember – I couldn't stay out all night."

By adding such players as Bilezikjian to his group – "Originally I played violin, mandolin and oud remember… I put a bit of icing on the cake, if you know what I mean" – Cohen gave notice that he had widened his musical palette, got a grip on his own work again and re-engaged his musical interest. By the time he got back into the studio he was primed utterly for the work in hand. When later asked to put a time period on the making of the album, Cohen reckoned that the gestation period – the actual writing – had taken three to four years while the birth – the delivery which of course included the actual rehearsal and recording of it, took the same amount in months. Obviously, particularly in writing terms, this was not concentrated amounts of time. Cohen's life, like anyone else's could not be consumed totally by work, even though as a novelist, poet, singer and songwriter he wore more hats than most. His civilian life continued alongside his artistic calling, of which he considered his 'slowness' as a 'protection'.

In terms of discography, *Recent Songs* came directly after the Spector trauma, and Cohen openly admitted that he had lost a grip on both himself and his work during that period. "Phil was too strong for me," he would acknowledge later. This album – in process, execution and result – would be as ordered and refined as *Death Of A Ladies Man* had been chaotic and incomplete. "I experienced no bad vibes," says Bilezikjian. "No cursing, no 'You son of a bitch', no 'you mutha…, none of that." Incredibly, he "… didn't even see Leonard smoking."

Beyond the authorship of the songs themselves, Cohen would take due credit for the co-production and direction of the record. He didn't want anyone to think that, unlike some other singers who were wont to go as far as to whistle guitar solos to their lead guitarists, he dictated every note of each part. He stressed in interviews promoting the album that the soloists were given their own space and did what they felt within given parameters. Like a film director in part relying on the quality of his chosen actor's inherent talent, Cohen saw the brief of making an album as "To gather together some very good musicians and give them a vehicle in which they themselves can express themselves."

Cohen would, of course, have final veto on any performance but would rarely have to exercise it to any extreme degree. He had after all, chosen the players himself and was justifiably confident in their (and his own) abilities and taste. "He let me do whatever it was I wanted to do," confirms Bilezikjian. "He trusted my sense of musicality'." Cohen would introduce his songs to the band by simply playing them live on a guitar in front of them. "He would be with a microphone and headphones and we'd all be wired up in our separate booths and we'd listen and add our part. I noticed his guitar playing was very unique… the way he did those arpeggios with his right hand… beautiful… that style was all his own."

Obviously not all the musicians would be continuously present at the sessions. Lewy would call them in when required, staggering their contributions as the sessions progressed. Once he was finally called to the studio, Lubbock got to observe Cohen first hand in a professional capacity. The well spoken Englishman liked what he saw. "He was enormously respectful of those around him; he was an absolute joy to be around," he says simply. Cohen's attitude was perhaps partly down to the notion that he had never considered himself a 'proper' musician and still felt, to a degree, privileged to have bona fide, Julliard school level professionals working on his untutored, and as he saw them, 'home made' songs. "He'd say, 'Listen to this and add what you can add'," says Bilezikjian. "He was very open and loose and cordial. He wanted us there because he wanted to see what each of us could bring to the pieces on our own. In a way, each of us was a writer."

Lubbock adds: "When he came to work, Leonard left his ego at the door. It's incredibly rare. Cohen's relationship with Lewy was good, like Henry's relationship was with Joni. But you have to remember that Lewy was basically an engineer so that was the basis of his relationship with Leonard. He wasn't producing Leonard as such. Leonard didn't really need a producer, he was his own producer. That was obvious." Bilezikjian saw things from a similar vantage point, but another way. "If you ask me, I think Lewy had more input than Leonard on that score," he says. "Probably Leonard had the final say. But you know I never even heard Lewy say 'Great take' or 'The oud was this, the oud was that'. I never had any kind of comment other than 'That was great'. Most of my takes at least were first takes… if they wanted a second or a third it was just to have the option… another feel… Because you know, nothing was scored, none of our parts were written down. So Leonard would just say, 'Let's see what else you can come up with, John…' On hearing his songs I immediately had a feeling of what I could add," he continues. "But he did not instruct me, as I would in his position. I would even write out the parts. But we – the musicians would merely listen to his chord changes, his melody and work out our individual roles within each song. The melodies were beautiful and the chords straightforward."

When it was time to add the orchestral parts, the string players themselves were brought in by Lewy and not Lubbock. The arranger himself was not consulted in terms of the personnel who would actually bring his arrangements to life. "It was early days for me, I didn't have a handle on that aspect yet," says Lubbock.

The tone of his lush string arrangements brought a fresh new sound to Cohen albums. Unlike the slightly avant garde jazz flavour of Lissauer's arrangements and the full-on string sound that Spector had employed, Lubbock's arrangements were straightforwardly romantic and sumptuous, bringing a patina of Elgar and Delius to bear beneath Cohen's plaintive Nashville croon. 'The Traitor' in particular had a moderately English renaissance era quality, at times sounding like the aural equivalent of a Waterhouse painting. "Part of my success as an arranger in Hollywood during the time I worked there was precisely because of the 'English content' of my arrangements, if you like," affirms Lubbock. "Nobody else was doing that kind of thing." No one, including the arranger, would hear the arrangements until they were played live at the actual recording sessions. Lubbock would not have been able to demo the arrangements in any form; the technology did not exist then. Home studios were a rare luxury and most arrangers had nothing in their place of work but a piano, a score sheet and a pencil with an eraser on the end. "And that's just how it should be," Lubbock states. "All this bullshit about having demos these days is just nonsense because that means everybody thinks they are an arranger and, of course, they are not. So nowadays they can screw around with what you've written and it's ridiculous... chances are the arranger will always come up with something more interesting than the artist he's writing for... because they are not an arranger... but back then nobody heard anything until they went in the studio. Not even Sinatra!"

Cohen was not complaining at the end result. After the previous debacle with Spector, *Recent Songs* was catharsis. "I really had to rediscover some sort of basis; something I knew about," Cohen said. "It was a coming home... a very rich period."

Aside from the introduction of Lubbock's plainly romantic strings on two of the songs, the album also employed other more familiar and redemptive sounds. The lush women's voices bathing Cohen's were made up of a small brigade of female singers, painstakingly overdubbed onto one another to create a virtual choir.

All instrumentations were ultimately informed by the songs and their author. "Leonard was the captain," says Bilezikjian. "We all played beneath him or maybe counter to him. That was my speciality – counterpoint. That gave more depth to the music and I think when people compliment me on my contribution to Leonard's music over the years that's why. And remember I wasn't used to this kind of music. But it just came out of me. And how did I come up with it? From God. It came from a divine area. It flowed. It was very natural."

As always, Cohen felt free to draw from divine and esoteric sources. One of the album's most spiritual pieces, 'The Guests', was based on a 13th century Persian poem and was chosen specifically to open the album simply because of the enthusiastic response it had evoked when Cohen played it to friends. It also defined the album for the author in that he saw each song as an individual 'guest'. Thus this first song served as an initial host, ushering in the rest of the album piece by piece. If the material would fail to seduce the public at large it did at least beguile those who helped give it shape and form. "I really came to love Leonard's songs," says Bilezikjian, who in the space of a few years would go from not even having heard of Cohen to performing his own versions of Cohen's songs during solo shows.

Although Cohen and his session crew had completed an elegiac, poised and quietly accomplished record, the very lack of tension in the recording process was perhaps apparent in the result. For all its artistry, *Recent Songs* sounded bland and MOR. Despite the occasional feisty outburst – as in the Mariachi influenced 'The Lost Canadian' or the Sinatraesque torch song beauty of 'The Smokey Life' – the album as a whole ploughed a self-indulgent, middling trough. Sadly, among the outtakes from the album was a version of 'Do I Have To Dance All Night', a weirdly powerful funky 'disco in the library' number, that would have provided some dynamic relief. Nevertheless, *Recent Songs* at least served higher purposes in that it was therapeutic for its author. Beyond the moribund tempo and overly meditative singing style, Cohen had once more found a space and balance within himself through his work. Yet in world wide terms no one was particularly interested. Even John Lissauer, on hearing the album at the time considered it… "spotty. I mean, *Death Of A Ladies Man* I'd been shocked at, it left me empty. But *Recent Songs* I thought was quite spotty."

The basis of some of the songs, in particular 'Came So Far For Beauty', was the ...*Rebecca* sessions and featured Lissauer on piano (although he was unaccredited for his contribution to the production of the song, he was listed as co-composer). Lisseur remained unembittered. "And of course it also had some versions of songs we'd worked on... But then I don't scrutinize records as such... I don't have time to really study other people's records..."

Poring over Cohen songs and their accompanying record sleeves was just what his audience had always excelled at, but for the greater record buying public, Cohen was simply becoming irrelevant. The Eighties were approaching, the new wave movement was superseding disco and Cohen was as hip as the Boer war.

Recent Songs was released in September 1979. That same month in the UK, sub-Bowie spin off electro phenomenon Gary Numan was number one in the singles chart with the fizzy electro rush of 'Cars'. His debut album *Replicas* reached the top of the album charts the same month. In the US, Led Zeppelin once again dominated the album charts after a barren couple of years. Cosmetically, and perhaps even cosmically, Cohen appeared to fit neither between, beside or even behind such competitive products. And yet this is what, on one level, all three acts were – songs for sale and backed by major record company investment and thus by default in direct competition with one another. Cohen himself was defiant. "My music will overtake the new wave," he said. "New wave is a kind of last ditch attempt to revitalise rock'n'roll in a commercial framework but there's nothing new that has been done...'

Such confidence was admirable but even within the trajectory of his own career, *Recent Songs* was neither a high nor a low for the now 44-year-old Canadian. Even for the average Cohen fan the new album could lazily and easily be construed as yet another meditative and mostly mid-tempo Cohen manifesto on the unbearably bearable anguish of love. This was sloppy journalism and no doubt based solely on the stately tempos and minor keys of the music alone, augmented by Cohen's sometimes potent but always limited range as a singer. In fact, as Cohen saw it, the record was very specifically about "Fulfilled love and the mechanics of love". If this was too complicated or subtle a notion for the average or casual listener – who perhaps related only to songs about falling in or out of love – then Cohen was polite enough to once again take the blame, admitting that "I try to make it as simple as I can… maybe sometimes I fail."

Even the artwork of the album was off putting, showing a garish illustration by Dianne Lawrence which appeared to be an amateur painting of Dustin Hoffman. It was, of course, a portrait of Cohen himself. The striking, if somewhat clumsy, picture would also be used on many of the posters advertising the album and incongruously, even on tour jackets. Politely received as the record was, a good, solid work such as *Recent Songs* was no longer – if it ever had been – enough. Reviews were respectful and sales were acceptable, but they were matched by a decline in Cohen's sales and profile world wide, although this was most obvious in North America. Europe and Canada were less fickle. Past collaborator Lissauer again looked on, insightfully commenting that… "Cohen comes from a European background, in the tradition of the French chanson, even. He came from *French* Canada remember, Montreal *not* Toronto. He had a European sensibility that was never gonna go over big in America. He would speak to me about guys like Yves Montand and Jacques Brel and especially Serge Gainsbourg. These guys were big influences on him. He had a European sensibility, not an American one at all."

As muted as its reception was, the album's release was nevertheless promoted by a tour which opened the following October. The touring band consisted primarily of members of Passenger: Roscoe Beck, Bill Ginn, Steve Meador, Paul Ostermayer, and Mitch Watkins. In addition there were the four freelance musicians, John Bilezikjian, Raffi Hakopian, Sharon Robinson and Jennifer Warnes. It was a culturally rich mix that encompassed slick LA session players and soulfully authentic ethnic – violinist Raffi Hakopian barely spoke English. Mirroring the cultural diversity of his group, the Cohen operation was global. Rehearsals for the tour took place in London at Shepperton Studios. The tour began in Sweden's Gothenburg, and went on to France, Belgium, Germany, Switzerland and England. Leonard and his band performed 53 concerts in 44 cities in less than 70 days with a comprehensive set-list of 45 songs to draw from.

Occasionally accompanied by Roshi, (who by now bore a striking resemblance to both latter day versions of the Dalai Lama and Hunter S. Thompson), the presentation on stage was much less obviously drink and drug fuelled than previous tours and somewhat slicker and generally less playful as a result. But their leader was still very much present in the moment throughout and very occasionally launched into improvisations of a non musical nature. "Leonard wasn't making up songs on the '79 tour, when Passenger was the back-up band," remembers Roscoe Beck, "but there could be big surprises. I think we were in Oslo one night, and right in the middle of the set, he said, 'You know my back-up band, they have music of their own.' And then he walked off the stage! We were totally unprepared for that moment. Or he might just start talking for five or 10 minutes in French. Anything!"

Other members of the group were slightly more rock punk. "Hakopian did some crazy things on tour," remembers Bilezikjian. "He bought a gas gun that fired pellets. And you know… he got carried away and… we ended up in a police station and I had to translate for him 'cos he knew very little English."

Cohen himself stressed that he did not like to tour for the sake of it but only when he had something new to say – i.e. a record to promote. He did not tour merely to "gather applause and money" although conceded that "that's not a bad idea". Once again the venture was well documented in sound and vision by filmmaker and old friend Harry Rasky. The aesthetics of his film, *The Song Of Leonard Cohen*, mirrored the band it was documenting. It was tasteful, thoughtful and saturated by a limited but potent palette of hues, its dynamic mostly maintaining a walking pace. The footage did, however, prove once and for all that the dapper Cohen never looked more handsome than when he was cradling an acoustic guitar made from battered wood. Rasky's film portrayed Cohen as a composed man in a quiet and constant flux, even when not engaged on the road professionally.

"I've been moving around a lot for the last ten years but I'm kind of tired of it now," he said from his home in Montreal, in a neighbourhood that was now a funky and predominately Portuguese locale. Rasky did a quick tour of Cohen's apartment, which was sparse, white and grey, its tidiness only slightly marred by the occasional book and magazine (some resting, as in almost every other house, atop the toilet cistern). Some of the furniture belonged to Cohen's now dead relatives – a small desk, a clutch of framed prints and photos. Smoking at a table that held a typewriter, some writing paper, a cup of pens and pencils, and an enigmatic petit plaster cast sculpture from the Twenties, Cohen clearly loved where he lived. "It's got everything you need – and nothing you don't," is how he summed up this home, perhaps also alluding to the kind of life he ultimately sought. When pushed on what motivated his seemingly constant wanderings, Cohen seemed almost indifferent as to the reasons behind his nomadic lifestyle. "I feel no sense of the quest or the Odyssey, there seems to be reasons to move but none of them are very profound... but now I don't wanna move around." When pressed by certain interviewers during this period about his ideas of destiny and mission, Cohen surprisingly revealed himself as someone who preferred to gaze anywhere but in the direction of his own navel. "I think the song is the most appropriate place to examine those kinds of questions... not in conversation." He was, though, as happy as ever to talk about one of his primary motivations – his fascination and fixation with the female. "One is deeply concerned with women," he told Rasky. "Of course I got completely obsessed by women. Have been since I can't remember. I don't know why." Pressed on this Cohen had no idea of the reasons behind this 'obsession' claiming he was 'too busy' to give it serious thought. Such a coy response might be considered lame in the extreme had it not been backed up by the immediate proof of the extensive schedule Cohen had embarked upon.

The tour travelled widely, excluding Spain for some reason. Cohen still had a much more than minor audience in almost every country in the world and most of the venues he and his band performed in were sell outs. The audience's reaction seemed largely to depend on the age of the audience. In France the demographic was younger while in the rest of Europe the ticket buyers included a smattering of well-dressed and middle-aged professional couples infiltrating the usual regiments of students and loners. Yet, however considered and elegant the performances were, there were still moments of frisson, as in Berlin that November when Cohen and the crowd locked horns over a failing sound system. Confronting the audience's aggression full on, Cohen even had the balls to quote Goebbels at them – "Do you want total war?!" The heavy irony of a Jew aggressively quoting one of the most notorious Nazis – in the very same sports arena where those very words had been originally spoken back in the early Forties – was lost in the angry crowd reaction that followed. Perhaps Spector had been right. Cohen could occasionally be 'rock punk'.

The heavy schedule was of course augmented by the odd TV appearance and the usual duties of radio and newspaper interviews, although press interest for this album was much lower than previous or later Cohen albums. On French TV Cohen and Raffi performed a stately version of 'The Guests'. Looking tanned and handsome in a pink T-shirt, the performance nevertheless confirmed the media's perception of Cohen as the dour and mysterious poet. A woman's face, presumably one of the other guests on the TV show, was superimposed live over Cohen as he sang. She appeared beguiled and poetically disturbed by the singer's ruminations and the effect was cloyingly corny. Yet, even if he cared at all, how could Cohen hope to manipulate the manner in which TV producers and journalists perceived and presented him? The problem was that many watching such a schlocky TV appearance would, of course, assume that this was exactly how Cohen was and how he *wanted* to be presented – as a brooding, old fashioned balladeer trapped in some poetic Pre-Raphaelite time warp.

Cohen had little time to consider such matters. On and off stage he was working as hard as ever and his labours were in addition once again being documented in sound and vision. Rasky's film portrayed an accomplished group of musicians that were on consistently good form and whose leader appeared consummately sober and professional, almost to the point of minimalism. Cohen was subtle. To introduce a solo during a concert, he would simply turn to the relevant musician in a courtly manner and cue them into the song via an almost imperceptible nod. Whilst even his obvious passion could sometimes seem constrained and mannered, he sang in a voice just above his most comfortable natural pitch, and the effort did at least give the material a slightly strained and subliminally hysterical edge. But while most relevant boxes were ticked – there were impeccable arrangements of fine, beautifully crafted songs, the performances were lucid, coherent and often moving, if rarely truly groovy or swinging – there was also something occasionally perfunctory about the exercise, a sense of treading water that mirrored the lack of dynamic on his latest album. Almost inevitably, to some observers Cohen was still merely a Sixties artist who had survived the Seventies and was about to be eclipsed by the Eighties. If in some venues the audience did not respond as enthusiastically as they once had, Cohen was still confident enough to put the blame on the public and not the band. "You can say it's our fault," he exclaimed after a mildly disappointing reception in Belgium. "We're tired, we've been on the road a long time… perhaps there is some special element that is missing from our presentation. I don't think so. I think it's the most passionate presentation I've seen in a long time. I'm afraid that in this case… the people are to blame."

Bilezikjian remembers that gig. "His guitar got out of tune that night," he says, "and I was closest to him. He was having trouble on stage tuning it. I knew what was wrong so I walked up to him and turned the peg that was out and he looked up to me and then to the audience. I saluted him with my right hand, just to be cute!"

Cohen had never, actively or consciously courted fashion but for a while, as in the late Sixties and early Seventies the two had got along purely fortuitously. Whatever the climate of fashion surrounding him was, as far as Cohen was concerned he was still following his heart and offering valuable and solid work as a consequence. "It's not important to me to describe myself to myself," he stated. "I have some work to do in the world and I try to do it the best I can and if I can find a public to it that is receptive to it I'm happy and if I can't I still continue to do it."

But to some, and particularly to those who worked in the music media, when you placed the overtly romantic poet/singer between punk and the new glam synthesizer dominated trend that was approaching, Cohen the troubadour and his courtly roving band of impeccable musicians – oud and fiddle and all – seemed by comparison a tad dusty and creaky. Yet, in retrospect at least, one could see Cohen almost as a pioneer of another approaching musical phenomena – world music. His band offered nightly a veritable spice box of musical flavours. Despite never baldly discussing it with his musicians, Cohen was eager to push the 'ethnic' elements of the arrangements by using an Armenian violinist and oud player. "I've always liked that kind of music," he explained, going on to cite the Russian ballads of Masha's youth. "Before my mother died she said to me, 'Why don't you play any of those songs we used to sing?'" he added.

The concerts in London were more a more relaxed and celebratory business. Although being particularly out of fashion there, sandwiched between the wake of punk and the oncoming tide of new wave, Cohen and band still easily sold out 3,000 seater venues. The average show had no support act, started at eight o'clock sharp – Cohen was among the most punctual perfomers ever – was close to three and a half hours long, including mass sing-alongs ('So Long Marianne') and up to eight encores, finally closing in a standing ovation. Despite the vagaries of fashion, by any other standard the tour was a rollicking success.

In London, a clearly moved Cohen thanked his audience for "... your interest in my work, for letting me live the life of the heart and not believing the shit they write about me." Maybe he *did* care how the media presented him. Buoyed by the passion of his people, Cohen announced that he planned to keep on playing that night "until they pulled the plugs out". Management finally threatened to do just that. The singer and his band eventually exited stage left under a modest hail of red roses.

The travelling company were close off stage too, often improvising group singing sessions on the bus as it sped down motorways into yet another European sunset. This was, after all a Leonard Cohen tour and in some sense this made him 'the boss'. But he did not make a show of his authority and bonded with his band as individuals, not as a mere group of hired hands. "Leonard would take the whole group out for dinner every week," remembers Bilezikjian. "And I would go and have French onion soup in France for breakfast with him and talk about the tour. We'd talk about the music… I felt we were buddies. I know he felt that way too. He knew he could trust me. I didn't go out with the women. I didn't do anything untoward. I believed in the tour. I tried to be as much help as I could. I was always on time, never late. Some of the other musicians were late for the morning bus call. I was always on time and I attribute that discipline to my training as a violinist."

The tour continued into 1980. No singles were released from *Recent Songs*, but another in the endless line of compilation albums was released in Germany that year – *Liebesträume – Leonard Cohen Singt Seine Schönsten Lieder*. This was the first example of Cohen losing control over his output. The packaging of the album was hideous; an overtly 'romantic' shot of a mandolin-playing buffoon perched on a boulder on a beach at sunset. The effect was tacky in the extreme, attempting to market Cohen as some James Last-style chocolate-box balladeer. Richard Clayderman album covers of the time seem like recruitment posters for the Waffen SS by comparison. Cohen was aghast when he came across a copy. "Well, that record made me very uneasy," he said. "It was the only record that has ever been released which I didn't design the cover and I didn't chose the songs. And I gave it my consent, it was just over the telephone. The head of the German record company said we want to put out a compilation… when I saw the album and the kind of treatment that they'd given the songs I was quite turned off by it…"

This album was released in the first year of the new decade, a decade when pop music and its image, particularly with the rise of the promo video, was paramount. And as the ghastly *Liebesträume – Leonard Cohen Singt Seine Schönsten Lieder* proved, in terms of image, Cohen's was in a crisis.

After a brief respite that Christmas, the tour took up again in March 1980, with Cohen and band, playing Australia for the first time. Starved of Cohen as they were, his Australian audience received him rapturously. On one occasion the audience actually re-assembled outside the Sydney venue in which Cohen and band had just played and applauded them as they boarded their tour bus. Asked why he had taken so long to play Australia, Cohen replied: "I take a long time to do everything, to get everywhere. I only tour every two or three years."

He was reflective in interviews, reminiscing about his old life on Hydra and his original Australian hosts there. "I knew George Johnston and his wife Charmian Clift very well because I lived in Greece in those days on the same island… The Johnstons were there. There were just a few foreigners there in those days. The Johnstons were central figures. They were older. They were doing what we all wanted to do which was to write and to make a living out of writing. They were very wonderful, colourful, hospitable people… I heard a lot about Australia. You're on a little Greek island and there's nothing much to do but sit around and talk. George was a magnificent talker. He used to talk about his life here. He was Australian, there's no question about it. Now that I've come here,

I see just how Australian he was. I don't know if I can characterise what an Australian is, but I know one when I meet one."

By March 14 the 'Recent Songs' tour was over and Leonard and band went their separate ways.

With no new album to record and no tour or promotion to attend to, Cohen spent much of the period that followed travelling, reading and quietly working. Suzanne had now relocated to France with the children to a house with an orchard that Cohen paid for, set in the mountain area of Luberon. Old Chelsea Hotel regular Barry Miles had befriended Elrod and spent a summer there in the early Eighties. "She seemed quite content. It was very nice place," he affirms. "We just sat outside eating cherries. Very pleasant. I'm sure we spoke about Leonard but it was so long ago."

Sharing custody of the children when he could, Cohen kept moving, occasionally returning to Hydra as he did in the summer of 1983. This was the year that another writer, the nomadic David Fagan, fell in love with the island. After visiting on a day trip he decided against re-boarding the boat that had brought him there and eventually made Hydra his home. Retaining an immortal spirit as it did the Hydra of the Eighties was still tangibly linked to the community that Cohen had entered more than 20 years ago. But the link to those golden summers was rusting and weathered as Fagan confirms: "I came to Hydra at what I would regard as the tail end of the really good artistic time of the island," he explains. "There was still good stuff around of course but there was a sense that it had peaked. Bill's Bar was still happening and you could go in there around this time and see Leonard Cohen and John Cleese and Rolf Harris, Joan Collins at the bar and no one would pay much notice. But that would be changing, alas."

It would take more than another decade for the ubiquitous fascination with celebrity in any shape or form to infect Hydra and for now many of the original, simple attractions still remained. Hydra was not merely of sentimental value to Cohen, it was even now a unique kingdom unto itself. No matter where he moved in the world and despite the coming and going of Elrod, the death of his mother and the ups and downs of his career, Cohen could still connect to something eternal in Hydra. The crime rate there was practically nil, still. 'Its so small you wouldn't be able to get away with anything," explains Fagan. "Everyone knows and sees what's going on. You couldn't get away with it. As soon as you open your window in the morning someone will see you and say, 'Oh, you got up early this morning, and your dog is out.' The Yayas, the grandmothers on the island, know exactly what is going on. It's like a big high school in some senses. Gossip is rampant. Some people live for gossip. Actually it can sometimes be a pain in the arse. And remember we're an island. You can't drive through and rape and pillage. We've no heliport, certainly no airfield. Boat is the only way to reach us. I can't remember the last time I locked the door to my house."

There were still no cars or motorbikes. Not only was the island's terrain unsuitable for motorised transport, laws had been passed banning even petrol powered scooters. Every islander had a 'donkey man' they could rely on if needed. Other primitive modes of transport wouldn't even work on the island. "No, we couldn't even have rickshaws," says Fagan. "There's not enough flat areas. It's all pebble stones and steps remember. Even wheelchairs don't work here." Daleks would not be invading Hydra any time soon.

Fagan's introduction to Cohen occurred that summer on a drowsy afternoon in Bill's Bar. "There was a Scottish tourist at the bar," he remembers, "and she was drunk. Leonard was doing what he usually does, which is sitting in a corner reading a newspaper. It was about two in the afternoon and she'd had too many Bloody Marys or whatever. And suddenly, very loudly she cried out to Leonard, 'Oi! You!! I nearly committed suicide twice because of you, you fucker'! And Leonard just giggled and nodded. It was fine."

The two men would eventually become friends and in the coming decades Fagan would let Cohen use his office for phone calls, emails and the like. Cohen's 'celebrity' didn't get in the way. "I knew of his work, sure but we wouldn't talk about that. I'd never bring it up."

CHAPTER EIGHT

No Good Genius

"You realize that whoever you are, Goethe or Edgar Guest, you're just really a guy hauling his guitar around. There's a certain shabbiness to the whole enterprise: seeking to be noticed enters into the work. On one side, you're the acknowledged legislator of mankind. On another, you're trying to cope – get through it all, make a living, keep the wheels turning."

LC

For the first three and a half years of the new decade Cohen had no books or records released. His last book, *Death Of A Lady's Man* had been published in 1978 to a relative critical silence, and was not even reviewed in North America. As far as his public profile went, Cohen had disappeared without trace but he was, of course, working continuously; in one sense Cohen was merely swimming under water. These were profound times for Cohen, as meaningful as any of the previous more publically celebrated years. It was a time of taking stock. His last few albums had been received unenthusiastically, particularly by Columbia. His record company, like any other major business, had a high turnover of personnel and some of the new staff there were conscious that Cohen was merely an inheritance from an earlier and now deeply unfashionable era. After the lukewarm critical reception and lack of sales of his previous three albums, no one was pushing Cohen for new record any time soon. As a consequence, as the first year of the new decade kicked in, Cohen had no recording sessions lined up, no promotional duties to fulfil and no pressing book deadlines to meet.

He did, however, undertake a mid-sized tour that began in October 1980, performing his last American concerts for five years as part of the *Bread And Roses* festival in Berkeley at the prestigious open air Greek Theatre on October 3 and 5. He then flew to Europe to perform for a stalwart audience spread over 29 concerts in France, Switzerland, Belgium, Holland, Austria, Germany, Spain, and Israel. The musicians on board were the same as the previous tour with the exception of Jennifer Warnes who was now concentrating on a solo career.

Although his own career was no longer in ascent, Cohen was far from starving. After this latest tour he could actually afford not to work for a while. While his record sales had tapered off the albums themselves were not particularly expensive to make so with all such deductions having now been paid off it's likely he was receiving royalty payments from the earlier releases by now. In addition he received income from sales of his books, many of which had been translated into a several different languages and gone into second and third editions. There were modest tour profits that he had no doubt put aside, bolstered by the occasional fees he would have received for allowing his concerts to be broadcast on television and radio. His main source of income was from songwriting and the publishing monies they generated, particularly the more popular cover versions of his songs which were played on radio much more frequently than his own versions. Agonisingly, he still did not receive publishing royalties for 'Suzanne' or the other two songs hi-jacked by Jeff Chase back in the Sixties. He had worked hard during the last 20 years and in the last decade such efforts had begun to pay off financially. He still in part provided financially for Suzanne Elrod and their children but, nevertheless, by the early Eighties, Cohen found himself modestly and temporarily comfortable in financial terms. This allowed him to pursue less financially motivated disciplines.

His restlessness continued to manifest as he moved from Hydra to Montreal to LA. He was alone and in company; spending quality time with Roshi and catching up with friends and old colleagues the world over as well as seeing his children Adam and Lorca when time, their mother and circumstance allowed.

In the winter of 1981 and 1982, he began another collaboration, Night Magic, co -writing with one time Lissauer collaborator and fellow Canadian Lewis Furey. Initially Cohen supplied words – a libretto – to Furey's music, an opera score, although Cohen preferred to think of the piece as a ballet. "It's not a rock opera... It's not even an opera. It's... something else," he offered helpfully at the time. "It will involve a corps de ballet, three principal players, backup singers. It's going to be highly choreographed. It's designed to be done on video tape – maybe a stage production later in Montreal or New York... Yes, we hope to do it later in New York." The project was completed and then filmed, directed by Furey himself. It would be carefully edited and dubbed over the next couple of years, aiming for the form of a film that Cohen ultimately hoped would combine the aesthetics of 'Brecht and Disney'.

Cohen's romantic life continued apace. Around this time he became involved in a relationship with Dominique Issermann, a Paris based French photographer. Issermann and her staunch work ethic had a bootstrapping effect on her new lover; and as a consequence he revaluated his attitude toward his work and how he *worked* at his work. He upped his effort, his discipline and the seriousness in which he approached his song writing. At the same time all of these processes were, oddly, expanded and heightened by something widely regarded as a novelty or a toy, a cheap Casio keyboard that Cohen had happened upon and become smitten with. In tandem with his continued studies of the Talmud, his ongoing Buddhist meditation and Issermann's influence, the Casio keyboard would revolutionise his writing.

The collaborative experience with Furey had also stoked an interest in film. In the spring of 1983 Cohen instigated yet another cinematic project – the filming of a series of short videos set to a handful of his songs all linked together as one 30-minute film entitled *I Am A Hotel*. Finance for the project was soon found and filming took place over six days that April, with some scenes featuring Cohen (as 'the resident') perched smoking in a flimsy hotel room miming along to newly recorded versions of 'Suzanne' and 'The Guests' among others. Cohen did not particularly enjoy the experience or the initial edit, but it was at least another new idea in yet another medium that was realised with considerable panache and professionalism. *I Am A Hotel* would air on Canadian TV almost a year later going on to win the Golden Rose award at the 24th International Montreux Television Festival.

By now Cohen's song writing muscle was twitching back to life. While the commercial response and the reaction of his own record company may have been indifferent to Cohen's albums during this period, during the early to mid-Eighties, despite the dabbling in film, libretti and his ongoing work in literature, he would nevertheless write and record some of the most memorable songs of his career.

While Cohen moved between the axis of Hydra, Montreal and Paris, between his children and Issermann, from the coffee cup to the cigarette, and to the notebook and guitar, those associated with him and his past work were getting on with their own careers and lives the world over. "I hadn't heard from Leonard for years," recalls John Lissaeur. "And it was 1983 before I heard from him again."

If times had been tough professionally for Cohen since he and the arranger/producer had last worked together, then they had been even more testing for Lissaeur. While he was never short of work, his experiences with the sharp business end of the music industry, as typified in the extreme by Marty Machat, had shaken his confidence and left him bruised. "Since *Songs for Rebecca*, I'd been busy in the meantime, recording Barbra Streisand, Manhattan Transfer, and I did a great album with a guy called Tony Bird which was like [Paul Simon's] *Graceland* before *Graceland*... And I'd been doing film scores... but the record business had been getting painful for me. I couldn't collect royalties... I seemed to be getting screwed left and right. It wasn't rewarding. I'd assumed I'd get paid for the good work I was doing but that wasn't the case. I had to sue for everything and still couldn't get it... and then I got the reputation as being the guy 'who does those art albums', you know, 'We're not making money from him'. And then disco hit and I wanted nothing to do with *that* so I stopped doing albums or at least slowed down. I'd gotten into films and doing music for television. Things changed."

Lissauer had put serious time and effort without payment or

compensation into the writing and recording of the aborted *Songs For Rebecca*. And yet when the project was pulled from under him by Marty Machat, in order to clear the way for Cohen to work with Spector, Lissauer was not even offered an explanation, neither by Machat nor Cohen. Unable to reach Cohen, Lissaeur had instead resolved to forget about the unhappy situation and had simply gotten on with his life. Still, insult was added to injury when elements of the tracks he had worked on with Cohen for the ...*Rebecca* project manifested themselves in the Lewy produced *Recent Songs* album. Lissauer was credited for a song writing contribution and for his piano and arrangement part on one track. Other versions of some of the ...*Rebecca* songs had also turned up on *Death Of A Ladies Man* (although only lyrics remained) but it was hardly surprising that Lissaeur did not even receive a 'thank you' on that album (even though the local liqueur store and pizzeria were credited). Despite all this the freelance producer/arranger, who was now in his early thirties and still living in New York, did not hold any grudges against Cohen whatsoever.

"Leonard and I had never had a problem," he says, having neither seen nor heard from Cohen since early 1978. "Time just passed and he was mainly in LA, Greece or Montreal and not New York but then I got that phone call out of the blue. I had just gotten remarried and I was in my house and when I picked up the phone I knew it was Leonard before he even spoke because of the sound of the breath he took. And he said 'John? Is it time for us to get back to work'?"

Cohen made no reference in the phone call to past events or to what he'd been doing since the last time he and Lissauer and been in a room together. This didn't seem to faze the producer even slightly. "You know, we both liked the camaraderie that came through hard work, the rolling up of the sleeves and the getting on with it."

Which is exactly what the two now planned to do. Cohen was ready to record again and he wanted Lissauer to produce and arrange. Although he had become jaded by the idea of making 'pop' records generally, Lissaeur considered Cohen an exception to the rule in more than artistic terms. He was also a forgiving friend. "Leonard was great at making artistic decisions but not business ones." The producer argues, "That's why he had Marty and Marty had been very successful at that.

As a consequence Leonard had a fine old life and he didn't want to rock the boat as far as Marty went. But I think in this case he had already said, 'Marty, we're doing another record with John', because it was clear from when he called me that it was on. We didn't have to demo tracks or present anything. We just got to it."

It had been 1979 since Cohen had last done any serious recording and he was eager to get back to the studio. During that first phone call, he told Lissauer he would be in New York the following week. "Let's meet up and I'll play you the songs," said Leonard. The producer continues: "So we met at the Royalton on 44th Street which was one of his favourite hotels in New York." The Royalton dated from 1898, was of Gothic design and renowned for its massive mahogany 'Round Bar', elements that would have obviously appealed to Cohen's taste. Lissauer wasn't expecting much in the way of a revelation when seeing Cohen again after so long. But surprisingly, he *was* surprised. "We went to his room and I was slightly taken aback to see that instead of presenting me with the new songs exclusively on a Spanish guitar as usual, he had this dinky little Casio keyboard with him." Such equipment was considered by serious musicians at the time as being closer to a toy rather than an actual instrument. Yet for Cohen, the portable keyboard would become as much a travelling companion as his Peter Jackson brand of cigarettes, notebook and copy of the Talmud.

Cohen, as his co-writing collaborations with Lissauer and then Spector had shown, had evidently become dissatisfied with the limits of writing alone on a guitar. And although he'd learnt the basics of piano playing as a child he'd made no serious effort to reacquaint himself with the instrument. Perversely, he had found his ideal musical collaborator – and the breakthrough in his writing that he'd been looking for – via something commonly found in a toyshop. "The Casio was a great discovery for Leonard because these machines allowed you to put one finger down and have a whole band come back at you," explains Lissaeur. "I mean I had a $35,000 Synclavier in the studio at the time and what Leonard had was kind of the (much) cheaper, more portable version of that. It was a 49-note keyboard instead of the standard 66, very small and must have cost about $99 on Broadway. And he'd be playing it on the bed with this insane boyish grin – he has the most infectious grin – and the keyboard would be playing 'ding ding ding ding'... All these miniature syncopated rhythms, bass and drum patterns... and this is how he came up with 'Dance Me To End Of The Love'."

Cohen had never really evolved his guitar technique, as singular and accomplished in itself as it was. And unlike many musicians, Cohen had little interest in technology beyond what it could do for him in terms of writing. The guitar was a basic tool for him as the typewriter or pen. Perhaps the same could be said for his singing voice. For whatever reason Cohen never took singing or guitar lessons (after the initial three flamenco lessons he'd received as a teenager) and never showed any conscious will to develop his musical 'chops' further than whatever progressions came naturally. At the same time he very consciously did want to expand his own musical vocabulary and the Casio was a readymade remedy for his own musical shortcomings.

Lissauer: "See he couldn't really play guitar in a strict chopping rhythm style, that wasn't his thing. So this little keyboard with its built in drum machine and bass parts which played fast and slow and was totally different to his style of European guitar playing... it helped him approach song writing in a totally different way. This was a joyous discovery for him. He was like a little boy in FOA Schwartz."

With producer and poet ensconced in the classically styled New York hotel room, Lissaeur would record Cohen's 'hotel versions' of his new Casio (and guitar, Cohen still also wrote on his first instrument) songs on a portable Sony Walkman, take them home and learn them by ear. "I'd write charts out based on these recordings," he says, "map out the structure and have charts with suggestions of instruments that maybe he hadn't heard, after all he was hearing these things on the Casio or a guitar."

Lissauer didn't consider Cohen's renditions definitive at this juncture. "I would say he was playing me kernels of songs at this stage and I would help him elaborate on them going as far as altering the chords and tailoring them. He might say, 'Oh what can we do with this, it sounds too ordinary, come up with a 'John chord'."

The two worked together as if they had last seen each other only last week and Lissauer adopted a professional and gentlemanly attitude in not asking for an explanation regarding their last work together. "*Rebecca* wasn't mentioned," he says, "not once... not a single reference to it, not a 'Geez man sorry about that' or 'Whatever happened to...' And if I'd been tempted to mention it I would have. But it was non-issue at that point. It would have only made him uncomfortable and there would have been nothing to be gained from that. The last thing I wanted to do was put an artist of Leonard's integrity in a corner or make him defensive or explain himself. And I always felt it was down to Marty anyway not Leonard. I guess us not mentioning *Rebecca* was admirable on both our parts."

Unlike during the production of *Rebecca*, Cohen did not ask specifically for his producer's direct musical contribution as far as the writing of the songs went. The essence of the pieces was already there but once again Lissaeur made a definite contribution. The collaboration was as discreet as the men involved. "It was the first time we'd worked that way, where I would help with chord changes... including a new song called 'Hallelujah'... just making the chords less simple and more evocative. Moving the songs along... because of our previous collaboration he was much more open to musical additions and changes."

Lissaeur would neither ask for nor receive any song writing credit on the album. Other than this tweaking and fine tuning by the producer, there were no other preliminary sessions, demoing or pre-production activities. The *Rebecca* songs had been taken on the road, tested, refined and forged before they were taken into the studio but on this project, Cohen and Lissaeur went straight from the hotel room to the studio. "I never had to present a budget," states the producer. "We never knew what would be exactly required and anyway I wasn't known for big budget albums." Unbeknown to the producer, this trait was actually something Marty Machat admired in Lissaeur. "My dad liked John," remembers Steven Machat. "He liked any producer that brought Leonard's records in on time and under budget." Unlike some major label albums being made in New York during the early 1980s, the new Cohen album was recorded under relatively Spartan and austere conditions. "We didn't have a limousine budget or a coke budget," laughs Lissaeur. "We simply did a few takes of things and then moved on to the next song."

Once the choice of songs to be recorded had been decided on, a group of core musicians was assembled. "There was a band I'd used on Loudon Wainwright's album," says Lissaeur, "a group called Slow Train, and the five of us went straight into the studio." Marty's only stipulation had been that Lissaeur use an 'affordable' studio and so he booked the project into NYC's Quad recording complex. "It was above one of the great strip clubs of New York, The Metropole Go-Go on 49th and Broadway. We were on the 14th floor. They were really enamoured of Leonard at Quad and I had brought some other projects there previously and we had a great relationship going so they gave us a good deal."

With Leanne Ungar engineering once more, sessions began in the late summer of '83. Cohen had been inspired by the new and complex technology he'd acquired in his inexpensive Casio and consequently Lissauer was aware that this album would rely on less 'traditional' or classical elements than previous Cohen albums. The work would also sound less ethnic. "We had various keyboards that I'd collected over the years and a very nice piano that I wanted," explains the producer, "and in the studio we would set up live and we would all just run through the songs, following the charts I'd done. Leonard was there throughout, singing along and playing guitar. We wouldn't end up using his parts at this stage it was just for the vibe. He always wanted to concentrate on his vocals and we'd take great care to record them later and separately."

The basis of three tracks was recorded on the very first day. This was a notably quick approach in an era when groups who expected to reach the higher echelons of the charts might take days just to set a drum sound in the studio. "When the song is fresh is when you get the best ideas," reckons the producer. "When you work them to death it makes 'em stale. You don't want to overpower them. Perfecting inspiration is an interesting concept. If you do that it can become fussy and you end up micro managing the details… I like to get an artistic, vulnerable and expressionistic performance."

Lissaeur noted little change in Cohen personality wise but did pick up on one important development: his voice had dropped 'a minor third'. Thus, *Various Positions*, as the album would become known, marked the birth of Cohen's 'new' voice. Until now Cohen's singing had reached for a mid-range plateau within his songs, and occasionally on the new album, still would. But in the main, from now on Cohen would sing from the gut, at a walking pace that both came and sounded natural. It was the voice of someone who had been tried and was tired. It was the sound of Lee Marvin crooning Baudelaire. The other previously noted development was that Cohen was now utterly besotted with 'new technology' as represented by his dinky home keyboard. It wasn't even as if he wanted the 'higher', more expensive version of the machinery that the domestic keyboard represented. Cohen would actually prefer to use the basic home model he was writing on in the studio. "I wasn't so keen on synthetic sounds," says Lissaeur, "but he was liking it, the drum machine that came with the keyboard in particular, so much. 'This is so good, yea, yea,' he'd tell me... he loved it and I would have liked to have used it less but it was effective so we had it on and it didn't hurt anything. On 'Dance Me To The End Of Love' we actually used the very keyboard that he'd written that song on. It didn't even have an audio output so we had to mike it up. We tried to do that song with real drums and percussion but he liked the simplicity of the Casio and had become accustomed to it. So after trying it other ways we went back to it and tried to make it work and added a lot of things over the top of it. But still, we ended up back there, with just that basic bass and drum sound from the Casio. That's what you're hearing on the record."

The musical key on this version sounds too high for Cohen's natural pitching (it would be lowered in its live incarnation) and has the effect of making him sound close to strained and desperate but this was not particularly a conscious or stylistic choice. Recalls Lissaeur: "That was just the key that the song was written in, on that Casio keyboard, literally the key his finger had hit. If we'd had to change that we'd have had to change all kinds of stuff. It was what it was because of the situation it was written in. We kind of underdid it. It could have been huge but we did it very calmly, didn't try to make it massive...to me it was a little art piece..."

In retrospect, sonically the album could be seen as Cohen in transition. He'd taken the previous blueprint of C&W music with heavily poetical lyrics as far as he could and the public would accept. This new album was reaching toward new production techniques and arrangements that were very obviously of their time but that with hindsight would not sound convincingly like either old or new Cohen. *Various Positions* could arguably – if harshly – be perceived as a demo version for the next Cohen album, a work on which he would finally refine and perfect the new edition of himself. Yet while Lissaeur's production occasionally sounded incomplete or unrealised, it did contain powerful versions of some of Cohen's greatest songs. "'Hallelujah' took two years," Cohen said. "Hank Williams wrote 'Your Cheating Heart' in 20 minutes."

Lissauer was there when Cohen presented – in the rawest form – what would ultimately become this most beloved and worthy song. "He wrote that on guitar and that's how he played it to me in the hotel. Remember that not all songwriters are necessarily accomplished musicians. Even Irving Berlin could only play piano in one key and had to have a lever built into to change key… he could hardly play but he was able to come up with great melodies and put together the musical stuff that made great songs…' Sometimes Lissaeur's arrangement of the songs – going so far as to change the odd chord – stepped over the line of mere arrangement and into the realm of actual co-composition. "That's true but I would never get into that," he says, ever self-effacing. "I would say I'm just the arranger."

The tune that would eventually become a hymn for the 21st Century began life humbly. "'Hallelujah' did stand out the first time I heard it but it wasn't remotely like it is now. I sat down with him at the piano and started playing these deep gospel chords arrangement of it, more like the way it eventually became… heftier… it was a real guitar song, that 6/8 time thing Leonard had done a lot of… very European sounding… and I said, 'Gee, lets make this slower and more bare and stark. And I suggested a choir of people. Not a *gospel* choir but just a choir of different singers. I didn't want a black gospel feel but something more akin to a non church like choir… It was easy to get…quite simple… we wanted to use drums… big drums but playing with brushes…very strong but soft… we didn't want any power ballad stuff… and the drummer was like 'You gotta be kiddin' me… brushes? But the result was outstanding because it was forced restraint. The power comes from its starkness. I said to Leonard, 'When we hear the voice at the beginning of this its going to be "Whoaaa"' and it *was*."

But even the impressive recording of the mighty song itself did not particularly raise gooseflesh in the studio at the time. To the musicians who brought the song to life, it was just another song, just another session. "These guys were from Tulsa," says the producer by way of explanation. "They were unflappably relaxed. They were the least jive guys. They were calm country boys... mellow, unflappable."

The song also brought a new figure into his life, an important friendship that was forged during the sessions when his producer introduced a beautiful new singer and musician into the proceedings. Anjani Thomas was a 24-year-old Hawaiian, by profession a backing singer and keyboardist. "I introduced her to Leonard. She was part of the choir on 'Hallelujah'," recalls Lissaeur. "More than any other musician on the sessions, from hereon Cohen and Thomas forged a bond that would endure for decades to come. Such friendships were not a given in this business – they were an occasional and blessed perk in a way of life that was defined by musicians coming together for concentrated activities of touring and recording and then for the most part, going there separate ways again once the job had been done. But then, with their familial atmosphere, Cohen sessions were apart from the norm. The sessions were effortless, flowing. We were happy to be in one another's company," says Lissaeur. "This was about beautiful and evocative. Not about trying to please the record company or Marty. I just wanted us to do something different that stood alone. I always hated records that sounded like they were aware of trends or other records. I think if you make records that are uncompromising they have a way of hanging out for a long time."

Despite this being the most obviously contemporary sounding record Cohen had made since his debut, Lissaeur was not aware of any other particularly contemporary musical influences. "We never played each other other records," says Lissaeur. "Between the two of us that was never an issue. We would never directly reference other records. We were really pure artists and we didn't want our record to sound like any other records."

Cohen himself, meanwhile, felt at the height of his powers. "When I was making *Various Positions*, it was the first time I could really see and intuitively feel what it was I was doing, making or creating in that enterprise," he would say. "After a long period of barrenness it all just seemed to click. Suddenly, I knew these weren't discrete songs I was writing. I could see – I could sense a unity; *Various Positions* had its own life, its own narrative. It was all laid out and all of a sudden it all made sense. It was almost painfully joyful."

The sessions began to wind down. As they did so they were, as ever, on time and within a reasonable budget, and unlike many other, more high profile, albums of the era this record began and ended in the same studio. "I always mixed in the same studio and I always mix with the engineer I record with," confirmed the producer. Though the final balance, or 'mix', of the recordings is often done in different studios, sometimes with additional or new engineers, this wasn't the case with Cohen. "Leonard would be there throughout," says Lissaeur. "Generally only people who were essential would attend. No roadies, no assistants, no management, no dealers, no yes men. I never brought my wife or girlfriend to the sessions although I remember Dominique Issermann coming in a time or two but even then she was photographing stuff, videoing the sessions. She was an artist in her own right, one of the team."

Once the album had been written, recorded and mixed, Cohen would give careful thought to the sequencing of the songs, prior to the album being mastered. He did not yet own a home computer or word processor – and so resorted to writing the song titles on separate strips of paper and physically moving them around on a table top. This curiously visual approach to what ultimately could be seen as a musical decision reveals a key component of Cohen's aesthetic nature. "After four or five tries, you usually come up with something that sounds right," he confided. He would, of course, listen to the songs in order before consenting to them as such to be set in vinyl forevermore. The album would then be mixed as one whole piece before being cut to vinyl and tape. "My involvement stopped with the mastering," says Lissaeur. "And we would always master with Bob Ludwig. No matter where he was. He was the best and purest that there was. After this I had no interest in the work because from then on stuff was decided by people who I didn't understand."

Ironically, in light of what was to come, during the sessions neither label nor management showed any interest in the record while it was being made. "Their presence was zero," confirms Lissaeur. "They never came to the recordings. Marty in particular knew that I'd had it with him. He wasn't artistic at all. He had no sense of art at all other than he recognised Leonard as being something special." Cohen himself was pleased with the work. He had entered the sessions an invigorated, inspired and hungry man. He left as satisfied as he ever was. "The pulling and the putting of the pieces together coherently, the being inside of that process and knowing, once I'd done that, it would be finished and I would have to leave it and go back to the world," was a process he found "joyful".

However, the tangible result of this happy process – the actual record – would fail to arouse such a positive response among the people who actually owned it. Soon after the album had been delivered to Columbia, Marty heard back that they would not be releasing it in the world's biggest market, North America. He relayed the bad news to a shocked Cohen who decided to visit the label boss, Walter Yetnikoff, himself. For someone who avoided such confrontations at almost any cost, this was a bold move for Cohen. (Cohen was wont to avoid any sort of confrontation except the most personal and vital ones. Business matters seem to have bored him profoundly.) Cohen finally got an audience with the legendary booze guzzling and coke snorting label president in his Columbia office. Cohen would repeat the account of his meetings for years afterward: "I went to see Walter Yetnikoff. After reviewing my dark double-breasted suit, Walter said, 'Leonard, we know you're great, but we don't know if you're any good', and he turned down *Various Positions* for US distribution because it wasn't contemporary."

Despite Yetnikoff being particularly vocal to Cohen about his dislike of the actual mixes (Cohen offered to let the label boss mix the album himself) it seems the record was ultimately rejected for not being what it *was* but for what it *wasn't* – *Various Positions* was turned down for not being 'current' enough or as the singer himself put it, "Somewhere along the line, I guess, quite justifiably I was designated as a singer who was not in the mainstream."

This was exactly the kind of news that Lissaeur did not want to hear. "The mixing thing – well, remixes were coming into fashion then so maybe that was something to do with it, although I maintain that the mixes were haunting," says the producer in his defence. "I couldn't even imagine how these meetings went… we weren't making records to sell records or to please the record company. We didn't even use compression! These record company guys were just lawyers. They had nothing to do with music, they were lawyers running art. We wanted something that would last, we didn't want to cheapen material. Subsequently this would get me a reputation within the record business as being difficult."

Cohen himself was not seen as being at all difficult. Worse, he was seen by some as simply irrelevant.

By the mid Eighties other artists of roughly the same generation were also going through commercial troughs. The once untouchable Dylan was widely deemed to have 'lost it'. Cohen, who for some years had counted Dylan as an occasional friend, defended him passionately. "Dylan, to my way of thinking, is the Picasso of song," he would say at the time. (Cohen, by comparison, may be seen as Matisse). "People came to me when he put out his Christian record and said 'This guy is finished, he can't speak to us anymore'. When you're talking about a man like Dylan you can never write him off. I would never write off a writer like Norman Mailer or a singer like Dylan or Ray Charles. Those people are always gonna come up with something beautiful."

Cohen left his record label's building having been unable to convince them to release his record. Never one to punish himself over business matters, he turned the problem over to the ever faithful Marty Machat and made a continued effort to look on the bright side, later acknowledging that, "I didn't find it depressing that I wasn't selling records. They were selling sufficiently so that I could take care of my needs, send my kids to school, pay the bills. I was able to satisfy my dictum that I set myself: to be paid for my work, but not to work for pay."

The record's producer was less philosophical and more openly disappointed. "It took so long for the record to come out, I was like 'What the hell happened?'" Lissaeur would bemoan. "They said it wasn't commercial enough. Well, one of those songs ['Hallelujah'] would go onto be one of the most recorded songs of its time and they said – of that song in particular – that it wasn't relevant. When they first heard 'Hallelujah', Columbia said 'What is this?' They didn't know how to market it, it wasn't Springsteen or even Kenny Rogers or Dolly Parton… it was just another art album. And Yetnikoff had not been involved in the signing of

Leonard, remember – he had inherited him. When they wouldn't release it I thought, 'That's it, I've had it with the record business. This record is so good that if people can't hear that… and if I'm wrong, if I think a record this good and its not deemed releasable then… I have no right to make records and I should just do films and television. And that's what I did. *Various Positions* marked the end of my desire to make records."

Unlike his disillusioned collaborator, deprived of a musical release, Cohen at least had another book in the wings. Having found himself "frozen" and with "his back against the wall" prior to the *Various Positions* sessions, he'd attempted to write his way out of his depression via a collection of Psalms that would be published under the title *The Book Of Mercy*. As *Various Positions* languishes in limbo his 'book of prayer' was published by McClelland & Stewart in April 1984. The cover bore a new symbol designed by Cohen himself – a 'coat of arms', that he called the 'unified heart'. The symbol used the 'transcendent star of David' as the blueprint and was, as Cohen saw it, "A version of the ying and yang or any of those symbols that incorporate the polarities… and try and reconcile the differences." Critical reception to the book, what there was of it, was puzzlement and confused Cohen's image further. It did however go on to win yet another award for its author, claiming the Canadian Author's Association Literature prize for Lyrical Poetry in July of 1985.

While Lissauer threw himself into film and TV work, Cohen attempted to record the psalms with Henry Lewy in a Hollywood studio. Reciting the words over a string quartet arrangement, this was Cohen's most explicit attempt yet at marrying pure words with pure music. Although he was often thought to simply be a poet who put his poems to music, Cohen was actually and technically a songwriter. Cohen did not see the lyrics to his songs as merely poems set to music, as he explained: "If you would set a poem to music you would definitely change something. The meaning may be intensified or changed but there would be a modification." He used the specific example of the Lord's Prayer, which had occasionally been set to music over the years. "Music defines it much more specifically… when you read it as a prayer it's really much more quiet, a whisper to the heart… in music its more majestic, wide…" Depressingly, these sessions were abandoned before completion.

That autumn, in September 1984 Cohen turned 50. Considered a landmark age by many, it meant little to Cohen. "[It was] just another day," he reckoned. "I don't think things radically change. We change by imperceptible degrees..." Meanwhile Marty had been shopping the unwanted album around and *Various Positions* was finally released in January 1985, well over a year after it had been completed. Columbia, who did not deem it worthy of release in North America, permitted Marty to license it to Passport Records, a minor independent label. Cohen was stoic in his acceptance of this demotion. "Sometimes they're hospitable to innovation and excellence and sometimes they're not. The music business is not terribly hospitable to innovation and excellence at the moment. It's the icy grip of the dollar right now."

To be fair to Yetnikoff, for an artist whose latest records had definitely not been doing the business, 'Dance Me To The End Of Love' was an off putting opener to the album. Swamped in reverb and augmented by female voices, the use of the Casio keyboard is startling in its baldness. It sounds electric rather than electronic, novelty noir rather than Kraftwerk cool, tacky rather than touching. Combined with the straining key in which Cohen sings, the fact that the song comes across at all is testament to its strength but it succeeds despite its production and not because of it. Cohen has said that the inspiration for the song was taken from a photograph of inmates in a World War II Nazi concentration camp but Lissauer disputes that Cohen would ever talk directly about the meaning behind his lyrics. "He would never talk about the meaning of his songs. If someone gets pushy he'll make some absurd thing up to put 'em off but in my experience he never talks about the inspiration or true meaning."

'Coming Back To You' is the first track of the album to successfully mix the Casio with live (and heavily gated) drums. It also introduces the 'new' Cohen voice, gravellier and truer sounding in this low register. This was a deliberate act of sequencing. Lissauer: "Next to 'Dance Me To The End Of Love', his pitching here is more comfortable and as a consequence it makes the song sound much more impressive and commanding."

'The Law' was more successful again, abandoning completely the familiar country traits and once more mixing electronic bass and drums with Cohen's voice, locking them into a groove that recalls Serge Gainsbourg's parallel work of the time. Lissauer: "The 'reggae' thing on the bass and groove came from me... I wanted to move it along, take it away from its folksy origin, add some spirit, contemporise it... inject a little edge into it."

'Night Comes On' in particular recalled the snowy chord progressions of the still estranged (publishing wise) 'Suzanne', and if the themes, structures and actual songs themselves sounded instantly familiar in some cases, their author did not see this as any great sign of weakness or deficiency. "Any writer really has only one or two songs and they are elaborated on over the years," said. The song seemed to be about his departed mother but again, the producer knew as little as anyone. Whilst confident enough to contribute musically, he kept out of the lyrical side of the process. "I would never question Leonard about his lyrics. I mean this guy was the greatest poet I had or ever will work with. I was amazed at the words and never second guessed them; just took them at face value. I would notice the tiny changes he'd make, the difference between a 'the' and a 'an'... but I would never suggest, 'Hey we should repeat that line in the first verse because that's the hook' ... never."

The obvious majesty of 'Hallelujah' was somewhat stifled, marred by the overuse of reverb and misjudged synthesiser, but shone through nevertheless. The recorded version was only a partial representation of a song whose original verses numbered double figures. On writing such long songs, Cohen explained that, "I have this writing method that involves a lot of blackened pages because I can't throw out a verse until I finish it... to the best of my capacity... because that's when you go behind the slogan, the easy solution..."

'If It Be Your Will' was the closest relative to the psalms in *Book Of Mercy*, and as such "needed a haunting and rich treatment. It was hymn like," opines the producer. And in comparison to the almost dry and brittle up close and in your face sound of *New Skin* this album was literally dripping in reverb. "His voice was so low and rich by now compared to when I had last worked with him. It didn't work 'dry'. These songs have a presence and we experimented to bring out that, to make them sound commanding. They were on a new level compared to the *New Skin* album *Various Positions* was more sombre, religious if you like… it was a darker thing and I went with it."

The rest of the album did not deviate far beyond this description and for its aural shortcomings it did at least did sound cohesive. Although CBS had not taken up the North American option on the album they released it in the rest of the world where it did as well as ever in the hottest and coldest of places, going top ten in both Scandinavia and Spain. Only the most faithful bought it in the UK where it sold respectably if sparsely. Its release in America on Passport Records – a moniker that Cohen may have taken as being somewhat ironic – confirmed CBS's gloomy predictions and it sold poorly. Cohen was by now almost completely perceived by the public as the princely poet of gloom; a living cliché – the old hippie guy failed by the Sixties who nevertheless insisted on crashing the party and bringing down everybody's buzz while doing so. Cohen acknowledged this image problem bravely but obviously felt up against the wall in this regard. In his defence he reminded the public that he was not the world's first introspective, 'moody' artist. "There's a whole tradition of music that comes from a place that is not a joke," he offered, somewhat clumsily. "I like comedians and films that are funny… it's not that I don't appreciate a good joke… but somehow the tradition I'm in comes from another place. It's not a more valuable place or a less valuable place, it's just a different place. I think a lot of my songs are more light hearted than people consider them to be."

Cohen had actually admitted to sometimes "indulging himself in a melancholy high", a strangely perverse addiction that in the coming years he would fight hard to kick. He has also revealed that when writing he would play the guitar and actually attempt to make himself cry. "I don't weep copiously but I might find a little catch in my throat… then I know I'm in contact with something that's a little deeper than when I started." There was perhaps some self suggestion at work here or even the resurfacing of the hypnotist's skills which he claimed to have lost as a youth. Like many people Cohen did not feel the need to define himself in such crass terms as 'pessimist' or 'optimist'. "I've never examined whether I'm an optimist or a pessimist. There are some things I expect the worst of and there are some things I expect the best of and they are often the same things." Cohen even considered such a stance as a 'luxury'. "Things come at me faster than I can possibly develop attitudes for," he explained. He would defend his songs against the predictable and recurring accusations of being 'miserablist', quoting from letters he has received from those who found great comfort in listening 'again and again' to these songs. "Perhaps the songs have a form and a mood that is melancholy," he admitted, 'but they are not meant to depress. On the contrary they can have an opposite effect. A healing effect."

The album's release did not provide Lissaeur with any sense of redemption. In fact it only compounded his predicament in an industry that he was doing his best to put behind him. "Marty, also, never paid me. Not a cent. He told me, 'By the way, you're not gonna' get any royalties until the cost of Leonard's videos are recouped.' And they had cost $400,000. I told him that this wasn't what I and Leonard had agreed and he said. 'Well that's the new trend, so take it or leave it kid.' And I did these albums without a contract, just based on a handshake with Leonard. And by this time Leonard has disappeared so Marty would say 'I don't care what you agreed with Leonard.' Marty would have done anything for Leonard but Marty was not to be trusted if you were anyone else." At least the promo video from the album – Cohen's first – was one of the best things to come out of the project. Beautifully directed by Isserman, it featured a dapper Cohen roaming a mental institute in beguiling sepia tones. Had it been shown it would have been one of the classiest things on MTV at the time.

Once again, the record needed to be promoted and 1985 saw lengthier touring, albeit with Cohen's smallest band of musicians since 1974. This was probably down to financial constraints. Since Yetkinoff had refused to release his latest album, no tour support from Columbia in North America would have been forthcoming. Consequently the Cohen Carney would have had to make many dates, specifically the American ones, pay for themselves. From January through July, Cohen clocked in 77 concerts in five separate tours, encompassing Europe (twice), North America (twice) and Australia.

Among the new personnel on the road was the musician introduced to Cohen at the *Various Positions* sessions, Anjani Thomas. Whilst rehearsing Cohen's songs, Thomas considered some of the chord structures – mostly simple but highly effective progressions of majors and minors – a little basic. "She felt she should educate me to the real meaning of music," remembered Cohen. Anjani's opinion of her boss was that, "He's never had formal training – he's a singer songwriter, not a player. I'll play what he wants but doesn't know how to ask for." Cohen freely admitted that he had a long standing problem finding his pitch when singing and the plainer the chord shapes that accompanied him, the better. "I just needed a triad," he stated, instructing Anjani to keep it simple. Anjani however, pushed him, achieving a pyrrhic victory of sorts. "I was so sure the major 7, the suspended 4th, the augmented… were better choices," she remembered. But Cohen not only wanted simplicity he *needed* it. There was some friction because of this. "It didn't go smoothly," says Cohen who eventually gave up and accepted his keyboard player's elaborated shapes. The situation would at least birth to 'Jazz Police', one of his most surreal and throwaway songs several years later.

On May 17, Furey and Cohen's collaboration Night Magic (with its tagline, 'Money, success, women and love… everything he's always wanted in one magic night'!) was premiered in Cannes. The audience response was middling and the film did not go on to enjoy even a healthy life on VHS but the soundtrack album, released in France, did at least win Cohen and Furey a Juno award for best 'Rock Opera' score. Outside Canada, Cohen felt most warmly appreciated in Europe and, by contrast, now rather dramatically considered his audience in North America to have 'evaporated'. In real terms, this was not quite true, particularly the 'live' market. Cohen would sell out New York's Carnegie Hall on his next trip there on May 5. His commercial decline was hardly comparable to even Sinatra's dramatic fall from grace in the late Fifties. Or was Cohen doing himself a disservice by comparing himself to other rock acts? His niche was closer to that of country artists like George Jones – important, respected artists who while rarely being in fashion or on MTV nevertheless had a claim upon the hearts of many, including the much put-upon John Lissauer: "Leonard is an artist and as such he can't be changing what he does to fit into the trend 'cos if you do then you're at least a year and a half behind your decision anyway. So I never understood why someone like Yetkinoff would turn around and presume to know what was real music in the midst of a middle room. He clearly did not."

The latest Army backing Cohen on tour consisted of the *Various Positions* players, Richard Crooks, John Crowder, Ron Getman (switching from harmonica to guitars), Ajani Thomas (doubling up on keyboards) and Mitch Watkins, a veteran of Cohen's 1979 and 1980 tours. The world's second biggest music market, Japan, would still not get a look in on this tour but other virgin territories were breached, with first time forays into Italy and Poland. The latter's March visit held a particular emotional resonance for Cohen. Indeed, Lithuania, where his mother had been born, had once been part of Poland. Cohen described the visit as 'alarming and touching'. This was for two reasons. "There had been a very large Jewish community there," explained the singer, "of three million who were destroyed in a couple of years during the war. So as a Jew I was curious, because there was a lot of cooperation to be able to do away with that many people." He was also aware of the countries current struggle, identifying with the Solidarity movement's protest against the Communist Government.

He was well received in Poland, again seeming to fulfil some sort of symbolic role for the oppressed citizens there. "I had no idea I had any place in the Polish culture at all," he would admit, sounding humbled. "But it was kind of alarming to find the crowds there and the kind of attention that I got there." This was in part down to the Polish singer/songwriter and disc jockey, Maciej Zembaty who since accidently finding a copy of Cohen's album in a film directors flat in 1972, had taken it upon himself to singlehandedly translate, record and introduce Cohen's songs to the Polish public. Many authors, song publishers and songwriters would have paid handsomely for such promotion but the particular quality of Cohen's work seemed to instil such devotion anyway. The Polish version of 'The Partisan' (not actually written by Cohen of course), became "… one of the informal anthems of Solidarity. It was sung in prisons, in detention camps, everywhere," says Maciej, who had met Cohen briefly on a stopover at Warsaw airport in 1981 and was of course profoundly excited and moved that the singer was finally coming to his country. "Leonard was the first well-known artist who came to Poland," he remembers. "It helped us very much. We had lunch together, and I asked him to accept an invitation to a party for the Polish democratic opposition. He accepted, and we had a wonderful meeting at the Canadian embassy."

More practically, Cohen's trip to Poland was due to the efforts of Polish promoter Andy Marzec. "I've always been a great fan of Leonard Cohen who was very popular among Polish students and young intelligentsia," he says. "Cohen's songs, ballads and poetry I'd been hearing on Polish Radio and I bought his albums whenever abroad. I still have his entire discography." Oddly Marzec had not heard the supposedly popular Polish versions of Cohen's songs, "… but the original pieces are hard to beat," he says. "At the time I worked at the Polish Artist Agency and I was responsible for bringing international artists to play in Poland. Mostly we promoted shows of Eastern European and Russian artists. But once it turned out that there was a budget to invite Western and American bands I quickly suggested we start promoting popular music. To support the idea I resorted to explaining the western artist's popularity, solid repertoire and the originality of the performers. I've proposed some names that were since brought over for shows: Bo Diddley, Elton John, Tina Turner, Kraftwerk and many more. This process required diplomatic skills but there was no duress as such – rather it depended my own enthusiasm and perseverance. I had to present the idea for Cohen to the board of directors of the Polish Artists Agency for them to either approve or reject it. When the motion passed they also decided on the financial offer made to the artist for playing shows in Poland. Once we finalised the negotiations with at that time Cohen's European Agent Flemming Schmidt of DKB in Denmark, me and my team were promoting all shows within Poland. Normally it worked as a week long tour – arrival, five shows all over Poland and then departure). In case of Leonard Cohen we did four shows: Poznan, Wroclaw, Zabrze, Warszawa."

Cohen's trip, seemingly of as much political significance as it was poetic and musical, was well documented. The Polish Akademickie Radio Pomorze in Szczecin published two 60-minute cassette-tapes containing the Warsaw concert complete with English lyrics, Polish translations and even some transcriptions of comments that Cohen made to his audience during the show. The underground movement also asked Cohen to invite Lech Walesa, then leader of the Solidarity movement, to the Warsaw concert. This would have had the effect of publicly aligning

Cohen with the movement and challenging the Government which had Walesa under 'town confinement' in the northern city of Gdansk. "I was totally unequipped for the kind of pressures that were put upon me," he explained months later. Although on one level Cohen's natural inclination was to agree to such a request, (and in doing so publicly embarrass the Government that had allowed him to play there), his band, whom Cohen was ultimately responsible for convinced him to decline. "Some of the guys in the band drew me aside," explained Cohen, "and said 'You know Leonard, we don't know what weird missionary adventure you're on but we're just getting paid by the week so don't say anything that's gonna' make it difficult to leave the country. Let's play the gig and get out of town.'"

With such a violent history still palpable in the very air of the country, tension during such a controversial trip was inevitable. At one concert in the city of Wroclaw, the venue's earlier role as the site of Nazi rallies visibly disturbed Cohen but, as ever, his daring dry humour neutralised the bad vibes. Halfway through the show (a ticket to which had cost some a month's salary) he told the crowd that he considered himself "... a better singer than Hitler". This seemed to puncture the tense atmosphere. A magazine was published to coincide with Cohen's visit, a large format 16-page booklet entitled *Alleluja!* Privately printed, it contained tablature for 12 songs including 'Suzanne', 'The Guests', 'Passing Through", 'Hallelujah' and 'If It Be Your Will'. Lyrics were printed in English and Polish.

The Polish visit seemed to define Cohen as much as a 'folk hero' as 'folk singer' in a country where 40 years before so many millions of his people had been persecuted and murdered. Although always left of centre in his political views, the visit to a real life Communist state cemented his negative suspicions about such a regime. As Marzec notes: "One has to take into consideration that Poland back then was still behind the Iron Curtain, with censorship, limited freedom of expression and an establishment convinced that some music might infect its citizens with the 'bug' of freedom, causing people to get rebellious."

The shows went off without a hitch, however, and the determined promoter enjoyed the experience greatly. "I became quite popular for a while as I had to do all TV, radio, media appearances to announce shows which meant back then that I had a status of temporary celebrity... but it also opened some doors and hopefully drew some attention to the situation of Poland back then."

Professionally the trip had been a pleasure too. 'In Leonard Cohen's case it was smooth sailing because his older songs were on the playlists of Polish Radio. The shows were promoting *Various Positions* and its biggest hit 'Dance Me To The End Of Love' which was very commercial, had a great video – what more could you ask for?" Lissauer confirms that, "That song was very successful. It was infectious, people really loved it, in Canada especially I remember."

Marzec found every aspect of the venture rewarding: "On a personal level it was also an amazing adventure as I got to spend a week with a man whom I admired, whose music I enjoyed. Some tried to put those shows into a political context but Leonard was extremely diplomatic about it and avoided being dragged in. The message he wanted to get across he shared from the stage. I never suffered any bad consequences though some were hoping I would for inviting the 'voice of freedom' to Communist Poland."

Ironically, as a promoter Marzec had a fear of the shows doing too well in advance. "I was worried about the tickets selling as immediately as they did because it meant being under pressure to 'get a ticket for someone at the last minute'. Having known the work of Leonard Cohen I knew he had to be a man of perfect manners and believed he would quite understand in case of any possible difficulties. It turned out that the entire touring party was a team of great people, interested in a new country, surprised by hospitality and warm welcome of audiences well acquainted with Cohen's music."

Cohen himself reckoned that, "People are really suffering under that regime... anyone who's ever seen a Communist government or ever felt it for a moment or seen its public presence... I hate it'. Cohen's unofficial Polish translator, Marzec mirrored his hero's sentiment. In fact he used it to defend Cohen's ''depressive effect' when he pointed out all too seriously that, "In Eastern Europe we are so depressed, Leonard Cohen doesn't bother us."

By sheer contrast, in the spring of 1985 Cohen found himself in Australia for the second time, warmly welcomed by the weather, the public and the media. He was by now comfortably introduced on TV show hosts as 'a living legend'. Walking onto *The Midday Show* to the strain of Monty Python's 'Always Look On The Bright Side Of Life' in May, Cohen appeared remarkably youthful, particularly in profile and silhouette. Although his voice was entrenched in its third, Lee Marvin-esque phase, physically he still bore a striking resemblance to the young poet of Montreal and Hydra 25 years ago. Such interviews, with their predictable questions about Bob Dylan ("I've rejoiced in his genius over the years," responded Cohen to one Australian host), Greenwich Village and Janis Joplin showed that although Cohen was revered and respected he was still seen, ultimately, as a 'survivor' of the Sixties. If such a perception was noticed by Cohen then he was far too courtly to express frustration at it, at least publicly. In fact he still seemed genuinely touched and appreciative that his work was being shown such interest. Australia was like every other country, other than the USA, in that it welcomed Cohen almost as one of its own. This was another of Cohen's ingrained talents – he was a natural, genuine 'world citizen', the kind of guy who could travel anywhere and give the impression that he had relatives in that country. One host put it to him that being Canadian he shared 'British stock' with Australians. "We studied the same things at school," he agreed. "We looked at the map of the British Empire and we were both red." Being Canadian also lent him natural currency in France and America and even Britain but with other countries it was harder to define the exact source of affinity.

To those with an interest in such stuff, it was public knowledge that Cohen and band were to be supplied with superior red wine by promoters backstage at every show on this tour. This was a contractual requirement. Although seemingly incongruous compared to other rock and roll backstage demands, this was in essence the escalation of a bad habit for the singer and one that would come to a head shortly before the end of the decade. When asked if he felt comfortable in his role as a pop/rock performer, Cohen answered, "It depends on the red wine. Sometimes I feel pretty good up there." Commenting on the success of his most recent concerts he thanked the vine: "The wine has been good to us."

By the first week of May Cohen and group were in America again. It was his first appearance there since 1980. He put this absence down, in part, to the obstructive mechanics of an industry, the record business, was in effect not set up for poetry in any guise. Cohen half joked that he now felt he had to get to his American audience not via but despite his record label. For all his natural grace and manners Cohen did sound pissed off at these circumstances, righteously frustrated and angry. The American Cohen interviews of the mid-eighties reveal a middle aged man at his most browbeaten and furrowed, with more than a hint of self-loathing thrown in to taste. In the May of '85, when asked what he would put down on an imaginary application form as his official occupation he replied, apparently seriously: 'sinner'.

He chose to wind down post tour at his apartment in LA. As ever, his work still maintained a healthy life independent of its creator, the songs utilised by strangers and friends alike. After giving a series of readings of his work in New York during the early part of 1986, he got wind that a long held hope of Jennifer Warnes and Roscoe Beck had finally came to fruition. 1986 would be the year that Warnes finally recorded and released *Famous Blue Raincoat*, an entire album of her friend's songs. This was the album that she and Cohen had talked about over so many dinners so many times in the last few years. Superficially, the finished product was in a much more contemporary vein than Cohen's recent albums (and, as a result, unlike those albums, it would age less gracefully). Unlike previous collected interpretations of Cohen's albums, *Famous Blue Raincoat* was no mere tribute or homage: it was a complete stand alone album in itself that just happened to have Cohen as the sole songwriter.

The album had had a difficult birth. Although she was an established artist and this would be Warnes' sixth album, she could not initially find a major label to finance and release it. This was a direct reflection of Cohen's low commercial stock in the US and to a lesser extent of Warnes' own commercial decline since 1982's monster hit, 'Up Where We Belong', a duet with Joe Cocker that was used to memorable effect in the soundtrack of the smash hit movie *An Officer And A Gentleman*. A deal was eventually found with the obscure Private Music label; even after, or especially after, Passport Records' moribund handling of *Various Positions* this would have been some compromise, as at the time, 'independent' labels had not seriously established themselves in

America. The fruition of the project had taken at least a couple of years of concentrated effort, mainly by Warnes and Beck, and Cohen was grateful for the effort.

The choice of songs spanned the timeline of Cohen's complete career, from 1969's *Songs From A Room* to '84's *Various Positions* and beyond. Warnes even introduced early versions of 'First We Take Manhattan' (originally entitled 'In Old Berlin') and 'Ain't No Cure For Love' (albeit both with different lyrics). The choice of musicians was just as varied and interesting as the variety of material. Guest contributors included the supremely gifted and terminally hedonistic rock blues legend Stevie Ray Vaughan on lead guitar as well as respected journeymen like David Lindley and Robben Ford, keyboardist Russell Ferrante, legendary arranger Van Dyke Parks and the man himself, with Cohen duetting with Warnes on 'Joan Of Arc'.

Produced by bassist Roscoe Beck, the record was well executed in the contemporary style with lush synth pads, metronomic drum tracks and clean, clinically soulful playing pulsing slickly throughout. But while it sounded more complete than *Various Positions* it failed to evoke anything like the atmosphere or sense of time and place that was so inherent on the originals. Warnes' voice, although much admired by Cohen and a proven commercial commodity, still sounded at times like a backing vocalist pushed to the front of the mix. She sang impeccably but failed to inhabit the lyrics with any apparent meaning, new or otherwise. However, in the context of the time and the still prevalent FM radio culture that was so important in America, the album presented Cohen's songs much more palatably than his own records had for at least a decade. The record was a success, commercially, critically and also kudos-wise for Cohen. In America it did respectable business in a highly competitive market, peaking at number 72 on the *Billboard* chart, doing well in the UK and going gold in Canada. Publishing wise, Cohen reaped a sound financial reward from his catalogue's partial reincarnation. The inner sleeve and subsequent CD booklet included a cartoon by Cohen of a torch being passed with the caption, (and original album title) *Jenny Sings Lenny*. "It has revived my name in certain record company offices around the world," he admitted cheerfully. "I was really happy with that album."

It was obvious he was touched too by the gesture. Warnes had spoken to him about the possibility for years but Cohen had merely acknowledged this as 'an expression of her friendship' and nothing more. He was moved by the actual materialisation of the record and in his usual courtly manner replayed the compliment: "I think she's a very good singer and a very underrated singer... there are very few people who could match her skills in song."

Cohen kept moving. That autumn found him in Paris recording a version of 'Take This Waltz', an adaptation of a Lorca's poem set to music for an album celebrating the 50th anniversary of Lorca's murder. He then travelled to Lorca's family home in Spain's Granada region to film an accompanying video. While there he met with Lorca's sister, Isabel, and remained friendly with her till her death.

Meanwhile, back in New York, *Sincerely L. Cohen*, a musical production of his songs, appeared in a small theatre. The production was part of a series entitled 'Word/Play' which usually presented writers performing readings of their own work. If the writer himself was not available or unwilling, then semi theatrical presentations of those writings would be performed. Barbra Vann was the director of this particular event and recalls that, "Kenneth Koch, who was a friend of LC's, suggested that we invite LC to take part. At that point I knew practically nothing about him. This was back in 1983/4. So we started with his published books, *The Energy Of Slaves, Book Of Mercy,* etc. I arranged excerpts in some kind of quasi-dramatic order, interlaced with his songs. I know LC was at a rehearsal or two, and he took the fee that was offered him for his appearance at the 'reading' and used it to pay for two of his excellent musicians to accompany us. I should say that he's the only writer in 26 years of this series who has not accepted the fee for himself. The event was such a success that I continued to alter it, change it, and rearrange it through the years. We always spoke to LC about it, and he always gave us permission to use the material – only suggesting that we add one or two newer songs each time."

In that same year at the urging of his son, Adam, who was a fan of the show, Cohen guest starred on the hugely hip and popular American cop show *Miami Vice*. Cohen played the black clad François Zolan, a senior executive in Interpol. Although he appeared in only two very short sections (appearing on screen for less than a minute), speaking French moodily into a telephone receiver, Cohen's dark presence was formidable. Incongruous as this appearance may have seemed it actually marked the precise point of turnaround in Cohen's image in North America. Directed and conceived by Michael Mann, *Miami Vice* entertained only the coolest of cameos – including guest spots by such luminaries as Miles Davis, Eartha Kitt, Frankie Valli, Bianca Jagger and Frank Zappa. If in some ways, 1985 had been a relative anno horribilis for Cohen, the positive reaction to the *Sincerely L. Cohen* production and the success of Warnes' album could be seen, rightly, as snowballing signs of an impending renaissance for the poet/singer/writer.

Yet even if being asked to guest on the hippest TV show in America did signify a greater opening in the zeitgeist for Cohen, there was always some disappointment to contend with. "In truth, I had a much bigger part," Cohen would recall. "I went down there and did my first scene and the assistant director rang me up and said, 'You were really great, truly wonderful'. And I said, 'OK, thanks a lot'. Then the casting director from New York called me up and said, 'You were fantastic, truly wonderful!' And I said, 'You mean I'm fired'. And he said, 'Yeah, we're cutting all your other scenes and giving them to another guy.'"

CHAPTER NINE

...Then We Take Berlin

"If you look at my anti-war songs they are also anti peace."

LC

Cohen's tenth album *I'm Your Man* was released in February 1988. Almost immediately it was described by critics (in the usual clichéd fashion) as his "comeback" album, but for once such a labelling wasn't completely hollow. After the commercial nadirs of *Recent Songs* and *Various Positions* and the Yetnikoff/CBS debacle, Cohen finally sounded like he'd rediscovered his centre of gravity.

Recorded in LA, Paris and Montreal and written primarily on a Technics home keyboard, in almost every aspect *I'm Your Man* marked not so much a progression but an evolutionary leap forward from Cohen's other recent, under-produced and poorly promoted work. *I'm Your Man* contained archetypal Cohen songs recorded in a truly contemporary yet original – and thus ultimately classic – style. This was arguably the first time he'd managed such a synthesis since *New Skin For The Old Ceremony* but even that fine album had tilted more toward experimentation than commercialism. Cohen's new musical canvas was rich and wide, with its bold and bald use of sequencers, drum machines, synclavier and synths all mixed exotically with the lingering eastern European textures of the bouzouki, the oud, and the heart rending (old Russian school) violin. The studio group here sounded like some new weird aural template from a parallel European state: Giorgio Moroder themes reproduced by a Romanian gypsy troupe.

While it was obviously classic Cohen, it glided and throbbed unhindered by any trace of the Sixties persona by which so many still stubbornly insisted on defining him. Admittedly he didn't sound exactly 'cheery' but neither did he sound beaten, warn down or droning. The mild sense of tranquilisation prevalent on many of his albums had been replaced by a dry, sardonic wit. The foreboding sexy dude grooving and growling through instant classics like 'I Can't Forget', 'First We Take Manhattan (Then We Take Berlin)', and the title track itself sounded like the best dressed depressive in the world. Such songs sounded like instantly minted standards, as if they'd been around an age already. In effect, they had. "This record took a long time to finish," the author admitted, sounding suitably fatigued. "I rewrote it several times, I failed several times in the studio... the recordings broke down, I broke down, I forgot what the songs meant I had to rewrite a lot of them. I didn't know what I was doing... it was a difficult time. I thought I had the record finished a couple of years ago... there were lyrics I'd been working on for years and when I came to sing them in the studio, they stuck in my throat. I couldn't get behind them anymore."

The cost and struggle for conviction was obviously worth it. On the finished work there was no doubt about the conviction of Cohen's delivery. Within the previous albums his voice occasionally seemed to be struggling for its pitch and sometimes circling the lyric, melody and their meaning rather than actually nailing it. On *I'm Your Man* each consonant, vowel and word was speared straight through with conviction and nailed stone cold to the cross. The voice itself was black Gucci, its recited lyrics tailored as impeccably as the finest Armani, and if the instrumentation was mixed up from an unlikely palette of aural colours then the whole was masterfully framed and unified by Cohen's perfectly poised and expensively ravaged voice. Whereas on Warnes' *Famous Blue Raincoat* the use of synths and sequencers sounded pedestrian beneath Warnes' rather anaemic voice, here they rubbed up against Cohen's authoritative growl perfectly.

That voice was now an undeniably powerful instrument with which to confront the "greed is good" mantra that rang so profoundly through these Thatcher-Reagan years. By the mid-Eighties, the cult of the coked up yuppie was in full bloated bloom and without being explicitly political, Cohen seemed to be in full frontal attack against such values, even though he himself was by now, ironically, dressed in the finest designer suits. The lyrics, by his own definition, read like a "demented manifesto". It was as if he were now using his albums like French resistance radio. The messages were encoded, but to those who knew the score, to those who like Cohen "lived on the frontline of their own lives", the quatrains and couplets made a quixotically perfect sense. "I wanted to write a very direct lyric... a very clear melody," he stated. For all their cinematic imagery their writer explained that such songs were "the opposite of fantasy... I can tell you that they are reportage... accurate and precise descriptions of actual events and actual states of mind. I think of myself as a reporter... as a journalist..."

The album took on the Eighties using the decade's very own musical vocabulary. No way was Cohen just another '60's survivor in cowboy boots and bandanna, picking archly away at his Spanish guitar, protesting poetically against the sins of Wall Street and Reagan whilst secretly hankering after the good old days of a villain you could trust, like Nixon. His musical armoury now throbbed with sleek technology and menace and the handsome, designer-suited dude in the Ray Bans was crooning the hippest lamentations to be heard on MTV. In a sense this was always who he had been, but with this album the vision and production co- incided perfectly. Not that this was a cynical, calculated attempt on Cohen's part to court favour. He was just being true to himself. "I never set out to make an Eighties album just like I'd never set out to make a Sixties album," he said. His discontent was obviously way beyond fashion. As he'd put it as far back as 1973's *The Energy Of Slaves*: "I've had to contend with all the flabby liars of the Aquarian age."

As ever, the order of the songs on the album was of paramount importance and this was the first album where its author had to consider the CD version in his sequencing. Previously, he had considered his works and their vinyl incarnations as having two opening songs and two closing songs (one on each side). With the new CD format there

211

was one start and one finish (discounting the shuffle button). 'First We Take Manhattan' was a very conscious choice to open this new record. "It was a very calculated risk to open with '... Manhattan' because I knew that a lot of people who knew my work would be alienated by the kind of music that was there but I thought [it] is such a powerful opening statement that it sets up the character of that whole record. The definition of 'that man' [as in *I'm Your Man*] was very clear in that song."

'Ain't No Cure For Love' was a single, presumably chosen as such for its majestic AOR sound, sounding closer to Jennifer Warnes' track than anything else on the whole album. The title itself was self explanatory but Cohen would explain the song's meaning further, adding that "... nobody can sustain surrender for a very long time and nobody can stand the distance either."

'Everybody Knows', the first recording in his discography for which Cohen was credited with playing keyboards, was a metronomically devastating breaking down of every illusion in the West, co-written with sometime backing vocalist Sharon Robinson, who contributed the music. "We had actually written one song before," she recalls, "a song called 'Summertime' which we wrote in a Tel Aviv hotel lounge in 1980 whilst waiting for our bus. That had been covered by other people – Diana Ross and Roberta Flack – but 'Everybody Knows' was the first song we wrote together that Leonard recorded." At this point in her life Robinson had ceased to work as a backing singer on the road in order to raise her family and, published by Geffen Music, made her living from writing for other artistes.

"I can't recall what precipitated it," she says, "but I know I was over at Leonard's house and he gave me a bunch of lyrics there. I took them home and developed a couple of versions that I thought would work." Robinson was not particularly intimidated by the sheer levity of the lyric or its length. "I just tried to get a sense of what he's getting at in the lyrics for my own satisfaction and try to find a musical take that supports it and doesn't overshadow it. There are a lot of layers of meaning in Leonard's lyrics and I try to leave space for the listener to get their head around what he's saying." Robinson wrote the chords and melody on a piano – "or maybe my old Wurlitzer 200" – despite the song fitting in perfectly with the style of the other Cohen/Casio compositions. "I take that as a compliment," she says, "because I try to understand what Leonard might need to do and how he might need to say it."

As with any song writing partnership the collaborative process took time and even though Robinson wouldn't suggest a lyric change, Cohen would often ask for the chord structure to be refined and modified. "It's ultimately his decision what we go for," confirms Robinson, "and I'm very conscious of the key I'm writing in. I try to begin writing in a key that Leonard will be able to sing the song in."

Robinson is an accomplished vocalist with a range wide enough to sing in a key close to Cohen's. Unlike John Lissauer, who would sing in his own natural key and then transpose the chords down to suit Cohen, Robinson could actually "… sing in his range and I think that makes the process truer, if you begin in a similar place to where its gonna end up. I would demo the songs in my home studio and mix it down to a cassette – something Leonard could play in his car and we would follow that up by getting together and breaking it down, remixing it in my studio, getting it into a place where he was extremely comfortable with it. He might say, 'I don't phrase like that', for instance… and I would always write in deference to his words, although he would sometimes come back and say 'I've changed a verse'! But it was a truly collaborative process."

Not every song Robinson and Cohen worked on was a success and even if it was, as with 'Summertime', Cohen himself wouldn't necessarily record it. But in this instance, Cohen's former backing singer had delivered something as powerful and potent as anything else on the album. On top of the elegant and relentless chord progression Cohen was again writing in character. Initially, the lyrics were written: "… on a napkin. I wanted to write a tough song. I had the feeling I was Humphrey Bogart. I began it in France, in Paris in a café at the 14th Arrondissement… I don't know who I thought I was at the time but it was somebody you couldn't put anything over on. "The oud refrain was improvised in the studio by Bilezikjian. "I just came up with it at the time," he remembers. "And Leonard still uses it today, when he plays the song live."

I'm Your Man was an instant classic, something Sinatra could have dealt with impeccably; indeed, there had even been talk of a 'Sinatra Sings

Cohen' album at one point but as with so many of Sinatra's more left field projects, it came to nothing.

'Take This Waltz' was an adaption of Lorca's 'Pepueño Vals Vienes' and an expanded version of the track that Cohen had recorded earlier in Paris for the Lorca tribute album. The album's oddity was 'Jazz Police', one of the more curious songs of Cohen's career and one of the few recordings that sounds as if it was written in the studio rather than being meticulously honed beforehand. It is also arguably more of a production piece than a crafted song in the Cohen tradition. The idea for the song began during the *Recent Songs* sessions, when Cohen was, after all, working with a fusion group. Passenger would apparently try to morph basic triad chords into augmented fifths or sevenths. This mildly irritated Cohen who wanted the band to merely embellish his basic chord progressions and not invert or modify them. Thus Cohen himself took on the role of 'jazz policeman'. This point of inspiration becomes somewhat lost in the actual song, which sounds more like a frantic, nervy aural portrait of a paranoid dissident. Musically, it's irreverent, playful, bordering on pastiche and placed amongst the sombre magnificence of the surrounding album, a refreshing comic relief. As to whether Cohen himself was a jazz fan, John Lissauer says that, "Jazz is basically an instrumentalist's medium. He had an appreciation of it but he wouldn't sit around listening to jazz when I knew him. He would know the odd thing but he was a balladeer, a writer, a poet. He might appreciate jazz in an impressionistic sense, like as in a cubist painting but he doesn't live there."

In 'Tower Of Song', Cohen explores the activity of his own song writing. He was sufficiently pleased with the result to exclaim somewhat disingeniously that it was "... the only real song on the album." The shadow of his youth was evident in the recording, in the sound of the pseudo fifties doo wop of the backing singers and the explicit reference to his hero, Hank Williams. This piece, "one of the three or four real songs I've ever written" according to its author, was almost abandoned in an earlier incarnation but Cohen clinched the lyric late in the day and recorded the vocal in one take.

He had laboured hard over the whole album, harder than any record previously. "I find it difficult to bring things to completion and when I do find a way to bring it to completion it's the only way it can be."

Since meeting Dominique Issermann in the early eighties, he had raised his game as far as his whole work ethic went, becoming more stringent, more ruthless, more demanding of himself. This song in particular was a comment on his change in attitude, "... a definitive statement about this heroic enterprise of the craft of song writing". He did actually dedicate the whole album, on the inner sleeve, to Issermann. Arguably, he could have also dedicated the work to the Casio and Technics home keyboards he'd become besotted with. Not only were their pre-programmed auto rhythms and melodies clearly detectable in the song structures, but the cheap sounding drum patterns and electronic bass lines were also actually used in the recording of the album, to startling and curiously moving effect.

Reviews for the album, released in the same month as Robert Plant's *Now And Zen*, The Fall's *The Frenz Experiment* and Fine Young Cannibals' *The Raw And The Cooked,* were generally positive and overwhelmingly welcoming.

If the album could be seen as an antidote to the snake poison of rampant consumerism of the era – *play at least once a day, preferably before shopping and with red wine* – then it was amusingly perverse to think that Cohen had appeared in *Miami Vice*, a TV show that on the surface at least seemed to epitomise coked up American imperialism less than two years previously. Oddly, one could imagine that the very character Cohen had played on the show – Zoltan – was the voice and face of the recent album, the actual man in 'I'm Your Man', the character now so successfully putting across Cohen's "demented manifesto". Having experimented generously with all kinds of drugs throughout his youth, Cohen was now vehemently anti-drugs and those who sold them. "I was thinking about this war on drugs and how my heart moves to a real reactionary position about drugs," he said that year. "I think there should be *real* war against the countries that are supplying dope to America, unless there is some really sinister conspiracy in high places in America which I doubt, that is that they want to destroy the black youth or the poor white youth, [but] I don't think such a conspiracy exists. But unless there is such a conspiracy, then what is happening is a real assault and a real attack on the future of the United States. I think it's much more tangible than any other kind of attack that is being described in any political circles. I think this is a real attack and I think it should be met with real force, with the full force of the American armed community. So I would really go in and bomb the countries that are supplying drugs to America."

I'm Your Man quickly went silver in the UK and gold in Canada and was number one in Norway for 16 weeks. In the all important market of America, where Columbia magnanimously deemed a Cohen album worthy of release this time around, it did better critically than any Cohen album had since the early Seventies but didn't quite do the businesses *Billboard* wise. It was, however, unanimously acknowledged as having reclaimed ground for Cohen, commercially, critically and kudos-wise. He would never outlive the clichés others insisted on applying to him and he had long since accepted this. "I recognise that I go around place to place with a guitar and that there have been guys doing this for a long long time but exactly how you fit into that... I don't know.. you just get up there and do it. It seems to me that these descriptions don't make it any easier... so I tend to resist these descriptions."

His co-writer Robinson was not present in the studio when their collaboration was recorded. "I think it's a Hollywood thing," she laughs. "They like to keep the songwriter outta the studio when they're doing your song." But she was more than pleased with its treatment. "I thought it was fantastic," she says, "and I was thrilled to have that piece on his album, it was terrific."

In advance of the record's release, Cohen had begun a two-month promo tour that January. His one-man tour of hotel rooms, cafes, radio stations and TV studios was a preliminary excursion, a reconnaissance before the full scale push of the full band musical tour. He had now adopted a unique approach to the often embarrassing travails of miming one's recent songs in front of a live TV audience. On February 16, on Belgium's *Mike* show, Cohen appears, dapper, dignified but slightly sinister, looking like a designer diplomat from some obscure eastern bloc state flanked by two upmarket call girls. There is a particularly moving lip synch through 'Take This Waltz', where Cohen, sandwiched between his Amazonian companions, endured nuzzling and hand clenching with the expression of someone who can hardly believe his luck. His canny professionalism also shows through, as is the seriousness with which

Cohen views these performances. He is alert to which camera is on him at any given moment – the girls stare ahead no matter what – and is aware also of his perceived failings as a performer, specifically the lack of dynamism in both his vocals and body movements. To combat this he sets up a living frame within which to project to the television audience. Many of his promo performances from this period are like mini dramatisations, four-minute plays complete with props. For one interpretation of 'First We Take Manhattan...' he employs an old radio microphone seemingly from World War II, a pile of documents, a clutch of papers, and a heavy desk.

Such manifestations of his songs are in effect live alternatives to the actual promo videos he was now making. Despite having a natural, unforced, almost Humphrey Bogart/Ben Gazzara-like presence on camera, Cohen was not particularly enamoured of the video culture in which he now found himself competing. Asked about the elegant, *cinema noir*-style promos that accompanied 'Dance Me To The End Of Love' and 'First We Take Manhattan', he casually admitted that he would never have allowed them to be made if such tools hadn't "... Become such a convention of the music business. The stuff I've done I've done as well as I can and I've worked with people I respect and I think some of the results are pretty good... but it's nothing I feel very urgent about." When asked if he felt the videos had added anything (to his work) he replied starkly: "No".

There would be further memorable TV appearances. On *Sunday Night Live* in February 1989 Cohen and band were joined by soul pop funk group Was Not Was, adding a mini choir of what appeared to be pimps to the line up. Legendary saxophonist Sonny Rollins also joined them on this occasion for 'Who By Fire', adding incendiary squalls that visibly moved Cohen who observed the jazz master's solo with obvious reverence. Yet, in promoting his most successful album in decades Cohen would sometimes hit a wall during the relentless interview schedule. Again and again he was, in effect, being asked to describe something he'd already explained so consummately, eloquently and beautifully in the song itself. To this end he would simply quote the lyrics back at the interviewer, explaining that he "couldn't put it any better than he already had". Such issues could only be explored in poetry, lyrics and music; in art and not during the artificial context that a press interview entailed. Such interviews were always worth hearing in themselves if only for the classic *bon mots* Cohen would utter. Sometimes he was funny without realising it: "No point in waiting for the nuclear holocaust," he told one interviewer straight faced, "that's just an alibi."

In April 1988 'Ain't No Cure For Love' was released as a single. While no hit, it helped to further maintain the most positive interest in a Cohen album since the mid-Seventies. Critics also noted, for the first time, the humour apparent within the work. This was a minor relief for Cohen who hadn't been taking himself *as* seriously for some time now. Revealing in an interview that he preferred the Sid Vicious version of 'My Way' to Sinatra's, he punctured the image of himself, adding, "I can't go round in a raincoat and fedora looking over my life saying 'I did it my way' – well, for 10 minutes in some American bar over a gin and tonic you might be able to get away with it."

Alongside Cohen's world wide renaissance, Steven Machat's minor grudge match continued. Steven seemed to live in a parallel world where all the qualities that Cohen were revered for were almost completely inverted. In February 1988, as was standard procedure, the promoter handling the bulk of Cohen's European shows, Flemming Schmidt banked a deposit in the Machat business account to cover 50 per cent of the anticipated revenues from Cohen's forthcoming European tour, an advance against what Schmidt and Cohen expected to make. Cohen, naturally, had to check in with what was now called Machat & Machat before the tour got underway. Unfortunately, at around the same time Machat Senior's health began to deteriorate rapidly, and Marty's predicament soon became public knowledge, amongst those in the industry at least. "Because he knew where all the money was buried, all sorts of people started coming out of the woodwork," remembers Steven bitterly.

For the first time in ages, Steven received a call from a panicky sounding Cohen. He was apparently terrified at the prospect of Marty dying and leaving his business concerns to his unhinged and alcoholic romantic partner, Avril. "I'm worried about Avril," he told Steven. "She wouldn't let me talk to Marty properly. She thinks that she is going to take over as my manager and I don't trust her. Your dad has all my money and I don't want Avril taking it." Machat Junior assured Cohen that he would take care of it. He immediately called his sick dad, told him the score and asked what happened next. Marty's reply was brusque and to the point: "Give him the money because he's a fuck." Even Steven, long desensitised by a life at the hard core end of music business was shocked at such a bald statement. He asked Marty what had prompted such viscera. "My father said: 'Because he's acting like I'm going to die.'" The following day, at Marty's insistence, Avril met Steven at LA's Chemical Bank with documents signed by Marty authorising the handing over of the Stranger Music publishing company, and all of its assets to Cohen. Steven remembers that instead of a straightforward "thank you", he instead received an enigmatic phone call from Cohen, seemingly still in Zoltan/Interpol character, telling Steven: "You have a best friend in me forever. I will never harm you and I will always be there for you."

This apparently gracious sentiment nevertheless raised Steven's heckles. "The telling point was that he volunteered this information at all," he says. 'Leonard, for all his faults, was not malicious, so why would he offer not to harm me? It suggested to me that he was thinking of harming me, and if he was thinking of it, he would probably do it." Ultimately, Steven decided to give his dad's favourite client the benefit of the doubt. "He still owed us money," reasoned Machat Junior and he figured Cohen, ultimately was decent enough to pay what managing commission he owed.

"My father never believed he was dying," recalls Steven sadly. "He felt short changed and became very quiet and withdrawn. This caused a lot of panic and fear in people around him." Cohen was clearly among those who panicked. Machat Junior didn't place all the blame on Cohen. "Dad could have solved everything peacefully before he went but he couldn't face the fact that he was dying."

Not even Marty Machat could negotiate himself out of the ultimate clause in the contract of life, and in April 1988 he died. His favourite client barely seemed to acknowledge the fact. "When my father died, Leonard never turned up to the funeral and didn't even bother to send his condolences, let alone some flowers. He never did pay me my commission. He ran off with Dad's secretary and all the books and records and all he had to do was talk to me. People still ask 'Why didn't you ever manage Leonard?' And I have to say that I don't know if it would have worked and more importantly if I had – if we both had agreed to that – then I would have simply been my father. And I'm not my father."

Kelley Lynch, Marty Machat's one time assistant, took over in an administrative capacity for Cohen and Steven was duly affronted by this. "She had given me the impression that she was a shoulder to cry on for me, but behind my back she was already working for Cohen. She was secretly squirrelling away the files and records in my father's office and took them with her when she went to California." Such underhand tactics seemed to work in Cohen's favour for now but these very traits in Lynch's character would be turned against Cohen himself before the decade was out, with financially catastrophic results. Meanwhile, for the next few years rancour would fester between Marty Machat's son and his father's one time favourite client. "Leonard was petrified that I was going to sue him over monies owed," says Steven. "But I was never going to pursue Cohen because I had too much on my plate as it was in the aftermath of my father's death and I really have never seen the point in pursuing former clients."

Kelley Lynch would eventually become Cohen's full time manager and remembers Marty Machat as "... someone I loved very much. We were very close. Mr. Machat was an extremely brilliant and sophisticated man... a perfect gentleman, a great gin player, and a very key player in the music industry." Publicly at least, Cohen never acknowledged any discomfort at being a player in such an occasionally barbaric industry. "I never came across mean spirited people for some reason," he said that year. "I haven't come across that real abrasive experience." It was his willingness to accept Lynch as his manager that would brutally put paid to this innocence within the next decade.

In the first months of 1988 Cohen began auditioning new musicians for the forthcoming tour and this, of course, included recruiting two female backing vocalists. One late morning in early spring, 30-year-old blonde and buttery Julie Christensen, in stretch pants and white shirt tied at the waist, rang the door bell of Cohen's duplex. Roscoe Beck had personally recommended her to Cohen. "I'd known the members of Passenger, the group who'd worked with Leonard in 1979-80 and 1985, when we all lived in Austin Texas," she remembers. "Actually, I moved to LA in 1981, but when those guys would visit out here, they'd headquarter at Leonard's house, and so I visited his house without having yet met the man." She was however, a long time fan. "When I was a young girl of 13 or 14 I had a big Judy Collins songbook that my mother and I would play and sing through and of course it contained a lot of Leonard's songs and photos of him. But I had only heard him sing 'Suzanne'. The songs that I learned off the pages of that book, however, stuck with me. I learned 'Suzanne' – poorly – on guitar in college."

The door of the duplex opened. A "dark and gracious" Cohen, dressed in a silk shirt and Armani trousers, received his auditionee personally. "Come in darling," he greeted Christiansen, "glad you could make it." Christiansen, who was "pretty emotionally raw at the time" following a romantic misadventure, remembers her potential employer as being charming and flirtatious. Technically, by the time she met Cohen personally, she had already actually passed the "singing" test. "I did 'audition', and Henry Lewy was there at the audition, but Leonard was still travelling and making preparations to tour. It was probably more important that Leonard and I met and that he liked me as a person and ally than my singing was," she explains. Once inside the duplex, Christensen greeted Roscoe Beck warmly and Cohen made them both coffees. She was then passed a guitar to perform an endearingly halting version of 'Suzanne' for its author. Cohen, charmed, had heard enough. "Well, that's not exactly it, darling," he told her, "but I'm flattered just the same... Shall we all go have something to eat?" Relocating to a Fifties style diner, Cohen let Christensen know what awaited them, should she take the gig. "This tour is going to be difficult," he told her. "Four or more shows a week. Booked pretty solid for ten weeks in Europe and then we have the coasts and Canada." Having recently completed a "hell-tour" in a van across the vast states of America, Christensen was more than up for it. "Leonard," she told him, "let's do it." The three celebrated the successful audition with a grilled cheese sandwich.

The world tour began on April 5 in Germany. The band from the 1985 tour was rebooted, consisting now of Bob Furgo on keyboards and violin, Bob Metzger on guitars and pedal steel guitar, Steve Meador on drums,

Stephen Zirkel on (occasionally fretless) bass, keyboards and trumpet, the faithful John Bilezikjian on oud and mandolin, Tom McMorran on keyboards, haloed by the dual luminosity of Julie Christensen and Perla Batalla on vocals.

Cohen was conscious of attracting a younger, fresh and expansive audience for the first time since the early Seventies. Commenting on the predominance of youthful punters amongst the audiences Cohen quipped, "I guess they need an older man in their life" but ultimately he didn't make any distinction based on age. "I see my own children at 13 and 15 and their emotional lives are passionate and highly developed... and we forget that. We forget that their feelings are as deeply developed as our own. The songs are acceptable to any age."

If he was amused that some people still insisted as seeing him as some sort of patron saint from the Summer of Love then he was still gracious enough to give them the very songs that, for some, exemplified such a status. He had no problem singing 'Suzanne' every night. "One is happy to do something that makes other people happy," he offered. "There are not so many opportunities in life to do that sort of thing." The latest live incarnation of 'Suzanne' was a much more muscular proposition than its ethereal, snow-tinted recorded version. In concert it now rocked purposefully, its sensuality tilting toward sexuality, as if the subject of the song, like Cohen, had learned to live strong and hard in a decade that seemed in direct contrast to the Sixties.

This was a prime time for Cohen live. Physically, at 53, he was at a personal peak (on stage at least), his voice low and worn but resonant and strong, the group behind and beside him stoked and young enough to rock out but sufficiently mature to hold back when needed. In Julie and Perla he had two beatific singers with high-class glamour sheen. After the recent commercial "wilderness" years, Cohen was relishing this very public return to form. The gigs kicked ass, the singer at their centre coming on righteous, with it and heavy. Clutching the microphone in a strong fist, and seeming to gnaw at the radio mike, Cohen grooved and growled through a two-hour, 20 plus song set. The newest songs in particular sounded exciting and electric but along with 'Suzanne', many older classics showed new strengths too. For 'Stranger Song' and 'Chelsea Hotel' he plucked in his inimitable way at a semi-acoustic, nylon stringed black Chet Atkins model Gibson guitar. (It was by now tuned two octaves down from concert C to compensate for the lowering of Cohen's voice.) For 'Tower Of Song', he shuffled seductively over to a Technics SXK350 keyboard, momentarily shrinking any hall down to the size of a bedsitting room.

Jarrko Arjatsalo, a long time Finnish fan, saw Cohen for the first time on this tour in Helsinki at the (sold out) 7,000 capacity Ice Hall on April 28. He was not disappointed. "My wife and I were speechless after the show," he remembers. "It was so different to listening to him on record. His concerts are... really special. This was his best tour, I think... his voice, the band, the mixture of instruments." This show was enough to convert Jarrko from dedicated fan into religious collector. "After this I started to look for more concert recordings, rare pressings that kind of thing... and I got in touch with others of a similar interest. [I] started to subscribe to newsletters and fanzines." Within a decade, this modest passion would ultimately lead to the most comprehensive and definitive Cohen website on the World Wide Web: *The Leonard Cohen Files.*

Although it was undoubtedly successful, with many of the shows being sold out, the tour was not particularly profitable financially and years later Cohen would joke that perhaps one of the reasons for this was the amount of Chateau La Tour (1982 vintage) that was drunk on the tour. "We were pretty much drinking up the profits," he admitted. Drinking each night before the show was a way for Cohen "... finding a way into the song."

"I stumbled on this vintage of wine," he said, "which produced a very acceptable kind of concert. And many of the musicians who drank this wine with me agreed."

Cohen had stumbled upon his very own kind of polypharmacy; the mixing of various drugs to produce a third unique substance often more powerful than those two drugs alone. For example, when cocaine mixes with alcohol in the liver it produces cocaethylene, a substance unique to this condition but more powerful than either of its base elements. Although Cohen certainly did not take any cocaine on this tour, the music, in effect, acted as the second chemical component that once mixed with the Bordeaux would produce a very particular high. When the tour was over, Cohen once again opened up a bottle but found it did not have the same effect. "It seemed to marry very well with the music," he said. One obvious side effect of this indulgence was that Cohen often appeared of ruddy complexion and looked bloated whilst being interviewed on TV during this period.

Despite the boozing, or perhaps because of it, it was a tight and passionate tour born out of Cohen's recent resurgence as a commercial and artistic force and from the familial vibe the group embodied. Some of the musicians in the touring band had been with him a decade. Cohen's generosity toward his friends was not just sharing fine wine with them. "In Spain he gave me a great opportunity," remembers Bilezikjian. "He said to me before the show, 'John, why don't you go out there and play something.' So I went out prepared to play one piece, a traditional piece for oud. The people went nuts... absolutely nuts.... 40,000 people in a bullring, going nuts at midnight! I finished the piece, had a standing ovation and I began walking off stage but the rest of the band at the side of the stage said, 'Go back John, do something else.' Well, the audience love me. Leonard finally came out with the band and on the mike he says to the audience, 'This is why I can't let him out on the stage.'" In Vienna, the appreciation of Bilezikjian's prowess was actually disturbing the song structures. "I remember my solos were getting ovations," he says. "It was disrupting Leonard's thing! It was such an appreciation."

For Christensen the tour provided benefits beyond just the musical. It was in effect a healing process for the singer, who at the beginning of the tour was just getting over a particularly toxic relationship. "Being around Leonard was a salve," she states. "It was like travelling with one's teacher... I (also) met Leonard's Zen teacher, Kyozan Joshu Sasaki Roshi, and I still study with Roshi and that group of people, though I don't call myself a Buddhist... I think that relationship between Leonard and Roshi, and the generosity, charm, humour, and grace that Leonard manifested in so many different situations during our travels is what I experienced, more than the management and promoters who made things happen day to day. In 1988, there was a lot of good energy around that tour from most corners, and my memory of most of it is very charmed."

Cohen hadn't been exaggerating when he'd warned Christensen about the rigours of this tour. The European leg alone consisted of 59 concerts through April to July of that year. It then immediately transferred to

North America and Canada, with Cohen and band performing a further 25 concerts. It closed on November 23.

By now, few mourned the disappearance of Leonard Cohen the novelist but Cohen himself did not completely discount the idea of another such book. "I'd like to. I'm always blackening pages," he said that summer, "but the novel takes a certain regime, you know, you need one room, one table, one chair, one woman." The conditions on such a massive world tour did not provide any of these requirements – in fact it was almost diametrically opposed to them. The recent success had solidified its own path. "I think as you get older you stop humouring yourself with alternatives – I know now I'm not going to be a brain surgeon or a forest ranger. There comes a certain point where you think 'I'm a songwriter living in Montreal' and you buy into it. Recently I've gotten very interested in song writing."

As the months following the huge tour turned to years, Cohen's life went on as before. He slipped in and out of relationships (he and Issermann finally parted around this time), he continued to work, travel and turn up at award ceremonies when he was invited and honoured. Yet no matter how successful he was, however newly beloved Cohen may have felt, like anyone he could not escape his past.

In 1990, Leonard met with his old antagonist, Steven Machat. In some ways Cohen must have felt he was being haunted by his dead manager, a ghost alive and feisty in the body of Marty Machat's only son.

The two met up at a Chinese restaurant on Wilshire Boulevard in LA. Cohen obviously had something on his mind as to Steven he looked visibly nervous. "He was drinking whisky, which I'd never seen before, and it was only 12 noon," recounts Steven. "He appeared terrified." Dutch courage or not, Cohen got straight to the point even though he avoided eye contact, informing Steven: "Your Dad ripped me off." The reason given for this was apparently because Machat Senior hadn't "worked" Cohen's back catalogue enough. Considering Cohen was one of the most covered contemporary songwriters still living, this was a curious accusation. Nevertheless, Steven maintains that, "Leonard told me he was convinced that my father had failed to exploit [his] copyright to its full potential. But to me it was all bullshit."

Steven's own take on the situation is that Cohen was attempting to justify to himself and the Machat estate his continued failure to pay the old management commission fees he owed them. Steven rejected this utterly, pointing out that in any case Cohen now owned his own publishing (and had recently and successfully reclaimed the songs he'd lost to Jeff Chase in the Sixties). The two also discussed other unsolved financial matters before Steven tried to bring the uncomfortable meeting to a close.

"I don't want the job, Leonard, in case you're wondering," he told Cohen, puncturing any assumption that he would want to take up where Marty had left off. "Someone else is welcome to manage you but why in God's name would you let Kelley be your manager?"

Steven did not trust Kelley Lynch who had now taken over Cohen's affairs completely. Instead he suggested that one of Cohen's most faithful live agents, the Danish Flemming Schmidt, take over the job. Cohen wasn't convinced, telling Steven that, "You remember the 1988 tour? Flemming extorted $100,000 from me. He wanted 20 per cent managerial commission, in addition to his promoter's fees. He thought he was doing extra work for me and wanted me to pay him. Because I don't like confrontation, I gave him $100,000."

Steven later confronted the agent with this statement. "Flemming told me that Cohen was lying," recounts Steven. "He said, 'Leonard asked me to take up the slack after your father's death. Leonard told me he would pay me a management commission. When I went to get the money after the tour, Leonard told me he couldn't pay me because he owed it to the Machats. So we settled on $100,000. The reason I settled was because I was still going to be his promoter.'" Steven believed Schmidt, and his initial negative impression of Cohen – at that first meeting back in the Seventies – though it had mellowed somewhat over the years – was now further confirmed. "I realised that I totally misunderstood what Cohen was about. Far from being the poet of the spirits, Leonard was a hustler using Buddhism as a facade. His trips to the monastery aren't for enlightenment, but to escape the nightmare he's trapped himself in."

Although Cohen was as ever plagued by depression during this period, his career was otherwise in re-ascent and his personal life as interesting, challenging and rewarding as it had ever been. It's hard to gauge what nightmare Steven was referring too. Still, Cohen was obviously disturbed by something during the meeting. Steven recalls that "He became increasingly uncomfortable and refused to make eye contact." Steven confronted Cohen directly regarding his suspicions over Lynch. "I said, 'Kelley is in love with you. You well know that she's a gossip and is untrustworthy. Leonard, you know she's been trying to imply that you, her and her boyfriend are in some weird three-way shit together. Yes, perhaps you are older and wiser than me, but you're going to get it. She will really fuck you if you don't act now to protect yourself." Cohen apparently at least acknowledged this, saying, "Steven, you're right. I am older and wiser. I'll be OK." Time would prove him wrong.

Aside from difficult meetings with the son of his dead former manager, Cohen's life was unfolding pleasantly; at least that's how it looked from the outside. His songs had recently enjoyed a new spurt of life in being covered by a slew of not just contemporary artists but by – every songwriter's dream – the younger generation too. The ultimate expression of this was manifest in the 1991 French *I'm Your Fan* compilation, conceived and co coordinated by two journalists at *Les Inrockuptibles*, France's leading music and style magazine.

JD Beauvallet, a co-founder of the magazine, remembers that, "Christian – the editor – and I were huge fans of Cohen and we were flummoxed that he wasn't considered more highly. Why wasn't he up there with Bowie and Dylan? He was considered something of a has-been almost, it was awful. Yet almost every young artist we spoke to every month seemed to be a fan of Cohen. So we came up with the idea of a tribute album by these people. We figured that would be more useful than actually putting together a compilation of Cohen himself."

The two went about the process with utter innocence and as a result found the whole exercise to be surprisingly straightforward. "Everyone who wanted to do it was very easy to work with; no one wanted an advance or anything. Some people never got back to us – Bowie, Eno and Morrissey didn't want to do it. Bur almost everyone else did. We licensed it all over the world and it was a great success."

This release was a watershed moment in terms of how Cohen was accepted by a growing (and increasingly financially powerful) "alternative" audience and the album was among the most successful and certainly hippest of Cohen tribute albums. Cohen himself was delighted. The possibility of a "bad" cover version didn't seem to exist for Cohen. "They are ALL GOOD," he would say empathically, years later. "My critical faculties go into suspension and I'm always happy... I never think 'Oh, they've murdered that song'." Many of the artists featured on the record have since slid into semi-obscurity but a few remain omnipresent in the greater consciousness of the pop public to this day.

One of the most successful tracks on the album was by John Cale. Singing soulfully in his Welsh tenor to his own gospel-esque piano accompaniment, Cale's rendition of one of Cohen's then lesser known songs was a revelation. It raised an obvious question. How come 'Hallelujah' wasn't a universally regarded classic?

CHAPTER TEN

That's How The Light Gets In
1992–1999

"You go your way/I'll go your way too."
The LC Poem, The Sweetest Little Song

Life had gotten in the way of Cohen's next album. Someone else's life. In 1990 Cohen's only son Adam was involved in a near fatal car crash in the West Indies. Cohen immediately had him flown home and then suspended everything to spend time by his son's Montreal hospital bed. Adam was in a coma for almost four months and his father read to him throughout, mostly from the Old Testament. Adam's full recovery took a year and his father paid vigil to his son for the duration. "My dad brought his own life to a halt," said Adam, who also admitted that before the accident he and his dad had not been particularly close.

Both of Cohen's children were now teenagers and Cohen was, of course, fascinated at their own burgeoning personalities. He had always been a reflective father. "It is only when you have children that you're truly forced to give up looking only at yourself and start worrying about some other lives. If you attempt to respond to a child, you can never think of yourself in the same way again. You stop being the centre of your drama, which becomes very secondary in light of your children's needs, of their urgency."

Adam's accident was the ultimate example and proof of such a sentiment and all work on a new Cohen album was suspended until his son was in the clear. "I was so grateful," he acknowledged after his recovery.

While Cohen proffered that, in general, he had little interest in leaving any legacy he was no doubt touched that Adam and Lorca were appreciative of his work. The former would attempt to follow in his father's footsteps, though there was a long line of casualties in this regard, in both the commercial and physical sense – Frank Sinatra Jnr, Julian Lennon and Jeff Buckley. As an artist in his own right, Adam at least seemed confident enough in his own abilities to acknowledge his father and his work as an inspiration rather than a threat. "I have such a tremendous respect and admiration and love for my father," he admitted. "I see him as having contributed so beautifully, nobly, and elegantly to his field that I take inspiration from him and share as many sensibilities as I'm capable of sharing with him."

Cohen was amused and gratified by the interest of his own flesh and happy to share with them an enthusiasm for music in general. "My children have memorised all the words, they quote me," he said happily. "They don't talk about them [Cohen's songs] as critics, they just tell me what they like and don't like. We talk more about other types of music."

Once Cohen was sure his son was in proper recovery, work resumed on the latest album. This was his ninth studio album and it wasn't getting any easier. "Even if the accident hadn't happened," he said, "it would have been late because once again I feel the songs aren't finished even though I thought they were. I still feel that an easy way to do all this must exist but I have yet to find it."

His daily routine, a pattern he had identified and refined years ago, was much the same as ever. "Usually I get up very early and meditate. I start at five in the morning. Then at seven I make a big pot of coffee, open a pack of cigarettes and start working or what is supposed to be working. I sit in front of my synthesizer, I have a scribble pad next to me and I play and replay the same songs until they take on a form in my eyes. That lasts a couple of hours and then stops. I start again in the afternoon."

This routine was more akin to the life of a writer than that of a modern era songwriter, or perhaps closer still to the life of a monk. Finally, as satisfied as he ever would be with the new material he had, Cohen headed for a slew of studios where between January and June 1992, he worked at the album that would be entitled *The Future.*

The work on the new album was not forged in one concentrated effort. The number of studios used ran into double figures and was spread between Montreal and LA, although the original plan was to record it in Montreal only, with the same personnel that had worked on *I'm Your Man.* The cast brought to bear on the album was akin more to a movie production and included both a choir and orchestra as well as Cohen's current high profile beau, Rebecca De Mornay.

De Mornay was at this time rising star in her own right, a successful actress who had recently broken through co-starring alongside Tom Cruise in the film *The Hand That Rocks The Cradle.* She was an exceptionally intelligent, semi-pneumatic blonde who looked like she'd escaped from a Raymond Chandler novel, and Cohen was smitten. "When I met Rebecca," he would recall, "all kinds of thoughts came into my mind, as how could they not when faced with a woman of such beauty? And they got crisscrossed in my mind. But she didn't let it go further than that: my mind. Except it did."

De Mornay was a constant and active presence in Cohen's life for a couple of years and unlike the previous women Cohen had loved, De Mornay was more than a passive muse to him. She even had a production credit on the album, relating to the mighty 'Anthem'. When pressed on this, and asked if the credit represented some sort of 'Spinal Tap' type activity, of letting 'the girlfriend' undue input into one's career, Cohen laughed and explained that as he saw it, a producer was less a technician and more someone who 'makes it happen'. "I was playing the song at her house," he explained, "and she said, 'I think it's finished now'. I had been working on it for ten years. She said 'let's record it right away'. So we called up studios and I said 'You produce it' and she said, 'Well what does that mean'? I said, 'You direct it. Direct the operation. You know, if my voice doesn't sound right... tell me and direct it.' And she did, you know, bring it into being... also she worked on the arrangements. She has a good sense of harmony and has written some pretty good songs herself."

Steven Machat briefly encountered the two at this time. "I bumped into Leonard when I was leaving a movie house in Century City with my family in 1992," recalls Machat quite vividly. "We'd just seen *The Hand That Rocks The Cradle* where Rebecca De Mornay plays the psychopathic nanny who stalks this family. Who should walk along but Cohen, who was holding hands with De Mornay, his girlfriend at the time. Cohen was extremely uncomfortable because he knew he had stolen from me and it was clear that he couldn't get away quick enough. Neither could my son, because he took one look at De Mornay and ran. He was terrified because he thought she was the nanny in the film! I would not come across sight or sound of Cohen again for another 13 years."

Cohen meanwhile, continued to labour in the studio. As final mixing began he felt the old relief at having gotten through the process once again. "I tend to get shattered as I bring a project to completion," Cohen said. "I have to discard versions of myself, and version of the songs, until I can get to a situation where I can defend every word, every line. I have to go to this naked and raw place. And it usually involves the breakdown of my personality, and I flip out... I can't go into crowds, I don't want to leave my house, I don't want to leave my room, I don't want to answer the phone, all my relationships collapse."

Released in November 1992, *The Future* was one of its author's strongest, cohesive and most coherent albums to date. The production served the individual songs perfectly and as a whole it sounded neither like a folk throwback nor as self consciously 'modern' as the previous two albums. It sounded like classic big budget AOR yet with lyrics by Lorca, Bukowski and Lowell, sang by an old wino from Skid Row who really wanted to sound like Ray Charles at The Apollo. It was an intoxicating and intoxicated effort. Indeed, the interpretation of the Irving Berlin classic 'Always' had been recorded whilst all concerned were sloshed. As well as changing the tempo from a waltzing 3/4 to a more rock'n'roll friendly 4/4, Cohen had the confidence to add his own lines to this rollicking version. He considered his interpretation to be the 'drunken version of it'. This was helped along by Cohen actually playing bartender in the studio, serving up an original cocktail of his own design to his fellow musicians. "It's called a Red Needle which I invented in 1976 in

Needles, California. It consists of cranberry juice, tequila, a little Sprite, and a lot of sliced fruit of any kind," explained Cohen. He had fond memories of this particular session. "It's very charming. I have a couple of improvised lines in there. I wouldn't have kept the track if it didn't have such exuberance. A number of the musicians told me it was among the happiest sessions they'd ever played. It was a good party, let me tell you."

The Future was Cohen's longest album to date, clocking in at almost an hour. It could have been longer still. "I have about fifty verses of 'Democracy' that I discarded," he admitted. "It examined many many themes. It was occasioned by the collapse of the Berlin Wall. It is a song where there's no inside and no outside; this is just the life of the democracy; it isn't imposed from above; it isn't connected to a Democratic victory nor a Republican victory. It's coming through a hole in the wall, you know, it's coming through a crack."

The general mood of the album was, as to be expected serious, sombre and despite the tequila, essentially sober. But there were lighter, more up-tempo moments as with the lock-in and moonshine crazed stomp of 'Closing Time'. "There's a lot of activity in that song, and I think that's the way we experience our freedom today. It looks like freedom but it feels like death, it must be something in-between, I guess, its closing time. I don't know about you, but I live a life that is totally consumed with ambiguity and conflict. I can't get anything straight... Closing time. The landmarks are down. The lights are out. The catastrophe has taken place. Don't wait around for it, you know."

'Anthem' was heard by a then young LA lawyer called Robert Kory, who would in the fullness of time go on to become Cohen's manager. "This is my favourite song," he says. "That line, 'There is a crack, a crack in everything/That's how the light gets in'... that just nails it for me. Perfect."

Cohen seemed to feel more confident about this album than any in a long time. In interviews he sounded newly assured and focussed. "'Ring the bells that still can ring'. It's no excuse," he explained of Kory's favourite Cohen song. "The dismal situation and the future, there's no excuse for an abdication of your own personal responsibilities towards your self and your job and your love. 'Ring the bells that still can ring'.

They are few and far between. You can find 'em. Forget your perfect offering. That is the hang-up. That you're going to work this thing out... The thing is imperfect and, worse, there is a crack in *everything* that you can put together – physical objects, mental objects, constructions of any kind. But, that's where the light gets in; and, that's where the resurrection is; and, that's where the return – that's where the repentance is. It is with the confrontation with the broken-ness of the thing..."

There was humour too, as always, most notably in a line within the mighty 'Waiting For The Miracle'. Another song co-written with Sharon Robinson, though she cannot remember anything about writing or recording it, the song towers above the rest of the album, lurching like a cyclopic Easter Island statue come to life, wading through some apocalyptic nightmare-landscape, rendering the line 'I haven't felt this happy/since the end of world war two' all the more hilarious in its deadpan incongruity.

There was a surprise too in that *The Future* offered Cohen's first ever instrumental on a studio album. The sorrowful and synthesized lilt of 'Tacoma Trailer' had originally been written "... for a theatre piece by Ted Allen," explained Cohen. "It was part of a long suite and I kept playing the music when I was in this trailer in Tacoma. That part of the suite attached itself and started to sound better and better. Then, I thought it would just be a nice moment to unwind from a very dense and literate album." Ironically, on an album that would spawn more than its fair share of songs that were used in films, 'Tacoma Trailer' was not one of them.

Sales, press and the reviews were good. 'What's new on Leonard Cohen's *The Future*... is his savvy use of strings and a peppery, mostly female choir," said the *Wall Street Journal*. "Cohen, with his voice now a rumbling bass whisper, offers his lines as if he were delivering commentary rather than a song, adding a dark punch to the poetry. In all, *The Future* is a neat piece of work.'

"Cohen is probably the only person ever to have sacrificed a thriving career as novelist and poet to become a pop star, and it shows," wrote *The Independent's* reviewer. "His lyrics have more depth, colour and polish than the next man's. Two of these new songs are anthems, hymns, ancient in their concerns, modern in their outlook."

NME summed up with, "When the last notes disappear into the ether the silence is practically deafening. Hardcore Leonard Cohen admirers will, no doubt, adore this with a passion."

Given that Los Angeles – where Cohen wrote and recorded much of the album – was at this time going through a violent (and arguably justified) maelstrom of riots, a series of events that were seemingly mirrored on *The Future*, Cohen was once again honoured by the press with the role of prophet. While Cohen himself didn't see himself as a sage he did agree with the idea that "any artist embodies an oracular function… if he's good he's working on a level that's better than he knows and better than he is." Asked generally about the wisdom of old age, Cohen wittily countered that the only advice he had to offer the young was to duck!

The Future cemented the newly commercial and critically reborn Cohen. Until relatively recently there had been a consensus that people who loved Cohen were ashamed to admit it, as to all intents and purposes Cohen was seen as a 'burnt out old hippy'. This falsity had finally been put to rest by *I'm Your Man* and killed stone dead by *I'm Your Fan*. Of course, Cohen had not even been a true hippy back in the 1960s and the bygone age of Aquarius was of little interest to him now, as the title of his new album proclaimed. "I'm not nostalgic," he said. "There are people I know who have a very finely developed sense of nostalgia and they can draw me into moods where I look at the past in a way that's uncharacteristic. I don't look at the Sixties as the good old days. People ask me, 'Isn't it terrible what happened to the ideals of the Sixties' and I have to say I don't know. Maybe it is, but during the Sixties I never thought it was so great either, with the amount of charlatanism and hustling that went on. There's really nothing to regret about its passing."

The success of the album more than justified Columbia releasing and promoting singles, even if Cohen remained a proven non-charter as a singles act. Indeed, in his own name, he'd never come close to infiltrating any singles chart anywhere. But by 1993, with MTV and more appropriately (in Cohen's case) VH1 both approaching their peak, it was more important to simply have a single out so that you could make a video for it and have that video played on TV. Thus 'Closing Time' was released as a four-track CD in Europe and, more importantly, accompanied by a promo video that took up where the gorgeous Issermann films for *I'm Your Man* had left off. Filmed in deep, rich black and white at Toronto's Matador Club, a country & western music venue that was an old haunt of Cohen's, the film was elegiac, arty, accessible and cool. Directed by Curtis Wehrfritz and in part edited by De Mornay, the promo film would go onto reap considerable VH1 airtime and even win awards.

"The story for 'Closing Time' was to cast a story of the sweet and damaged all locked in a bar called the Matador," recalls its director. "The bull fight here is among the characters themselves, with the dizzy spirits presiding above. It was shot in black and white film and designed in a collaboration with my long time friend and cinematographer Miroslav Bazak. Shot over three days, the video included a separate location for the rooftop love-making scene and an additional shoot at Robert Desrosier's Dance studio where we filmed a stunt woman for the falling sequences. I recall that I asked the stylist to bring many bandages and neck braces as I wanted a *leitmotif* of damaged characters to reflect the toughness of their journeys. On the day of the shoot Earl Pastko showed up dejected and defeated; turns out he had an eye injury just the day before that included an eye-patch. It was all I could do to convince him how happy I was. I believe his injury created a better scene and sometimes I wonder if he just was practicing his form of method."

Wehrfritz considered Cohen to be "one of the poets of the century" and wanted to portray him a little differently than Cohen was used to. "I was able to negotiate with Mr. Cohen with regards to the portrait of him smiling," he says. "I think his usual portraits have left a lasting impression throughout his career but in meeting and working with him I found his generosity front and centre at all times. I suggested that we could try to play loose on the handle and seek an element of this trickster character he possesses within our tiny kingdom of 'Closing Time'. He agreed, and I think that is one of the first times I have seen him share that side of himself with us. I was seeking a connection with him and the story was unfolding as though he was watching and telling the story at the same time. Incidentally, it is one of the longest videos of all time at six and a half minutes and proudly it won the Juno award, the equivalent of a Canadian Grammy."

Columbia – who by now surely acknowledged Cohen as both great *and* good – were right behind this particular phase of Cohen's work and he made himself as available as ever for promotion. "There has been a softening in the offices of power," Cohen acknowledged, obliquely referencing his past skirmishes with his label. Even the unwieldy 'Democracy' was released as a radio only single and accompanied by one of the most perfunctory promo videos ever released by a major record label. While working fine as an album track, the duration and wordiness of the song rendered it clearly unsuitable for radio play. The video hardly helped broaden its chances on TV – it appeared so amateur as to be home made, featuring poorly shot clips of Cohen reciting his lyrics as if he were enduring an eye test at his opticians.

'The Future' was also released as a single (promo only, in Spain) and this time the attendant video was a major improvement on its predecessor. Perhaps taking its cue from the famous Cohen quote "A pessimist is someone who thinks it's gonna rain. We'll I'm already soaked", it featured the singer, now resembling an older and slightly crumbly Harrison Ford, actually *dancing* as water poured onto him from above. His movements, vaguely arthritic yet sinuously suggestive, are oddly compelling to watch.

Considering the basically uncompromising and visceral nature of the album, *The Future* did well, charting in several countries, drawing good press and solidifying Cohen's reputation in every aspect. If anything, it improved his image. He now came across, both in demeanour and interview, as something closer to a wise old statesman rather than a randy old man. To the casual reader of any of the Sunday supplements that featured high profile pieces on the now 58-year-old Cohen, the 'ladies' man' of yesteryear now seemed much more preoccupied with politics than pussy. But while Cohen had moved on lyrically for this album, he wasn't exactly a shrivelled old sexless eunuch just yet. "The idea that your creative impetus is over by 30, that you immolate yourself on this pyre of energy and sexuality and can then go back to cleaning up and doing the dishes... it just ain't so," he said while promoting the album. "The fire continues to burn fiercely as you get older. It's passionate."

Another world tour commenced in April 1993, starting in LA and moving on to Europe for 26 dates that would take the group (much the same personnel as in 1988) into late May. (Once again Cohen and co would not visit Japan). The red wine was once more flowing backstage and the whole trip had the air of a family outing. The then recently married Julia Christensen remembers one of Cohen's gestures particularly fondly. "My husband and son came to visit several times during that tour, thanks to a stipend Leonard generously made available for that purpose," she recalls. "I would not have done it differently. To work with Leonard is an honour almost equal to being a mother, and I'm glad that I was able to do it."

Apart from the addition of new material from *The Future* and an interesting new philosophy in terms of arrangements, there were few musical refinements compared to the last tour. "We have a joke in the band," revealed Cohen, "[which is] Orbisonising. That is, to take Roy Orbison's approach to the old tunes." Other than this (and there was little aural evidence of the Big O's influence), the tour was business as usual, with Cohen selling out some of the same venues he had been playing since the early Seventies, including his and his band's London home from home, the Royal Albert Hall. Cohen was clearly energised by his new album, as he always was. Officially the show ended at 10 p.m. but the encores continued until close to 11.30. The *Independent* noted that, "He does go on a bit in the end, though, and by the fourteenth encore his evident good humour and self-satisfaction have become slightly, well, *depressing*."

Backstage at the aftershow parties, Cohen – "the Mel Brooks of misery" and now apparently resembling Dustin Hoffman's Ratso from *Midnight Cowboy* – still got merry, still signed autographs, still flirted with his fans and was still going to bed drunk every night. In early June the American and Canadian leg of the *Future* tour began. Although having imbibed the usual ration of wine before going on stage, Cohen never seemed even slightly drunk during these shows. He was as sharp as ever in his onstage banter – "Thank you for your incoherent screaming," he told the crowd at a sold out Manhattan show – he never fluffed a lyric and with each night's concert lasting at least three hours, the same length as shows by Bruce Springsteen at his peak, Cohen's dedication to the art of performance was undimmed. The tour finally folded just before August, '93. Cohen was exhausted, burnt out, knackered. But rather than book into a hotel for a week to aid his comedown, or going on an extended golfing vacation, he made plans to retreat to a monastery. He would not tour again until 2008.

A memento of the 1988 and 1993 tours was released in July 1994. *Live In Concert* was another 'best of' compilation, albeit delivered in live form with many versions sounding superior – aged, refined, matured – compared to their original, somewhat undernourished, recorded versions. He dutifully promoted the anthology, revealing candidly that his relationship with De Mornay was by now over. "She got wise to me," he explained without ceremony.

Sometime in 1994 Leonard effectively moved full time to Mount Baldy. He had no set plans to leave. "I'd been drinking three bottles of wine a night on the tour and one of the things I was looking for was a rest." The Chateau de la Tour 1982, as well as a near addiction to caviar, had both served their purpose for Cohen, aiding and abetting him in each night's challenge during the tour while at the same time doing its own work on the singer, in all its negatives and positives. Although he hadn't been completely self-indulgent of late – he'd given up smoking for over two years and the only drugs he now took were prescribed antidepressants – Cohen still felt defeated. "I was wrecked," he said on entering the retreat. "I didn't know what else to do."

Additionally there was a feeling that his life had become too chaotic that drew him to the, ironically, anything but restful (in the physical sense) regime of the monastery. "I didn't really have any other place to go," he admitted. Cohen was checking in for a physical change of pace and a spiritual audit: "Someplace where I could tidy myself up." Other times he would refer to the monastery simply as "a hospital".

Cohen was a desperate patient; sick, so he believed, of not getting what he wanted and of not wanting it if and when he did get what he thought he wanted. He'd felt for years that some object of desire, some truth, some wisdom was eternally evading him and that if only he could truly embrace this intangible 'thing', he would be free of his distress and suffering. Never content with his lot, Cohen was haunted by the ever present feeling that there was some other, better way of living forever escaping him. Simply put he was yet another western guy with desires that couldn't be satisfied. But for a person as sensitive and as poetically attuned as Cohen, such feelings resulted in a tangible psychic agony. In attempting to escape this pain, Cohen threw himself into his work, into drinking, into medication, into sex. Such activities had been a balm for years and had even brought him a kind of fame and fortune, but by the mid-Nineties the medicine was no longer working. At this point in his life the balm had become an irritant. The tried and tested remedies were making his condition, as he perceived it, much worse. When he checked into Mount Baldy he not only considered himself a victim of depression, anguish and suffering but saw himself as a 'specialist' in all three.

The specialist still entertained the occasional visitor. Outside the grounds of Mount Baldy, enough interest remained in Cohen to attract journalistic interest. Cohen was still earthbound enough – maybe more so than ever in some respects – to comply with promotional duties and more than a few journalists took a pilgrimage up the mountain to interview him. Among them was well respected Swedish journalist Stina Lundberg, who travelled to meet Cohen in 1997 as part of the promotional bandwagon for the latest CD, yet another compilation, this one clumsily entitled *More Best Of Leonard Cohen.*

"I was offered the interview with him," remembers Stina, "and to be honest I wasn't that enthusiastic. As you know, most interviews with artists promoting their CD… well, you wait in a room with hundreds of other journalists, waiting to go in and meet the artists… it's a bit like going to the dentist. So I told Leonard's people I wasn't interested. Some time went by and then a friend mentioned to me that Leonard was actually in a monastery. So I went back to his people and said, 'OK if I can go to the monastery I'll be most happy to do it.' And I was very, very surprised that he said 'yes'."

The resulting film is even more intimate than *Ladies And Gentlemen* from decades before, showing at one point Cohen in baggy long Johns, dressing as he listens to talk radio in his small room. The chemistry between he and Stina is apparent. Both clearly enjoy each other. Cohen seems the perfect host, offering her food and whisky and even a performance of an early version of 'A Thousand Kisses Deep' on the keyboard he has set up in his room. Stina, a veteran interviewer of many 'big names' was, on meeting Cohen pleasantly surprised and utterly beguiled by her latest subject. "I wouldn't have said I was a Leonard Cohen fan," she says, "but I liked his music and loved a few of his songs already. But I'd never been to a concert of his and from a journalistic point of view I wasn't especially keen on him because he wasn't hard to get. I was always after the hard to get. In Sweden he was a familiar presence on the TV and in the magazines, he wasn't, you know, particularly exclusive."

Stina travelled with her one man film crew from Switzerland to LA, losing much of her equipment on the way. This meant that although they were only a few hours from Mount Baldy, they had to replace equipment at short notice. This and the fog and a general confusion about how they were to find the monastery delayed their scheduled appointment with Cohen. Far from being put out by their non arrival at the monastery, this turned out to be merely an opportunity for Cohen's charm and relaxed attitude to manifest. "I remember calling him," says Stina, "telling him we were very, very late and so forth... and he said 'Just take it easy, I'm waiting for you, take your time, don't worry...' He had a very, very nice attitude. You know, often in these circumstances you are treated as shit by the managers surrounding the so called star etc., but Leonard's attitude was so, so special, it made it so nice."

When Stina and her assistant finally did make it to the top of the fog shrouded mountain, Cohen was again nothing but light and sweetness. "As soon as we finally met him he was like, 'Oh, how are you, do you need a rest, something to eat...' He was treating me like a long lost relative coming to meet him or something."

The filmed interview is a joy to watch. Cohen is courtly and charming, giving Stina a tour of the monastery, which appears on camera as a hybrid of sanatorium, military boot camp, and holy retreat. He is warm and open in his responses to her questions. He explains that by his own definition, "A monastery is a place where they make you so tired you give up pretending."

It was also a place where the daily routine was so exhausting that it was in fact designed to "overthrow a 21 year old". Cohen was now in his mid-sixties. He was however, despite the years of drinking, still physically fit and in many routines – keeping in shape, watching his diet, his work – he had never lacked discipline. Yet this sense of surface order, his "cover story" as he termed it, which he presented to the world, seemed superficial to him in that it masked an "interior sense of deep disorder". Cohen's condition was desperate and its treatment called for measures just as desperate. Located in the San Gabriel Mountains 40 miles east of Los Angeles and prone to snow and freezing thin air, Mount Baldy offered such measures 'in spades'.

He talked Stina through the daily routine in painful detail: "Well, actually, each day was more like two days," he says. "If you are a senior monk with specialised duties, you get up at 2.30 a.m. The general wake-up is 3 a.m. I would get up a little earlier so that I could brew some coffee and smoke a couple of cigarettes before getting into the day. Then the bell would ring and one would get into robes and go into the meditation hall. Then there would be chanting for an hour, then two hours of sitting meditation, then breakfast in formal silence with a ritualised use of bowls and napkins, then a 15-minute break before the work bell, when you would turn up for the duties of the day. These really involved the maintenance of the facility – plumbing, shovelling snow, painting walls, making candles, cleaning and cooking." Almost unbelievably such a day would sometimes not end until midnight. Incredibly, as ever, Cohen still wrote. "There were moments I could scribble… I was cooking mostly."

For someone who had a self confessed "great appetite" for the company of women, and for the expression of friendship through sex, Mount Baldy must have been the best and worst of places. It was no secret that for years Cohen had been, like most men, obsessed with the female. But Cohen's hunger was more public than that of your average Joe and much more clearly articulated. "I wanted that immediate affirmation of… the possibility of escaping from the sexual loneliness… the pure loneliness of living with an appetite that you couldn't ever satisfy. That drives everybody crazy." Cohen had experienced a rare moment in recent history – the Summer of Love in the Sixties – when there had seemingly been a two-way open line of communication between the libidos of men and women. But even then, especially since then, Cohen had got to worrying that the quenching of this particular kind of loneliness was maybe all he wanted from women. As he'd admit, "Anything after that, I was ready to negotiate."

Although he had matured somewhat since the golden era of free love he'd once known, perhaps the recent experience with Rebecca

In Paris during the early Nineties. (RENAUD MONFOURNY/DALLE/RETNA)

Cohen, the band and the crew in Warsaw, 1985. (COURTESY OF ANDRZEJ MARZEC/AMC ARCHIVE)

Cohen, with promoter Andy Marzec, in Poland during 1985. (COURTESY OF ANDRZEJ MARZEC/AMC ARCHIVE)

A Polish press conference in 1985. (COURTESY OF ANDRZEJ MARZEC/AMC ARCHIVE)

On the 1979 tour with Sharon Robinson and Jennifer Warnes. (RICHARD MCCAFFREY/MICHAEL OCHS ARCHIVE/GETTY IMAGES)

Sharon and Cohen on the last day of mixing *Ten New Songs* in LA, 2001. (COURTESY OF GREG GOLD)

Cohen with Sharon Robinson in 2001 (COURTESY OF SHARON ROBINSON)

In LA with Jennifer Warnes, 1998. (ALBERTO MANZANO).

Performing at the Glastonbury Festival in June 2008. (REX FEATURES)

Former U.S. President Jimmy Carter with Cohen during the state funeral for former Canadian Prime Minister Pierre Trudeau on October 3, 2000 in Montreal. The funeral was held at the Notre-Dame Basilica in Montreal. (PIERRE ROUSSEL/LIAISON)

Performing with Javier Mas, 2009. (PA ARCHIVE/PRESS ASSOCIATION IMAGES)

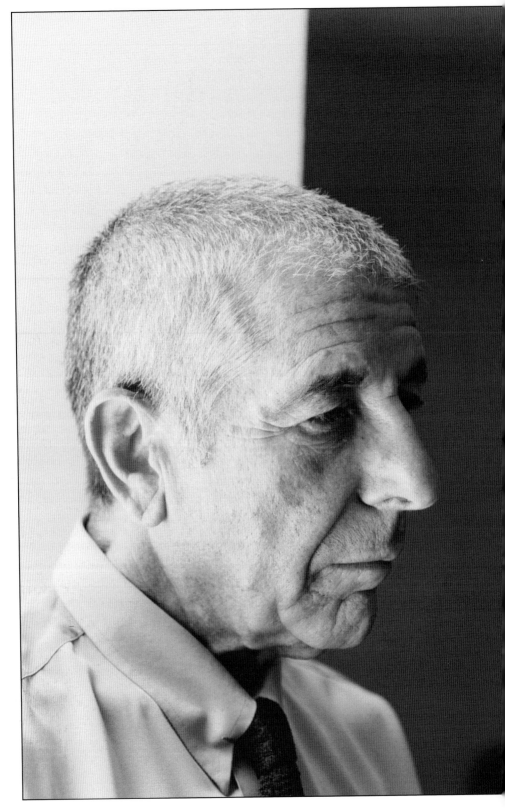

Facing the third act. (CHRIS BUCK/CORBIS OUTLINE)

De Mornay had convinced him to attempt to deal with the root of his perceived loneliness, to investigate its causes rather than its symptoms.

In 1997, asked bluntly if he still had a sex life, he explained that, "It seems inappropriate," and whilst celibacy was not mandatory the monk's life was so harsh that, "If you've got the strength after one of those days to lay down with someone... then go for it but it's not the appropriate place." When pressed further if such a condition bothered him he said: "When you're really studying something you want to avoid distractions." He professed that he still had many friendships, male and female, that he hadn't cut himself off from the world nor from old girlfriends. "I had brunch with Rebecca a few months ago and I said to her, 'I want to thank you for letting me off the hook so gracefully... and I know why you did, it's because I gave it my best shot'."

During the Mount Baldy interview with Stina, there seemed to be a definite sparkle in the monk's eye. "Oh, I don't think he was flirting with me in particular," says the blonde, blue eyed Swede modestly. "I think he was like that with everybody!"

Stina left deeply impressed and enamoured by the man. "The only negative thing I can remember is that me and my cameraman were fighting a lot on the way," she laughs, 'but when we met Leonard that dissipated instantly. We all felt very welcome and at ease."

Cohen occasionally went down the mountain to attend to business. He still had a working office in LA and sometimes went out for a coffee and a cigarette at a favourite café. Chris Darrow, the bass player who had played on Cohen's debut album, happened to live in the town at the foot of Mount Baldy. One afternoon he was attending an art show in town. "Roseanne, my friend's daughter, had been running around there saying 'I just saw Leonard Cohen!" recalls Chris. "I said, 'Where?' She said, 'I saw him sitting outside the Greek restaurant called Yanni's in Claremont'. So I walked a block and a half up the street and there he was sitting outside in front of the restaurant having a Greek coffee with a woman and they were both smoking and they had robes on and he had his hair shaved. But it was obvious who he was."

Although Darrow had kept track of Cohen's career, the two had not shared time and space together since that afternoon at Columbia's recording studio, way back in 1966. "I just walked straight up to him," says Darrow. "I said, 'Listen, I'm Chris Darrow and I was in Kaleidoscope and... do you remember me'? And he said, '*Remember* you? You guys saved my life!' And he went on to say, you know, 'I can't tell you how grateful I was for you guys to be there because it helped turn the record around...' And he was very nice. We had a conversation and I told him what I was doing and he told me what he was doing and it was very pleasant."

Such a chance meeting could serve as a kind of bookend to the slight relationship Darrow and Cohen had. But it caused the bassist to reflect on what that solitary studio session meant to him. "The Leonard Cohen sessions are part of my history," he says, "and his as well. I have had an opportunity to be at the right place at the right time, a great many times in my life... I feel grateful that I was chosen, over anyone else in the world, to play on the records that I played on. It does mean a great deal to me on a day-to-day basis, because playing music is what I am supposed to do. The sum total of my musical history fuels me to keep on going and to try and get better, until I can't play anymore. Leonard Cohen is a good example of that, himself. Guys like Segovia, Duke Ellington and BB King are examples of the kind of musician that I aspire to be. No one performance defines who you are, but the totality of your career gives you what you are leaving behind, your heritage. The rest is history."

Down in LA, Cohen's son Adam was making steps toward his own musical history. Cohen had called up John Lissauer and asked him for a favour. "He said, 'Listen my son is pretty good, can you work with him?'" remembers Lissauer. Adam and producer did some demos from which the former secured "a very nice record deal and then chose to use another record producer," recounts the once more Cohen spurned producer. "But he got a very good deal based on those three songs we did together."

Back in his cabin atop the mountain, 6,500 feet above sea level and after five years of militaristic discipline, Cohen was finally thinking about moving on. "I had the feeling it (the monastic regime) wasn't doing any good... it wasn't really addressing this feeling of distress that was the background to all my feelings, activities and thoughts... it was a lot of work for very little return." In some ways the time spent seemed to compress and compact some of the most basic inner patterns that Cohen himself found so displeasing about himself. In 'Titles', a poem he would eventually finish five winters later, he wrote about his time at Mount Baldy: "I hated everyone but acted generously and no one found me out."

The central revelation of his final Mount Baldy experience was almost ironic, an exquisite Zen joke. "I discovered I had no religious aptitude," said Cohen, sounding cheerfully grateful. "That I wasn't really a religious man." In fact, such a revelation was anything but negative. Surely the point of the retreat and its rigorous regime was in part to force and cajole the subjects toward a state of awareness. If, ultimately that awareness was merely the recognition that they would never become truly enlightened or if it was simply that the last place they belonged was actually in a monastery, then their time had been well served. As Cohen put it, "One of the goals of the activities it to discard a goal."

There was some tangible, corporeal evidence of Cohen's time on Mount Baldy, however. On August 9, 1996, he was officially ordained as a Zen Buddhist monk and given the Dharma name of 'Jikan', which translates as Silent One, and three years later, in January 1999, he visited Mumbai in India. Now 64 years old, his continuing spiritual road trip brought him from California to the subcontinent to meet the Hindu guru Ramesh S. Balsekar. Cohen had been impressed by the books of the 81- year-old sage and had travelled to meet the guru to imbibe the Vedanta tenets of Balsekar, who resided in a sea-facing apartment off Breach Candy. These very specific engagements aside, Cohen had no set plans once he'd settled in Mumbai. "It's been a kind of escape from my monastery," he said, "It's my first time in India, but I can't say how long I'll be here – it could be five minutes, five months or five years."

Cohen was befriended by a fan on his trip – Ratnesh Mathur – and Mathur took great pleasure in showing Cohen the sights and sounds of his hometown. The two visited art exhibitions, Mumbai's oldest synagogue and when Mathur played 'I'm Your Man' in the car, Cohen happily sang along. He eventually left India that April.

Once he'd returned to Roshi, Cohen soon decided to leave the mountain. He was initially concerned at how Roshi would take the news and permission was granted by him only reluctantly. A formal dinner followed, with all the senior monks in attendance after which Cohen finally left Mount Baldy. "I felt like I'd been there long enough...

I found myself saying to Roshi, 'I think its time to go on down the hill for a while.' He said, 'How long?' I said, 'I don't know.' He said, 'Well, goodbye.'"

Roshi would later tell Cohen, "When you left, half of me died."

Although Leonard Cohen had returned to his 'civilian life', happily referring to himself as "a failed monk" (indeed, his publishing company was titled Bad Monk), he was not quite yet back on 'Boogie Street' in the generally accepted meaning of the phrase. In fact, to those who thought Cohen had spent the last few years trying to escape such a state, he would later offer that it was impossible to leave it in the first place. He considered even the rarefied altitude of Mount Baldy to be part of it all. "A monastery is just a *part* of Boogie Street," he said. "In fact, on Boogie Street you go back to your flat or apartment and you eliminate the rest of the world... so in a way there is more respite from Boogie Street on Boogie Street."

Now cured by Roshi and his fellow monks of 'the illusion of being sick', and coming back down the mountain in his jeep to rejoin the business and entertainment Mecca that is the Hollywood end of Los Angeles, Cohen offered that "It's very nice here", while seeming genuinely ambivalent about how he – perhaps as a brand name or a commercial commodity – was perceived in this, the Babylon capital of showbiz. "I never stayed in show business. I guess I should have if I'd wanted to have established a certain kind of career but I never had any appetite for that," he mused. Paradoxically, immediately after leaving his monk's life Cohen's desire now was to return to the little room, the room (invariably with white walls and grey floors) where the songs – the songs that had actually made him famous – were born.

Depression, even clinical depression, had been a constant throughout Cohen's adult life. He wore it through most of his adult life like a late flowering birthmark, a stain that coloured his life and work, sometimes to his advantage. Depression... "was a part of every process," he explained. "It was the central activity of my days and of my nights. It was dealing with the prevailing sense of distress and anxiety... anguish... that prevailed." This prevalent and debilitating condition seemed to have lifted somewhat by the time Cohen had returned to his LA duplex apartment. He did not, however, rush out to the nearest bar just yet or throw himself back into any deep social lifestyle. Even away from the mountain he continued to leave a solitary – if no longer isolated – life, just as he always had. At the same time he was well aware of the expectations foisted upon him, of his legacy. It was just that who he was known as seemed increasingly to Cohen as more like who he'd *been*.

"I hardly ever get a chance to hear my old songs," he reflected. "Sometimes I hear one on some generous retrospective radio station when I'm in town, but I don't feel like that person any more. I stand in awe. People say the very early songs were the most important. I listen to them like I'm listening to someone else. I have a lot of respect for the young heart who produced those visions."

He still wrote both songs and poetry – had never stopped in fact – and now counted drawing among his daily activities. He'd taken to drawing a self portrait every morning for several years and no doubt saw this – to quote the father of Keats – as yet another "social act of the solitary man". Cohen had even considered writing another novel at this point in his life and had submitted a 'humorous' book to his publishers based around his monastic life. But he'd soon withdrawn it, opting to rework the material. Once down from the mountain Cohen began to re-enter a more regular civilian existence. He went travelling again, and began co-coordinating his next musical move with his manager Kelley Lynch. This would turn out to embrace both the past and the future with a Zen like equanimity. Cohen was also returning to his professional life accompanied by one of his oldest companions – a packet of cigarettes. When he'd entered Mount Baldy years earlier he did so as a newly reformed non-smoker, but in the first few months of his stay there he'd taken up smoking again. He remembered clearly "... attending a lecture where one of the members of the audience stood up to tell the author how their book had inspired them to clean up their act – and, yes, how they'd even quit smoking." The author replied, "Well, what's the point of living, then?" Cohen summed up the anecdote with the usual comic timing that seemed to turn the most serious quip into a punch line of sorts: "Naturally, I went out and bought a pack of smokes right away."

CHAPTER ELEVEN

Back On Boogie Street

"Boogie Street is what we're all doing... we're all on Boogie Street. We believe that we leave it from time to time ; we go up a mountain or into a hole but most of the time we're hustling on Boogie Street one way or another'."

LC

"I believe one of the highest moments of stress one can experience is when one is unemployed. I can undertake a new tour, but what I would like to do is make another record. I like to work and I like to go on tour, to drink, to sing. I hope I don't die tomorrow because I have a good many new ideas that I would like to continue working on." Such was Cohen's mood as he re entered the world as a monk. Jikan had spent most of his adult life in thrall to and a victim of his moods but this affliction had recently lifted somewhat. For years he was happy to explore vices that might free him of his residual anguish – speed, fine wine, tobacco – and Cohen had actually abandoned his *prescribed* medication recently whilst on the way to an airport.

In an attempt to combat his depression, Cohen had taken pretty much everything his doctors had thrown at him. "I was involved in early medication, like Desipramine. And the MAOs [monoamine oxidase inhibitors], and the new generation, Paxil, Zoloft, and Wellbutrin," he would recount cheerfully, "'I even tried experimental anti-seizure drugs, ones that had some small successes in treating depression. I was told they all give you a 'bottom', a floor beneath which you are not expected to plunge."

The most popular, even fashionable of pills – Prozac – had been swiftly abandoned by Cohen because it had obliterated his libido. Eventually he had decided to abandon everything. "[I] threw out all the drugs I had. I said, 'These things really don't even begin to confront my predicament.' I figured, 'If I am going to go down I would rather go down with my eyes wide open.'"

At the same time he had cut down on his drinking, imbibing in a modest fashion and savouring his tipples rather than bingeing. His caviar habit had receded but he was once again an avid consumer of (Vantage) cigarettes and (Godiva) chocolates. Either through the careful balance of rejecting and submitting to the use of these substances or as a result of merely hanging in there, it was around this time that Cohen's depression lifted. "The anguish just began to dissolve," he declared. "I just think my brain changed. I read somewhere that some of the brain cells associated with anxiety can die as you get older… gradually, within a small space of time, by imperceptible degrees, this depression lifted."

Although still officially an enlisted 'spiritual marine' within the Mount Baldy regime, throughout 1999 Cohen travelled extensively and ended up honing to perfection the lyrics for what would be his next album at his house on Hydra. The actual recording of what would be Cohen's tenth studio album began in late 1999 although the official starting date was given as May when, shortly after attending one of Sharon Robinson's son's piano recitals, he and she met at his LA duplex. "The day that we embarked on the project," remembers Robinson. "He invited me over to his place and we sat in his kitchen without speaking for a long time. He lit incense and he put on some chant music and we just sat there and meditated or something for a while. It was Leonard's way of setting up a tone or a headspace that we were going to be working from. That's how I see it in hindsight."

For Robinson, herself a sometime follower of Roshi, such a scenario was not as alien as it may appear to the casual observer. "We had been very close and had mediated together before so it didn't strike me as terribly odd, and I just said 'Ok, I'm gonna go with this, I see what's happening'."

Perhaps in some way this encounter was Cohen's version of a kind of cosmic job interview. "Collaborations happen so rarely in my case," he pointed out, and although she was in effect waiting for him when he came down from the mountain, there was no absolute certainty that Cohen was even going to continue an active recording career. "We didn't have an idea that there would be a record," said Cohen. "We just wanted to get together and write some songs together, because the process has always been very peaceful, so we wrote one and then two and then three. She has an extraordinary penetration of my lyrics."

Robinson confirms this. "It's not that we set out to make an album," she says. "We just started working on things and it just happened."

Nevertheless, it soon became apparent that both she and Cohen were involved in something major and crucial. Robinson's input would be profound; she would eventually produce, co-arrange, co-write and sing on the album. A secondary, purely practical reason for Cohen's wish to defer much of the new album's recording, instrumentation and co-composition may have been because since leaving Mount Baldy officially in June he had also been involved in the overseeing and preparation of another album entirely. For some time he'd wanted to release a document of his 1979 tour and he'd recently been listening to old sound board tapes and approving rough mixes from those very shows in anticipation of the release of this new live album.

Meanwhile, on a day-to-day basis throughout late '99 and during the first days of the new millennium, Cohen was mostly preoccupied with the creation of a completely new work. Now living back in the LA duplex that he shared with his daughter Lorca and her numerous pet dogs, Cohen responded favourably to almost all the demos that Robinson had built around the lyrics – often handwritten on A4 lined paper – that he had presented to her. In some cases, as with 'A Thousand Kisses Deep', she was not even aware that those lyrics already informed another completely different version of a song, a song Cohen was happy to discard. "I didn't know there was another version of that," says Robinson surprised. (Cohen had gone as far as recording demos of some songs while at the monastery but Robinson has no memory of hearing any.) "But after listening to my demos, he thought that that was what the actual finished record should sound like."

The decision to stick with the preliminary recordings was not a given choice – certainly not for a major label recording artist of Cohen's stature. Rather than halt their garage work and reconvene to a larger commercial studio with a band as might be expected, Cohen and Robinson took the brave and quietly audacious step of merely carrying on as they were. "The way the album came about is linked to the actual sound of it," Robinson explains. "The album had a unique path and it wasn't done the way an album is normally done. It was also recorded pretty much in the order that it plays in. The last song on the album is the last song we wrote together for instance."

Apart from Cohen and Robinson, few other musicians would be present on the record. In fact the sole cameo was limited exclusively to Bob Metzger's electric guitar spot on 'In My Secret Life'. There were hints throughout the record that musically Cohen had gone for what had once been termed 'trip-hop', not that he would have used such a term himself. His musical interests and vocabulary were still rooted in the classics. "We had several models in the back of our minds when we were working on the music," he said. "A slow R&B song may be referred for 'In My Secret Life', a country song might be referred to for 'That Don't Make It Junk', the model of a protest folk song might be referred to for 'Land Of Plenty'."

Whatever the terminology used to inform and describe the album, the result would be a strangely sub-marine sounding work that sounded less like the work of a duo and more like the result of two halves of the same whole exploring some psychic sea bed together. "Leonard and I were working extremely closely during that time," affirms Robinson. "[Engineer] Leanne [Ungar] was involved but basically [Cohen] was pushing everybody else out of his life during the period of time we were working. So this was his idea and it was his choice about how to get this thing done; it was how he wanted this to work."

One might have expected that on coming down from a monastery, no matter how sociable its atmosphere, Cohen would have wanted to surround himself with a big old style jazz band for his new album. Then again, being centred on community living, his time at the 'retreat' had encouraged anything but solitude. In many respects there was no distinct line between Mount Baldy, Mumbai and LA for Cohen; his practice continued wherever he was, whatever he was doing. "The recording was some kind of extension of his time at Mount Baldy," says Robinson. "He was still very reclusive during this time… he wasn't interacting a lot with other people and this was very intentional. He was totally focussed on the record."

This focus would endure over the coming two years during a process where Robinson's meticulous attention to detail would mirror Cohen's famously painstaking work ethic, in this case limited to honing the lyrics and their metre although he did offer the occasional melodic idea. The resulting insular and almost womb-like feel of the album's sound was down to one very good reason – much of it was recorded in Robinson's three-car garage that was adjoined to her house. "I turned it into a studio space*," she laughs, 'but it did used to be a garage! And I'd record the basic raw audio there and I'd take it over on hard drive [a portable Cheetah 10,000 Seagate device] to Leonard's studio where we'd work on sounds and arrangements. We'd tweak things basically and he would also, ultimately work on his vocals there."

Cohen's set up was similar to Robinson's except that Cohen's space was *above* the garage (and christened Still Life Studio). A rough mix of Robinson's tracks, confirms Leanne Ungar, was "… put onto two tracks of [Leonard's] eight- track Tascam tape, the other six left for Leonard's vocals." Ungar showed Leonard how to operate the appropriate machinery and once he'd got the hang of it, she left him to his own devices.

This simple, ergonomic and economically efficient set up suited Cohen's particular state of mind at the time. "The record was created in very relaxed conditions, because it was made in the study above the garage," he'd recall. "I would rise early to record it because I like to work before the birds begin singing and the dogs start barking and the traffic noise becomes unbearable. I was used to rising at two or three o'clock in the morning and I worked dressed only in my underclothes, in very

* Subsequently called Small Mercies Studio.

calm and pleasant circumstances. For that reason, it was much easier to complete than my previous records."

It was also, of course, cheaper. But while Cohen's home studio was well equipped it was definitely not acoustically sophisticated compared to professional recording environments. "Occasionally Leonard would forget to turn off the jacuzzi that is adjacent to the studio," remembered Ungar, whose job it would then be to remove such unwanted noise from the recordings. The team of three approached the writing and recording of the album from various positions.

"Sometimes Leonard would play me a Casio beat that he wanted the song to start with," explains Robinson who would then modify and expand on the pattern via Midi and pro-tools, often replacing each individual drum sound – snare, hi-hat, tom – individually. "If he had a musical direction that he wanted to start with, then I would come back and construct a track around that or if he didn't have a specific idea I'd come up with the idea myself." When working in unison the two would begin the day at noon until around seven in the evening although, like Cohen, when she worked alone Robinson could also begin very early and go on until very late.

As the recordings progressed, Robinson and Cohen would pause periodically to consider the possibility of bringing in live musicians to replace or augment certain synthesized parts. But when it came to it, Cohen rejected on the idea. "At a certain point," says Robinson, "he felt that it might ruin something good that we had. He's a big fan of not spoiling what you have already by trying to buff it to perfection. Additionally, he liked the consistency of the record that we had and didn't want to spoil that by bringing in additional musicians."

Cohen and Robinson were also aware of the almost infinite possibilities such working methods presented but when faced with an initial drum loop or beat, Cohen employed the Jack Kerouac maxim – first thought, best thought. Working in such a low-fi manner was nothing new. Beck had perhaps popularised the home-made ethic most notably with his debut album in the mid-nineties, and coincidentally Beck's stepfather – the string arranger David Campbell – had contributed to *The Future* and would also score one song on the current album. Nevertheless, these methods were usually the exclusive preserve of upcoming bedroom-based musicians purely because they couldn't afford sufficient studio time to record anywhere else. In Cohen's case he was still signed to Columbia/Sony with, to date, 12 million CD sales alone. He had a healthy nest egg in the bank that amounted to millions (or so he believed) and the home-made approach was therefore both quixotic and audacious. That said, Bruce Springsteen, who certainly had no need for frugality, had released two full-length studio albums recorded in his own home – 1982's sublime *Nebraska* and 1995's *Ghost Of Tom Joad* – and Tom Waits had dabbled in lo-fi too.

Despite adopting a recording method more familiar to much younger musicians, the obvious advantage Cohen had over his lo-fi contemporaries was twofold. Cohen was working with two strong and experienced colleagues – this was Ungar's sixth album with Cohen, Robinson was a Grammy winning songwriter – and he was by now in possession of one of the most unique 'singing' voices on the planet. Not only did Cohen's lyrics have an almost biblical gravity and a weight of conviction to them that bordered on the physical but he now also had the perfect instrument to deliver his words. There was no doubting the sheer heavy currency and authenticity of Cohen's singing voice, however it was captured. It would have sounded God-like on an answering machine. Next to the obviously synthetic but exquisitely recorded backing tracks, the power of his voice and words, along with the muscular precision of the songs themselves, made for a beguilingly odd and powerful mix. Simply put, very few recording artists of Cohen's experience and means had ever recorded an album in such a relatively inexpensive manner before, because they simply didn't have to and thus it hadn't occurred for them to do so. Those young bucks like Beck who *had* recorded albums in their garage did not have the life experience that Cohen had. Thus, *Ten New Songs,* as the album would come to be called, was both unique among Cohen's catalogue and as an album in itself. "This was something that Leonard talked about," says Robinson, "and something that he wanted to preserve. That contrast between the electronic thing that I was bringing and his very natural and rich voice – although he would never describe it that way. It was the human quality versus the electronic. He really was enjoying that contrast and it was something he wanted to keep."

The album was also the first of Cohen's to be recorded completely digitally, but it was unique amongst the Cohen canon for another reason too. While all of his albums had featured female voices in counterpoint and harmony to his own, this work would feature Robinson's expensive sounding soulful sheen alone. "That was something that came out of my demoing the songs first," she explains. "I would initially sing and play everything, at the time not knowing if we were bringing in other musicians or singers. Of course as it turned out, we didn't so my voice stayed because Leonard liked what he was hearing." She did not feel daunted by her multi-tasking on what some were now referring to as Cohen's 'comeback' album. "Leanne [Ungar] was of course there and at times we had two studios running at the same time. We got into a routine where I'd be writing a song while she and Leonard were over at his studio lining up tracks or working on the technical aspect of something we'd already finished. The three of us became a little factory I guess you could say."

Robinson usually put down her vocals first, sometimes using up to 20 tracks to do so, with Cohen singing 'on top' (or perhaps 'underneath' is a more accurate description) afterwards. This was a reversal of the way vocals were usually recorded on Cohen albums although sometimes he would in turn mute Robinson's voice and sing alone. He was still using a German microphone; by now it was the vintage model Neumann 87. Having trained himself to rise early back at Mount Baldy, Cohen not only had no problem recording his vocals in the pre-dawn hours but relished it. "It was very relaxed at those times," he said, 'to come in and find the right place to stand or sit and have the right drink or smoke in your hand, lean back, go back, erase, go forward. It was a very luxurious way to do vocals."

Cohen explained that he was concerned with finding the right mood in which to sing each song because his aim was to have the voice represent the song rather than just reveal it. "He does a few takes to get the *attitude* he wants," says Robinson. He was also aiming for a certain neutrality of sound, allowing the listener as much freedom as possible. He wanted it to have '… an agreeable groove… you can lean on it, relax into it. There are doors and windows you can enter if you have the time."

Once Cohen's vocals were completed they would be transferred by Ungar from his set up to the more expansive and advanced computer system at Robinson's garage. At no point during the process did Robinson herself ever question the lyrics she was presented with and had to sing. "I always considered it an honour to be working with him," she states. "Wherever he is as an artist, that's really his choice. It's not there for me to critique. As a voice on his albums I'm there to be subservient to his voice." In fact, Sharon's vocals on the album are at least if not more dominant – in terms of parts sung and individual tracks – as Cohen's own vocals. Some critics remarked that it sounded more like a Sharon Robinson album with Cohen guesting. The producer herself does not agree with this diagnosis: "I'm just honoured to be a part of it."

It was now early 2001 and with all the recorded parts deemed complete it was time to mix the components into a whole. Initially the team attempted to transpose the digital tracks to analogue tape and mix in a regular commercial studio but they were unhappy with the initial results and soon regrouped back at Cohen's studio where the mixing of the entire album – incorporating the balance and EQing of scores upon scores of individual tracks – was completed in three weeks. The finished whole was then sent to Bob Ludwig's Gateway mastering studios in Portland, Maine, where the album was mastered to CD and vinyl editions.

Despite the fact that this was Cohen's first new album since 1992 and that the record was musically untypical and therefore a risk in the marketplace Columbia/Sony were apparently very happy with the finished album. "They loved it," says Robinson. Their belief in Cohen and his new work would be borne out by the worldwide marketing they would put behind *Ten New Songs*. But first there was a little exercise in the raising of public awareness. To some Cohen was by now purely a mythical figure; beyond the good and the dead but hardly relevant. A gentle and classy reminder would be sent out to the public prior to the new album, both because Cohen wanted it so and because it wouldn't hurt his sleeping audience to be reminded what they'd been missing the last decade.

Thus, in February 2001, with *Ten New Songs* more or less in the can *Field Commander Cohen* was released. An exquisite time capsule from another epoch, this live album, culled from Cohen's "best ever tour" (his own opinion), with his then group Passenger brought the reborn ghosts of two 1979 English concerts into what was (with the horror of 9/11 a mere seven months away) now the final days of an ostensibly securer and safer era. Cohen had not had a notable release for some time and this 'new' album made many realise that they had missed him; a bit like an elderly uncle in the spare room whose wandering off into the hills years ago had hardly been noticed at the time. But *Field Commander Cohen* and the accompanying rumours of another new album in the offing reminded us just how unique Cohen's voice had been – in both senses of the word. Reviewing the album, the *New York Observer* noted that: "Mr. Cohen's voice is warm and strong throughout, and still has some of the high end that is not so evident on his last two studio albums... As for the classics showcased on *Field Commander Cohen,* Mr. Cohen offers up his best-known lyrics almost wistfully." *Rolling Stone's* critic opined: "The band relaxes and stretches... despite his famously miserabilist image, what comes over most strikingly is his wry and often overlooked sense of humour." *The Times* added: "Elaborately and yet simply awesome'... the songs still shine."

The title song itself was from another age, a time when politics had yet to debase itself completely and when pop singers like Cohen still went off to (three day) wars. Cohen recalled the origin of the song in detail, noting its very first appearance in his notepad all those years ago. "Let's see, I went to Asmara after the Yom Kippur War which was in '73, wasn't it?" he would reminisce. "No, this little notebook predates that by a couple of years. There is an entry written on March 14, 1971, in the coffee shop of the Hilton in Acapulco, and one in Suzanne's writing, on June 1, 1971. It also contains the first draft of 'Love Is A Fire' which was published in *The Energy Of Slaves,* in 1972."

Impeccably packaged, recorded, engineered and mixed, the album was nevertheless perhaps a little slick sounding for some tastes, a little too muso like, lacking the atmosphere of a hall or the ambience of an audience to be a truly classic live record. Still, it was received gratefully if modestly among the faithful and provided a neat segue to the next record in that it featured Sharon Robinson's debut appearance as Cohen's backing singer.

While *Field Commander Cohen* fulfilled its reconnaissance mission around the world, *Ten New Songs'* artwork was prepared for release. As with *Various Positions*, Cohen would provide the cover art himself in the shape of a lo-fi, grainy self portrait of him and Robinson that perfectly represented the record's content. "We were just sat at Leonard's computer," laughs Robinson, "and he just took one of those webcam pictures with the basic camera that was attached to the computer. Of course, he does everything with a lot of thought and care and I remember him composing the shot. But at the time I don't think he intended it as the album cover – he was just taking a picture." Cohen and Robinson look so close as to be related in the picture, a gang of two. "Well, we were very close during the making of that record, that's for sure," confirms Robinson who in the early summer of 2001 accompanied Leanne Ungar and the 66-year-old Cohen on a 'pre-promotional tour' (as his label incongruously termed it) of Europe.

This tour consisted mainly of the trio hopping from one five-star hotel to another in short bursts; one day in Madrid, the next in Berlin, the next in London where Cohen would do the usual interviews with the usual journalists (albeit some now young enough to regard Cohen as a bona fide legend). The trip was not just the usual round of TV and press chats, it also required the three to be present at 'meet and greet' events with local Sony licensees and album playbacks for distributors, sales and promo staff. Cohen and his collaborators were personally raising awareness of an album that was not scheduled for release until October 16. Perhaps Sony was worried that Cohen was in danger of becoming merely 'great' again and were eager to raise both industry and press awareness and anticipation for an album that was almost as unclassifiable as it was unique. After all, it was still a rare occasion indeed for anyone to hear Cohen on the radio.

His once light hazel eyes now transformed into a soulful downy grey, Cohen did his duty and looked every inch as one would hope. He sat meditatively in anonymous luxury hotel suites, Armani suited and unbooted – he was often barefoot – a cigarette and its smoke issuing from a lined and kind mouth beneath smart, cropped grey hair growing back into a classic Roman style. One weathered hand held the cigarette, the other hand sometimes threaded a "comboloi" (a Greek string of beads similar to a rosary). Cohen played the role of Cohen beautifully for his adoring press and was as gracious and self-effacing as one would expect of a man now officially a monk, often deferring the attention away from himself and to his friends. "Did you see the young black woman who was here?" he asked during one interview. "She is Sharon Robinson. We made this record together. We met in 1979 and have been close ever since then. I am godfather to her son, so our families have always been linked. In addition, she is a very good sound engineer as well. Sharon has done most of the music on this record. I gave her the lyrics and she worked on the melodies or did the choruses, but everything was done with excellent mutual understanding."

Although the album would be credited exclusively to Cohen, the songs within were very much a collaborative effort, the result of a direct partnership. And Cohen went out of his way to let this be known. Robinson had composed the music to all of the songs although the lyrics remained, obviously, 100% Cohen. The voice in which he sang the songs was now an immovable force, the aural equivalent of an Easter Island statue – as unwieldy as stone yet flecked with moss and down of greys and greens. The music ebbed and flowed around its parched timbre like an iceberg. Indeed, often the musical accompaniment that surrounded Cohen's sandblasted croon seemed purely secondary and was in danger of being sucked into the heavy gravity of the voice, like light collapsing into a black hole. It was the voice of someone who had lived and of someone who was committed to documenting that life. Cohen was less prosaic in explaining the evolution of his instrument, blaming the beautiful degradation of his "golden voice" on "about 500 tonnes of whisky and a million cigarettes… 50, 60 years of smoking".

Ironically it was around now – at 68 years old – that Cohen seriously stopped smoking. "I was having trouble getting the smoke down," he would chuckle, "so I had my throat examined. It's a very disagreeable procedure. They put a camera up through your nose and… anyway the doctor looked at it and had a scowl on his face… so I said 'OK, do I have it?' And he said 'No, but you're on the royal road'. So I thought I'd better give up the smokes." Spooked, Cohen gave up immediately but found that the practice of not smoking would become harder to maintain as time went on. Cigarettes for him were more than a mere nicotine buzz, they were a symbol of life and its possibilities, just as his guitar and famous blue raincoat had been.

Released in late 2001, *Ten New Songs* was well and warmly received. "Life's a bitch and then you die, but in Cohen's case, nowhere near as early as he imagined," said *NME*, giving Cohen's 'comeback' a seven out of 10. "It was worth the wait," reckoned *Uncut*. "Although the tone of these odes and meditations is mournful, at the age of 67 Cohen's pessimism about the human condition is tempered with reconciliation. He'll never be cheerful, but a Zen-like serenity pervades every song." *Playboy's* reviewer wrote: "[It] features his raspy bass voice at its seductive best. His lyrics make relationships mysterious, even mystical, which is testimony to his poetic powers."

In Europe, little changed and as ever he was received as a lost saint. There were high profile features in the Sunday supplements and across the broadsheets. Cohen was back and it felt good to have him so. He looked cool still, a man many thought they had lost to the mountain top had now returned dapper and slim. The Duke of Doom was still trading in dry wit, still agreeably serious and still writing too much. 'A Thousand Kisses Deep' had, according to Cohen, "... many many verses... the verses that made it into the song did so because they fit the metre of the melody." Here was Cohen the master craftsman again, showing that he still took his work seriously whilst simultaneously seeming effortless in his seriousness.

Some critics wanted the album so much to be Cohen's 'rap album' and whilst his corroded croon barely registered as singing it still carried the sunken melodies efficiently enough to impart their power. One disappointed fan described the album as sounding like something "some guy on a subway had burned to CD in his own apartment". This could surely also be taken as a skewed compliment. As a whole, the album ploughed inexorably through all other contemporary musics or tastes. Its sparseness directly reflected the singer's own refined aesthetic more baldly than ever. It sounded boiled down, coal compressed to diamond, essence of Cohen, now wearing the robes of a holy man in Armani, a sage in aviator shades

Ten New Songs charted well in the usual places – the hottest and the coldest countries – and had been inexpensive enough to make that it soon recouped its costs and then some. Although still signed to a major worldwide record company – Sony had swallowed Columbia some time before – there was actually very little commercial pressure on Cohen by now. Big labels like this could often afford to subsidise 'prestige' acts. Cohen explained that as there was little at stake financially either way, the record company could put out almost anything by him with little promotion and it would still sell, making a "modest profit". His label faithfully trailed the album with a single in Europe: the low major minor waltz of 'In My Secret Life'. Again, there was little expectation of any Cohen single competing with other Sony acts, the Mariah Careys of this world, but such an exercise helped maintain interest in the 'mother' album and it was also an opportunity to film a video, even if this medium's potential – in Cohen's case – was also limited. "MTV don't want anything to do with me," he mused, "but they have content laws in Canada so it gets shown there."*

Beyond his agreeableness in playing the game, it was as hard as ever to locate any kind of compromise in Cohen's work and life. If he was playing 'the game' then it was by default. Interviews had never seemed like hard word for Cohen and the ones conducted as promotion for *Ten New Songs* portrayed a man apparently at ease with his lot. Asked by one interviewer if "you don't care if it ends or goes on", Cohen paused for a moment, considering his answer before saying simply, "Not really".

The album sold steadily in the months following its release and Cohen continued to fulfil any promotional duties asked of him. Although this entailed a much less intense itinerary than on its pre-release, he was still doing interviews into the earliest months of the New Year. Generally, just as he had done exactly 20 years previously, 2002 was a year when Cohen himself stayed under the radar in terms of public profile. The

* Like many countries keen to retain their national identity in areas of the arts, percentage of videos shown in Canada had by prior agreement to be from Canadian artists.

events of September 11 had no doubt shaken Cohen and he may have taken time to consider how his – or anyone's work – could address such a meaningful an attack upon the "western code".

Meanwhile there was a plentiful archive to re-master, repackage and re-release and in the summer of 2002, Sony/Columbia put out *The Essential Leonard Cohen* as part of the "Essential" series of upgraded reissues they embarked on with artists of Cohen's vintage and prestige. The series was in itself a project of the "Legacy" branch of the label and this latest compilation placed Cohen in the company of, among others, Miles Davis, Bruce Springsteen, Bob Dylan and 'Weird Al'Yankovic. The two-disc set spanned all of Cohen's output to date with the glaring exception of *Death Of A Ladies Man*. Cohen was not merely a passive party in its release either; he oversaw the Bob Ludwig mastering session in Maine, proving that he still had an active interest in his old work. Aside from this, 2002 was a devoted quiet, behind-the-scenes time for Cohen. He continued to potter about among the plots and fields of words that would make up his next book. He continued to indulge his passion for producing artwork, daily drawing to paper and experimenting with graphic software on one of his many computers in his various homes. His next album was in its early stages and there were plans for a truly a collaborative effort with his latest romantic partner and long time backing singer Anjani Thomas. Cohen's activities were carried out in rooms and studios beyond the pen, camera and recorder of the journalist and biographer Short of performing live, he'd given of himself in every sense during the expansive and extensive press campaign for *Ten New Songs* and for the time being at least he would refuse all interview requests.

That November, Cohen's sister Esther visited her brother on a sunny LA evening and they spent time together in his backyard. With Adam also present they all posed for photographs in the Californian sunset, sipping champagne and comparing mythologies. The snapshots (taken by Thomas) hint, among other things, both at Cohen's past and at another path he might have taken had his life not panned out the way it did. His son, Adam resembles a slightly more expensively groomed, camper looking version of Cohen's younger self. Sister Esther, attractive and with an expensive hair-do and smart pink jacket, looks like the kind of bright and supportive woman who would have made the perfect wife Cohen never had. Cohen himself looks like an amiable old geezer, neither thin or portly, with an air of easy authority. He stands, hands in pockets like someone comfortable with himself and their lot, someone who goes to the dentist often and has a good medical plan. Standing in the warm air of his attractively untidy back yard, he looks like a man who has lived a full, rich life yet there is little of the artisan or poet about him. He has the air of a retired diplomat or perhaps a cosmetic surgeon who paints on the side. He could almost have been the man to have inherited his uncle's Montreal clothing business.

There were the usual awards and the usual surprises too in a year when Cohen lived up to his Roshi given name of 'To Be Quiet'. For a start, 'Hallelujah' had begun to take on a new lease of life. The John Cale version of the song had appeared in the computer animated fantasy film *Shrek*, released in late 2001. The movie was enormously successful, opening up a new franchise of sorts, and once its cinema run was over it was released on DVD, sales of which had continued to grow, bringing Cohen's plaintive ode into the living rooms of literally millions of families. The soundtrack to the film was also selling in its millions and included a version by of the song by Rufus Wainwright. Though no one knew it at the time, this was in fact the beginning of a whole 'Hallelujah' phenomena that would grow and grow.

In January 2003 Cohen received the rank of Companion of the Order of Canada, presented to him by former ABC journalist and old friend Governor General Adrienne Clarkson. "He has the distinction of creating a body of work that has remained contemporary and significant through three decades of shifting musical and aesthetic tastes," she said in a statement from her office in which she also described him as "a venerated dean of the pop culture movement." Cohen himself did not attend, the reason given being a summary of his life so far: he was "out of the country, travelling and writing".

These very activities, as well as the work on a new album, took up Cohen's days throughout the year. Yet even as he submerged himself in his personal day-to-day endeavours, the interest in Cohen and his work continued to manifest itself outside his own personal control. His songs continued to be covered by various singers in various countries and although he'd never accepted a commission to score the soundtrack to a whole movie himself, his recordings continued to appear in films throughout the world. In 2003 *alone* there were at least 14 uses of Cohen's original recordings and/or songs appearing in everything from a Greek TV series (*Amateur Man*) through a French financed high profile movie (*The Life Of David Gale*) to a Canadian feature based on one of Cohen's own books (*The Favourite Game*). While Cohen was rarely heard on the radio he had no problem seeping into the bedrooms of the unenlightened through a wide range of popular TV shows and fine films. For the more literary minded, there were still the books. While Cohen barely raised a cropped head in public during the year, at least four of his books were reprinted in various languages, including for the first time a Chinese edition of *Beautiful Losers*.

In late June there was yet another 'tribute' show at Prospect Park in Brooklyn. Conceived and executed by legendary A&R man/producer Hal Wilner, the show consisted of numerous singers with a fondness for the Cohen oeuvre in a show that was called "Came So Far for Beauty, An Evening of Songs by Leonard Cohen Under the Stars". The performance was just that; with Nick Cave, rising fop superstar Rufus Wainwright, Linda Thompson and old Cohen backing vocalists Perla Battalla and Julia Christensen among others, reinterpreting many of the classics from the Cohen song book to a capacity crowd. Cohen himself did not attend although his sister did. While the show itself was nothing unique – variations on the theme of performing and presenting Cohen's songs and poetry without the involvement of Cohen himself had been happening for decades – it was unique in that this was the first time that Cohen's songs could *only* be heard in such a fashion. For the first time in years – although there had been rumours – Cohen actually had no definite plans to tour himself. Some said he considered himself totally retired from the stage. Nevertheless, as the renewed and growing interest in Cohen's legend and songs became apparent, there was once again a very real public hunger to see Cohen in person. Unfortunately for his fans, although still lean, Cohen was anything but hungry now and financially at least had no reason to ever work again. Or so he thought.

Meanwhile, there were other compilation albums, tribute singles and albums, references to Cohen in books and autobiography, biographies, fan festivals, scripts based on his song titles, TV and radio documentaries that appeared through 2003 even as he disappeared from public view, though there was one final glimpse. A relatively quiet year ended, for those that were watching, with a Christmas card from Cohen – a self-drawn design depicting a guardian angel overlooking two children crossing a bridge was donated for commercial use to the world wide charity War Child.

2004 was yet another quiet year profile wise for Cohen although it did see the release of his eleventh studio album, *Dear Heather*, which was as low key as the record itself. Cohen declined to do any interviews to promote the record and this didn't help either its sales or profile in late October. Musically, the work was a gentle mish-mash of various sources drawn together to make an unsatisfying whole. Cohen obviously did not feel like rehearsing a band and going into a commercial studio to record a fully realised album in the conventional manner, and one might have expected, following the critical and commercial success of *Ten New Songs*, that he would have extended the working methods used on that album and recorded another album in a similar vein, again with Robinson and Ungar. Instead he went for an almost collage approach.

"I produced three of the tracks," Robinson points out, "but on the rest of the album I didn't appear at all. He was just doing his thing, trying different methods as usual." The three songs to which Robinson contributed the music, production and vocals were the Bryon adaptation 'No More Go A-Roving', 'The Letters' and 'There For You', none of which would have sounded out of place on *Ten New Songs*, largely because they sprung from the same sessions. This was not a problem in itself but alongside other material that clearly came from totally different sources, the tracks sounded discordant. The record also appears unfinished and plain incomplete compared to any other Cohen album in his catalogue, nowhere more so than on the final track, a remixed live version of the hoary old standard 'Tennessee Waltz', circa 1985.

There were moments, however. The eerie, lustful lament/mantra of 'Dear Heather' itself was an intriguing and affecting experiment, and Cohen was still working on new ideas for combinations of his and women's voices. "On the song 'Dear Heather', for some odd reason

I wanted to hear a woman's voice," he said, "and I wanted to sing background myself but... I told Anjani, 'Try and sing it as if you're not a really good singer'.

The album was haunted by ghosts. Three of the songs were dedicated to fallen friends: Irving Layton, who was still alive but grievously ill with Alzheimer's disease, the Canadian poet A.M. Klein, who'd died in 1972, and recently departed R&B singer Carl Anderson.

Some of the songs were based on traditional ballads while some took their texts wholesale from the work of other poets (as in the opening track's direct use of the Byron poem and in Franck Scott's 'Villanelle For Our Time' – the only track to have survived the Mount Baldy demos and recorded there in Cohen's cabin in 1999. On 'To A Teacher' Cohen even quoted himself from as far back as his first poetry collection, *The Spice Box Of Earth*. The basic tracks of 'The Faith' dated far back to 1979's *Recent Songs* sessions and credited the long retired and now ill Henry Lewy. 'On That Day' addressed the events of September 11: 'Some people say/They hate us of old/Our women unveiled/Our slaves and our gold'.

The whole patchwork made for unsatisfying listening, particularly after the seductive totality of *Ten New Songs* and even *Field Commander Cohen*. In fact both of these recent albums could be identified as the twin stools between which *Dear Heather* had so heavily fallen. Cohen for once sounded truly sad, nostalgic and *old*, seemingly unable to pull together a singular focussed concept. This suggests it would have been more useful and honest to market the album as a collection of outtakes and curios rather than a completely new album, and brings into question the motives behind the release; indeed, the original title of the record had been *Old Ideas*. Cohen sounded almost too comfortable in his discomfort and the sound of a band to help filter his intensity into something more musically palatable was a much missed factor on the album, even if those close to him didn't see it so.

"The music to 'Undertow', 'To A Teacher', 'Dear Heather', 'Villanelle For Our Time' and 'Because Of' is all Leonard's doing," explained Thomas. "What gives his arrangements such a cool vibe is that the drums and bass play in time but he doesn't quantise the keyboard pads or solos... they're mostly in the pocket but a lot of it is laid back or spilling over the beats. This gives it a very relaxed feel, just the way a live band would interact."

This was arguable but the actual sounds employed on the record certainly did not inhabit the same musical space that a group would have. Previously this hadn't been an issue; the use of inexpensive sounding electronics had worked as an alternative to a live group and not as a substitute. Still, the experience was a learning curve for Thomas who in time would employ her new experiences to much greater effect on a future solo album. "When singing Leonard's lyrics, my aim is to not over-emote or under-report. Sometimes it's tricky because a vocalist's natural inclination is to milk a great song for all it's worth. Leonard taught me to rein it in, sing less and let the story tell itself. It's the greatest bit of advice anyone has given me about my voice."

Both press and public were much less enamoured – if even aware – of the record than of *Ten New Songs*. "Some songs are virtually unadorned with poetic imagery and fall flat; in others, Mr. Cohen uses his calmly sepulchral voice for speech rather than melody. The production is homemade," observed *The New York Times*. "If this is the end," noted *Stylus* magazine, "then I'm sorry to report that *Dear Heather* is a particularly dour, unsatisfying way to end such an intriguing career." Other reviews were favourable and the record even charted higher in *Billboard* than many of Cohen's previous albums (peaking at 131 for one week) but this did not reflect long term sales. It was apparent in the reaction to the album that there was a sense that Cohen was treading water.

With regard to criticism Cohen himself reckoned that, "Other people can determine whether a piece of writing or a piece of art is useful or not. I tend to evaluate my own work on a basis of utility and that feedback comes from other people… the occasional letter from someone that says the work has helped them in one way or another and one is pleased that the work has some utility."

As ever his friends were naturally supportive. "Sometimes critics have complained it sounds like the music is tacked on to a lyric without much thought or care," admitted Thomas. "[But] this couldn't be further from the truth. Every track is given due time and consideration; if it doesn't make the grade it isn't released. It's no secret that for Leonard, writing is a long and arduous endeavour. Do they really think he would give up on a hard won lyric when it came time to arrange it?"

Some commented that the album, so moss stained by death and loss, was in fact Cohen's eulogy. At 70 years of age, Cohen had more than earned the right to retire at last. Yet such a move would have cast his re-emergence into the greater world after Mount Baldy as a futile step, a pyrrhic return. In fact, Cohen would not be allowed to retire. He was about to be forced back into his work, the world and towards a greater fame and fortune than he'd ever known. And this was purely as a consequence of one mighty cosmic joke.

CHAPTER TWELVE

Hallelujah

"Somehow, just in the nature of things, you know, the disappointments accumulate, and the obstacles multiply and you sense the destruction of your body, and your mind, and you feel here is the last arena – 'arena' is too big, the last boxing ring, or the last Ouija board, where you can examine some of the ideas that have intrigued you. That have seized you..."

LC

On October 6, 2005 Steven Machat remembers being in New York when he spied the curiously literate *New York Times* headline: 'Leonard Cohen's Troubles May Be A Theme Come True.' Like many others around the world, Machat was shocked at the story therein which stated that Cohen had been royally robbed, ripped off, turned over and was now apparently close to being completely broke. It transpired that over a period of years Cohen's long standing manager, Kelley Lynch, had raided his life savings and systematically spent millions of Cohen's dollars. While Cohen was ensconced at Mount Baldy his retirement fund had in effect become her pocket money. After selling millions of records and thousands of books, having sold out hundreds of concerts the world over and having personally generated millions of dollars in revenue, Leonard Cohen at 70 didn't have enough money to buy a modest house in Ohio.

As the authorised signatory on his account Lynch had had complete access to Cohen's cash and had used it to go on spending sprees, purchasing antiques, property and various other miscellaneous goods and services. Cohen was apparently a man who trusted those in his employment to check his accounts for him, and had very little idea of his bank balance at any given time. He was not given to checking on his account at the ATM and did not bother opening the statements that came in the mail.

The theft was brought to his attention by a friend of his daughter's who suspected Lynch's activities and, on finally checking with the bank, Cohen was hit hard in the face with the facts. "It's the oldest story in Hollywood I would think," said a weary but resigned Cohen, when asked about the ensuing litigation. "I had a bit of money and I didn't watch it... I never had... my indifference presented a temptation to a number of people to pilfer these accounts."

Machat's warning to Cohen way back about the wisdom or otherwise of getting involved with Lynch in any capacity – not just romantically – had been proved right. Cohen now publically admitted to a casual affair with Lynch but countered that there was "nothing urgent about it" and that like millions of other brief trysts around the world throughout history it was primarily motivated by "alcohol and familiarity".

At least the years of Buddhist training had apparently paid off insofar as Cohen seemed to have little animosity toward the accused. If Cohen's conduct and image had been a mere pose all these years, then this was the one instance ripe to explode it. But Cohen did not break down, threaten, scream blue murder, fly into a frothing rage or attempt to round up a lynch mob for Lynch. Indeed he seemed unusually calm considering the circumstances. He was even tender toward her saying, "She was more than my girlfriend... she was a friend...a very helpful person."

Confronted with the old adage that one shouldn't mix business with pleasure Cohen responded somewhat innocently that he had never considered his work a business or a career. "It was *all* a pleasure," he said. In public, at least, Cohen did seem remarkably sanguine about the loss. He was never angry or accusatory, and his stock answer to the calamity was the dry one liner, "It's enough to put a dent in your mood" but when pushed he admitted that, "I don't know what helped me deal with it… I guess it just hasn't hit me yet."

The whole business in some ways read like an acutely ironic Zen joke: materially wealthy man goes to monastery to escape material world. Leaves monastery to find out material world has been stolen from him. Now poor man has to embrace material world again to regain fortune. The amount stolen – over $5 million – was perhaps so large as to be incomprehensible to Cohen. Although he was allegedly left with only $150,000 in his account, on a day to day basis little in his life changed. "I was still eating every day. There's still a roof over my head. I live the same kind of life most of the time." Apart from of his own personal living expenses he had to maintain his various homes around the world but this would have been the extent of his monthly expenses. Both his children were grown up and financially independent and Cohen did not even own a pet. The legal rigmarole associated with the case seemed to bother him more on a day to day basis than the lack of financial abundance. Dealings with lawyers, forensic accountants and tax specialists are rarely to a poet's taste, and these matters exhausted and bored him. Cohen sued Lynch immediately for fraud, theft and mismanagement. He also found himself new management. Lynch had after all, taken considerably more than her allotted 15% commission.

Machat observed from a distance and was not sympathetic. "You have to let go of your ego to become enlightened. But when you put yourself in the centre and you become the victim throughout the entire episode… you've missed the entire point. You're not the victim; you're a participant in the causality of life. Everything has cause and everything has effect… he wants to be a victim. It's easier for him that way because then he doesn't have to stand tall."

Cohen's new management was the Montreal based firm of Macklam & Feldman but, more importantly, his new lawyer was Robert Kory. There was a slight history between the two. As a philosophy student at Yale, while "learning to meditate" the young Kory had bought a collection of poems by Cohen. "I came to him through his poetry not his music," affirms Kory who still reads the work today. Cohen was then popular among Kory's clique in the late Sixties if not with America at large. "Within my peers, he was fashionable," he remembers, "but no, he wasn't broadly popular." Although 'Suzanne' – presumably the Judy Collins version – would become omnipresent among the circles in which Kory and his pals moved, Kory was not much of a fan of Cohen the singer to begin with. "I didn't focus on his albums or music as such... not till later."

Now, more than 30 years later, as Kory began working with his new client (this had actually begun in November 2004) the seasoned lawyer quickly came to realise that Cohen was "incredibly unique. His poetry embodies music to some extent and it's so lyrical that it just lends itself to songs. I mean that's rare, in a contemporary poet." Kory grew to love the music of his client. "My favourite is 'Anthem'," he says. "That line, 'There's a crack in everything/that's how the light gets in'... that nails it for me. Remember, I approached Leonard through poetry as a philosophy student." The two had met briefly backstage at one of Cohen's North American concerts. "It meant more to me than it did to him," states Kory. "I'm sure he wouldn't even remember it." Kory would ultimately go onto become a pivotal figure in Cohen's life and later career but for the next three years his services would be limited to helping Cohen through the Lynch debacle as both a lawyer and a friend.

Kory was introduced to Leonard by Anjani to whom he was briefly married in 1988. "I decided I would help him and defer my fees in doing so," he says. "This was a strategy on my part, an investment if you like. I work with entrepreneurs. If I think a client has integrity I will go with them and they can pay me later. Leonard had integrity." Kory believes Lynch's behaviour was motivated purely by greed. "She wanted a fantastic lifestyle and to do that she ransacked Leonard's accounts. The amazing thing is how she hid this from him and how she explained her wealth to other people which she did by attributing her new found money to a side business she had set up. I wasn't surprised at Leonard's calm reaction, no. It proves the depth of his spiritual practice and sincerity."

Meanwhile, interest in Cohen's work, his legacy, his myth, his absence from the stage and most of all in his songs continued without Cohen's direct participation. All of this appreciation was evident in a film that premiered in Toronto in September 2005. Based on a January 2005 Sydney Opera House tribute show (Hal Wilner's *Came So Far for Beauty* production) and an earlier performance in Brighton UK, the performers featured included Nick Cave, Jarvis Cocker, The Handsome Family, Beth Orton, Rufus Wainwright, Martha Wainwright, Teddy Thompson, Linda Thompson, Antony, Kate & Anna McGarrigle, with Cohen's former back-up singers Perla Batalla and Julie Christensen making cameos. The climax of the film includes a typically malodorous performance of *Tower Of Song* by U2, (with Cohen guesting) which was filmed specifically for the movie in New York during May 2005. "A very graceful moment," said Cohen generously. After debuting in Canada, it was subsequently released in various other countries during 2006 and 2007 and garnered great critical and media attention, arguably more for Cohen than for the film itself. At the beginning of the U2 clip, in a brief interview segment, Cohen was explicit about the possibility of his return to the stage. "It becomes more attractive to me," he said, "the more I drink." Again Steven Machat was not convinced by this latest wave of renewed attention. Asked why Cohen's work had not only endured but thrived into the 21st Century Machat was typically contrary. "Leonard is successful because people like to be depressed and his music is a tool for that."

Indeed the happily miserable masses continued to honour Cohen. In Toronto in February 2006 Cohen was inducted into the Canadian Songwriters' Hall of Fame. The ceremony was accompanied by the usual blurb: "The 2006 Canadian Songwriters Hall of Fame inductees exemplify the profound wealth of talent that exists in Canada. Our songwriters have helped define our cultural and musical landscape," Hall of Fame chair Peter Steinmetz said in the official statement. Aside from Gordon Lightfoot, who sat next to Cohen at the preceding dinner, the other inductees were much less well known on an international level, Gilles Vigneault being the other main inductee alongside Cohen. 'Suzanne', 'Bird On The Wire', 'Ain't No Cure For Love' and 'Hallelujah' were among the actual songs being 'inducted' that night, as were 'La Manic' by Georges de La Tour, 'La Fille De L'ile' by Felix Leclerc, 'Mon Pays', 'Pendant Que' and 'Si Les Batteaux' by Gilles Vigneault, 'Put Your Hand In The Hand' by Gene MacLellan, 'Sugar Sugar' by Andy Kim (co-written with Jeff Barry) and 'Sweet City Woman' by Rich Dodson. Such names and titles illustrated how far Cohen had come. With the exception of 'Sugar Sugar', only his songs were well known world wide.

Cohen had truly transcended his roots, rising away from his cultural origins to achieve a kind of universality in his work. In some ways, being recognised as specifically Canadian aided and abetted this. Although he could now stand beside the greatest American songwriters – Cole Porter, Bob Dylan, Sammy Cahn, Smokey Robinson, et al, he was still considered a *Canadian* songwriter and in doing so was a big blue crusty whale in a lake full of trout.

The man who turned up at the event was still recognisably Cohen but did look his age. Wearied by his recent legal hassles, he appeared a little more lined than usual, his hair thinning, white and close cropped, his suit worn but sharp. He was generous with interviews to promote the occasion. "I'm not really drawn to these kind of events," he told one journalist. "I don't think anybody really wants all that attention. I love the attention given to a song or a concert – something you've actually done and worked at and sweated over, but this, where you're somehow being honoured, they're always tricky." He admitted that he had left the decision to attend or not to his current (and as it would turn out temporary) manager, Sam Feldman.

Sat for the concert between Gilles Vigneault and Cohen's now confirmed romantic partner Anjani Thomas, Cohen had the presence of a royal monk among the dressed up crowd. He looked almost daintily saintly as he took to the stage to formally accept his award and he wept as he did so, tearfully explaining, "One of the reasons one avoids these things is because they summon some really deep emotional responses. This happens to an artist or a writer very rarely, where you have in front of you the unconditional acceptance of your work."

Examples of his work were then presented exquisitely to him and the audience. Cohen was again visibly moved at three performances of his greatest songs. The now seemingly omnipresent Rufus Wainwright did a sombrely camp 'Everybody Knows', a scarecrow like Willie Nelson performed an appropriately bare bones, latter day Johnny Cash style version of 'Bird On The Wire' but the highlight was undoubtedly a barefooted kd lang performing a tenderly soaring, string caressed version of 'Hallelujah'. Her powerfully fluent performance in particular moved Cohen and his belle, both only a few feet away in the audience. "We were just in tears after that," recalled Thomas. "It was a magnificent performance. Just laid that song to rest, I think." At the song's end lang left the stage to embrace Cohen in the front row. Trading Buddhist exaltations and kisses, Cohen seemed genuinely humbled by the power of his song and lang's transcendental recital of it. With the ceremony over, a wearied Cohen and Thomas forsook the after-show parties and retreated to the King Edward Hotel bar, where further respect was paid. "kd lang passed through and Rufus was there and Gilles Vigneault and a lot of the entertainers came by," remembered Cohen. "It was very warm. The sense of community, which we [songwriters] don't often have, prevailed."

The legions of Cohen fans around the world, the very same ones who had campaigned for him to receive the Nobel Peace Prize the year before were delighted at the rise in their hero's profile and his impending productivity, even if the reasons for it were his pressing financial problems. Cohen, now 71, was astonishingly pragmatic about the situation in which he found himself. "There's always been a relationship [between work and money], you know," he said. "I've had a family and other people to look after in my life; it takes a certain amount of work to do that." Cohen had long stated that he wanted to be paid for his work and not work for his pay and acknowledged that, "I've been able to do that all these years; I understand that it's rare and it's a blessing, But, you know, I've always understood the connection between labour and wages."

Although Cohen was not actively pursuing a follow up to *Dear Heather* at this time the work continued to appear in its familiar guises. The successor to Cohen's last major book release, the *Stranger Song* anthology released in 1993, was the *Book Of Longing* which was finally released in May 2006.* Lavishly illustrated with Cohen's own illustrations, the author himself wasn't sure what the book was exactly – a biography, a collection of lyrics, an anthology of poems? In the final analysis he was happy to accept the critics' view of whatever *they* thought it was, suggesting with typical amiability, "Critics can be useful". When pressed, he would define the collection as a "Light hearted book... with a kind

---

* Such was the delay in the book actually appearing that Cohen confided that within his circle it had become known as The Book Of Prolonging.

of innocence about it. It doesn't pretend to be much and that's what I like about it."

Throughout its pages, Cohen wrote 'God' as "G–D", which is in fact the traditional Hebrew style. Cohen used this particular script as a "gesture of respect". The colourful collection was well if not rapturously received but would eventually be translated into scores of languages and also become the subject of a Philip Glass musical. The volume was in some ways as much a book end as a book in that it was a minor monument to a certain kind of life recently lived and now done with. This latest collection was the ashes, evidence and proof of the man Cohen no longer was. He had finally outlived and thus transcended all the labels critics and public had saddled him with. He was no longer the fasting rake, the negligible gigolo, the horny orphan or the randy holy man. Although apparently ensconced in a solid relationship with Anjani, Cohen stated that with the very release of *Book Of Longing* he had "… exhausted my longing now".

The work in song continued parallel to the poetry, as always. New as yet unreleased songs, *Book Of Longing* and the poem 'Puppets' were both put to music and recorded as demos but with no album in the offing they soon receded into the great netherworld of unreleased Cohen oddities. A much more corporeal expression of Cohen's recent song writing was present in the exquisite *Blue Alert*, a soft, jazzy album of ballads released that summer by his romantic partner Anjani Thomas. With lyrics by Cohen and music by Thomas, the recording is gorgeously and voluptuously stark – it brims with space, smoke and air – and as 'producer' this was Cohen's executive decision. "I tried to put other instruments in there but it just clouded it," he explained. Although he would sometimes speak with full authority as far as his role as producer went, Cohen also characteristically downplayed it. "All I had was an honorary veto… Anjani really produced it herself." Cohen's main role was going through the texts that Anjani had herself cherry picked from his notebooks and which Cohen referred to good naturedly as her "pilfering". Then, at her request, Cohen would modify, refine and complete these choices to suit her voice. The very title itself came from a few random lines he had scratched into the pages of a notebook that for some reason jumped out at Anjani.

Initially Cohen was actually reluctant to give these particular lines up. "I knew it was good and since good ideas come rarely… [I thought] this has some potential but… [still] I wasn't using it at the time." Commenting on Anjani's role as a singer – one criticism of her delivery could be that it was too clean, too perfect, too pure – Cohen tactfully pronounced that, "At one point her voice dropped down from her throat into her heart… This is where she went from being accomplished to… experimenting with the deepest resources of her talent."

Old Cohen cohort John Lissauer was briefly back on board as arranger for a couple of the songs. He'd spent years since his last work with Cohen in the wilderness as far as record producing went, and prior to getting this call from Cohen for *Blue Alert* Lissauer hadn't heard from Leonard in 15 years. "I knew Anjani very well of course. [He had introduced her to Cohen as a backing vocalist back on the *Various Positions* sessions]. So I did a few arrangements on there and I played clarinet and some sax. I was just hired as an arranger and performer." Little had changed, as ever. "I always find Leonard the same. He'd gotten greyer and I had gotten balder. He's the same guy, just as sharp, just as humble and generous and funny. We look back and chuckle at some things we did but generally we don't reminisce too much. We're moving forward kind of people."

This may have been true in the personal sense but in terms of his career (not that Cohen would ever have termed it as such) what the public unanimously wanted now was the old (i.e. younger) Cohen. Meanwhile the inexpensively made *Blue Alert* justified itself in terms of sales although it was perhaps too tasteful and perverse to emulate the kind of Norah Jones level of success that some at Columbia/Sony may have hoped for.

Apart from the sublimely pretty record itself, most mouth-watering of all was the fact that Cohen actually joined his partner in live performance on a handful of modest stages to help promote the record. A witty, nervy and obviously proud Cohen introduced his beau at Joe's pub in NYC to launch the album and that spring and summer saw Cohen making onstage cameos in Toronto and on Polish TV. Cohen was proceeding back to the stage a poco a paco; baby step by baby step.

Meanwhile his past continued to be recycled in all its essential and inessential forms; alongside the never ending compilations of and tributes to his own work, that August Jennifer Warnes' *Famous Blue Raincoat* album was re-released in expanded and remastered form.

By the end of a series of overly eventful years, despite the newly attendant and unexpected financial pressures put upon him Cohen was no closer to officially confirming any proper live dates. Indeed, as a self avowed fan of amnesia, he had long forgotten how to play many of his own songs. A Swedish journalist visiting him at home that year had asked him to play something for her. Cohen politely picked up an ever present nylon stringed acoustic guitar (they served an additional role as furniture in all of Cohen's homes) and out of hospitality finger picked some half familiar chord sequences for his guest. But the result was rough and unburnished, like the sound of a beautiful old car trying to start up after spending too may Montreal winters in a garage. "I'm just foolin' around," Cohen told the journalist almost apologetically, as his fingers attempted to make a connection between strings and memory. "Just remembering... I forget what these are... I've really got to remember them again." Having failed to recall the chord patterns of 'If It Be Your Will' Cohen gently gave up and put his guitar back against the white wall.

The prospect of a world tour at this point seemed beyond him. "I've been blessed with amnesia," he offered in a kind of defence. "I barely remember anything of the past now." In a sense, this was a Zen triumph for the poet. He'd long strived to live exclusively in the moment. "The cordiality of the moment is much more important than the content," he would profess, somewhat enigmatically. In interviews given at this time, he seemed utterly sincere in his lack of interest in the idea or 'myth' of Leonard Cohen, which was like all myths rooted in the past. "I'm not interested... I have very little interest in the man I was then." He did however have a clear opinion of where he stood in the pantheon of great American songwriters. Asked not unreasonably, to compare himself to Irving Berlin, Harold Arden and Cole Porter he admitted, "They are better than I am. They know more about music than I do."

Cohen recognised that his musicality was limited in comparison to these masters but nevertheless felt that he worked his small patch of allotted land as diligently as he could. Of the fruit it bore, he considered 'If It Be Your Will' and 'Hallelujah' to be his best two songs. His soon to be future guitarist Javier Mas, a truly consummate musician would, on working with him, actually be impressed by Cohen's technical knowledge. "He knows a lot," he would point out. "A lot. He even speaks about it in the lyrics of 'Hallelujah', 'The major fourths the minor fifths.' He knows his way around alright."

The main difference, as Cohen saw it, between himself and 'the greats' was a certain cynicism he harboured. At some point during 2006, Cohen kept running into Louis Armstrong's 'Wonderful World'. Coming at him in supermarkets, over the radio in his jeep and as the soundtrack to adverts on TV, the song seemed to be needling him. The unapologetically straightforward love of life that the song conveyed, albeit in a mysteriously majestic manner, was something Cohen himself wanted to have a crack at. "I heard it and I thought 'Why don't I leave a couple of songs like that behind me?'" The problem was that such pure feelings of joy did not present themselves to Cohen during the writing process. And if nothing else, he saw his job as specifically dealing with whatever energies came to him through the keyboard, the guitar and the typewriter. And in "such final moments", he pointed out, "you don't get to choose... you go where the smoke is."

At this juncture in his life Cohen's weekly LA routine included a regular Friday night Jewish dinner, with guests asked to arrive around 6.30. Even in the third act of his life, Cohen was still curious about the Jewish religion. "I would like to study Judaism," he said now. "I feel that my own Jewish education was really quite superficial from a certain point of view... there were aspects of the whole tradition that were not emphasised."

To anyone looking casually in from the outside, despite his recent financial catastrophe Cohen appeared content enough with his daily routine. He'd found a modest means of recording that seemed to suit both his current needs and the demands of a loyal, sizeable audience. His children were healthy and grown, and as much their father's friends now as his offspring. Roshi, although ancient, was still healthy and thriving, still travelling the world and teaching. (In 2005 Cohen had taken tea with his old friend on his 99th birthday.) Other stalwart companions had not made it that far. On January 4, 2006, Irving Layton had died at 93 years of age after suffering with Alzheimer's disease. Cohen: "He was a wonderful friend and many people would agree that he was Canada's greatest poet and a great champion of poetry."

Despite the old guard moving on Cohen still had plenty of good friends around the world and in Robert Kory he had an experienced lawyer who was as efficient as any manager Cohen had ever had.

Cohen was, not unsurprisingly, ever aware of his own mortality. When asked if he was surer now of anything than he had been at 17 he answered gleefully, "Death!" Of all his living spaces Cohen considered his house in Montreal as his base, his true home, the place where his children were raised. As the cliché went, he had "No plans to tour at present" and as the media silence around *Dear Heather* had proved, Cohen was much less available for interviews than before, feeling he had little left to say. Even in the course of day-to-day conversation, Cohen felt that, "I never say anything that even remotely matches what I say in my work." As a live performer, he felt comfortably retired from the distant military rigours of touring.

And yet, unbeknown to Cohen's pining audience, in 2006 Rob Hallett of the AEG worldwide live agency had flown to LA to persuade Cohen to play live again. "I'd been a fan since the early Seventies, when my sister brought home a record," recalls the enormously successful live agent. "I was instantly grabbed by it. I loved the poetry of it. I was listening to a lot of other stuff, like Cat Stephens, Led Zeppelin, but Leonard stood out for me. I then saw the *Bird On The Wire* movie and this was about the same time I was getting into girls. What impressed me about that movie was that Leonard had all these girls after him but he was very literary. I liked that. I'd always enjoyed reading and even writing my own bad poetry and there were lines from Leonard's poems that really became mantras throughout my life."

Hallett had seen Cohen live as many times as possible while he was growing up, buying multiple tickets to the Harvey Goldsmith promoted Albert Hall shows in the late Eighties and early Nineties. Now that he too was in a position to book and promote such concerts, Hallett... "Just wanted him back. He was a legend and I loved his work and yet there was a chance he was going to be forgotten."

A powerful and well respected player in the industry, Hallett had little trouble in securing an audience with his prey. "I got through to him via Robert [Kory] and flew over to make my pitch. I was nervous prior to the meeting; remember this was my boyhood hero! And well, I didn't try to be cool or anything, I shook Leonard's hand and we hugged and I told him 'I love your work and have for years, since I was a kid, and there were lines you wrote that helped me get where I am today if anything did at all.' He didn't say much but he was touched. He also probably though, 'Who is this weirdo?' And I did babble on a bit. And remember I've met and worked with some of the biggest names in pop and rock music… Anyway, I finally calmed down and gave him my pitch."

Hallett's offer, together with his enthusiastic sincerity and obvious faith piqued the interest of both Cohen and his manager. In an age where the traditional mechanisms of the music industry were breaking down and CD sales were on the decline, live performance had become one of the biggest money earning opportunities for many an artist, and particularly for one in Cohen's position. Interest in Cohen's new work – perhaps not surprisingly given the relatively poor quality of *Dear Heather* – was far outweighed by the demand for his older classic catalogue.

Kory had recognised this at around the time of the *I'm Your Man* film. "We had so many queries about when was Leonard gonna play live that I simply said to him, 'This is a headache. How shall we deal with it?' Leonard allowed me to look into the possibility of a tour, I certainly didn't suggest that he tour. I knew people at Live Nation like Flemming Schmidt and I knew John Meglen at AEG from way back in the Eighties. So I spoke to both and Meglen told me, 'You know we have a new guy here, Rob Hallett, who keeps calling me every six months begging to make an overture to Leonard'. And that's how we met up with Rob who was obviously a true fan and a very endearing man'.

Whatever the intricacies behind the story, Cohen recognised Hallett's interest. Kory suggested Hallett organise a small tour for Anjani's *Blue Alert* album. The agent did so and all were impressed.

Hallett was now finally in a position to make a more realistic offer. This he did. "They listened and liked the idea and said they'd think it over," recalls Hallett. "Pitch over, I did something I have never ever done before or since. I got out a camera and asked to have my picture taken with Leonard. I couldn't help it. I said 'Leonard, I'm your fan!'"

Kory laughs at the memory of this. "That was so unusual for a man at Hallett's level to be so obviously a fan too. He was quoting Leonard's *poetry* – not even his lyrics! Very unusual and very endearing."

Kory and Cohen were charmed and impressed by Hallett. Kory noted that if they decided to go with Hallett's proposal then his assignment would now be accented toward Cohen's very own forthcoming 'never ending tour' rather than pushing the singer forward in a studio context although the two pursuits were not mutually exclusive. As well as this course working out better financially for the manager and Cohen, above all Kory was happy to do whatever it was that his client and friend needed him to do. "I don't have any ambition for my client," stated Kory, "That's not my managing style. I consider it a great honour to listen to my client and Leonard shares with me the subtle intuitions about the directions he wants to take and this always involves a commercial interface with complex kinds of issues. So it's my responsibility to listen and see if I can work out a path which allows that intuition to flower. That's what I do." As with any healthy relationship, the two did not always agree on everything unanimously. "Yes, we disagree. We have very frank discussions but there's rarely ever a pressure to act... and there's a high level of mutual respect so we consider things and... we find ourselves going forward and then sometimes things seem not to be working out and we both wonder how we could have taken another road but then the road turns out to be great... it's great.'

In accepting Hallett's offer, at least in a preliminary capacity, Cohen's focus and raison d'être would move from his traditional focus as a studio based singer/songwriter and transfer him to a position of living out on a nightly basis the role of the myth and living legend that so many considered him to be. "Leonard was very ambivalent about this," says Kory, 'and all a tour would entail. He told me that if we did do it then I would have to iron out everything he hated about touring, which was everything except singing on stage. I agreed to that and in the event, we did cut out everything he hated about touring."

In July of 2007 yet another B-road branched out in Cohen's work when a travelling exhibition of his artwork titled *Drawn To Words – Works On Paper* had its premiere at the Drabinsky Gallery in Toronto. The accompanying press release informed us that: "Drabinsky Gallery,

Toronto, in association with the Luminato Festival, Toronto, and the Richard Goodall Gallery, Manchester, UK, is proud to present the world premiere exhibition of works on paper and annotations by Canadian poet, songwriter and novelist, Mr. Leonard Cohen.

Drawn To Words features more than 30 pigment prints of drawings and sketches selected from Mr. Leonard Cohen's extensive private archive stretching back over 40 years. Images from *Drawn To Words* will include portraits, nudes, objects and landscapes, many of which are annotated with Cohen's personal notes, observations and musings. Some feature recognisable characters from his songs, while others reflect his changing moods through revealing self-portraits.

"Drawings that capture views from his Montreal apartment, alongside pictures drawn during his five-year seclusion (1996–2001) as a Zen Buddhist Monk at Mount Baldy Zen Center are included in the collection.

"Mr. Cohen has kept journals and sketchbooks since the mid Sixties. As his music career developed, he continued to sketch and draw at every available opportunity and his visual work shares many of the same qualities and themes found in his music and poetry – the light and shade of human emotion, dark humor, social commentary, sexuality and politics. At least one of Mr. Cohen's original journals will be on display during the exhibition.

"Throughout his career, Mr. Cohen's art has always been highly private. Only when some of his drawings appeared in his collection of prose and poetry, *Book Of Longing*, published in 2006, did his worldwide fan base get a glimpse of this side of his creativity. We are honored to make this exceptional work available to a wider audience through the publication of these limited edition pigment prints mastered by Nash Editions, California.

"Each will be signed, numbered and dated by Mr. Cohen and many will carry personal text."

The artist himself was less reverential than his art dealers (whose job it was after all to promote and sell the work). Cohen referred to some of the drawings as mere 'doodles' and also revealed that that 'as a curious exercise' he had drawn a self-portrait every morning for a number of years, annotating them with the first thought that came to mind. Kory was more supportive of the work. "I think it's real. I collect light and space artists from California and I see the value in Leonard's work. It's another expression of his poetry."Whilst he was as unsure of the validity of his artwork compared to that of his songs, Cohen saw no problem in spreading his art across so many media. As far as he was concerned, the poetry, songs, lyrics, novels and drawing were all rivers heading to the same ocean. "We're drawn to the truth," he explained, "when we hear it. And when we see it, we're hungry for it… and we're surprised when we see it because it manifests itself in so many ways in so many different forms… it's so precious when you hear it that you're immediately drawn to it. So, I tend to be wary of confining this expression of truth to one kind of artistic activity."

Unfortunately for Cohen his work and creative expression did not exist exclusively within the pure air of art and reason. As basically a pop/rock/folk singer songwriter, no matter how high and true his ideals and aims, Cohen's roots – just like those his rock and roll brethren – was mired in the much less romantic swamplands of the music industry.

Steven Machat liked to think by now that as far as his own life was concerned, Cohen was merely a one time main player now consigned to the past. But in 2007, while Machat was holidaying in Jamaica, he received an email from Cohen's former European promoter Flemming Schmidt who wanted Steven's help in persuading Leonard to start touring again, a tour that Flemming wanted to manage and promote. Against his better nature, but ever curious to engage with the enigmatic Cohen, Machat decided to lobby Cohen on Schmidt's behalf. In September 2007, he and his father's one time favourite client met up in LA at Cohen's house on Tremaine Avenue. Immediately on entry Machat was disturbed at how tidy the place was. "The music was filed, the guitars on stands and even the fridge was organised." He was also slightly paranoid. "In the background was a man that Leonard described as his handyman, but I think he was present to listen in and make sure I didn't attack him."

After the inevitable small talk the conversation turned to religion. When Cohen told Machat he would have to leave soon for the temple, his guest admonished him: "I thought you were supposed to be a Buddhist? Why do you care about a Jewish festival? I thought we had put that kind of stuff behind us." Cohen, sounding out of character, apparently replied:

"I want to keep all my options open. Maybe Buddha, maybe God." (Elvis Presley had a similar philosophy of hedging his bets, once stating that he wanted both the Jewish star and the Christian Cross on his gravestone for the same reason). Maybe Machat needed reminding that Cohen had never actually proclaimed himself a Buddhist. As recently as 2006 Cohen had clearly stated that, "I never became a Buddhist... I bumped into a man many years ago [Roshti] who happened to be a Zen master. I wasn't looking for anything exalted or spiritual. I had a great sense of disorder in my life... of chaos... disorder... depression... and I bumped into someone who seemed at ease with himself. It was the man himself who attracted me. If he'd been a teacher of physics in Heidelberg I'd have learned German and studied physics." Buddhism then was just "the uniform" that Cohen would have to acquire to "hang out in Roshi's scene". Yet for some reason on this occasion Cohen declined to argue the point with Machat.

Whatever the course of conversation, Machat was disappointed that he and Cohen couldn't seem to connect in any fundamental way. Perhaps if they did, Steven would in some fashion be reunited with a piece of his father again. Before Cohen departed for the temple, the pair did at least share an agreeable lunch. Yet still, never quite able to relax in Cohen's company, Machat brought up the painful subject of Kelley Lynch. "For once," Machat reported, "Leonard looked me straight in the eye. 'You were right about her,' he said. 'She stole everything and you warned me. She really is crazy. All my money is gone. She started believing this money was hers and she started spending it. All of it. When I got back from my pilgrimage, I went to withdraw money from my bank and was told there was no money left in the account to cover the draft. I was speechless. I didn't know where to look, where to turn or what to think.'" As a trained lawyer Machat had been confused about the ensuing case and told him so, picking Cohen up on various outstanding legal points. There were too many illogicalities to the case for Machat to be satisfied that Cohen was merely a straightforward victim. Perhaps Cohen wasn't being as forthcoming as Machat would have liked or perhaps ultimately the minutiae of the Lynch episode merely and thoroughly bored him. Machat was plainly suspicious and felt sure that Cohen was hiding something profound, something important that would confirm every doubt Machat had ever had about his father's one time trophy client. Whatever the ultimate truth of the case, the financial blow had at least one obvious and practical effect on Cohen. He had decided to tour again. "I'm going to have to go back to work," he told Machat as he showed him the door. "Wish me well."

Machat was piqued. Back home he went as far as to contact Lynch and ask the accused directly for her side of the case. "Predictably I got a radically different story and one that was just as intriguing – possibly more so," he says. In the final analysis Machat had little sympathy for either Cohen or Lynch but perhaps this wasn't the point. He had hoped the latest meeting with Cohen would have been the beginning of some sort of reconciliation between him and Cohen and ultimately a way of reconnecting with Marty. But he found his dad's old client as distant as ever. "He really hurt me," says Steven. "He knew secrets about my dad and he never spent one minute talking to me about it."

Kory was aware of Machat's interest in Cohen but saw it as purely mercenary. "When Leonard got back on his feet again, Steven came into the picture," he states. "Steven is another whole different story. I wouldn't rely on anything he says."

Cohen had never been interested in looking back at the best of times and with the prospect of a new tour a definite possibility, dealing with ghosts from his past or even his missing millions was the last thing on Cohen's mind. Machat's suggestion that Cohen go with Flemming Schmidt both as a manager and a live agent was doomed before the idea was even aired. Unbeknown to Machat, the offer that Hallett had made to his boyhood hero was one that Cohen could not refuse.

Although the singer was typically reticent at first, since his initial pitch in Kory's office Hallett had been steadily working at persuading Cohen to re-enter the live circuit. Cohen, although touched by the interest and humbled by the agent's very personal efforts, was still reportedly reserved in the extreme. He was wary of going on the road for various reasons; one of his chief worries being that no one would remember him. "It took some time," conceded Hallett, "[but] Leonard was trying to make some of the money back that had been stolen. At first he said, 'I don't know if anyone wants to see me. You must be joking'."

However genuinely unimpressed by the notion, Cohen was not dealing with some awestruck rookie with stars in his eyes. Hallett was a successful veteran of the industry who had worked with many showbiz legends. He'd recently put Prince on stage for 21 consecutive nights at London's enormous O2 Arena and in the Eighties had managed worldwide Duran Duran's concert career at their global peak. He was also obviously a deep admirer of Cohen and a long time fan of his work who wanted the now 73-year-old poet back on world stages sooner rather than later if only for his own personal satisfaction. To this end Hallett politely yet firmly persisted. It took him almost 24 months. He offered Cohen a sweet deal – out of his own pocket, Hallet would actually cover the (sizeable) cost of rehearsals (usually this would be the record company's responsibility) and then and only then if Cohen decided to go ahead, AEG would structure the deal to make sure Cohen got a higher cut of the profits than was standard in the touring industry. If Cohen got as far as rehearsals and still didn't feel like touring that was fine too, he would owe Hallet nothing. "I told him, we'll go our separate ways and that's life, and it as an interesting thing to try."

If the conditions offered were out of the ordinary, then this merely reflected their unusual character of the star of the show. Cohen was by this point a bona fide living legend. In March 2008 he was inducted into the Rock and Roll Hall of Fame by long time (albeit fairly secret) admirer and contemporary poet of the street Lou Reed. Both one time notorious speed freaks now appeared at the ceremony looking more like courtly academics on the brink of old geezerdom, two old sons of Allen Ginsberg made good. As Reed introduced Cohen by reading from his own selection of Cohen's verse, the shabby bedrooms of the Chelsea Hotel and their once mutual fascination with Nico – now long dead – seemed eons ago. As a dapper Cohen took to the stage in a tuxedo, looking like Harrison Ford's embalmed grandfather, and composed himself atop the podium there seemed to be an inevitability to the whole occasion. Yet this was not so. Cohen's career, particularly in North America had never been one of steady ascendency. In the mid-Eighties it had been on the verge of disappearing all together. There was a time when the industry, and CBS president Walter Yetkinoff in particular, had very publicly written Cohen off by refusing even to release his albums. But now, post 'canonisation' and post the 'Hallelujah'

rebirth and after all those miles and years on from the sun baths of
Hydra and the Montreal cafés of his youth, this latest honour somehow
seemed as natural and as timely as Easter in April. It was an unnaturally
natural evolution. In some ways it was down to the fact that Cohen
had come to be recognised as someone who had been around since the
Sixties and yet had enough integrity and vitality in his current work
and reputation to ensure that he was light-years away from other artists
of a similar vintage, many of whom had long ago been consigned to the
third ring of entertainment hell and the Hades of the Vegas nostalgia
circuit. Nobody spoke of Cohen in the same breath as Neil Sedaka,
Paul Anka and Barry Manilow. There was no true comparison between
him and Paul McCartney. Brian Wilson in concert was less a musical
experience and more a voyeur's exercise in curiosity and duty. And
while Cohen did not orbit in the same rarefied heights as Dylan, he
still field-commanded a much larger audience that old peers Donovan,
Judy Collins and Buffy Sainte-Marie and was still as a human and artist
– even if it was often by imperceptible degrees – moving forward. Some
of his old associates looked on, gently surprised at the way it turned out.
"It's not what one would have necessarily expected," says Barry Miles,
"having met him all those years ago at the Chelsea. But good luck to
him. After losing all that money in that way he did, I think he kind of
deserved all of this."

Few knew it but as Cohen accepted his induction from a small raised
podium that March he was mere weeks away from returning to the
greater world stage. While initially sceptical, Cohen had been unable
to deflect Hallett's confidence from the off and although it took him
almost two years to commit to any kind of tour he had actually been
considering possible musicians for such a venture from Hallett's earliest
call. As the concept of a tour became a definite possibility, the actual
auditions for a new group had finally begun in LA. Roscoe Beck had
never really left Cohen's orbit and Cohen had asked him to take on
the duty of musical director for the new endeavour. Sharon Robinson's
presence as a backing singer was another given. Stalwart Bob Metzger
was on board too. Among the newest musicians, there was the Spanish
guitarist Javier Mas. Cohen had phoned Mas at home some months
before, waking the Spaniard from a deep sleep. In the classic showbiz

tradition, Mas, a long time fan of Cohen, had not believed who was actually on the other end of the phone and thought a friend was playing a joke on him. He'd actually hung up on Cohen before realising that it really was him.

As a member of Cohen's group Mas' background, experience and credentials were typical of what Cohen wanted in that they were untypical. Mas was a multi-instrumentalist who played various stringed instruments, his main one being the bandurria.* Mas was a born musician and as his body grew, so did his repertoire of instruments. As a devoted Kinks fan in the sixties he played drums, before moving to 12-string and six-string electric guitar. Unlike the musicians who had trooped into the Spector sessions almost two decades before, Javier certainly knew who Leonard Cohen was. "The first money I ever made from music was from playing Leonard Cohen songs on the beach," he remembered fondly. As an accomplished, professional yet mostly unknown musician Mas was in some ways at the other end of the spectrum to Cohen "I can read and write music," confirms Mas, "but I prefer to play from the heart. I close my eyes and play."

Two new backing singers – the Webb sisters – were augmented by Sharon Robinson. The sisters had clinched the gig, according to Mas "because they played a harp at the audition". The nine piece band began rehearsals at a Los Angeles studio complex, and Cohen was a spare, dignified and economical presence during the sessions. Although Roscoe Beck was given the title of official band arranger and musical director, it was considered by some that his main role was more as a potential buffer between Cohen and group rather than as an actual interpreter of Cohen's specific musical requirements. Both Mas and keyboardist Neil Larsen were also gifted and experienced musical arrangers, as was Sharon Robinson. It was more Beck's particular dynamic and long friendship with Cohen that sealed this particular deal rather than him winning any kind of musical competition. However, although Cohen wasn't averse to letting his musicians know when

---

* Originally chosen, so the guitarist claims because when his grandfather took him to the guitar shop at age nine, the shop assistant exclaimed, "The guitar is bigger than him!" And so instead passed him a handier Bandurria.

he liked something he disliked having to dictate too stringently and hated confrontation of any kind, particularly in a professional situation. During rehearsals and on tour he could therefore dilute any tension – if it arose – by going through Beck. The choice of musicians was so impeccable that such situations were unlikely but if Cohen didn't like something, and it wasn't a major issue, then his response would be slightly delayed and carefully considered. "He would wait for the moment to tell you," said Mas. "Either in private or if not then he wouldn't address you directly in front of the rest group. He'd never say, 'Hey Bob, I don't like that!' No. He'd say something like, 'Say friends, can we try and play something like this', and we'd know what he meant without him picking on one particular person. It's not that he's being diplomatic, he's being kind. But also clever, 'cos if someone makes you angry you're not gonna' play what they need."

During a lunch break, Mas got his first opportunity to speak with the man face to face. The guitarist was understandably nervous, not about his playing but as to how it had been received by Cohen. Mas needn't have worried. "He told me, 'You play beautiful Javier. Don't worry. You play only what you feel. Don't worry for nothing. If you don't feel it, don't play it'. It was just what I needed to hear."

Mas was impressed by his new boss in every way. "He was beautifully dressed, always," he says. "And so polite. Beautiful manners. He was not one for small talk. Once the rehearsal was done he would go, not hang around. I never saw him angry. He was cool. Perhaps he did get angry and shout in his private life but I never saw that. I don't like to think of him like that. He was a gentleman from the moment I met him."

Although Cohen had the core of his band, he kept on auditioning and rehearsing. In the earliest stages, nothing was definite. Hallet kept his faith, admitting only that, "When it got to half a million dollars did I start getting a little nervous."

AEG would ultimately put $3 million into the Cohen enterprise without him even ever agreeing to step on stage. "They had serious faith," says Kory, "and let me tell you, every penny of that money went into the band. Nothing went to Leonard's personal living expenses. It all went into the band. If Leonard told me, 'I want the band in suits' then we got them fitted for suits."

The band rehearsed for two and a half solid months. "The longest time I ever rehearsed in a band," confirms Javier. "I would go over my parts alone in the morning, in my room and I would play with my eyes closed so I could really learn the part. Then we would all meet at the rehearsal space in the afternoon and practice through to the evening. I would record the sessions and then again next day, I would play them back to myself in the morning and try to fix anything I didn't like. I would listen to my improvised parts with the band and work out which parts I liked, and then have them as actual parts. But those parts would come from improvisations, not theory. And Leonard is the same. We are not into theory, we operate from the heart."

Eventually Cohen felt he and his new band had something fit for public consumption and Kory called Hallet to the LA rehearsal complex to see the direct result of his personal investment. The agent was as boyishly excited as he had been on his first introduction with Cohen. "Can you imagine," says Hallet, "my own audience with Leonard Cohen? They put a sofa in front of the stage and I just sat there beaming. It was so great." Obviously Hallett was impressed. The band was raring to go. Cohen was still cautious but also intrigued and excited by the various possibilities on offer. Plus, he had little to lose. He and Kory soon let their new agent know that he could book and announce a modest run of concerts in smallish venues in a particular region only. A delighted agent wasted no time in doing just that.

Cohen was back in business and he needed a new team around him. The obvious choice had been standing in front of Cohen for the last four eventful years. "I did not become Leonard's manager until the spring of 2008," says Kory. "I had negotiated a deal with AEG, the band was beginning rehearsal, the tour was being booked. Leonard asked who should manage him, and then said his vote was for me to do it, if I could work out the time." Kory took the job offered without hesitation. "As a client," he says. "Leonard is exceptionally appreciative. He understands what my sphere of responsibilities is and how they create the platform for him to really enjoy his work on every level...The rest is history."

Kory and Cohen signed a contract legalising their new business status and Kory instructed their new agent as to his next move. Hallet had a strategy based specifically on Cohen's preference. "He said he wanted to do 18 shows, low key shows before anything major. I booked him just that and I attended every show. I still have a great photo from the first gig that shows a billboard from outside the venue. It says something like "Tonight, The Counterfeit Stones, Tomorrow, The Australian Doors, Thursday, Leonard Cohen and Band', Friday, The Bootleg Beatles'."

That very first show, Cohen's first since 1993, was on May 11, 2008 – both Pentecost and Mother's Day – at the Fredericton Playhouse, in New Brunswick, a beautiful venue with a modest (for Cohen) capacity of exactly 709. The band and entourage arrived several days earlier and actually used the venue prior to the show itself as a giant rehearsal space, practicing from ten till four with a break for lunch each day. The show, although only modestly advertised was of course packed out, mostly by Cohen freaks alerted via the internet.

This was literally a dream come true for Hallet. "It was wonderful, of course it was. And it wasn't that he was particularly nervous on the first dates, although he was but you wouldn't have picked up on it if you hadn't known. It's just that with that great band and the audiences, he became more confident as the show went on."

Audience members reported that the show was confident and tight, with a dapper Cohen betraying no nerves, only a witty Zen like calm that he would refine throughout the coming tour to the point of a stand up act. "I last stood on this stage 15 years ago," he would quip, "as a young boy of 61 with a head full of crazy dreams."

Appeasing Cohen's wishes, Hallett had booked the first bunch of dates exclusively in small Canadian theatres. This was so Cohen could "work himself back into the routine". It became immediately apparent that the modest venues could have sold out multiple times over. "So we were about $3m (£2m) in and 16 shows in Canada and we knew that we had a monster on our hands," says Hallett. Ultimately, according to US figures, the 2008 tour would gross $36m (US) and would be among the top 20 grossing tours of the year. Money was a major part of the return. Roscoe Beck asked Cohen directly, "Are you going on the road just because you're broke?" And he said, 'Well, that might have something to do with it.'"

As the initial small leg of the tour progressed Hallet was already planning the next stage. "I thought, perversely, that his music would be better suited in arenas. It is too reverential in theatres, too church-like. I wanted us to upscale." Cohen was anxious about going too fast too soon. "We had one minor difference of opinion at the start," concedes Hallet. "He came to me and said that his son had told him 'You can't do more than 90 minutes these days dad, you gotta get off then.' I told him, 'Leonard with all respect, I'm your fan. And you haven't played in an age. We want to see you do everything, I'd pay to see a four-hour show! No disrespect but Adam is wrong. Trust me'. And he went for it. And he was more than up to it. Trust me, Leonard is a young boy."

Indeed although Cohen obviously looked *old* he was also ageless. The personnel on stage represented something like the Doctor Who tradition in reverse. While the supporting cast changed over the decades the central character remained the same. Cohen was certainly ageing but also appeared somehow weirdly immortal. It was soon apparent that Hallet's instincts had been more than on the money. Not only was there an audience for Cohen in concert but it was an audience that was seemingly voracious; it was an audience that seemingly couldn't be satisfied. On the early leg of the tour the group would be *greeted* to the stage by a standing ovation. "We knew pretty early on that what we had here was a monster," says Hallet. "As word started spreading the offers came in and didn't stop coming in, festivals, arenas, all over the world. With Leonard's approval we just kept on adding dates. It was a monster."

Working with his boyhood hero had not reduced the lustre of Cohen's appeal for Hallett. "Leonard is a lovely man," he says. "Every word that comes out of his mouth is sincere. And getting friendly with him, getting to know him, working with him. It didn't affect my relationship with his work at all except that it deepened it." On stage the group were instructed to play almost as softly as they could. As Roscoe Beck put it, "If you can't hear the lyrics, then the point of doing it at all has been missed. We're there to support Leonard." Mas concurred. "It's one of the best things that's happened to me as a musician. We're playing so soft. The volume is low. I never played like this with a band in my life."

Obviously, Cohen's voice was the vessel for the lyrics and while in terms of frequency it was not a particularly typical rock and roll instrument, it held a power of projection that was as effective and powerful as it was untrained and natural. "I played with him acoustically for two months in a hotel room," Javier would state. "You hear the man... he has a big sound. It's a huge voice. But frequency wise... on stage, it's not the loudest instrument. But it mixes well, it's complemented so well by the girls' voices and the banduria."

An impeccably tailored and intensely sober Cohen was calm at the centre of it all, the very eye of the hurricane itself. As the venues and audiences got bigger he continued with the tradition he had began almost 40 years ago by preceding some of the songs with spoken word extracts from the songs themselves. Often the verses would be from texts unused in the actual songs, as with 'A Thousand Kisses Deep'. In appropriate places – such as in Montreal or France – he would recite the verses in French.

Asides from the overwhelming interest, love and gratitude that Cohen felt from each audience every night he also had every reason to feel confident and buoyed because of the group that surrounded him. The band were closer to family by now and between them could cover an impressive range of instruments. For instance, Cohen had the use of up to *five* backing vocalists if need be. Their singer did not sleepwalk through the sets either as his bass player noted: "It's heads-up at all times. We may land on a chord and he just may feel that it's not time to come in singing yet, just emotionally it's a nice moment, and he'll decide to extend that moment another bar. We have to be ready for that, we have to be ready for anything. A lyric change, an added bar, a different song."

Whilst the likes of Beck melted amiably into the background on stage, other members – particularly the newer recruits – brought a fresh lustre to the show. The Webb sisters in particular had a naturally laid back and sexual presence that shimmered. Mas was also a natural star beside Cohen. The diminutive maestro had the air of an authentic gypsy on stage and his solos were one of the most exciting components of a show that was occasionally in peril of becoming a somewhat pedestrian musical experience. Mas primarily played a nylon 12-string guitar, custom made for him and his particularly small and nimble fingers by Tacoma. He sometimes wished that the band took more risks. "Leonard is confident in what he does, if he played just alone with a guitar it's gonna be beautiful," explained Mas. "And you know, it's a pleasure to accompany him." Mas spoke for the many who would have loved to see Cohen perform solo – just his voice and guitar – at least once during the three hour set. Javier lobbied on their behalf. "It's my fight," he said, "to get Leonard to do this. But to begin with he had a problem, with his age, you know, his fingers and the precision needed to play. But I'm asking him always to do this, play by himself for a song. Maybe have the girls accompany him. 'Cos you know, I play with him alone in a room and it sounds so powerful and true. But on this tour we had problems – mine was to stop smoking and his was to play the guitar again!"

Like every other musician who had come into close contact with Cohen's guitar playing in the last four decades, Javier was initially intrigued and puzzled by his boss's style. "I couldn't work it out at first. It's so particular. There is a kind of tremolo thing happening. I tried to play that way and now I got it. It's essentially a Spanish style, a more classical version of Flamenco. He makes it work for him so well and the way it is under his voice. So I'm always saying 'Come on, play some more songs, 'Avalanche' maybe? The other day we were alone together and I played him the guitar part of 'Joan Of Arc' and he was freaking out, laughing, 'cos that style of playing is very simple and very difficult."

As an accomplished musician himself Mas did not question Cohen's overall musical ability or why as a guitarist Cohen had limited himself throughout his life to exactly the type of guitar he had started using as a boy. "I think Leonard always uses nylon string guitars precisely because that was his guitar at the beginning," says Mas. "You know, he has become accustomed to nylon strings. Maybe he plays with metal strings some times, but I believe all his life was playing nylon and so it's natural that he feels comfortable with that and this and the sound from those type of strings really helped his songs and his playing."

Not only did Cohen not ruminate on his own musicality or lack of, he was also not particularly vocal as regards the chops of his band mates either. "He doesn't say much about my playing," continues Mas. "I think he likes my music and what I do, obviously. He treats me with the type of respect you would use to treat a master, that is he really leaves me free to do just what I feel. When I look at him he always smiles and that means he likes it, no? Sometimes we talk about technique itself, in particular the special Spanish way of playing the guitar. He has got that nice tremolo playing that makes an incredible sound in his songs, and that's one old Spanish technique. But if we really talk about music we only talk about the expression of soul in music, and how difficult it is to do that. As I told him it is important to be honest with yourself first and then you will be so with the people. I think music expresses your interior motives and feelings, technique is only one means of bringing this out."

As the Cohen live experience moved around the world and circulated in bigger and bigger venues – "In Dublin he filled an arena," remembers Hallett, "in the pouring rain. And people were *dancing* in the rain as I knew they would, given the chance" – many of Cohen's old associates, friends and lovers were sucked in to watch their Leonard Cohen from afar along with all the other Joes. "It was a great show I must say," comments Tony Palmer. "I saw him at the O2 in London. But no way could I get backstage as much as I tried." Veteran Cohen interviewer Stina Lundberg was one of many unable to get backstage but she saw the show with thousands of others. "I thought it was just marvellous," she says, this being the first time she had actually seen Cohen do his thing. "For quite some years I hadn't enjoyed going to concerts. They bored me. The sound is not so good etc., but Leonard's concert wasn't boring for one minute or second. It wasn't too loud, the sound was just perfect, the group were amazing, each one individually. I was worried he wouldn't be able to do the songs justice any more, you know, at his age, but he was marvellous. He had such a personal approach. Although I think he said 'Thank you' too many times. I'd liked to have seen him and Sharon afterwards perhaps but you could not get back stage."

Many didn't bother trying and just enjoyed the spectacle for what it was despite not always being completely blown away by what they heard. One close associate of Cohen, who prefers to remain anonymous, reckoned that, "The group didn't groove at all. It was too polite, it didn't swing, too MOR." John Lissauer: "I saw him play in New York two or three times recently and the shows are great and the musicians are great... it's slick and polished but that's what he does. It's a great show for the audience... maybe for us purists we could use more naked Leonard...

some of those darker things from the early years I would have liked to see but that's where he's at now. That's the level he's at."

During the tour a deep and unique rapport between Mas and Cohen gradually became apparent. This was manifested no more obviously, strongly or explicitly than in the opening song 'Dance Me To The End Of Love'. Mas was as shocked as the audience when one night Cohen got to his knees during the first verse and serenaded the seated guitarist as he would a woman. Cohen, of course, had a history of engaging his female backing singers, of almost courting them mid-song. For some reason he had now turned his attention to the 60-year-old Spaniard. The audience reaction was as intense as Mas's embarrassment. "The people went totally crazy," he recalled, delighted. The undertones weren't sexual but they were strangely romantic and this was not a familiar situation for a Spanish dude like Mas to find himself in. Cohen gave no warning of his move, and the first time he dropped before the seated guitarist, Mas did all he could with his facial expressions to tell Cohen, "Don't you do that!" The source of embarrassment wasn't just a matter of gender. "For me, he is a man I admire and he's also older than me... he's up there you know! I don't like to see him on his knees. And so. I'm like 'Get up from there!' and he give me this naughty little boy look, smiling and saying, like 'Fuck you Javier'."

Cohen would routinely spread the love throughout the later verses of the song, singing to Sharon and the Webb sisters but he just couldn't resist returning to his seated victim before the song's end. By this time Mas expressed his feeling through his fingers and strings rather than his agonised facial expressions. The pair now duetted via a call and response, Mas answering Cohen's vocal verses with his own guitar flourishes. It was a courtlier version of David Bowie mimicking fellatio on Mick Ronson's guitar back in the Ziggy Stardust era. As then, everyone loved this dynamic piece of rock theatre. "We had a nice thing going on," attests Mas simply. Without quite overegging the nog, Cohen would return to the routine throughout the three and a half hour show. Mas learned to accept it but never got over his initial embarrassment. He didn't like to see Cohen prostrating before him. "I would clean his shoes," said Mas, "but he's a humble man and he likes to serve." Neil Larsen told Mas: "People are expecting a Leonard Cohen show, a show of songs but now you're giving them a performance. Something theatrical." Despite this concession to rock and roll theatre Mas states that, "Nothing is choreographed but everything has a purpose with Leonard. We start the shows based on a pure... feeling. We do what we feel and this becomes part of the arrangement." Beyond all of this, what was most striking about each performance was that Cohen seemed to be present in each moment of every song at every gig. Unless Cohen had missed a calling as one of the great stage actors of his time, then the utter sincerity, focus and commitment of his singing was a rare and holy joy to behold.

Remembering his own experience of the meaningless backstage meeting in LA in 1988, Kory instigated a much tighter tour ship this time round. "It's why I've been so adamant on this tour about a closed tour policy," he explained. "These backstage meetings after a concert are unsatisfying for those who go backstage but particularly for the artist. Leonard doesn't need that if he's performing at the level he's performing at and if he's delivering the kind of tour we're delivering. So cutting out these kinds of meetings is for the benefit of all. It's for the benefit of the audience, ultimately, who pay every night. So we have this policy and there are no exceptions, because if you start making exceptions for somebody then you have to make exceptions for everybody. And the numbers of touching stories we get, from old friends and so forth... and of course Leonard would love to see everybody but it's just not physically, humanely possible."

Nevertheless, Cohen was taking graciousness to the max. In public at least, he appeared to be supernaturally peaceful, almost beatific. In interviews he was almost always polite and authentically grateful, recycling the well worn war stories of old and at times his demeanour and conversation came across as bland. But then Cohen had been through it all by now, his life having rivalled the most elaborate cinematic biopic. He was an urban Jewish kid from Montreal who had found fame, fortune and almost lost both. Now he had reclaimed these along with a rare kind of personal individuality rarely seen in anyone, much less a pop folk singer. In 2009 Leonard Cohen, the odd and old (even in the Sixties) looking poet that Columbia Records had been reluctant to sign back in 1966, was selling out major venues in almost every country in the world. His reaction to this subtle phenomenon – beyond a "general gratitude"

– was a non reaction. When pressed he admitted that he still didn't take anything for granted even when things were going so successfully. "I don't analyse the mechanics," he said humbly. "I'm just glad that it's going well." He had by now a thick skin and although he preferred praise to criticism, in some ways he was if not indifferent but above it all. "I'm ready for both."

"Leonard has always been slow steady and consistent," says Lissaeur, "and that's why now he's getting all this adoration. People say, 'Oh gee, you're fabulous' but they're just catching on, he's been fabulous for forty years."

In December 2008 a consummate manifestation of Cohen's timelessness appeared when the winner of a UK TV talent show took 'Hallelujah' to number two in the UK singles chart over Christmas. Versions by Jeff Buckley and even Cohen himself followed (with Cohen getting his first ever top 40 single chart entry, hitting number 36). By now Cohen's very own hymn seemed to be almost everywhere and recorded cover versions of it numbered in the hundreds. Despite being unappreciated at the time of release, Lissaeur was proud of the contribution that *New Skin* and *Various Positions* had made. "Three or four of the songs from *Various Positions* are now the cornerstones of the Cohen live experience," he points out, although this is arguably down to the songs themselves and not their original recorded incarnations. With regard to 'Hallelujah', Lissauer recalls that, "At the time I thought we had made one of the great achievements. It was one of the most special and inspired works of music that people would ever hear. But I was shocked when at the time Columbia didn't want to release it. I thought 'This is really special'. I didn't know it was gonna be a hit. I just thought this was gonna touch everyone. And it did, in particular other singers and songwriters. But now everyone knows this song."

By mid 2009 the Cohen tour machine was running like clockwork and had become by far Cohen's biggest, most profitable and comprehensive tour ever. Reviews were routinely praiseworthy and the public ever adoring; it was as if it was just enough to have Leonard Cohen on stage in person. There was the occasional minor expression of boredom from the audience as there always had been. At some of the later shows small numbers of people could always be seen leaving before the end and in

Granada that September during a lull between songs one lone voice excruciatingly cried out in Spanish, "When can we go home?" But these were mere trifles compared to what was to come.

On September 18 Cohen collapsed on stage in Valencia due to dehydration brought on by food poisoning – the first time ever that he had cancelled a show due to ill health. Cohen soon recovered and was back on stage a couple of days later in Barcelona, where Cohen webmaster supreme Jarkko caught up with his idol. Cohen was looking particularly thin since returning to the stage in recent years but by now he was almost gaunt. "He was still a little ill," he recalls Jarkko. "There was something wrong with his stomach. A few of the guys in the band also had food poisoning but he had it the worst. Still, he wasn't eating much when we sat down with him. Mostly he eats soups. The others in the band ate very well, but Leonard just ate soup and one piece of bread."

For many years Cohen had an acute awareness of his own body and its weight as much as he had had of his own father's who was, by his son's admission, a portly man. In his youth and middle age, when Cohen fasted and exercised, the effect on his small frame was flattering and empowering, the weight loss defining the edges of his physique, particularly on his face. But now, as a man in his seventies, his austere appetite made him look almost frail. "I think also, his time at Mount Baldy reinforced this attitude," says Jarrko. "The diet there was very sparse compared to your average person's. But when we saw him in Barcelona, yes he much thinner than at the start of the tour." Cohen was now careful about what he put into his body. He no longer smoked and rarely drank. "I find that even a glass of wine interferes with my mood," he confessed.

The 2009 tour ended, of all places, in Las Vegas in December 2009. *Spin* magazine commented that, "Live, Cohen is the consummate gentleman, effortlessly gracious and impeccably mannered. And from the first syllable of 'Dance Me To The End Of Love' to the last consonant of 'First We Take Manhattan', everyone was treated with complete respect. He even kneeled before the audience on numerous occasions, as if begging for their acceptance. Cohen was just as gracious to his nine-piece band, from the fedora-topped multi-instrumentalists to the cart wheeling back-up singers, and he twice took time out to introduce them and emphasise how important he considered their participation."

Reviews, good or bad, were irrelevant by now. Almost every show was a sell out and in 2009 alone the tour grossed $21 million. In a classic Karmic twist the theft from Cohen of $5 million by Lynch had turned out to be an investment for him. Even Steven Machat had finally come around to his old antagonist, explaining that his published recollections on Cohen were merely "… my views as I looked back and re-lived our collective past. As for Leonard and me in the present, I have nothing but respect for him as well as any man who can get up off the floor after what the ex-secretary of Machat and Machat [i.e. Lynch] did to him and go out, smile and love life as well as share that true love of life. He is a winner. For man's true measure of success is solely based in survival. No matter what a church or state says. Leonard became a man that all of us should hope [to be], that we have that strength inside us to roll with the valleys of life as well as enjoy the peaks."

For all the accolades, all the sell outs and all the love, Cohen had still not played in Japan, a country where even the sleaziest of LA poodle hair soft rock combos sold out tours on a regular basis. Everyone played Japan. Except Cohen. "I'm not sure why that is," ponders Kory. "It is odd. Maybe the work hasn't really translated well over there. I know he is more popular in Korea than he is in Japan." Yet Cohen had many attributes that went over big in Japan: Buddhist sensibility, a sharp sense of expensive style, a measure of excellence. Kory: "I don't know why he's never played there… perhaps the promoters don't get it."

With no fixed responsibilities until next spring Cohen now returned to his civilian life. There was talk of recording new songs as there always had been but his main occupation during what was only a break – the next leg of the tour was scheduled to begin next March – was to rest and reflect. These days he frequented his home in Hydra less and less although it was still used occasionally by his children. The magical island had eventually succumbed to tourism. Those original characters still linked to the Golden Age of the island who remained there nowadays shunned the port bars, avoiding the celebrity snappers and the rowdy sightseers by sticking to the more obscure haunts in the less well known alleyways and gullies of the island. "People own houses here who have been coming here years and years and they don't know Hydra at all," lamented David Fagan who barely saw or heard from his old friend

Cohen. "Unless you spend a winter here you're not really living on Hydra."

Although he hardly spent time there anymore, Cohen was still very much part of Hydra's myth, his history with the island almost a part of its topography. "He's our local hero!" exclaims Fagan, "but on the rare occasions he does return, people don't hassle him. We respect him. And of course, he comes and goes unannounced; people don't look for him."

Cohen still spent time in Montreal when he could but to all intents and purposes LA was now his home.

At this stage in his life awards, prizes and nominations seemed to follow Cohen around like seagulls trailing a trawler. There are far too many honours to list but among the most ironic was surely the fact that Cohen's appearance in Las Vegas was voted show of the year there for 2009. "You imagine that," exclaimed a delighted Rob Hallet. "It's like John the Baptist conquering Babylon. Leonard sent me a simple e-mail when I told him the news. He wrote: 'It's. All. Your. Fault'."

Cohen's past continued to resurface in the present in ever fascinating forms and guises. Tony Palmer had recently rediscovered the long lost *Bird On The Wire* movie, or the remains of its basic materials at least. "Some 294 cans of film were discovered in a warehouse in Hollywood, in rusted up cans that sometimes had to be hammered open," remembers the director, "and these cans were shipped to me by, of all people, Frank Zappa's manager, I believed at first that nothing could be salvaged. The cans did not contain the negative (still lost), some of the prints were in black and white, and much of it had been cut to pieces and/or scratched beyond use. But when I finally opened one box and found most of the original sound dubbing tracks, I knew we had a hope of putting the jigsaw back together."

Palmer would go on to painstakingly restore the film for a full domestic DVD release in 2010 with a unique cover. "The Picasso Estate," explains Palmer, "has given permission, in what I am told are unprecedented circumstances, for use of the great Picasso Dove of Peace as the main logo of the film and on the front cover of the DVD. Looking back after 38 years, my admiration for Cohen as a poet, a singer and as a man, remains undiminished. The original film was made with love, and I hope that quality once again shines through the restored film."

Meanwhile, in New York John Lissaeur had discovered the similarly AWOL *Songs For Rebecca* mixes. "We thought they were long lost," he says, "but not long ago we found rough mixes of all the songs, in a stash at my warehouse. I thought they would be ruined because the oxide on all these old quarter inch tapes disintegrates. However we were able to get 99% of the material off of the tapes into digital, eight songs with a vocal. They sound great. So I sent them out to Robert [Kory] and Leonard and we'll see if anything comes of it. I'd still like us to do one more record. A beautiful, artistic, pure statement. I know that the poet in him is still lurking in these monumentally exquisite verses that could be put in a setting that was winding down... like a suite... Leonard with an orchestra."

With the spring 2010 dates postponed due to a sudden back injury sustained by Cohen, there was now unexpected free time for Cohen to consider another album. According to Jarkko: "He strained his back while exercising. Of course, he insisted on doing the shows anyway but the doctor warned him that if he did he had a huge risk of damaging his back permanently and spending the rest of his life in a wheelchair."

Even without the signs and signals his physical form were sending him Cohen was obviously aware of where he was in his life. He had recently taken to quoting Tennessee Williams' maxim that, "Life is a fairly well written play, except for the third act". Now that Cohen was in the midst of that third, uncharted phase he was supremely conscious of what would happen next. "The end of the third act," he said almost joyfully, "when the hero dies – and I'm speaking about how each person considers himself the central figure of his own drama – that – from what one can observe, seems rather tricky." He also quoted his dead friend Irving Layton. "Irving said, 'It's not death I'm worried about, it's the preliminaries'."

Although famously healthy in his appetite for the company of women throughout his life, Cohen had never actually married or seemingly found his life long soul mate. Rather he seemed to have found perfect partners for specific phases of his life. Now approaching his late seventies, he was ambivalent about his own romantic relationships and almost rejoicing in his own general vagueness as to regards his life and history. "I'm not a sentimental guy," he quipped, "and I'm blessed with a certain amount of amnesia. I don't really remember what went down... I don't review my life in that way."

Cohen used his new free time to take tentative steps into LA studios, recording with members of a band for the first time since the Nineties, and there was evidence of brand new songs already. Cohen had taken to performing two virgin tunes 'Feels So Good' and 'The Darkness' at his most recent concerts. Musically, in his current band's incarnation at least, they were middle-of-the road, gospel inflected C&W blues but lyrically they were as strong, direct and as affecting as anything he'd ever written. Seemingly bathed in an ultramarine moonlight 'Feels So Good' appeared to be about the joy felt in finally feeling nothing and in the black sunshine blues of 'The Darkness' Cohen seemed, as in Picasso's final drawings, to be facing death head on and making vital art out of it. Cohen appeared even more in the moment when performing this new material on stage, clearly empowered still by the act of writing and expressing it.

"Leonard has been in the studio," confirms Kory, "and he's been asking people to come in. It's not going to sound like *The Future* or *Dear Heather*. I can't say too much, I don't want to jinx it except that it is great."

Another year, another Hall of Fame. This time it was the songwriter's version and on June 17, 2010 Cohen was inducted in a ceremony at New York's Marriott Marquis. His acceptance speech was raspy and to the point, utilising an abridged verse from 'Hallelujah' and the usual bouquet of thank yous. He was more verbal later the same night when asked about his impending album. "God willing it will be finished next spring," Cohen told *Rolling Stone* magazine, "I'm producing it." He revealed that most of the 10 or 11 songs on the album were composed before embarking on the marathon tour that began in May 2008. "One song was written on tour, the rest were written before," he said, noting that he wrote some tracks with long-time collaborator Sharon Robinson and others with his long-time companion Anjani Thomas. Asked what the album would sound like Cohen replied: "Something good, I hope." He added that he was listening to much the same music as he had been for the last few years "...Tom Waits, Van Morrison, Bob Dylan, Judy Collins."

Kory was at the ceremony with Leonard. "We had such respect for the other artistes there," he says. "And yet you couldn't really compare Leonard to any of them. He's a poet first and foremost. And the other inductees loved Leonard. There was such a mutual respect. But he's unique among them all. What he is dealing with, essentially, is poetry."

What was also unique about Cohen was that unlike many of his fellow inductees nothing in any of his work – either in song, poetry or literature – had ever utilised cliché.

At 75 years of age Cohen was looking forward to another massive world wide tour and the completion and release of his twelfth studio album. By the standards of the rock'n'roll industry Cohen was ancient and this was an almost freakish achievement. Yet by other measures – as within the realm of blues music, literature and the arts – it was more common for a man of Cohen's maturity to still be working. It was even frightening to think that compared to Roshi, a professional holy man who had travelled the world and worked into his late nineties, Cohen was still a relatively young man. Perhaps it was true after all. Perhaps a poet *did* become immortal through his work. The very words that Cohen had written and published as a young man, as a middle aged man and as an old man still chimed, rang and resonated within the hearts of millions around the world. And furthermore Cohen was still beguiled, fascinated and nourished by this very phenomenon. As he had written so many many years ago on Hydra, with the sun on his face and with Marianne still by his side:

"In my journey I know I am somewhere beyond the travelling pack of poets / I am a man of tradition / I will remain here until I am sure of what I am leaving."

Selective Discography

New Skin For The Old Ceremony
Is This What You Wanted, Chelsea Hotel #2, Lover Lover Lover, Field
Commander Cohen, Why Don't You Try, There Is A War, A Singer Must
Die, I Tried To Leave You, Who By Fire, Take This Longing, Leaving
Green Sleeves
August 1974

Death Of A Ladies' Man
True Love Leaves No Traces, Iodine, Paper-Thin Hotel, Memories, I Left
A Woman Waiting, Don't Go Home With Your Hard-On, Fingerprints,
Death Of A Ladies' Man
November 1977

Recent Songs
The Guests, Humbled In Love, The Window, Came So Far For Beauty,
The Lost Canadian (Un Canadien Errant), The Traitor, Our Lady Of
Solitude, The Gypsy's Wife, The Smokey Life, Ballad Of The Absent
Mare
September 1979

Various Positions
Dance Me To The End Of Love, Coming Back To You, The Law, Night
Comes On, Hallelujah, The Captain, Hunter's Lullaby, Heart With No
Companion, If It Be Your Will
February 1985

I'm Your Man
First We Take Manhattan, Ain't No Cure For Love, Everybody Knows,
I'm Your Man, Take This Waltz, Jazz Police, I Can't Forget, Tower Of
Song
February 1988

The Future
The Future, Waiting For The Miracle, Be For Real, Closing Time,
Anthem, Democracy, Light As The Breeze, Always, Tacoma Trailer
November 1992

Ten New Songs 2001
In My Secret Place, A Thousand Kisses Deep, That Don't Make It Junk,
Here It Is, Love Thyself, By The Rivers Dark, Alexandra Leaving, You
Have Loved Enough, Boogie Street, The Land Of Plenty
October 2001

Dear Heather
Go No More A-Roving, Because Of, The Letters, Undertow, Morning
Glory, On That Day, Villanelle For Our Time, There For You, Dear
Heather, Nightingale, To A Teacher, The Faith, Tennessee Waltz
October 2004

LIVE ALBUMS

Live Songs
April 1973

Live In Concert
July 1994

Field Commander Cohen
February 2001

Live In London
March 2009

Live At The Isle Of Wight Festival
October 2009
(DVD & CD Package)

COMPILATION ALBUMS

The Best Of Leonard Cohen (Greatest Hits)
November 1975

Liebestraume – Leonard Cohen Singt Seine Schonsten Lieder
(Germany only)
December 1980

More Best Of Leonard Cohen
October 1997

The Essential Leonard Cohen
October, 2002

Greatest Hits
July 2009

TRIBUTE ALBUMS

Famous Blue Raincoat
1986

I'm Your Fan
1991

Tower Of Song
1995

Acknowledgements & Sources

Thank you's: Greg Gold, Michael Brandon, Robert Kory, Javier Mas, Cathy Boyce, Sharon Robinson, Jarkko Arjatsalo, Michael, Margaret, Bernard, Juan-Luis Salmeron, Charlotte Greig, John Williams, Olga Perez Brana, Jim Devlin, Chris Charlesworth, Chris Allen, Stephen Dunthorne, Anna Powell, Harvey Kubernik, Helen Tremaine, Steven Machat, Fidel, Pablo Gonzalez, Kate McKenna, Clair Woodward, Doug Thorp, Carl Bevan, Walter the Spanish hairdresser and Jose & Manolo at La Solana restaurant, Benimamet, Valencia, Spain.

Interviewees: Robert Kory, Sharon Robinson, Javier Mas, John Lissaeur, Steven Machat, Jarkko Arjatsalo, Curtis Wehrfritz, Tony Palmer, Rob Hallett, Julie Christensen, Anne Riise, Andrea Schwarzwaelder Dolfino, Andrew Darbyshire, John Miller, Dan Kessel, Justin Pierce, Andrzej Marzec, Kelley Lynch, Oscar Brand, John Williams, Ruth Wiise, Chester Crill, Stuart Brotman, Chris Darrow, Barry Miles, John Bilezikjian, Stina Lundberg Dabrowski, Barbara Vann, Devra Heichert, Jeremy Lubbock, Bill Mays, Al Perkins, Venetta Fields, Donald Fagan, JD Beauvallet and Art Munson.

Websites

http://www.webheights.net/speakingcohen/main.htm

This a truly exhaustive source of interviews, critiques and transcripts of almost every radio, press, and television piece associated with Leonard Cohen since the 1950's and was a major reference point during the research for this book.

http://www.leonardcohenfiles.com/

Newspapers & magazines

Q, Mojo, New Musical Express, Melody Maker, Sounds, Spin, The Times, The Sunday Times, The Independent, The Guardian, Rolling Stone, Creem, Blitz, B-Side, The Canadian Forum, Canadian Jewish News, Commentary, The Daily Telegraph, Les Inrockuptibles, Details, El Mundo, Financial Post, Globe & Mail, Goldmine, GQ, The Independent On Sunday, The Observer, Interview, Macleans, Mix, Musician, New Yorker, The New York Times, Playboy, Sunday Express, The Tamarack Review, Toronto Star, Toronto Sun, Vox, Wall Street Journal, Zig Zag.

Bibliography

Cohen, Leonard. *Book Of Longing* (Penguin, 2007)
Devlin, Jim. *Leonard Cohen In His Own Words* (Omnibus Press, 1998)
Devlin, Jim. *In Every Style Of Passion* (Omnibus Press, 1996)
Machat, Steven. *Gods, Gangsters & Honour* (Beautiful Books, 2009)
Nadel, Ira. *Various Positions: A Life Of Leonard Cohen* (Random House, 1997)
Rasky, Harry. *The Song Of Leonard Cohen* (Souvenir Press, 2010)
Ratcliffe, Maurice. *The Complete Guide To The Music Of Leonard Cohen* (Omnibus Press, 1998)

Index